MW01201622

Shōbōgenzō

Shōbōgenzō

The Treasure House of the
Eye of the True Teaching

A Trainee's translation of
Great Master Dōgen's
Spiritual Masterpiece

Rev. Hubert Nearman, O.B.C.
Translator

Shasta Abbey Press,
Mount Shasta,
California

First Edition—2007
© 2007 Shasta Abbey

This edition reformatted—2022

ISBN: 978-0-930066-36-9
Imprint: Shasta Abbey Press

Shasta Abbey
3724 Summit Drive
Mt. Shasta, California 96067-9102
(530) 926-4208

Volume II of III

This Volume contains Chapters 30 to 70

Acknowledgments

Considering the scope and length of this work and the demands, both monastic and scholarly, that it puts on any translator, a reader may well wonder what could possibly motivate anyone to take on such an enormous task. Whatever may be the motives for other translators, mine has been quite simple. I had finished translating the various texts that were included in *Buddhist Writings on Meditation and Daily Practice* (Shasta Abbey Press, 1994) and asked Rev. Daizui MacPhillamy, my editorial consultant at the time, whether Rev. Master Jiyu-Kennett had anything else she wanted me to translate for her. He took my question to her, and, he said, he was dumbfounded when, without a moment's pause, she replied *"The Shōbōgenzō,"* for such a monumental undertaking would obviously take me many years to complete, not only because of its length but also because of its reputed obscurity and even incomprehensibility. Simply because she was my Master, I agreed to her request, knowing that I would never have taken on such a task for any other reason. It has been my monastic offering to the Sangha over some fourteen years. During that time I have had the great good fortune to live at Shasta Abbey, a traditional Buddhist monastery where the life that Dōgen extolled is practiced. I wish to express my deep gratitude for all the assistance my fellow monks have given me, and in particular:

—Rev. Master Jiyu-Kennett, Abbess of Shasta Abbey when the initial volume of the first eleven of Dōgen's discourses was published. (This has been reworked in light of the whole of the present book and is not simply a reprint.) She can never be thanked enough for opening the Way of the Buddha, and of Dōgen, to an immeasurable number of people;

—Rev. Daizui MacPhillamy, whose sharp intellect and broad experience in the Dharma provided me with critical editing and consultation, but who sadly died unexpectedly before he could work with me on the last half of the discourses;

—Rev. Ekō Little, successor to Rev. Master Jiyu-Kennett as Abbot of Shasta Abbey, who has given me the unflagging support, encouragement, and assistance needed to complete the work;

—Rev. Oswin Hollenbeck of the Eugene Buddhist Priory for help with the introduction and who, together with Rev. Meikō Jones of Portland Buddhist Priory and Rev. Chōsei Swann of Shasta Abbey, read and commented on a number of the discourses;

—Rev. Fidelia Dolan who not only transformed electronic information into formats that could be made available to all, but also worked tirelessly as my editorial consultant after Rev. Daizui passed on, and helped me find ways to convey Dōgen's medieval Japanese and Chinese into hopefully comprehensible English;

—Rev. Meian Elbert, Rev. Shikō Rom, and Rev. Veronica Snedaker, who brought the book to completion;

—and to all the monastics, known and unknown, who have kept the Buddha's Transmission of the living Dharma vibrant down the centuries.

May the merit of this work benefit all beings.

Acknowledgments for the reformatted edition

The reformatting of this edition into three volumes to enable the use of print-on-demand services was undertaken by Rev. Lambert Tuffrey of Throssel Hole Buddhist Abbey, UK.

Contents

Volume III of III

The *Shōbōgenzō*

A Trainee's Translation
of Great Master Dōgen's Spiritual Masterpiece
Translator's General Introduction

The *Shōbōgenzō* is the recognized spiritual masterpiece by the thirteenth-century Japanese Sōtō Zen Master Eihei Dōgen. It is comprised of discourses that he gave to his disciples, in person or in writing, at various times between 1231 and his death twenty-two years later at age fifty-three.† These discourses cover a wide range of topics pertinent to those in monastic life though often also relevant to those training in lay life. He discusses matters of daily behavior and religious ceremonial as well as issues involving the Master-disciple relationship. He also explores the deeper meaning that informs the so-called Zen kōan stories, which often puzzle readers by their seeming illogicality and contrary nature.

I have translated the title as *The Treasure House of the Eye of the True Teaching*, though a fuller, more comprehensive rendering would be *The Treasure House for What the Spiritual Eye of Wise Discernment Perceives from the Vantage Point of the True Teachings of Shakyamuni Buddha and His Heirs*. The term 'Teaching' in the title is synonymous with the Buddhist use of the term 'Dharma', which refers not only to what the historical Buddha taught to His disciples but also to the Truth that flows from the Unborn and which all things give expression to when they are functioning directly from their innate True Self. However, it does not address what may be a scholar's particular interest in producing a translation, though it is

---

† The present translation is based primarily on Kawamura Kōdō's edition of Dōgen's complete works Dōgen Zenji Zenshū (Tokyo: Shunjūsha, 1993), in consultation with the editions by Tamaki Kōshirō, Dōgen Shū (Tokyo: Chikuma Shobō, 1969), by Ōkubo Dōshū, Kohon Kōtei Shōbōgenzō (Tokyo: Chikuma Shobō, 1971), by Terada Tōru and Mizunoya Oko, Dōgen (Tokyo: Iwanami Shoten, 1972), and by Masutani Fumio, Gendaigoshaku Shōbōgenzō (Tokyo: Kadokawa Shoten, 1975).

obvious that translating anything from medieval Japanese and Chinese requires special academic training: hence the subtitle "A Trainee's Translation of Great Master Dōgen's Spiritual Masterpiece". That is, it is intended primarily for those who practice Zen Buddhism rather than those whose interest is purely academic.

There are various ways in which Dogen's discourses can be presented, each having its particular advantages. The way I have chosen is simply to divide the discourses into those that were completed before his death and those that were still in draft form when he died, ordered where possible chronologically by the date when the discourse was given.

The discourses were originally written out by hand, primarily by his chief disciple and amanuensis, the Second Japanese Sōtō Zen Ancestor, Kōun Ejō. Most of the discourses have a two-part postscript (printed in italics, usually at the end of a discourse). The first half indicates who the recipients of the discourse were, along with when and where it was presented. If this is signed, it will customarily be by Dōgen. The second half supplies a short account of when and where the copy was made. These copies are most often signed by Ejō, though three were signed by Giun, one of Ejō's Dharma-heirs who later became the fifth abbot of Dōgen's Eihei-ji Monastery.

The majority of the discourses focus on exploring the spiritual significance of some topic drawn from Buddhist Scriptures or Chinese Chan (Zen) texts. Dōgen's commentaries on these texts are not lectures as would be understood in academic circles, but are talks that arise from a Zen Master's deepest understanding of the spiritual meaning and relevance of his topic to Buddhist training and practice. They come out of Dōgen's mind of meditation and are being presented to his monastic and lay disciples, who are presumably listening from their mind of meditation.□

The discourses carry a strong flavor of the conversational and the personal, and he enriches them with colorful Chinese and Zen phrases, as well as with medieval Chinese and Japanese colloquialisms. When translated literally, many of these metaphors and figures of speech may well have little meaning for English-speaking readers. However, by the thirteenth century they would have been a common way for a Buddhist Meditation Master to refer to That which is the True Nature of all beings. The function of these metaphors is, to some extent, to 'ground' a Master's disciples by providing them with a colorful and more easily remembered image instead of some more abstract, 'intellectual' definition. They point to the Great Matter for which one trains in Serene Reflection Meditation, which is to awaken to one's True Nature.◻

Dōgen sometimes uses a manner of speaking that closely resembles a dialogue. One specific instance occurs in 'A Discourse on Doing One's Utmost in Practicing the Way of the Buddhas' (*Bendōwa*), his earliest dated text in the *Shōbōgenzō*. The major part of this particular discourse consists of an imaginary dialogue between Dōgen and a potential disciple. While it takes the form of someone asking questions and Dōgen giving answers, it is not a catechism. That is, it is not a series of formal questions and answers. Rather, the questions arise from an attitude of mind which has misgivings about the efficacy and worth of the type of seated meditation that Dōgen advocates. Dōgen's responses, by contrast, arise from a place that lies beyond the intellective, duality-based mind and are aimed at helping the questioner to recognize that duality and to let go of it. Hence, the attitude of mind of both the questioner and the Master is as important as the specific question being asked. For the translator, one challenge in rendering Dōgen's text is to convey to the reader the attitudes implied in the exchanges between the two.

These interchanges between a Master and a potential or real disciple are not speculative in nature, but invariably have the purpose of helping disciples find that spiritual certainty which is the hallmark of a genuine kenshō, 'the seeing of one's Original Face', that is, the direct experiencing of one's innate Buddha Nature. This is not the same as having an intellectual understanding or intuition, since the experience takes one beyond those functions associated with the so-called rational mind, which are the foundation and authority for those who are not dedicated to spiritual pursuits. Furthermore, the certainty arising from a kenshō is not speculative in nature or the product of rational persuasion or a form of blind faith.

Dōgen's teaching in the *Shōbōgenzō* is neither confined to nor limited by conventional mental categories, which is why practitioners of Dōgen's type of meditation are admonished to be willing to be disturbed by the Truth, that is, to have not only their intellectual preconceptions questioned but also to have their reliance on solely what makes conventional, worldly sense called into question. Despite the view of some that Dōgen is therefore 'anti-intellect', once the spiritual certainty arises in those who are doing the training, the previous need to depend solely on the 'boxes' fabricated by their intellect disappears. Or as several Meditation Masters describe it, once we give up 'the walls and fences' that our intellect constructs from the bits and pieces of experience, this dependency disappears, and we metaphorically 'drop off our body and mind' but without rejecting the intellect itself or denying its natural and useful functions.

Conventions

In the present work, when a common word is used having spiritual significance, I have employed initial capitals to signal to the reader that word X is not intended literally but is part of a code which Zen Masters have used to convey spiritual meaning. Indeed, when people spiritually awaken, this is customarily signaled by their expressing their understanding in some unique and personal way. When the use of this code is ignored or overlooked by a translator, a kōan story may well become totally unintelligible and give rise to the erroneous notion that Zen promotes the indescribable. To avoid this, I have added some footnotes intended to point out places where the code may not have been spotted by readers.

An example of this may occur in a dialogue in which a Master and his disciple use the same words but with a totally different meaning. For example, a Master and his disciple are having a discussion, and the Master tests his disciple's understanding of what his True Nature is by asking, "Do you get It?" with the disciple answering, "No, I don't get it." The Master's question is a spiritual one: "Have you got to the heart of your spiritual question?" to which the disciple's reply reveals that he is still attached to conventional, worldly ways of thinking.

Elements of Style

In the present translations, four stylistic elements are used whose purpose may not be immediately apparent:

First is the capitalizing of words that would not usually be proper nouns, such as 'Original Nature', 'the Self', 'the Truth', 'It', 'One's Original Face'. Such words refer either to one's own Buddha Nature or to That which is the spiritual source of one's Buddha Nature. For instance, there is a difference between the term 'good friend' which refers to a Buddhist who has the ability to teach and train others in Buddhism (usually synonymous with a Zen Master), and the term 'Good Friend', which is another name for one's Buddha Nature.

Second, a word that is underlined is to be understood as emphatic within the context of the particular sentence in which it occurs. Were the text to be read aloud, the underlined word would be given emphasis.

Third, Dōgen sometimes abruptly changes his topic within his talks. Whereas many of these shifts are signaled by some introductory word, such as 'further' and 'also', which appears at the beginning of a new paragraph, in some instances this is not the case. Thus it has seemed advisable to aid the reader by inserting a plum blossom asterisk (ˋ) between paragraphs where a sudden shift might otherwise prove disconcerting.

Fourth, single quotation marks are often used in the sense of 'so-called', 'what I (or someone else) would call', or 'the term' or 'the phrase', in addition to their customary use for marking a quote within a quote.

Special Terms

Dōgen often alludes to 'training and practice'. This consistently refers specifically to doing seated meditation, applying 'the mind of meditation' to all one's daily activities, and attempting to live in accord with the Precepts of Mahayana Buddhism, that is, the Precepts as spelled out in Dōgen's *Text for a Precepts Master's Giving the Mahayana Precepts* (*Kyōjukaimon*) and *The Scripture of Brahma's Net* (*Bommō Kyō*). Similarly, references to 'studying' denote training under a Zen Master, and do not signify the undertaking of a scholastic regimen.

To render the Japanese word *tennin* (or *ninden*) I have used the phrase 'ordinary people and those in lofty places'. Some translators render it as 'gods and men'. There is the danger that some readers may therefore assume that it means 'immortals and mortals'. However, in a Buddhist context it refers to those who are in the celestial and human realms among the six Realms of Existence, the four others being those of beasts, those in a hellish state, those who are hungry ghosts, and those who are asuras (heaven stormers). Those in the celestial and human realms are potentially able to hear the name of Buddha and absorb the Dharma, whereas those in the other four are so preoccupied with their suffering that it is exceedingly difficult for them to believe that they can transcend their suffering long enough to hear the Teaching and thereby free themselves from their spiritual obsessions.

Dōgen often uses the terms Mahayana and Hinayana (translated as 'the Greater Course' and 'the Lesser Course'). A widely voiced view is that references in Mahayana writings to those who follow a Lesser Course denote practitioners of the Theravadan Buddhist tradition. The Theravadan tradition, however, was not active in medieval Japan during Dōgen's lifetime. Also, the Pali Canon upon which the Theravadan tradition is grounded was known to Dōgen through Chinese translations and was held in great esteem by him. Allusions in Dōgen's writings to 'those who follow the Lesser Course' are clearly to persons whom trainees may well encounter in their daily life. Thus it is likely that he is referring to shravakas (those who merely seek to gain an intellectual understanding of Buddhism) or to pratyekabuddhas (those who undertake some aspects of Buddhist practice but only for their own personal benefit).

The Issue of Gender and Sex

This issue is sometimes raised in regard to translating medieval Chinese and Japanese texts into English. It involves the attitude of Buddhism in general, and Dōgen in particular, toward women in spiritual life. While it is true that in some cultures during some periods negative social attitudes toward women have unfortunately colored the practice of Buddhism, Dōgen's view is unequivocal: males and females are spiritual and monastic equals, for enlightenment knows no such distinction as sex. The English language, however, has not yet developed a universally accepted way to express what is gender neutral. When Dōgen refers to monks or laity in general or as 'someone who', it should be understood that he is including both males and females, even though the English pronominal reference is, for brevity's sake, 'he', 'him', or 'his': I have used 'she', 'her', and 'hers' only where the sex of the person is known to be female.

Appendices

Two appendices have been added to the book. The first is a listing of the Japanese names of the major figures in the various kōan stories along with their Chinese equivalents. The second is a glossary of words and idiomatic phrases, such as hossu and kōan, which need some explanation because they do not have an easy equivalent in English.

On Kōan Stories

Dōgen makes wide use of stories from Zen kōan collections. Since these stories may strike some readers as strange or incomprehensible, the following observations may prove helpful.

Originally, the term 'kōan' meant 'a public case', and in Chinese Zen referred to a notable, authenticated instance when a disciple came to realize his or her True Nature. By Dōgen's time, the term 'kōan' had become synonymous with the spiritual question which epitomizes that which keeps disciples, as well as anyone else, from directly experiencing what their Original Nature is. It is the spiritual doubt that keeps someone 'looking down'. The kōan stories, then, are usually accounts of how a particular trainee's doubt was resolved.

In these stories, the spiritual problem of a trainee often involves a habitual acting counter to at least one of the ten major Mahayana Buddhist Precepts on either a literal or a figurative level. That is, in some way the disciple will have persisted in taking the life from someone or something, in taking things that are not given, in giving in to covetous feelings, in saying that which is not so, in trafficking in something that intoxicates or deludes, in putting oneself up and others down, in insulting others, in giving in to anger or resentfulness, in being stingy, or in acting in a disrespectful manner toward Buddha, Dharma, or Sangha.

When reading such dialogues, it is prudent to consider what the mental attitude of the questioner is and not just what is being asked. This is important because the question asked arises from a particular frame of mind. Determining who is asking the question (and sometimes where and when) will help clarify what this frame of mind is and, therefore, what is really being asked, since the answer given will not be an absolute one, independent of the questioner, but one that speaks to the questioner's mental attitude and perspective. This is sometimes referred to in Zen writings as 'two arrows meeting in mid-air', one meaning of which is that the questioner thinks he knows what the target, or goal, is and has 'shot his arrow' of discriminatory thought at that target only to have his 'arrow' deflected by the Master's response so that, to mix metaphors, the disciple's 'train of discriminatory thought' is derailed. At the same time, the Master's 'arrow' points to a way for the disciple to go in his Buddhist training.

However, in some cases the roles are reversed: the Master asks the disciple a question or 'invites' him to respond from a perspective beyond the discriminatory mind. If the disciple has truly awakened, he will respond appropriately from the mind of meditation and not from the discriminatory mind of duality. In such an instance, the 'two arrows meeting in mid-air' is an expression for their oneness of mind.

The stories may follow any of several different patterns or their combination. Almost all will involve at least one of the following three patterns:

In the first, a disciple will ask the Master a question which arises from a reliance on dualistic thinking to comprehend his own spiritual doubt. This encounter with the Master will often occur in the context of a formal spiritual examination ceremony, but this will not always be made explicit in the text. The Master will then do or say something which cuts through the disciple's confusion and points him directly toward 'seeing' his Original Nature. What the Master does or says arises from a source that transcends the dualistic, intellective mind: it is not a philosophical, doctrinal, or 'rational' answer to the question. If the disciple is 'ripe'—that is, spiritually ready to shift his perspective away from reliance on what his intellect is doing so that he can realize That which transcends intellect—he has an experience referred to by some such phrase as 'realizing the Truth' or 'awakening to his True Nature'. In some kōan stories, the trigger for this experience may not be directly supplied by the Master but by some other external condition, such as seeing peach blossoms or hearing a piece of tile strike bamboo.

In the second, a Meditation Master initiates an exchange with a disciple who is still in doubt, and tries through his conversation with the disciple to steer him toward facing up to what his spiritual problem is. In such dialogues, the Master's questions may seem upon first reading to be casual ones. In kōan stories, when a Master asks a question, he is not trying to engage the disciple in some social interchange: his question will have a deeper purpose or meaning, which the disciple may or may not pick up on. If the disciple fails to 'get it', the Master will usually persist in his questioning until either the disciple has an awakening or until the Master decides that the disciple is still not yet 'ripe' enough.

In the third pattern, a Master-disciple interchange occurs, but with a disciple who has already awakened to the Truth. In such an instance, since what the disciple is saying or doing no longer arises from the mind of duality, there will be some clear indication of the Master's approval.

In those cases where the disciple is still in doubt, one useful clue as to what his spiritual problem is can be found in how the Master addresses the disciple. For instance, in one story, a monk who is given to striving too hard is addressed as 'Shibi the Austere Monk'. In another, a monk who has become entangled in erudition through his academic pursuit of studying Scriptures is addressed by his Master as 'you who are a learned scholar of considerable intelligence'.

In identifying the disciple's spiritual problem, it is helpful to determine what the disciple's attitude of mind is, and not to treat his questions or responses on a purely informational level. Once the disciple's spiritual problem has been identified, how he responds to his Master will reflect that problem until he has an awakening, at which time he may compose a poem which expresses the change in perspective that has emerged.

Another aspect which may be difficult for the reader to fathom immediately is the relevance of the Master's actions in word or deed to what the disciple's problem is. Since such actions are not 'pre-planned' but reflect the on-the-spot skillful means of the Master, it can only be said that whatever is done will arise from the mind of meditation, will be free of any dualistic tendency, will not break any of the Precepts, and will arise out of his compassion for the suffering of the disciple. In one famous kōan story (Nansen's cat), the roles are reversed: Meditation Master Nansen puts himself in a spiritually unsupportable position by trying to teach his monks to keep to the Precepts by seriously breaking one himself, and it is his chief disciple who points this out to him.

Another topic that arises from the kōan stories deals with who the participants are. The Master is easily identified. On the other hand, the one who asks a question is often referred to simply as a monk. In such cases the person is most likely a junior monk, one who has not yet been Transmitted and who is asking his question at a ceremony called shōsan. This is the formal spiritual examination ceremony which is customarily held twice a month in Zen monasteries during which junior trainees ask a question that reflects their present spiritual state.

When the monk asking a question is specifically identified, this refers to a senior monk, one who is already Transmitted or who will be Transmitted. These are monks who will ultimately function as a Master, and often as the founder of a temple or a lineage. Whether in the kōan story they have already been Transmitted or are still juniors can only be determined by the nature of their question.

Applying the Principles

To see how the preceding principles apply to an actual kōan story, the following one, taken from Dōgen's *Bendōwa*, is given with my exegetical remarks in square brackets. The kōan story itself is given in indented text:

> Long ago, there was a monk in Meditation Master Hōgen's
> monastic community named Gensoku, who was a subordinate under
> the Temple's administrative director. Master Hōgen asked him,
> "Director Gensoku, how long have you been in our community?"

[Although Gensoku is not the director, he is apparently acting as though he thought he was, thus breaking a Precept by 'putting himself up'. Hōgen's question is not a casual but a leading one, arising from his compassionate sensitivity to Gensoku's spiritual suffering from pride.]

Gensoku replied, "Why, I've been in the community for
three years now."

[Gensoku tacitly acknowledges recognition of his importance as self-evident and
responds in a casual manner. Had he not been absorbed in his pride, he might have
responded, as would be expected not only from a novice but also from any Chinese,
by some such statement as "You flatter me by addressing me by too exalted a title,
considering that I have been training here for only three years now." Had he already
had a kenshō, his response, though not predictable, would not be impolite or
disrespectful in tone but, on the other hand, would probably not be a conventional,
'socially correct' one either.]

The Master asked, "As you are still a junior monk, why
have you never asked me about the Buddha Dharma?"

[Hōgen gently corrects Gensoku by now pointing out his actual position as a junior
monk. He then asks another leading question, which implies that Gensoku thinks that
he is above all other novices and does not need instruction.]

Gensoku replied, "I will not lie to Your Reverence. Previously, when I was
with Meditation Master Seihō, I fully reached the place of joyful ease in the Buddha
Dharma."

[The delusion underlying Gensoku's pride begins to emerge more clearly, for he
claims to have attained a spiritual state which he has not yet reached. This is what
Hōgen had probably surmised and which had led him to engage Gensoku in this
dialogue. Gensoku is now breaking the Precepts by saying that which is not so and by
having sold himself the wine of delusion.]

The Master said, "And what was said that gained you entry
to that place?"

[Hōgen now probes directly into the heart of Gensoku's problem.]

Gensoku said, "I once asked Seihō what the True Self of a
novice is, and Seihō replied, 'Here comes the Hearth God looking
for fire.' "

[The nature of the question and the response suggest that this interchange had occurred
as part of a shōsan ceremony (referred to above) held before the assembled monks,

during which novices ask a Meditation Master a question which presumably reflects their current spiritual understanding. Because at this point Gensoku is still operating from the mind of duality, it is likely that the question was asked from the intellect rather than from the heart. The significance of Seihō's response will be discussed later.]

> Hōgen responded, "Nicely put by Seihō. But I'm afraid you may not have understood it."

[Gensoku had heard Master Seihō's words but had not grasped their import. Hōgen makes a complimentary remark about Seihō's comment. Had Hōgen suspected that Gensoku had already had a kenshō, it is unlikely that he would have done this, but instead might have made some remark that on the surface looked as though he were disparaging Seihō, such as "That old rascal! Is he still going around saying such things?" but which Gensoku would see as being the way a Master may acknowledge another Master whilst avoiding judgmentalism.]

> Gensoku said, "A Hearth God is associated with fire, so I understand it to mean that, just as fire is being used to seek for fire, so the True Self is what is used to seek for the True Self."

[Gensoku has worked out an intellectual interpretation of Seihō's remark, and therefore thinks that this type of understanding is what constitutes awakening to one's True Self. Gensoku's error is in thinking that there are two True Selves: the one that seeks and the one that is sought.]

> The Master said, "Just as I suspected! You have not understood. Were the Buddha Dharma like that, it is unlikely that It would have continued on, being Transmitted down to the present day."

[The Master now sets Gensoku straight as to where he is spiritually, in order to shake up his proud complacency and break through his deluded view.]

> Gensoku was so distressed at this that he left the monastery. While on the road, he thought to himself, "In this country the Master is known as a fine and learned monastic teacher and as a great spiritual leader and guide for five hundred monks.

Since he has chided me for having gone wrong, he must
undoubtedly have a point." So, he returned to his Master,
respectfully bowed in apology, and said, "What is the True Self of
a novice?"

[Leaving the monastery when asked to confront one's spiritual problem 'head on' is
not an uncommon occurrence in kōan stories. Similarly, the turning about in one's
heart by recognizing that it is oneself who may be wrong is a crucial moment in the
life of a trainee. Here it marks Gensoku's letting go of his pride, so that he now returns
with the appropriate attitude of mind for asking his spiritual question, which now
arises from his heart-felt need to know the truth, and without any preconceptions.]

The Master replied, "Here comes the Hearth God looking
for The Fire." Upon hearing these words, Gensoku awoke fully to
the Buddha Dharma.

[What a Meditation Master says or does at a formal spiritual examination ceremony
in response to a spiritual question is often multilayered in meaning and application.
Since it is not intellectually contrived but arises from the Master's spiritual depths, it
may in some way speak not only to the questioner but also to others who are present.]

[In Master Seihō's original remark to Gensoku several layers of meaning
were occurring simultaneously. On one level, he was inviting Gensoku to give up his
attitude of self-importance and 'play' with him; hence, the form in which the response
was given: it forms a first line for a couplet and would have been spoken in the
equivalent of English doggerel, the translated version read to the rhythmic pattern of
dum-dum-di-dum-dum dum-di-dum-di-dum. If Gensoku were open enough, he would
have come up with a second line, such as 'Burning up his false self upon the funeral
pyre'.]

[On another level, Master Seihō was pointing Gensoku toward his spiritual
problem. A 'Hearth God' is the title given to the temple boy whose task it is to light
the monastery lamps. Thus, Seihō was saying in effect, "You are acting like a temple
boy, not like a monk, and are seeking for that which you already have—in your case,
the spiritual flame of your training."]

[Hōgen uses the same words and intonation as Seihō did, but context brings out a third level of meaning, which Gensoku now hears, "Here comes the one most innocent of heart whose practice lights the way for all of us, truly seeking That which is the True Light (The Fire)." Gensoku, upon hearing this, realized that this is what he has been truly seeking—not social position or erudition—and awoke to the Truth where the distinction of self and other completely drops away.]

[In the original Chinese text, as given by Dōgen, the words used by Seihō and Hōgen are the same, but the context indicates that there has been a shift in meaning from how Gensoku interpreted these words when spoken by Seihō and what they implied to him when reiterated by Hōgen. To convey that difference in meaning in English, the two quotes are translated in a slightly, but significantly, different way. In other kōan stories where the same phrase is used in two different contexts, the translation will also attempt to convey the shift in meaning, rather than leave it to the reader to puzzle out from a mere repetition what that shift may be. While footnotes have occasionally been supplied to help readers over such difficult points in a kōan story, the translator has not attempted to supply full explanations of these stories, trusting that the preceding guidelines, plus the footnotes, will be sufficient.]

On 'The Meditative State
That Bears the Seal of the Ocean'

(Kaiin Zammai)

Translator's Introduction: This is one of the most subtle discourses in the *Shōbōgenzō*, due in part to the influence of the *Avatamsaka Scripture* on Dōgen's way of expressing his points. It is primarily devoted to a line-by-line analysis of a poem attributed to Shakyamuni Buddha, which ends with the phrase *kaiin zammai,* 'the meditative state that bears the seal of the Ocean'. This term is traditionally applied to the meditative state that Shakyamuni Buddha is said to have entered in order to expound the *Avatamsaka Scripture* and, by extension, to the meditative state that all Buddhas and Ancestors enter when They give expression to the Dharma.

The term 'seal' is an allusion to a carved seal bearing its owner's name. It is used to authenticate a person's signature. For instance, when someone is Transmitted in the Zen tradition, the Transmission documents which the disciple writes on silk at that time are then 'signed and sealed' by the Master as proof of the authenticity of the Transmission. By extension, the meditative state referred to in this discourse is one that bears the seal of the Ocean, which means that what the meditator is giving expression to is genuine Dharma. In the context of this chapter, 'to seal' carries a meaning of 'to authenticate as genuine'.

All of the Buddhas and Ancestors invariably enter the meditative state that bears the seal of the Ocean. As They swim about in this meditative state, there are times when They give expression to the Truth, and times when They experience the Truth directly, and times when They put It into Their daily practice. The merit of Their doing Their practice upon the surface of the Ocean includes Their having penetrated to the very bottom of the Ocean. They make Their practice upon the surface of the Ocean Their practice that plumbs the depths of the Ocean. They are not concerned with wistfully seeking out ways to make Their wandering about through birth and death return Them to the Source. Instead, They have broken through former obstructions, as if They were passing through barrier gates or piercing through the joints in a cane of bamboo. This liberation is characteristic of each and every Buddha and Ancestor, for They are the various streams that have flowed into the meditative state that bears the seal of the Ocean.

The Buddha once said in verse:

> *Merely of various elements is this body of Mine composed.*
> *The time of its arising is merely an arising of elements;*
> *The time of its vanishing is merely a vanishing of elements.*
> *As these elements arise, I do not speak of the arising of an 'I',*
> *And as these elements vanish, I do not speak of the vanishing of an 'I'.*
> *Previous instants and succeeding instants are not a series of instants that depend on each other;*
> *Previous elements and succeeding elements are not a series of elements that stand against each other.*
> *To give all of this a name, I call it 'the meditative state that bears the seal of the Ocean'.*

We need to make a diligent effort to fully explore these words of the Buddha. Arriving at the Way and entering into the realization of the Truth do not necessarily depend on listening to someone else or on speaking with someone else. And we have heard of those whose knowledge is broad who have realized the Way upon hearing four lines of Scripture, and those who have knowledge as extensive as the sands of the Ganges have been known to realize the Truth through hearing a single line of a Scriptural verse. And what is more, the Buddha's present words are not about seeking one's inherent enlightenment in what lies ahead, nor are they about grasping after one's first awareness of enlightenment within some experience. In general, even though making one's inherent enlightenment manifest is the meritorious behavior of a Buddha or an Ancestor, the various kinds of enlightenment—such as the first inkling of enlightenment or the full experience of one's inherent enlightenment—are not the only things that make a Buddha or an Ancestor what They are.

Just as the Buddha said:

> *Merely of various elements is this body of Mine*
> *composed.*

At this time, the Buddha was speaking from within the meditative state that bears the seal of the Ocean. From within this state, the various elements simply exist as they are, which He expressed as there 'merely being various elements'. He called this moment 'the composing of this body of Mine'. The integrated form which is composed of the various elements He accordingly calls 'this body of Mine'. He did not consider this body of His as a single unified form, for it was composed of various elements. Thus, He spoke of this bodily composition as 'this body of Mine'.

> *The time of its arising is merely an arising of elements.*

This arising of elements never leaves 'arising' behind.[1] For this reason, 'arising' is beyond what we can know through direct perception and beyond what we can know through intellectual discrimination. It is what He spoke of as, "I do not speak of the arising of an 'I.'" By His not speaking of an 'I' that arises, other people have learned not to engage in perceiving or differentiating about any arising of self within such elements, nor do they think about or discriminate between individual arisings. What is more, when there is transcendent 'mutual seeing', there will be a going beyond the realm of 'mutual seeing'.[2]

'Arising' invariably refers to the arrival of a specific moment, for time is what arises. Just what is this 'arising'? It must surely be arising in and of itself. This arising is already a moment in time. Never did He say that it fails to expose what Skin and Flesh, Bones and Marrow really are. Because this is the arising of 'being composed of', it is this body of His that arises, it is an 'I' that arises, and it is 'merely being various elements' that arises. It is not only hearing sounds and seeing forms and colors; it is also the arising of an 'I'. It is this arising of an 'I' that one does not speak

---

1. That is, the arising of elements is not a single event but something that keeps on occurring at each instant of now.

2. Transcendent mutual seeing refers to an understanding that goes beyond Master and disciple mutually recognizing each other as being 'such a one'.

about. 'Not speaking about something' does not mean 'not expressing something', for being able to express something is not the same as being able to put it in words. The time of arising is synonymous with the appearance of 'these elements'; it does not refer to the twenty-four hours of a day. These elements are what the time of arising is, and they do not compete with each other within the three worlds of desire, form, and beyond form. As an Old Buddha once put it, "Suddenly, fire arises." Through this expression, He was saying that there is no waiting about for this arising.

Another Old Buddha once said, "What is this ceaseless time of arising and vanishing?"[3] Thus, in that this arising and vanishing is our experience of the arising of an 'I' and our experience of the vanishing of an 'I', the process is unceasing. In entrusting the Matter[*] to Him, we need to discern the real meaning of His stating the ceaselessness of this process. We continually chop up this unceasing time of arising and vanishing, which is the very lifeblood of an Ancestor of the Buddha. In the unceasing time of arising and vanishing, who is it that arises and vanishes? As to the 'who' that arises and vanishes, it is the 'who' that is on the verge of being able to realize enlightenment within this body. That is, it is the 'who' that manifests this body, the 'who' for whom the Dharma is expressed, the very 'who' in the past who was unable to grasp what Mind is. It is "You have gotten what my Marrow is," and it is "You have gotten what my Bones are," because the 'you' is the who that arises and vanishes.

> *And as these elements vanish, I do not speak of the*
> *vanishing of an 'I'.*

The very moment when He does not speak of the vanishing of an 'I' will be the moment when those elements vanish. The vanishing is the vanishing of the elements. Though we speak of our own vanishing, it will actually be that of the

---

3.   Although, on a conventional level, this remark is a question, in the context of Chinese Zen Buddhism it would be understood as the assertion, "The What is this ceaseless time of arising and vanishing," the 'What' being used as an epithet for That Which goes beyond any name we can assign to It.

*   See Glossary.

elements. Because they are elements, they are beyond defilement, and because they are beyond defilement, they are untainted. To put it simply, untainted is what the Buddhas and the Ancestors are. And They say that you are just the same, for who is not a 'you'? All those for whom there existed a previous moment and for whom there exists a following moment will be a 'you'. And They say that 'I' is just the same and, since previous moments and following moments all constitute what an 'I' is, who is not an 'I'?

In that vanishing of the Buddha's, He was adorned with all manner of hands and eyes.[4] This was His great, unsurpassed nirvana, which is spoken of by some as His 'death', and which is described by others as His 'entering into extinction', and by others still as His 'entering a place of abiding'. While the ever so many hands and eyes are spoken of in these ways, they are nothing other than the meritorious function of the Buddha's vanishing. He said that on the occasion of His 'I' vanishing, He did not speak about it, and on the occasion of His 'I' arising, again He did not speak about it. Yet even though these were simultaneous when He was alive, they may not have been simultaneous once He was dead.[5]

This vanishing refers to the previous elements having already vanished, and it refers to the vanishing of future elements. It refers to the previous moments of the elements and it refers to the future moments of the elements. It refers to the previous and future elements, which are our thoughts and things in operation, and it refers to the previous and future moments, which are also our thoughts and things in operation.[6] Their 'not depending on each other' refers to our thoughts and things in operation and

4.   'Hands and eyes' is an allusion to the myriad ways in which Avalokiteshvara, who is the embodiment of the innate compassion of one's Buddha Nature, sees and offers aid to those who cry out for help.

5.   In this context, 'alive' refers to the time when we believed in the delusion of a separate self, and 'dead' refers to the time when we have relinquished that self because we have realized our True Nature.

6.   The phrase 'our thoughts and things' refers to whatever arises, persists for a while, disintegrates, and vanishes, be it the thoughts that we perceive as being within our mind or the things that we consider to occur in the physical world.

their 'not standing against each other' refers to the operating of our thoughts and things. Our letting them not stand against each other and our letting them not depend on each other is our realizing eighty or ninety percent of the Truth. When this vanishing turns the four elements* and the five skandhas* of our being into hands and eyes, there is our taking them up and there is our dedicating them.[7] When vanishing turns the four elements and the five skandhas into our course of action, then we step forward and both Master and disciple mutually recognize each other as being 'such a one'.* At just such a moment as this, even the statement "Our whole body is hands and eyes" is insufficient. Even "Our whole being, through and through, is hands and eyes" is insufficient. In sum, 'vanishing' is the meritorious activity of an Ancestor of the Buddha.

Now, as to the expressions 'not standing against each other' and 'not depending on each other', you need to realize that 'arising' encompasses 'arising in the beginning, middle, and end'. "Officially, there is not space enough for a needle, but privately, a horse and cart can pass through."[8] 'Arising in the beginning, middle, and end' is not something that depends on vanishing, nor is it something that stands against vanishing. It makes thoughts and things suddenly arise in places where they had previously vanished, but it is not the arising of what has vanished; it is simply the arising of thoughts and things. Because it is the arising of thoughts and things, it does not stand against anything or depend on anything. Further, one moment of vanishing and another moment of vanishing are not something mutually dependent, nor are they something mutually opposing. Even vanishing in beginning, middle, and end is simply

---

7.   This sentence has a double meaning: First, by recognizing the impermanence of all thoughts and things, we dedicate our temporal being to expressing compassion. Second, by dropping off body and mind (the vanishing of a concern with self), all that remains is the dedication of oneself to expressing compassion for all beings. This double meaning of 'vanishing' as 'recognizing impermanence' and 'dropping off a concern with self' carries through the rest of this paragraph.

8.   This saying by Meditation Master Sōzan Honjaku can be paraphrased as, "Officially, the Teaching is above any personal considerations, but on an individual level, It permits of broad provisional applications."

vanishing. As a Master once remarked, "While we are encountering something, it does not stand out, but when our attention is drawn to it, then we recognize its existence." Vanishings occur suddenly in the place of previous arisings, but they are not vanishings of arising, they are vanishings of thoughts and things. Since they are vanishings of thoughts and things, they do not stand against each other, nor are they mutually dependent.

Whether vanishings are what constitutes 'all of this' or whether arisings are what constitutes 'all of this', the Buddha chose the phrase 'the meditative state that bears the seal of the Ocean' to give all these various things a name. It is not that training and enlightenment are not 'all of this', it is simply that He called this untainted state 'the meditative state that bears the seal of the Ocean'.

Meditative states are what manifest right before our eyes. They are our realization of the Way. They are the middle of the night when we grope behind us for our pillow. They are our groping behind us for our pillow on such a night.[9] And our groping about for our pillow is not something we do just for billions and billions of myriad eons: it is our being within the Ocean, constantly doing nothing other than giving expression to the Teaching on the Flowering of the Wondrous Dharma.[10] Because we do not speak of the arising of an 'I', we are within the Ocean. Its former surface, which is myriad ripples that follow from the slightest movement of a single wave, refers to our constantly giving expression to the Dharma. And Its later surface, which is a single wave that follows from the slightest movement of those myriad ripples, is the Teaching we give on the Flowering of the Wondrous Dharma. Even were we to reel up and cast out a thousand foot or ten thousand foot fishing line, such a line would, alas, just hang straight down.[11] 'The former surface' and 'the later surface' refer to that surface of the Ocean which we are on. It is as if we were to speak of the front of our head and the back of our head. What we call the front part of our

---

9.   The meaning of this metaphor is explained in detail in Discourse 32: On Kannon, the Bodhisattva of Compassion *(Kannon)*.

10.   'The Teaching on the Flowering of the Wondrous Dharma' refers to our way of expressing the Dharma that the Buddha voiced in the *Lotus Scripture*.

11.   In other words, the wondrous Dharma is like an ocean that is bottomless in its depth.

head and the back part of our head is adding a head upon a head.[12] It is not that there is a person inside, for the Ocean of one's being is not some abode of a worldly person nor is it some place beloved by a saintly person; it is one's Self alone within the Ocean of one's being. It is simply our constantly and openly giving expression to the Dharma. This 'within the Ocean' does not pertain to Its center, nor does it pertain to Its inside or outside; it is our constantly and endlessly dwelling within It as we give expression to the Teachings that are the Flowering of the Dharma. Though we do not take up residence in the east, west, south, or north, we do return, our boat empty yet fully illumined by the Moon's Light. This genuine refuge is our returning to our Original Nature. Who could say that this is our day-by-day conduct of 'staying in the water'? It is simply the Way of the Buddha manifesting in the Ultimate. We treat this as the seal that seals water. Put another way, it is the seal that seals limitless space. And put another way still, it is the seal that seals the mud. The seal that seals the water is not necessarily the seal that seals the Ocean, for above and beyond this there can be a seal that seals the Ocean. We call these the seal of the Ocean, and the seal of the water, and the seal of the mud, and the seal of the Mind. Having been directly Transmitted the seal of the Mind, we seal the water, and seal the mud, and seal the boundless space.

Sōzan Honjaku was once asked by a monk, "I have heard that it says in the Scriptures that the great ocean does not give lodging to corpses. Just what kind of an ocean is this?"

The Master responded, "One that contains all that exists."

The monk then asked, "Then why doesn't it give lodging to corpses?"

The Master replied, "What has ceased to breathe is not connected with It."

---

12.   That is, just as one cannot separate the surface of the ocean from the rest of the ocean, so one cannot separate the front of the head from the back of the head, as if they were separable objects.

The monk asked, "Given that it contains all that exists, why is something that has ceased to breathe not connected with it?"

The Master said, "The functioning of all that exists is something other than ceasing to breathe."

This Sōzan was a monastic brother to Ungo Dōyō. The fundamental thrust of Tōzan Ryōkai's teaching has found its true mark in this account.[13] Now the phrase, 'I have heard that it says in the Scriptures,' refers to the genuine Teaching of Buddhas and Ancestors. It is beyond the teachings of ordinary worldly people and of saintly ones. And it is beyond the teachings of the Lesser Course,[*] which are connected with the Buddha Dharma.

The Great Ocean does not give lodging to corpses.

'The Great Ocean' does not refer to the Innermost Sea or to the Outermost Sea, for instance, nor does It refer to the Eight Seas or any other similar ones.[14] This is not something for those of us who are studying the Way to have doubts about. And not only do we recognize as an Ocean that which is not an ocean, but we also recognize as an ocean that which is an ocean.[15] Even if you were to insist that the ocean in either case is what is being referred to, it still would not be the Great Ocean. The Great Ocean does not necessarily refer to the deep pools whose waters contain the eight virtues, nor does the Great Ocean necessarily refer to such things as the nine abysses of salt water.[16] Since Its various elements will enter into the composition of all of

---

13.   Sōzan and Ungo were both Transmitted disciples of Tōzan. Sōzan's line died out shortly after his death, whereas Ungo's has continued up to the present day and is known as Sōtō Zen, the name referring to the teachings of Sōzan and Tōzan.

14.   The Eight Seas, which include the Innermost Sea and the Outermost Sea, are associated with Mount Sumeru.

15.   An Ocean that is not an ocean refers to a metaphoric ocean, whereas an ocean that is an ocean refers to ocean in an everyday, worldly sense.

16.   The eight virtues of water are its being sweet, cold, soft, light, pure, odorless, not harmful to the throat, and not harmful to the stomach. 'The nine abysses' refers to nine vast underground rivers in China.

these, why must the Great Ocean always refer only to deep waters? This is what prompted the monk to ask, "Just what kind of an ocean is this?" And, since the Great Ocean was still unknown to ordinary people as well as to those in lofty positions, he spoke of It as 'the Great Ocean'. Someone who would ask such a question is one who would attempt to put into words his attachment to the word 'ocean'.[17]

As to Its not giving lodging to corpses, the phrase 'does not give lodging to' can mean "If you come with a clear head, you act with a clear head; if you come with a dull head, you act with a dull head." A corpse is dead ashes: its mind does not change no matter how many times it encounters the springtime. What he called 'a corpse' is something that no one has ever experienced, and that is why they do not comprehend what it is.

The Master's saying, "One that contains all that exists," expresses what the Ocean is. The point he is making is not that there is some single thing that contains all that exists, but rather that It is all contained things. And he is not saying that the Great Ocean is what contains all existing things, but rather that what is expressing 'all contained things' is simply the Great Ocean. Though we do not know what It is, It is everything that exists for the moment. Even coming face-to-face with a Buddha or an Ancestor is a mistaken perception of 'everything that exists for the moment'. At the moment of 'being contained', although it may involve a mountain, it is not just our 'standing atop a soaring mountain peak', and although it may involve water, it is not just our 'plunging down to the floor of the Ocean's abyss'.[18] Our acts of acceptance will be like this, as will our acts of letting go. What we call the Ocean of our Buddha Nature and what we call the Ocean of Vairochana* are simply synonymous with 'all that exists'.

---

17. That is, the disciple is asking his question because he is not sure that he understands what Sōzan is talking about, but not because he doubts the validity of what Sōzan is saying.

18. Dōgen borrows these two lines from a poem by Meditation Master Yakusan, which Dōgen had previously quoted at the beginning of Discourse 11: On 'Just for the Time Being, Just for a While, For the Whole of Time Is the Whole of Existence' (*Uji*). Here, he is expanding on what he said in that discourse.

Even though the surface of the Ocean may not be visible to us, we never doubt its existence in our daily conduct of 'swimming about'. For example, the monk Tafuku—one of Jōshū's Dharma heirs—once described a grove of bamboo as, "One or two canes are crooked, and three or four canes are aslant." Although his daily monastic conduct led him to see all that exists as a bunch of errors, why did he not say, "A thousand crooked canes! Nay, ten thousand crooked canes!" Why did he not say, "A thousand groves! Nay, ten thousand groves!" Do not lose sight of the underlying principle that is present like this in a grove of bamboo. Sōzan's expression, "One that contains all that exists," is synonymous with 'all that exists'.[19]

Although the monk's question, "Why is something that has ceased to breathe not connected with it?" might be viewed, albeit mistakenly, as arising from doubt, it could have been just what his mind was concerned with. When Master Rinzai said about Fuke, his elder brother in the Sangha, "I have long had my doubts about that fellow," he was simply recognizing who 'the person' was about whom he had long held doubts.[20] In what exists, why is something that has ceased to breathe <u>not</u> connected with It and how can It <u>not</u> give lodging to corpses? Herein, why something that has ceased to breathe is not connected with It is that It already contains all that exists. Keep in mind that 'containing' does not mean 'keeping' and that 'containing' is synonymous with 'not giving lodging to'. Even if all that exists were a corpse, it might well be that not giving lodging to it would forthwith span ten thousand years, and it might well be that 'not belonging to It' is this old monk Dōgen playing one stone in a game of *Go*.

What Sōzan said is, "The functioning of all that exists is something other than ceasing to breathe." In other words, whether all that exists ceases to breathe or does not stop breathing, a corpse would still be unconnected with It. Even though a corpse is a corpse, if it had behavior that was in harmony with all that exists, it would contain all—it would be containment. The journey before us and the journey behind

19. That is, the It is not something separate from what It contains since both the contents and the container are identical with It.

20. Rinzai's remark was not derogatory, but was a common way among Zen monks of acknowledging that someone—in this case, Fuke—was 'such a person'.

us, which is part and parcel of all that exists, each have their own functions, and ceasing to breathe is not one of them. In other words, it is like the blind leading the blind. The fundamental principle of the blind leading the blind includes 'one blind person leading one blind person' and 'a mass of blind people leading a mass of blind people'. When a mass of blind people are leading a mass of blind people, all contained things contain all contained things. Further, no matter how many Great Ways there are, They are beyond 'all that exists', for we have still not fully manifested our meditative practice, which is the meditative state that bears the seal of the Ocean.

Written at Kannondōri in Kōshōhōrin-ji Temple on the twentieth day of summer in the third year of the Ninji era (May 21, 1242).

Copied by me during the first year of the Kangen era (1243).

Ejō

31

On Predicting Buddhahood

(Juki)

Translator's Introduction: This discourse is based on the prediction by Shakyamuni Buddha that all sentient beings will ultimately realize Buddhahood. In Japanese, this prediction is called *juki*, a technical term that needs to be translated in slightly different ways depending on context. These can include the principle of predicting Buddhahood, the conferring of a prediction of Buddhahood, and affirming someone's realization of Buddhahood, among others. Towards the end of the discourse, Dōgen writes the word *juki* using a different character for *ju,* which conveys the meaning of receiving, accepting, or acknowledging the prediction.

The Great Teaching which Ancestors of the Buddha have Transmitted one-to-one is the prediction of Buddhahood. Those who have not trained with an Ancestor of the Buddha have never encountered this Teaching even in their dreams. The timing of this prediction varies. It is predicted even for persons who have not yet given rise to the Mind of Wisdom, and it is predicted for those who are not yet aware of their Buddha Nature, and it is predicted for those who are aware of their Buddha Nature, and it is predicted for those who have a sense of a personal self, and it is predicted for those who are beyond a sense of a personal self, and it is predicted for all Buddhas. All Buddhas preserve and rely on the predictions of Buddhas. In your training, you should not think that after you have had the prediction conferred on you, you will become a Buddha, nor should you think that after you have become a Buddha, you will receive some affirmation of it. At the time when the prediction is conferred there is one's becoming Buddha, and, at that same time, there is also one's continued training and practice. There is the affirmation of Buddhahood that resides within all Buddhas, and there is the affirmation that is above and beyond Buddhahood. This affirmation is given to oneself, and it is given to one's body and mind. If one then gives up on continuing to learn about 'the Great Matter* of the affirmation of Buddhahood', then one is giving up on learning through practice, and thereby sets aside 'the Great Matter of the Way of the Buddha'. The prediction of Buddhahood is

---

* See Glossary.

present before one has a body, and the prediction of Buddhahood is present after one has a body. There is the prediction of Buddhahood that we can recognize, and there is the prediction of Buddhahood that we do not recognize. There is the prediction of Buddhahood that others become aware of, and there is the prediction of Buddhahood that others do not become aware of.

By all means, you need to realize that when you affirm your prediction of Buddhahood, your true Self will manifest before your very eyes, for affirming the prediction of Buddhahood is synonymous with the manifesting of your true Self. Therefore, what Buddha after Buddha, Ancestor after Ancestor, and Successor after Successor have inherited is just this prediction of Buddhahood. And further, there is not a single thought or thing that is excluded from this prediction. So how could the great earth with its mountains and rivers, along with Mount Sumeru and its vast oceans, possibly be exceptions? There is not the least person, be it Mr. Chang's third son or Mr. Li's fourth son, who is beyond it.[1] The prediction of Buddhahood that we thoroughly explore in this way is something that we can express in one phrase, that we can hear in one phrase, that we may misunderstand in one phrase, and that we may comprehend in one phrase. It is our doing our practice in all earnestness and our giving expression to the Dharma in all sincerity. It is what instructs us to step back and what instructs us to step forward.[2] Our being able to sit here today whilst wearing the kesa* could not have come about had we not been able to receive the prediction that has come to us from the distant past. Because we have put our hands in gasshō* and placed the kesa upon our heads, what has manifested before us is the prediction of our Buddhahood.

---

1.   Chang and Li are common Chinese family names and, much like the western names Smith and Jones, are used to refer to anybody in general. Third and fourth sons also represent individuals who are not apt to hold a position of importance within a family. Hence, the allusion is to 'anybody and everybody'.

2.   In Zen parlance, 'stepping back' is associated with sitting in meditation and reflecting on one's True Nature, whereas 'stepping forward' is associated with going forth and doing one's daily deeds from the mind of meditation.

The Buddha once said:

Although there are many forms for affirming Buddhahood, to summarize them briefly, there are eight:

First, you recognize it yourself, but others do not
recognize it,

Second, everyone else recognizes it, but you do not,

Third, both you and everyone else recognize it,

Fourth, neither you nor anyone else recognize it,

Fifth, those close to you perceive it, but those distant
from you do not,

Sixth, those distant from you perceive it, but those
close to you do not,

Seventh, both those close to you and distant from you
perceive it,

Eighth, neither those close to you nor distant from you
perceive it.

The affirmation of one's Buddhahood is just like this. So, do not occupy yourself with thoughts that your Buddhahood cannot be affirmed because it has not been recognized or appreciated by the living spirit within that smelly skin bag* of yours. And do not say that the prediction of Buddhahood cannot be readily given even to those humans who have not yet awakened. In ordinary, worldly ways of thinking, people have customarily been taught that they will receive this prediction when they have completely fulfilled their training and practice, for that is what is critical to their becoming a Buddha, but in the Way of the Buddha this is not what is taught. When someone gives heed to a single phrase whilst following a good spiritual friend or gives heed to a single phrase whilst following some Scriptural work, this will be the cause for their receiving a prediction of Buddhahood, because this is the fundamental practice of all the Buddhas, and it is the practice that puts down good roots amidst all the hundreds of things that sprout up in one's life. If I were to express in words what the prediction of Buddhahood is, I would say that all who receive the prediction are persons who will indeed realize the Ultimate.

Keep in mind that even a single mote of dust is unsurpassed, that even a single mote of dust is transcendent. Why would the prediction of Buddhahood not include a single mote of dust? Why would the prediction of Buddhahood not include each thought and thing? Why would the prediction of Buddhahood not include all the myriad thoughts and things that arise? Why would the prediction of Buddhahood not include training and enlightenment? Why would the prediction of Buddhahood not include the Buddhas and the Ancestors? Why would the prediction of Buddhahood not include one's doing one's utmost in practicing the Way? Why would the prediction of Buddhahood not include great realization and great delusion? It is just as Meditation Master Ōbaku said to his disciple Rinzai, "When my tradition comes down to you, it will greatly flourish in the world." And it is just as Meditation Master Enō said to his disciple Nangaku, "You too are like this, and I too am like this." The prediction of Buddhahood is a mark of the Dharma. The prediction of Buddhahood is "How could it be otherwise?" The prediction of Buddhahood is a face breaking out in a smile. The prediction of Buddhahood is birth and death: it is coming and going. The prediction of Buddhahood is the whole universe in all its ten quarters. The prediction of Buddhahood is the whole universe's never having been hidden from us.

Gensha Shibi was once walking in attendance with his Master Seppō, when Seppō pointed to the ground right before them and said, "This plot of land would be a fine place to erect a seamless stupa for me."

Shibi asked him, "And how high would it be?"

Thereupon, Seppō looked up and down as though measuring it.

Shibi then said, "There will certainly be great good fortune for all ordinary humans, as well as for those in lofty positions, from such a stupa. And yet, my venerable monk, it is as if you have not encountered the prediction of Buddhahood on Vulture Peak even in your dreams."

> Seppō responded, "Well, how would you put it?"
> Shibi replied, "Seven feet or eight feet."[3]

Now, in Shibi's saying, "And, my venerable monk, it would seem that you have not yet encountered the prediction of Buddhahood on Vulture Peak even in your dreams," he was not saying that the prediction of Buddhahood on Vulture Peak did not exist for Seppō, nor was he saying that Seppō had received the prediction of Buddhahood on Vulture Peak. He was saying that it seemed as if the venerable monk had never encountered the prediction of Buddhahood on Vulture Peak even in his dreams.[4]

We need to use our Eye to see the prediction of Buddhahood on Vulture Peak from a higher perspective. Shakyamuni Buddha put it in words as, "I have the Wondrous Heart of Nirvana, which is the Treasure House of the Eye of the True Teaching, and I am entrusting It to Makakashō." Keep in mind that, in harmony with the time, when Seigen gave the prediction of Buddhahood to his disciple Sekitō, Makakashō was likewise receiving Seigen's prediction of Buddhahood, and Seigen was also conferring Shakyamuni's prediction of Buddhahood. Thus, it is clear that Buddha after Buddha and Ancestor after Ancestor have had entrusted to Them the Treasure House of the Eye of the True Teaching. Accordingly, Daikan Enō, the Sixth Chinese Ancestor of Mount Sōkei, had already conferred the prediction on Seigen. Once he had received the prediction from the Sixth Ancestor, Seigen became the real Seigen who preserved and relied upon the prediction of his Buddhahood. At this time, what all the Ancestors up to the Sixth Ancestor had learned by exploring the Matter through their training was being put into practice through affirming the prediction of Seigen's Buddhahood. This has been described as:

---

3. A seamless stupa is a funeral monument carved out of solid rock that serves as a repository for someone's remains. When it contains the remains of a Master, it is considered to be the body of a seated Buddha six feet tall. Shibi's saying "Seven feet or eight feet" was a statement that expressed deep love and respect for his Master.

4. By this statement, Shibi was affirming the 'no self' of his Master.

> *Clear and bright are the tips of all the things*
> *that sprout up;*
> *Clear and bright are the true intentions of the*
> *Buddhas and Ancestors.*

Since this is so, how can the Buddhas and the Ancestors not include 'all the things that sprout up'? How can all the things that sprout up not include 'me' and 'you'? Do not be foolish and think that you can see or recognize all the thoughts and things with which you are personally endowed. This is not the way things are. The thoughts and things that we recognize are not necessarily our own possessions. What we possess is not necessarily something that we ourselves see or are aware of. So, do not be skeptical, thinking that since the prediction is beyond anything we now know, or see, or think about, we are not in possession of it. What is more, what we call the prediction of Buddhahood on Vulture Peak is Shakyamuni Buddha's predicting of Buddhahood: it was given from Shakyamuni Buddha to Shakyamuni Buddha. While it would be reasonable not to give the prediction to someone whom you are not yet sure of, the underlying meaning is that there is no obstacle to affirming the prediction of Buddhahood for someone who has already received that prediction. Even where there has not been an affirmation of Buddhahood, it is not superfluous to predict someone's Buddhahood. There is nothing lacking nor is there anything superfluous: this is the principle of predicting Buddhahood that all Ancestors of the Buddha have given to all Ancestors of the Buddha. This is why the Old Buddha Unchō Tokufū said:

> *From past to present, Masters have raised their*
> *hossu* to point the Matter out,*
> *Great their wish, deep and subtle, and not, I dare say,*
> *easy to explore.*
> *Were it not for this Truth which Masters have given*
> *through their Teaching,*
> *From what perspective, pray, could we talk about It?*

Now, to thoroughly explore Shibi's point, in his reckoning how high a stupa made from solid rock is, he used the expression "How high?" Thus, it is not that Shibi is dissatisfied with Seppō's looking up and down. It is simply that—thanks to Seppō— even though there will certainly be great good fortune for all ordinary humans, as well as those in lofty positions, nevertheless, Seppō's way of looking at the stupa is not what Shakyamuni Buddha's prediction of Buddhahood is about. That which gains Shakyamuni Buddha's prediction of Buddhahood exists in the expression 'seven feet or eight feet'. In our looking closely at Shakyamuni's real prediction of Buddhahood, we need to examine it by means of the expression 'seven feet or eight feet'. So, setting aside for the moment whether the expression 'seven feet or eight feet' is on target or not, the prediction of Buddhahood must unquestionably encompass the prediction of Seppō's Buddhahood as well as the prediction of Shibi's Buddhahood. Further, one should express the height of a stupa by proffering the prediction of Buddhahood. Should anyone proffer something other than the prediction of Buddhahood, it will not be an expression that conveys the Buddha Dharma.

Whenever we recognize, hear, or state that the Self is truly our self, then, beyond doubt, the prediction of Buddhahood will fully manifest our spiritual question. When we are face-to-face with the prediction of our Buddhahood, we will immediately do our utmost in practice, for this is in harmony with the prediction of Buddhahood. In order to ultimately realize the prediction of Buddhahood, just as ever so many Ancestors of the Buddha have done, one trains in order to manifest one's genuine enlightenment. And utilizing one's strength in the effort to affirm one's Buddhahood brings forth the Buddhas en masse. This is why Shakyamuni Buddha said in the *Lotus Scripture,* "Only because of Their relationship to the One Great Matter do Buddhas appear in the world." This means that, on a higher level, it is the transcendent Self, which goes beyond one's personal self, that receives the prediction of the transcendent Self's Buddhahood. This is why Buddhas receive the affirmation of Buddhas.

Generally speaking, when it comes to giving the prediction, there are those who predict it by raising one hand, and those who predict it by raising two hands, and those who predict it by raising a thousand hands and eyes, and those who are given the prediction. On one occasion it was predicted by the raising of an udumbara blossom, and on another occasion Shakyamuni predicted it for Makakashō by holding aloft a gold brocade kesa, but neither of these ways is a required way of doing it. There are various ways of conferring the prediction. There can be a prediction of one's Buddhahood from within, and there can be a prediction of one's Buddhahood from without. The principle of thoroughly exploring 'within and without' will be found by exploring the affirmation of Buddhahood through your training with your Master. To learn the Way as an affirmation of Buddhahood is equivalent to a single iron rod extending for ten thousand miles. To sit with the stillness of a mountain as an affirmation of Buddhahood is a single instant being equivalent to ten thousand years.

Our Old Buddha Shakyamuni once said in verse:

> *One after another, They were able to realize Buddhahood*
> *And, turning to the next, They were able to confer the*
> *prediction of Buddhahood.*[5]

The realization of Buddhahood spoken of here undoubtedly implies 'one after another', and 'one after another' refers to realizing Buddhahood bit by bit. There is a 'turning to the next' in the predicting of Buddhahood. 'Turning to the next' is a turning that begets a turning, and 'turning to the next' is a next that begets a next. It is, for instance, creating a next, and creating a next involves performing an action. That action is beyond the deliberate, calculated creation of a self, beyond the deliberate, calculated creation of circumstances, beyond any measured concoction, and beyond any deliberately created state of mind. By relying on the principle of 'turning to the next', you should, by all means, thoroughly investigate both your creating circumstances and your not creating circumstances. And by relying on the principle

---

5.   A verse based on a passage in the Lotus Scripture, which speaks of a Transmission line that will pass
      through five hundred monks. 'The next' refers to one's disciple, that is, someone who is next in the
      line of succession.

of 'turning to the next', you should thoroughly investigate both what you are concocting and what you are not concocting.

Now, the emerging of Buddhas and Ancestors is due to Each having been turned to through performing some action. The coming from the West of the five Buddhas and the six Ancestors was due to Each having been turned to through performing some action.[6] And what is more, the toting of water and the carrying of firewood has continued on by a turning to the next. To live your life as "One's very mind is Buddha" is a turning towards the next. When you enter nirvana as "One's very mind is Buddha"—and entering once or twice is nothing extraordinary—you will pass through ever so many nirvanas, and will realize ever so many realizations of the Truth, and will manifest as signs and marks ever so many signs and marks.[7] This is nothing other than realizing Buddhahood by one after another, and entering nirvana by one after another, and predicting Buddhahood for one after another, and one after another realizing what 'turning to the next' is. Turning to the next is not something that is inherent, but is simply something that is all-pervasive, penetrating all. Now, Buddhas and Ancestors mutually recognize each other, face-to-face, and this face-to-face mutual recognition is what is meant by 'one after another'. There is no room in which to turn away from or evade turning to the next in the giving of the prediction by a Buddha or in the giving of the prediction by an Ancestor.

---

6. The five Buddhas are the Five Dhyāni Buddhas of esoteric Buddhism, each of whom represents a particular aspect of the Cosmic Buddha. These Buddhas are: Vairochana, the Eternal Buddha; Akshobya, the Immovable Buddha; Ratnasambhava, the Jewel-Born Buddha; Amitabha, the Buddha of Immeasurable Light; and Amoghasiddhi, the Fearless Buddha. The six Ancestors is an allusion to Bodhidharma as the First Chinese Ancestor through Daikan Enō who was the Sixth.

7. 'Signs and marks' is an allusion to the thirty-three signs and eighty distinguishing marks of a Buddha.

It was an Old Buddha who said:[8]

> *Now that I have heard from the Buddha*
> *That we have received His glorious prediction of our*
> *Buddhahood*
> *And that through His turning to the next, we have had*
> *His assurance conferred upon us,*
> *My body and mind are filled with joy.*

This is saying that the glorious matter of Shakyamuni Buddha's prediction is, beyond question, what Kaundinya heard from the Buddha. What has filled his body and mind with joy is that he has also received an assurance, which he has just now heard from the Buddha through His turning to the next. The next that is turned to will be the 'I now' who hears and the assurance will not be limited to some 'self' or 'other' of past, present, or future. It will be heard of from the Buddha and not from someone else. This lies beyond delusion and enlightenment, beyond sentient beings, and beyond earthly realms with their grasses and trees, for it will be what one hears from the Buddha. It is the glorious matter of His predicting our Buddhahood, and it is our receiving His assurance through His turning to us as 'the next'. The principle of 'turning to the next' never gets stuck in some cranny even for a moment but, bit by bit, fills the body and mind with joy. The joyous assertion that is extended through this turning to the next is undoubtedly in harmony with the body, which is seeking far and wide for the Master, and it is also in harmony with the mind, which is seeking far and wide for the Master. Further, because the body, beyond question, thoroughly permeates the mind, and the mind, beyond question, thoroughly permeates the body, Kaundinya spoke of his body and mind being filled. In other words, it is what permeates all worlds and all directions; it permeates the body and permeates the mind. This, then, is a particularly great joy. This joy clearly gladdens us, whether we are

---

8.   The Old Buddha is Ajnyata Kaundinya, one of the five ascetics who associated with Shakyamuni before His enlightenment. As recorded in the Lotus Sutra, Kaundinya was the first of five hundred to receive this prediction after the Buddhas enlightenment.

asleep or awake, deluded or enlightened. Even so, although the states of being asleep, awake, deluded, or enlightened are intimately connected with each other, they do not stain or defile each other. This is the glorious matter of predicting our Buddhahood, which is our being turned to and receiving the affirmation.

        Shakyamuni Buddha, through speaking to Bhaisajyaguru, the Bodhisattva* Lord of Healing, addressed eighty-thousand other bodhisattvas, saying, "O Lord of Healing, within this great assembly of countless heavenly beings, dragon kings, yakshas, gandharvas, asuras, garudas, kinnaras, and mahoragas[9]—both human and nonhuman—as well as male and female monastics, and male and female laity, you can see those who are seeking to be shravakas,* those who are seeking to be pratyekabuddhas,* and those who are seeking the Bodhisattva Way to Buddhahood. If such as these, who are all standing before the Buddha now, should hear but a single verse or line from My Teaching, which is the flowering of the Wondrous Dharma, and take joy in It for even a moment, I will give them all a prediction of their Buddhahood. Beyond question, all will realize supreme, fully perfected enlightenment."

So, within this assembly of countless beings, even though the wishes and levels of understanding of these countless heavenly beings and dragon kings, of those in the four categories of Buddhists, and of those in the eight categories of nonhumans may differ, who would have them hear one line or verse which would not be the Wondrous Dharma? How could any of you take joy in non-Buddhist teachings even for a moment? His phrase 'such as these' means those who are the flowers of the

---

9.   'Dragon kings…mahoragas' comprise a list of quasi-mythical beings who were originally given to violent or seductive acts but who, upon conversion to Buddhism, became spiritual guardians, each type having governance over some protective function. Hence, they may manifest as some human or non-human being fulfilling that function. Together with the heavenly beings, they are known as the eight categories of non-human beings.

Dharma. His phrase 'who are all standing before the Buddha' means all who are within Buddha. Even though humans and nonhumans may hold mixed beliefs concerning the myriad thoughts and things that arise, and even though there are those who have sown karmic* seeds for hundreds of later sproutings, they will still be included in 'such as these'. 'Such as these' means 'all those to whom I have given a prediction of Buddhahood'. 'All those to whom I have given a prediction of Buddhahood' is correct from head to tail. Accordingly, it is the proper functioning of supreme, fully perfected enlightenment.

> Shakyamuni Buddha, in addressing the Lord of Healing, also said, "Further, after the Tathagata's extinction, if there is someone who hears a single verse or line of My Teaching, which is the flowering of the Wondrous Dharma, and that one were to rejoice in It even for a moment, I would predict supreme, fully perfected enlightenment for such a one as well."

What would be the time span implied by the phrase 'after the Tathagata's extinction' that was just spoken of? Would it be within the forty-nine years after His enlightenment or would it be within the eighty years of His whole life span? Let's say for the moment that it is the eighty-year span. When the Buddha said, "If there is someone who hears a single verse or line of My Teaching, which is the flowering of the Wondrous Dharma, and that one were to rejoice in It even for a moment," was he referring only to what is heard by those who are keen-witted and not to what is heard by those who are dull-witted? And does it matter if they hear it correctly or not? If we express this Teaching for the sake of others, it should be expressed as, "If there are any people by whom It is heard," and so on. And do not treat them as being either keen-witted or dull-witted. What you should say is, "Although that which hears His Teaching, which is the flowering of the Dharma, is the profound and immeasurable wisdom of Buddhas, when some hear It, It is invariably experienced as one phrase, and when others hear It, It is invariably experienced as one verse, and when still others hear It, It is invariably experienced as one moment of joyousness." Such a moment will be Shakyamuni Buddha's once again giving His prediction of their realizing supreme, fully perfected enlightenment. There is His giving His prediction one more time and there is His giving His prediction to all. Do not entrust some stumble-footed, worldly, third son of Chang with the task of spiritual prediction. Experience it through painstaking effort that is in harmony with your training. Then you will be 'someone who hearkens with joy to a single line or verse'. There is no time to waste by treating Skin and Flesh, Bones and Marrow as if one were sticking a head upon one's own head. His witnessing someone's being given the prediction of supreme, fully perfected enlightenment is the Buddha's wish being fulfilled. And it will be the same for all us skin bags. Through this prediction, the hopes of the multitudes are fulfilled. And it would be like this if anyone hears it.

Buddhahood has been affirmed by holding aloft a pine branch, by holding aloft an udumbara blossom, by holding aloft twinkling eyes, and by a face breaking into a smile. And there is the example from the past of its having been affirmed by passing on a pair of sandals. These are some examples of this Dharma's being something that speculative and discriminatory thinking are unable to fathom. There is the affirmation of "I myself am also like this," and there is the affirmation of, "You yourself are also like this." This principle can be stated as, "One can give the prediction of Buddhahood in the past, present, and future." Because past, present, and future are encompassed within the prediction of Buddhahood, Buddhahood is realized in the prediction of one's own Buddhahood and it is realized in the prediction of the Buddhahood of others.

Vimalakirti,* in talking with Maitreya,* said, "O Maitreya, it is said that the World-honored One has given you the prediction that in some lifetime you would realize supreme, fully perfected enlightenment. In which lifetime are you able to receive His prediction? Is it in the past, or in the present, or in the future? If you say it was in a past lifetime, such a past life has already gone. If you say it will be in some future life, such a future life has yet to come. If you say that it is in your present lifetime, there is no present lifetime that abides. If it is as the Buddha teaches, then you, dear monk, at this very moment, are living and aging and perishing. If you are able to receive His prediction on account of your no longer being alive, then no longer being alive would be the right state to be in.[10] But, then again, within such a 'right state', one cannot receive a prediction and one cannot realize supreme, fully perfected enlightenment. So how, Maitreya, will you receive the prediction in any lifetime? Will you do it by being able to receive the prediction in life just as it is? Or will you do it by being able to receive the prediction in death just as it is? If you say you can get the prediction by means of life just as it is, there is no such thing as 'life just as it is'. If you say you can get the prediction by means of death just as it is, there is no such thing as 'death just as it is'. All sentient beings are like this, and all thoughts and things are also like this. The wise and holy among the multitudes are also like this. And you, Maitreya, are also just like this. If you, Maitreya, are able to receive the prediction, then all sentient beings should also be able to receive the prediction. And why is that? Well, because 'That Which Is as It Is' is free of duality and free of any differentiations. If you, Maitreya, can realize supreme, fully perfected enlightenment, all sentient beings can likewise realize it. And why is that? Because all sentient beings are already manifestations of enlightenment."

What Vimalakirti is saying here is not something that the Tathagata has said is not so. While this is true, Maitreya's being able to receive the prediction was already a settled matter. Therefore, the ability of all sentient beings to receive the prediction must likewise be a settled matter. If there is no affirmation for sentient beings, there cannot be any affirmation for Maitreya, because all sentient beings are manifestations of enlightenment. It is enlightenment that receives the prediction of enlightenment. Receiving the prediction is our life this very day. Thus, because all sentient beings have given rise to the same intention to realize Buddhahood, their receiving the prediction will be the same and their realizing the Way will be the same.

---

10.   This refers to the intermediate stage between death and rebirth.

Even so, Vimalakirti, by your assertion, "Within this 'right state', one cannot receive a prediction," you seem not to know that the 'right state' is simply one's receiving the prediction, and you do not seem to be saying, "The 'right state' is precisely what enlightenment is." Further, you said, for example, that one's life in the past has already gone, one's life in the future has not yet come, and one's life in the present does not abide. But the past is not necessarily something that has gone, the future is not necessarily something that has not yet come, and the present is not necessarily something that is not abiding. Although you may say that you are studying such notions as 'already gone', 'not yet come', and 'not abiding,' in terms of past, future, and present, by all means you need to state the principle that what has not yet come is past, present, and future. When we recognize this, then we will understand the principle that our arising and our perishing both realize the prediction, and we will understand the principle that our arising and our perishing both realize enlightenment. When all sentient beings realize the prediction of their Buddhahood, Maitreya, too, realizes his prediction.

Now, O Vimalakirti, I would like to ask you, "Is Maitreya the same as any sentient being or is he different?" Try to say, and we'll see! You have already said that if Maitreya obtains the prediction, all sentient beings will also obtain the prediction. If you are saying that Maitreya is other than a sentient being, then sentient beings cannot be sentient beings and Maitreya, likewise, cannot be Maitreya. But that won't do, for at this very moment, you too could not be Vimalakirti! If you were not Vimalakirti, then this expression of yours would be useless. So, we can say that when the prediction of Buddhahood causes the lives of all sentient beings to exist, there are the lives of all sentient beings and there is Maitreya. The prediction of Buddhahood can cause everything to exist.

Written in the summer of the third year of the Ninji era, on the twenty-fifth day of the fourth lunar month (May 26, 1242) at Kannondōri in Kōshōhōrin-ji Temple.

Copied by me on the twentieth day of the first lunar month in the second year of the Kangen era (February 29, 1244) while I was residing in the quarters of the Abbot's assistant at Kippō-ji Temple in Etchū Province.

On Kannon, the Bodhisattva of Compassion

(Kannon)

Translator's Introduction: The name Kannon is a shortened version of Kanzeon (Skt. Avalokiteshvara), 'The One Who Heeds the Cries of the World'. This Bodhisattva goes under many names and has taken many forms in India, as well as in other East Asian Buddhist cultures. Originally, Avalokiteshvara was iconographically represented as being male, but after the figure came into China, it was often pictured as being female, although not exclusively so. From the standpoint of Buddhist iconography, the male aspect represents the personification of compassion, whereas the female aspect represents compassion in action. However, Buddhas and Bodhisattvas are said to have the ability to shift between these two functions, depending on which seems to be the more spiritually helpful in a given situation. For a translator writing in English, this presents a problem of how to refer to Kannon: as He or as She. Since a choice has to be made, I have chosen to use masculine grammatical forms simply because, historically, this Bodhisattva is Indian in origin, where the figure is traditionally considered to be male and the name is grammatically masculine in gender.

The compassion that is represented by Kannon has no limitations in its functioning, as the dialogue between the two brother-monks, Ungan and Dōgo, expresses. It is like eyes that see everything and hands that offer help everywhere, even in the darkest of times. Some readers may find it difficult, on occasion, to follow what Dōgen is driving at in this discourse. To put it simply, when it comes to conveying what the innate compassion of one's Buddha Nature is, it is difficult to express what is essentially beyond words to convey, and conventional ways of talking about the innate compassion of one's Buddha Nature do not meet the mark. Therefore, even though Ungan and Dōgo successfully found a way of expressing what the compassion of Buddha Nature is like, the way that they put the matter goes beyond conventional ways of understanding what is said. At times Dōgen explains what they mean by using the *via positiva* (saying what something is like) and at other times he does this by using the *via negativa* (saying what something is not like).

Ungan Donjō once asked Dōgo Enchi,[1] "What use does the Bodhisattva* of Great Compassion make of His ever so many hands and eyes?"

Dōgo replied, "He is like someone in the night who reaches behind himself, his hand groping for his pillow."

Ungan remarked, "I get it, I get it!"

Dōgo asked, "What did you get?"

Ungan said, "That His whole body is hands and eyes."

Dōgo replied, "What you have said is very well put. Still, it only expresses eighty or ninety percent of the Matter."*

Ungan responded, "Well, so much for the likes of me. How about you, my elder brother in the Dharma, what do you make of it?"

Dōgo replied, "That His whole being, through and through, is hands and eyes."

In expressing what Kannon is, many voices have been heard before and after this incident, but none of them equal the words of Ungan and Dōgo. If you wish to explore through your training what Kannon is, you should thoroughly investigate what Ungan and Dōgo are saying here. The Bodhisattva of Great Compassion spoken of here is Kanzeon Bosatsu, 'The Bodhisattva Who Heeds the Cries of the World', who is also known as Kanjizai Bosatsu, 'The Bodhisattva Who Observes All Things Free of Attachments'. Through our training, we study Him, or Her, as the father and mother of all Buddhas. So do not consider Him to be inferior to the Buddhas, thinking that He has not yet realized the Truth, for in the past He was the Tathagata known as 'The Clarifier of the True Dharma'.

So, let us now take up, and thoroughly explore, the words spoken by Ungan, namely, "What use does the Bodhisattva of Great Compassion make of His ever so many hands and eyes?" There are Buddhist traditions that make a point of honoring

---

1.   Ungan and Dōgo were both Dharma heirs of Yakusan Igen.

*   See Glossary.

Kannon, and there are Buddhist traditions that have not yet seen Kannon even in their dreams. The Kannon that existed for Ungan was in complete harmony with Dōgo's Kannon. And this was not so just for one or two Kannons, but Ungan was likewise in harmony with hundreds of thousands of myriad Kannons. Only Ungan's assembly allowed Kannon to truly be Kannon. And why is that? The difference between the Kannon of which Ungan spoke and the Kannon of which other Buddhas spoke is like the difference between being able to put It in words and not being able to put It in words. The Kannon of some Buddhas merely had twelve faces; this was not so for Ungan. The Kannon of some other Buddhas merely had a thousand hands and eyes; this was not so for Ungan. The Kannon of still other Buddhas had eighty-four thousand hands and eyes; this was not so for Ungan. How do I know this to be true? Because when Ungan speaks of the Bodhisattva of Great Compassion using His ever so many hands and eyes, his phrase 'ever so many' does not mean merely eighty-four thousand hands and eyes. How much less did he limit it to some particular number, like twelve or thirty-two or thirty-three! 'Ever so many' is synonymous with 'beyond count'. The phrase 'ever so many' is not limited as to what sort or how many. Since it is not limited to any sort or amount, you should not limit it, not even by calculating it to be an unbounded, limitless amount. You need to explore through your training that the underlying meaning of the phrase 'ever so many' is just like this, for it has already gone beyond the bounds of the immeasurable and the unbounded.

Now, in taking up Ungan's phrase 'His ever so many hands and eyes', Dōgo did not say that it did not reveal the Matter, so it must have contained the underlying principle. Ungan and Dōgo were in complete harmony with each other and stood shoulder-to-shoulder, having already trained together under Yakusan for forty years. During that time, they had discussed accounts from both the past and the present, rooting out what was not correct and verifying what was correct. Because they had trained together in this manner, when on this day they stated 'His ever so many hands and eyes', Ungan was making a statement and Dōgo was verifying it. Keep in mind that 'His ever so many hands and eyes' was being discussed by both of these Old Buddhas alike. Both Ungan and Dōgo are clearly in accord concerning 'His ever so many hands and eyes', so Ungan now asks Dōgo what use Kannon makes of them.

Do not consider his question to be the same as the types of questions raised by academic teachers of Scriptures and scholarly writers of commentaries, or by the 'thrice wise and ten times saintly'.[*] This question has elicited a spiritual affirmation: it has elicited 'hands and eyes'. Now, there may well be Old Buddhas, as well as more recent Buddhas, who have realized Buddhahood through the force of Ungan's having said, "What use does He make of His ever so many hands and eyes?" Ungan could also have said, "What does He accomplish by making use of His ever so many hands and eyes?" And he could also have expressed the Matter as "What is it that He does?" or "What does He put into motion?" or "What is He expressing?"

> Dōgo replied, "He is like someone in the night who reaches behind himself, his hand groping for his pillow."

To express the underlying principle, Dōgo gives as an example someone who is groping behind himself for a pillow in the middle of the night. 'Groping for' means 'searching for'. 'In the night' is a way of saying 'being in the dark', just as we might speak of 'seeing a mountain in the light of day'. That is, 'using one's hands and eyes' is like someone in the night reaching behind himself, his hand groping for a pillow. We need to investigate 'using one's hands and eyes' on this basis. And we need to examine 'in the night' from the perspective of 'in the light of day', as well as from the perspective of when it is nighttime, and we need to examine it from the perspective of a time that is neither day nor night.[2] When people grope for a pillow, even though they do not understand it as something resembling Kannon's using His hands and eyes, we do not and cannot escape from the principle that it is just like that.

Can it be that the 'someone' who is 'like someone who' is just a word in a simile? And further, is this 'someone' an ordinary, everyday person or might it be someone who is no ordinary, everyday person? If we study it as being an ordinary, everyday Buddhist, then there is something we need to investigate in 'groping for a pillow'. Even a pillow has some shape or design that needs our inquiry. And 'the night' might not simply be 'the night' which ordinary people and those in lofty positions

---

2. That is, 'being in the dark' and 'seeing something in the light of day' are metaphors, and do not refer to a temporal night and day.

mean by 'day and night'. You need to realize that what is being said is not about getting hold of the pillow, or about finding the pillow, or about pushing the pillow away. If we investigate what underlies Dōgo's saying, "in the night, reaching behind himself, his hand groping for a pillow," we need to see, and not disregard, the eyes that show you the night. A hand that is groping for a pillow has not yet touched its edge. If reaching behind with the hand is essential, then is there something essential that needs to be reached with the eyes? We need to clarify what 'the night' means. Would it refer to the realm of hands and eyes? Is it in possession of human hands and eyes? Or is it just hands and eyes alone, flashing like bolts of lightning? Is it one or two instances of hands and eyes being right from head to tail? If we examine the matter in this way, then the use of ever so many hands is present. But who is the Bodhisattva of Great Compassion? It is as if all that is heard is 'the Bodhisattva of Hands and Eyes'. If that is so, then we should ask, "What does the Bodhisattva of Hands and Eyes use ever so many Bodhisattvas of Great Compassion for?"

You need to realize that even though hands and eyes do not stand against each other, they are making use of That Which Is, and That Which Is is making use of them. When That Which Is expresses Itself in this way, even though the whole of Its 'hands and eyes' are never hidden from us, we must not look for a time when It expresses Itself as 'the whole of Its hands and eyes'. Even though there are Its hands and eyes that are never hidden from us, and even though these hands and eyes do exist, they are not our self, nor are they mountains and oceans, nor are they the countenance of the sun or the countenance of the moon, nor are they "Your very mind is Buddha."

Ungan's words, "I get it, I get it!" are not saying, "I understand Dōgo's words." It is an "I get It, I get It!" in relation to his having made a statement about the hands and eyes that That Which Is makes use of, which will be Its making free use of the here and now, and Its having free entry into this present day.

Although Dōgo's expression, "What did you get?" is another way of <u>his</u> saying, "I've gotten It," it is one which does not stand against Ungan's "I get It." Even so, Dōgo had his own way of putting "What did you get," a way that means "I've got It and you've got It." Would this not be equivalent to "Our eyes get It and our hands get It?" Is it referring to an understanding that has emerged or to an understanding that has not yet emerged? While the understanding implied by "I get it" is synonymous with the 'I', you need to consider that there is a 'you' in "What did you get?"

What has come forth as a result of Ungan's statement, "His whole body is hands and eyes," is a plethora of Kannons who, in speaking of 'someone in the night reaching behind himself, his hand groping for his pillow', are exploring it by stating that one's whole body is nothing but hands and eyes. These Kannons indeed are Kannons, even though They have not yet been able to put it into Their own words. When Ungan said, "His whole body is hands and eyes," he was not saying that hands and eyes are the Dharma Body which exists everywhere. Even though everywhere is the whole universe, the hands and eyes of our body at this instant will not be the Everywhere that is everywhere. Even though the hands and eyes of our body can perform the meritorious actions of the Everywhere, they cannot be the hands and eyes that leave the marketplace with stolen goods. The meritorious activities of hands and eyes will be beyond the sort of seeing, behaving, and expressing that judges rightness. These hands and eyes are already described as being 'ever so many', so they are beyond a thousand, beyond ten thousand, beyond eighty-four thousand, and beyond the immeasurable and the unbounded. Not only is it like the whole body being hands and eyes, it is also like giving voice to the Dharma in order to rescue sentient beings, and like letting loose the Light throughout the nations. Therefore, you should explore through your training that it must be, as Ungan put it, that your whole body is hands and eyes. So, even though he says to use your whole body as hands and eyes, and even though he says to change your demeanor, now being active, now resting, do not let yourself be disturbed by this.

Dōgo replied, "What you have said is very well put. Still,
it only expresses eighty or ninety percent of the Matter."

The main point of what Dōgo said here is that Ungan's expression is very well put. 'Putting it very well' means that what one says hits the mark and that it clarifies the Matter, with nothing left unexpressed. When what has not been expressed before is now finally expressed so that nothing remains that has not been expressed, it will still only be expressing eighty or ninety percent of the Matter.

Even if your exploration of the intent behind what Ungan said were one hundred percent, if you are still unable to put It in words, then your have not thoroughly explored the Matter. And even if Ungan's way of putting It was eighty or ninety percent of the Matter, it was still his expression of It, which might be eighty or ninety percent on the mark or one hundred percent on the mark. At that very moment in time, Ungan might have stated the Matter through hundreds of thousands of myriad expressions, but his abilities were so wondrous that he offered only a bit of his abilities and expressed a bare eighty or ninety percent of the Matter. For instance, even if he had had hundreds of thousands of myriad abilities to bring forth the whole universe, what he actually said would surpass his leaving the Matter unsaid. At the same time, were he to take up just one of his abilities, it would not be an ordinary, worldly-wise ability. The meaning of this eighty or ninety percent is like this. Even so, when people hear the statement by an Ancestor of the Buddha that someone has expressed eighty or ninety percent of the Matter, they understand it to mean that it is only eighty or ninety percent because it does not come up to an expression that would be a hundred percent of the Matter. If the Buddha Dharma were like this, It would not have reached us today. You need to explore through your training that the so-called 'eighty or ninety percent' is an eighty or ninety percent of 'hundreds of thousands', as if we were speaking of 'ever so many'. Dōgo had already stated 'eighty or ninety percent of It' and he certainly knew that It must not be confined to a literal eighty or ninety percent. We need to explore through our training that this is the way that the Ancestors of the Buddha speak.

When Ungan said, "So much for the likes of me. How about you, my elder brother in the Dharma, what do you make of it?" he said "so much for the likes of me" because he wanted Dōgo to put into words what he called 'only expressing eighty or ninety percent of the Matter.' Although this is his 'not leaving any traces behind', it is also 'his arms being long and his sleeves being short'.[3] "While I have not yet exhausted the ways of saying what I have just said, I leave the matter as it is" is <u>not</u> what his expression "So much for the likes of me" means.

---

3. Another way of expressing this is that, although his words leave no karmic wake (not leaving any traces behind), his intention in asking the question is obvious (his arms sticking out from his sleeves).

> Dōgo said, "His whole being, through and through, is hands and eyes."

These words of his are not saying that hands and eyes, as independent entities, are what one's whole being is through and through. What he is saying is that one's whole being, through and through, <u>is</u> hands and eyes. As a consequence, he is not saying that one's body is what hands and eyes are. Since 'with His ever so many hands and eyes' means 'using His hands and using His eyes',[4] His hands and eyes are, of necessity, the whole of Him being hands and eyes, through and through. In asking, "What does He do with His ever so many bodies and minds?" there will be the response, "His whole being, through and through, is whatever He is doing." What is more, it is not the case that Ungan's expression, 'whole body,' is not quite complete whereas Dōgo's expression, 'whole being, through and through,' is thoroughly complete. Ungan's 'whole body' and Dōgo's 'whole being, through and through' are not open to any discussion of their comparative value, <u>and</u> the 'ever so many hands and eyes' that was stated by each of them is an expression of That Which Is.

Thus, the Kannon of whom our old Master Shakyamuni spoke only had a thousand hands and eyes, or twelve faces, or thirty-three bodies or eighty-four thousand bodies. The Kannon of Ungan and Dōgo had ever so many hands and eyes and is beyond any talk about quantities. When you explore through your training the Kannon of Ungan and Dōgo, which has ever so many hands and eyes, then you, together with all Buddhas, will realize eighty or ninety percent of Kannon's meditative state.

Given on the twenty-sixth day of the fourth lunar month in the third year of the Ninji era (May 27, 1242).

---

4.   The Chinese character, read as yō in Japanese, when functioning as a preposition means 'with', and when functioning as a verb, means 'to use'.

Now, since the Buddha Dharma has come from the West, many Ancestors of the Buddha have spoken about Kannon, but they have not equaled Ungan and Dōgo, and for that reason, I spoke only about this Kannon of theirs. As Yōka Genkaku said in his poem, "The Song That Attests to the Way":

> *Not stuck on seeing just one single thing: this we*
> > *call being a Tathagata;*
> *Such a one can be called a Kanjizai, one who*
> > *regards all things just as they are.*

This is evidence that even though the Tathagata and Kannon manifest in Their particular bodily forms, They are not separate beings.

And there was also an exchange between Mayoku and Rinzai concerning the true Hands and Eyes.[5] These are just a couple of cases among ever so many. There is Ummon's statement, "There are the Kannons who, upon seeing the forms of things, clarify Their minds, or who, upon hearing the sounds of things, awaken to the Way." What sights and sounds are not encompassed within Kanzeon Bodhisattva's seeing and hearing? And in Hyakujō's words, "There is His gateway for entering into the Truth." Among the assembly in the *Shurangama Scripture*, there are the Kannons who have fully realized the Way. And among the assembly in the *Lotus Scripture*, there is the Kannon who manifests everywhere. All these Kannons are identical with the Buddhas and They are identical with the great earth with its mountains and rivers. Yet, at the same time, They are but one or two of the ever so many hands and eyes.

Copied by me on the tenth day of midsummer in the third year of the Ninji era (June 9, 1242).

Ejō

---

5.   This exchange is recounted in the Translator's Addendum immediately following this discourse.

Translator's Addendum from
Book 3, Kōan 44 of Dōgen's Chinese *Shinji Shōbōgenzō*

Once while Mayoku Hōtetsu was training in Rinzai's community, he asked Rinzai, "Which is the true Eye of the Compassionate One with a Thousand Hands and Eyes?"

Rinzai replied, "Which is the true Eye of the Compassionate One with a Thousand Hands and Eyes? Well, quick, you tell me! Speak right up!"

Thereupon, Mayoku pulled Rinzai down off his chief monk's seat in the Meditation Hall and sat himself down in Rinzai's place.

Rinzai got up off the floor and said, "Well, how do you do!" Mayoku was about to respond, when Rinzai suddenly gave out a Zen shout, pulled Mayoku off the chief monk's seat, and sat back down on it.

Mayoku got up off the floor and [since he had been bested] left the hall.

33

On Arhats

(Arakan)

Translator's Introduction: The Sanskrit word *'arhat'* means 'one who is venerable' or 'one worthy of respect'. It is used in Buddhism to designate someone who has arrived at an advanced spiritual stage that is marked by being completely free of defiling passions. The term, however, has somewhat different meanings within the various traditions of Buddhism, ranging from the highest level of spiritual attainment (one who is a living Buddha) to one who is just on the brink of entering Buddhahood. While the concept of the arhat has occupied a central position in Southern Buddhist traditions, it tends to be given a secondary position in Mahayana traditions, with the bodhisattva ideal being primary. Dōgen's discourse, however, covers much broader and varied applications of the term, thereby embracing a more universal perspective.

> "With all their desires already completely spent and having
> gone beyond all defiling passions, they have succeeded in reaching
> what truly benefits them, and, having brought to an end the bonds
> to existence, their minds have been set free." [1]

This describes what the great arhats are, for arhathood is the ultimate fruit of those who study the Buddha Dharma. These are the Buddha arhats who are called 'Those of the Fourth Stage'. [2]

'All their desires' is equivalent to a wooden ladle with its handle broken off. Though, up to now, the ladle has been used many times, an arhat's complete wearing out of self is the whole body of the Wooden Ladle springing forth. 'Their having succeeded in reaching what truly benefits them' is synonymous with Its whole Body emerging from the crown of their head.

---

1. This is Shakyamuni Buddha's definition of arhats found in the opening passages of the Lotus Scripture.

2. See the 'Four Stages of Arhathood' in the *Glossary.*

'Their having brought the bonds of existence to an end' is the same as their never concealing anything anywhere in the universe. And we need to investigate thoroughly that the way in which their minds perceive the forms and characteristics of things, once their minds have been set free, is synonymous with 'high places being naturally in balance up high, and low places being naturally in balance down low'. Because of this, they have their own tiles and stones for their walls and fences.[3]

'Being set free' is synonymous with their mind's manifesting all functions. Their not returning to their defiling passions is synonymous with defiling passions not yet arising, which is spoken of as 'defiling passions being obstructed by defiling passions'.[4]

Further, an arhat's marvelous spiritual abilities, wise discernment, meditative states, giving voice to the Dharma, leading others, and letting the Light of Truth shine forth are not to be likened to abilities discussed by non-Buddhists, quarrelsome bedeviling people, and the like. Teachings about an arhat's ability to see such things as hundreds of Buddha realms are never to be associated with the views and opinions of ordinary, worldly people. The principle of this is: "Although we have just said that a barbarian's beard is red, there is also the fact that a person with a red beard is a barbarian."[5] 'Entering nirvana' is an arhat's practice of getting inside his, or her, own Fist.[6] Thus, the Wondrous Heart of Nirvana is a place which an arhat does not turn

---

3,   That is, they have their own way of thinking about things.

4.   'Defiling passions being obstructed by defiling passions' means that when an arhat sees defiling passions arise in others, he or she keeps defiling passions from arising in response, because the arhat sees the suffering that will arise from giving in to such passions.

5.   A saying by Meditation Master Hyakujō, referring to two ways of saying the same thing. In other words, a person who has such properties is an arhat, and an arhat is a person who has such properties.

6.   That is, operating from the place of enlightenment within.

away from or shun. Arhats who have entered their own Nostrils are those we call true arhats: those who have not entered their own Nostrils are not arhats.[7]

It was said in olden times in the *Lotus Scripture*, "We today are also true arhats, and, by our voicing of the Buddha's Way, we can help all to hear It." The main point of 'we can help all to hear It' is that we can help all things to be voices of Buddha. Why would anyone stop at just listening to Buddhas and Their disciples? When all those who are conscious of It and have knowledge of It, who have Its Skin and Flesh, Bones and Marrow, proceed to help others hear It, that is what I would call 'helping all'. Our 'being conscious of It and having knowledge of It' is synonymous with the grasses and trees of our native land and with the tiles and stones of our walls and fences.[*] What we hear is the rising and falling away of all these things, their flourishing and fading out, their births and deaths, their comings and goings. But the basis of helping all to hear the Buddha's Way by means of our voicing It is not simply exploring through our training that the whole world is an ear.

Shakyamuni Buddha once said the following, "If any among My disciples would call themselves arhats or pratyekabuddhas,[*] but have not heard or realized the fact that the Buddha Tathagatas only instruct bodhisattvas,[*] they are not the Buddha's disciples, nor are they arhats, nor are they pratyekabuddhas." The Buddha's saying that He only instructed bodhisattvas means "I, along with the Buddhas in the ten quarters, know this well, for each Buddha on His own, together with all Buddhas, has been able to exhaustively explore the True Form of all things, which is what supreme, fully perfected enlightenment is." Thus, to consider oneself to be a bodhisattva or a Buddha must accord with considering oneself to be an arhat or a pratyekabuddha. And

---

7. 'Someone entering his, or her, Nostrils' is a common Zen Buddhist metaphor for someone who has awakened to the Truth: such a one has gotten 'a whiff of It'.

* See Glossary.

why is this? Because to think of oneself in this way means that one has heard and recognized the fact that all the Buddha Tathagatas only instruct bodhisattvas.

Long ago it was said, "In the Scriptures of the shravakas,* arhat is the name given to those who have realized Buddhahood." What is said here is confirmation of what the Buddha said. It is not simply the preaching of some faint-hearted scholastic commentator, but expresses a universal principle in the Way of the Buddha. You need to explore through your training the principle of calling an arhat someone who has realized Buddhahood, and you need to explore through your training the principle of calling someone who has realized Buddhahood an arhat. Apart from the effects of arhathood, nothing else remains, not even a single mote of dust or a single thought or thing—still less does fully perfected enlightenment remain as something separate from arhathood! Apart from supreme, fully perfected enlightenment, again, nothing else remains, not even a single mote of dust or a single thought or thing—still less do the four stages and four results of arhathood remain as something separate from supreme, fully perfected enlightenment![8] At the very moment when an arhat is carrying all thoughts and things upon his shoulders, all these thoughts and things are truly beyond being 'eight ounces or half a pound'.[9] And they are beyond mind, beyond Buddha, and beyond material things. Even the Eye of a Buddha cannot see them, look as It will. So, we need not get into discussions about eighty thousand eons before and eighty thousand eons after. All that remains to such a one is just the complete Dharma.

---

8. The four results of arhathood refer to the results that arise from attaining each of the four stages.

9. That is, they are beyond our ability to measure.

Shakyamuni once said the following:

> If any of these male and female monks should tell themselves, "I have already realized arhathood and am in my final embodiment, which is ultimate nirvana," and therefore give up their intention to seek supreme, fully perfected enlightenment, you should, by all means, know that such as these are all braggarts. And why? Because if there were monks who had truly realized arhathood, they would not have arrived at such a state unless they trusted this Dharma of Mine.

What is said here confirms that those who are able to trust in supreme, fully perfected enlightenment are arhats. To have trust in this Dharma, of necessity, is to depend on It. One who has truly realized arhathood is beyond such statements as "I have already realized arhathood and am in my final embodiment, which is ultimate nirvana," because such a one is intent on seeking supreme, fully perfected enlightenment. To aspire to seek supreme, fully perfected enlightenment is to take delight in one's Eye, to sit there facing a wall, and, in facing the wall, to open one's Eye. Though we may say that fully perfected enlightenment encompasses the whole world, it is 'gods appearing and demons vanishing', and though we may say that it extends over all of time, it is 'the mutual throwing of self and other into the moment at hand'.[10] We call one who is like this someone who is intent on seeking supreme, fully perfected enlightenment. Thus, such a one is intent on seeking arhathood. Aspiring to seek arhathood is being satisfied with gruel and being satisfied with rice.

---

10. The two quotes are from a poem by Meditation Master Engo, which Dōgen quotes on page 293 of Discourse 22: On the Everyday Behavior of a Buddha Doing His Practice (*Gyōbutsu Iigi*). The first describes the arbitrary way that thoughts and things arise and disappear, and the second describes how arhats function.

Meditation Master Engo of Mount Kassan once said the following:

After those of old had caught the drift, they would go off into remote mountain areas, living in huts fashioned of mallows or thatch, or in rock caves. For ten or twenty years they would dine on rice boiled in a broken-footed pot. For the most part, they would forget human society, having taken their leave of its defiling domains forever. In our present age, I dare not aspire to live like that, so I simply conceal my former name, cover my tracks, and keep to what I ought to do, which is to become an old monk, all skin and bones, living in accord with what I have realized, and making use of what I have received as it accords with my abilities. Wearing away my old karma,* I would adapt myself to the age-old ways. Had I any strength to spare, I suppose I would extend it to others, creating conditions for the development of wise discernment, and training myself to stand on my own two feet and to ripen naturally. It would be as if in some wilderness covered deep in tall grasses, I set about to hack out one whole real person, or at least half a one. Then, knowing that I too have It, together with all others, I would rid myself of birth-and-death, ever benefiting more and more those who are to come in the future, that I might repay my deep indebtedness to the Buddhas and Ancestors.

However much I may restrain myself, I suppose I cannot prevent the frosts and dews of my years from ripening the fruits of my karma. And so, I will need to reenter the world and adapt myself to accord with circumstances, opening up and entrusting myself to ordinary people and those in lofty positions, but without letting my mind manipulate me into seeking for gain. And how much less could I possibly enslave myself to the influence of the nobility only to become a mediocre, fawning teacher who acts to deceive the common folk, who scorns the saintly, who courts gain, who contrives to win a name for himself, and thereby creates for himself the karmic consequence of living in an Avichi hell of unremitting suffering! If only I could go through the world in such a manner as to produce no karmic wake—though I may not have the chance— would I not then be an arhat who has left behind the defiling world?

Accordingly, a genuine monk here and now <u>is</u> an arhat, one who has left behind the defiling world. If you would know what an arhat is, know that it is like this. Do not let yourself be led astray by the words of Indian scholastics. Meditation Master Engo of China was an Ancestor of the Buddha who had inherited the True Transmission.

Hyakujō Ekai in Hungchou Province once said, "When our eyes, ears, nose, tongue, body, and mind, each and every one of them, no longer covet and are no longer tainted by thoughts and things, either material or immaterial, we call this 'accepting and keeping to a four-line verse', as well as 'the fourth stage.'"[11] It is impossible for any of us to change our eyes, ears, nose, tongue, body, and mind into something different from what they are, for they are completely, from top to toe, beyond our fathoming. As a consequence, such a one's whole being is naturally beyond covetousness or stain, and the whole of all thoughts and things, material and immaterial, is beyond covetousness or stain. It means that one's accepting and keeping to a four-line verse is naturally beyond coveting or staining <u>anything</u>, and we call this 'the fourth stage'. And the fourth stage is that of an arhat. Thus, the eyes, ears, nose, tongue, body, and mind that fully manifest before us here and now are what an arhat is. From beginning to end, such a one will be naturally free from delusion. 'Arriving immediately at the barrier gate' is synonymous with accepting and keeping to a four-

---

11. 'A four-line verse' is a common reference to Scriptural Teachings given in verse by Shakyamuni Buddha.

line verse.[12] Accordingly, it is the fourth stage. Right from the crown of his head to the bottoms of his feet, his, or her, whole body fully manifests It and there is not the slightest thread or hair that has been omitted.

In short, were I to express the Matter,* how would I word it? I might put it this way: When an arhat is in a worldly state of mind, all thoughts and things serve to obstruct him. When an arhat is in a saintly state of mind, all thoughts and things serve to liberate him. By all means, you must realize that an arhat and all thoughts and things are fellow trainees. When an arhat has already awakened, he is restricted by 'being an arhat'. This is why, since before the time of the Lord of Emptiness, arhats have been Old Fists.[13]

Given to the assembly on the fifteenth day of the fifth lunar month in the third year of the Ninji era (June 14, 1242), while residing at Kannondōri in Kōshōhōrin-ji Temple in the Uji district of Yamashiro Province.

Copied by me on the sixteenth day of the sixth lunar month in the first year of the Kenji era (July 11, 1275).

Ejō

---

12. 'The barrier gate' is a common Zen Buddhist metaphor for the unobstructed gateway into realizing enlightenment.

13. The Lord of Emptiness refers to the first of the Seven Buddhas, the One who lived during the Age of Emptiness, that is, before duality had first arisen. 'Old Fists' implies that arhats, from beginningless time, have been embodiments of Ultimate Reality.

34

On the Cypress Tree

(Hakujushi)

Translator's Introduction: The subject of this discourse derives from a kōan story in which a monk asks Meditation Master Jōshū what Bodhidharma's intent was in coming to China. Jōshū responds by alluding to a tree called a *'hakuju'* in Japanese and a *'pai-shu'* in Chinese. Even though these two words are written with the same Chinese characters, they designate two different types of tree: the Japanese *hakuju* tree is an oak (a deciduous tree), whereas the Chinese *pai-shu* tree is a type of cypress (an evergreen conifer).

In China, since at least the time of Confucius, the cypress has been paired with the pine tree. Because these two trees, unlike all others, do not lose their foliage even in the severest of winters, they have been used as a common metaphor in China for friends who remain constant in adversity. When this metaphorical meaning is applied to Jōshū's alluding to the cypress, it describes the intent behind Bodhidharma's coming to China, namely, to find a true spiritual friend (disciple) who would remain constant in adversity. The one he found was Eka, who proved his constancy by standing in the courtyard outside Bodhidharma's quarters in the ever-deepening snow and then later proffering his 'severed arm' to the Indian Master as evidence of his commitment. (This 'severing' may refer to giving up one's attachments rather than to a literal, physical act.) The nature of the relationship between Bodhidharma as Master and Eka as disciple becomes clearer when Bodhidharma is seen to represent the pine (a common metaphor for the Eternal) and Eka is seen as the cypress. In a subsequent kōan story, this relationship is expressed as the Empty Sky and the cypress tree.

Jōshū was of the thirty-seventh generation after the Tathagata Shakyamuni. He was sixty-one years old when he first gave rise to the intention to seek the Truth and left home life behind to explore the Way. At that time he made a vow, saying, "Even if someone is a hundred years old, if that person is spiritually less advanced than I, I shall offer that person Teaching. And even if someone is seven years old, if that person has spiritually surpassed me, I shall ask that person for Teaching." Vowing thus, he drifted southward like a cloud.

While wandering about in search of the True Way, Jōshū chanced to arrive at Mount Nansen, whereupon he went to make his prostrations to the Abbot, the monk

Nansen Fugan, who happened to be in his quarters, resting, when Jōshū came for his initial interview.

> Nansen immediately asked him, "Where have you just come from?"
>
> Jōshū replied, "From the Hall of the Auspicious Image."[1]
>
> Nansen asked, "And have you seen the Auspicious Image?"
>
> Jōshū replied, "I have not yet seen the Auspicious Image, but what I have encountered is a reclining Tathagata."[2]
>
> Thereupon Nansen immediately arose and asked him, "Are you a novice that has a Master not?"
>
> Jōshū responded, "A novice that has found his Master."[3]
>
> Nansen then asked, "And just who is that Master of yours?"
>
> Jōshū replied, with all sincerity, "Though the early spring is still cold,[4] as I was doing my prostrations, I could not help but reflect on how grateful I am for the health of your august body, Venerable Monk. It is like ten thousand blessings."
>
> Thereupon, Nansen called for the Head Monk of the Meditation Hall and told him, "Put this novice in the special place!"[5]

---

1. The name of a temple building on Mount Nansen.

2. Nansen's question has a double meaning. Taken on a conventional level it simply refers to a statue of the Buddha that is in a particular temple hall, whereas on a spiritual level it is asking Jōshū whether he has had a kenshō yet. Jōshū's response takes the latter intent.

3. That is, as his subsequent remark implies, he already regards Nansen as his Master.

4. Jōshū's reference to the early spring being cold is his way of expressing how young and inexperienced he is in training with a Master.

5. The 'special place' is an area in the Meditation Hall directly behind the senior monks. New novices who had already demonstrated their understanding of what monastic life is about were seated there.

Thus it was that Jōshū took up residence with Nansen, and, for thirty years, did his utmost to practice the Way, without once going off to some other temple. He never idled away a moment or engaged in other pursuits. Then, after he had been Transmitted and received the methods for teaching others how to train in the Way, he took up residence in Kannon-in Monastery in Jōshū Province for another thirty years. While he was Abbot there, the things he did and how he did them were different from the behavior of ordinary monks in other places.

On one occasion, he composed the following verse:

> *In vain do I gaze upon the smoke from the hearths of my*
> *neighbors on all sides.*
> *Jam-filled buns and rice cakes, for a year now, have*
> *parted company from me.*
> *Thinking about them today, I can only swallow my spit.*
> *Periods of mindfulness are few, bemoanings all too*
> *frequent.*
> *Among hundreds of families, not a single good and*
> *friendly face is to be found.*
> *Those who come by merely say, "I've just dropped in for*
> *a cup of tea."*
> *Unable to have any tea, they leave in a snit.*

How sad that a smoking fire in his own hearth was rare, that even a one-dish meal was so scarce, and that he had not had a varied meal since the year before. When anyone from among those hundreds of families came, they were in search of a cup of tea, and those who were not in search of a cup of tea did not come at all. There was not one from amongst those hundreds of families who came bringing tea.[6] Occasionally, there

---

6. 'In search of a cup of tea' is a Zen Buddhist metaphor for someone seeking a Master in order to get 'enlightenment' but, in Jōshū's case, none were willing to stay and train. 'Bringing tea' is an allusion to those who come to a Master and selflessly offer their training, or to someone who has had a kenshō and seeks to have it confirmed.

was a novice who came to look at 'the wise one',[7] but there was not a single dragon elephant* who wished to be his equal.

On another occasion he composed a verse:

> *When I think about those throughout the country who*
> *have left home life behind,*
> *How many can there be whose state resembles my*
> *state in life?*
> *Earth for a bed, broken reeds for a mat,*
> *An old elm branch for a pillow, and nothing at all for*
> *a coverlet.*
> *Before His revered image, there is no Peaceful Breath*
> *incense to be burned,*
> *And from the ashes all I smell is the scent of cow*
> *dung."*[8]

From what he said, we should recognize the spotlessness and purity of his temple, and we should learn from these traces that he left behind for us today. There were not many monks in his assembly, maybe twenty at most. His Monks' Hall was not large, lacking both a front hall and a back hall.[9] It had no lighting at night and there was no charcoal for wintry weather. Sad to say, the conditions there could be described as the way that old folks live in their declining years. And the deportment of Old Buddhas was like this.

---

7.   This is an allusion to the custom of monks, and novices in particular, to go traveling to other monasteries during the summer months in order to train under a Master other than their own.

*   See Glossary.

8.   Peaceful Breath was a type of incense made from a tree resin and widely used in temples throughout China. The cheapest forms of incense were made from cow dung.

9.   The front hall contained meditation platforms which were used by temple officials and guests. The back hall traditionally contained a washstand and was used as a cleanup area for the monks who lived in the Monks' Hall.

Once when a leg on his meditation platform broke, Jōshū tied a charred log to it and it lasted for years. Whenever an officer of the temple commented that the leg needed to be repaired, the Master would not permit it. This is a good example, one rare in any generation.

Customarily, the rice for their gruel was so thinned down that there was not even a single grain of rice in it, so the monks would distract themselves at meals by turning their gaze towards tranquil windows or towards the dust in some crack. Sometimes they would gather nuts or berries, which both the assembly of monks and the Abbot himself would use for their daily sustenance. We trainees of today should praise this deportment, and though we do not surpass the Master's deportment, we should make our attitude of mind one of fond respect for the past.

Once, when Jōshū was addressing his assembly, he said:

> For thirty years, I lived in the south intent on nothing but doing seated meditation. If any of you wish to realize the One Great Matter,* you will encounter It by pursuing the principle of doing seated meditation. If after three years, or five years, or twenty years, or even thirty years, you can still say that you have not realized the Truth, take the skull of this old monk and make it into a pot to piss in.

That is the kind of vow he took. Truly, doing the practice of seated meditation is the straight road of the Buddha's Way. We should follow the principle of "Just sit and you shall see what happens." Later, people would say of him, "Jōshū was truly an Old Buddha."

> Great Master Jōshū once had a monk who asked him, "What did our Ancestral Master Bodhidharma come from the West for?"
> The Master replied, "For a cypress tree in the courtyard."

The monk then said, "Venerable Monk, pray, do not use some physical object to point it out to a person like me."

The Master said, "I am not pointing it out to you by using a physical object."

The monk again asked, "Well then, what did our Ancestral Master come from the West for?"

The Master replied, "For a cypress tree in the courtyard." [10]

Although this particular kōan* sprang from the mind of Jōshū, ultimately it is what all Buddhas have habitually put into practice with Their whole being. In doing so, They skillfully lead trainees by asking, "Who is the One in Charge?" [11] The main points that you need to recognize at present are the principles that a cypress tree in the courtyard does not refer to a concrete object and that 'a cypress tree' is not one particular person. This is why, when the monk said, "Venerable Monk, pray, do not use some physical object to point it out to a person like me," Jōshū replied, "I am not pointing it out to you by using a physical object." What venerable monk is limited to being a 'venerable monk'? Because he is not so limited, he will be Jōshū's 'I'. And what I is limited to being that 'I'? And even if he were so limited, he would still be referring to a person. And what physical object would not be limited by Bodhidharma's intention of coming from the West, since a physical object must certainly have been what he intended by coming from the West? [12] Even so, his intention in coming from the West was not dependent on some physical object, nor was it necessarily for the Wondrous Heart of Nirvana, which is the Treasure House of the Eye of the True Teaching, that the

---

10. That is, Bodhidharma came to find a true spiritual friend who, like the metaphorical 'cypress tree', would be constant in all adversity.

11. 'The One in Charge' is another name for one's Buddha Nature.

12. That is, Bodhidharma did not come searching for a physical object in the form of a botanical tree. Rather, he came searching for a physical object in the form of a true spiritual friend, and happened to find such a one in the person of Eka.

Ancestral Master came from the West. Nor was it for someone's heart or mind, or for a Buddha, or for some concrete thing.

Now, "What did our Ancestral Master Bodhidharma come from the West for?" was not the monk's asking some idle question, nor was it a matter of two people being able to see things alike. It was a matter of one person—namely, Jōshū's monk—who had still not been able to experience a mutual encounter with his Master, so how much could he himself have actually realized?[13] Or, to put it another way, the monk had always been 'that kind of person'. Therefore, even though he was mistaken time after time, because he was mistaken time after time, he was paying close attention to his mistakes in making mistakes.[14] Would this not be his hearing what is false and his taking its ramifications in hand?

Because his openhearted spirit was devoid of any attachment to duality, the monk was a veritable 'cypress tree in the courtyard'. When there is no physical object, there can be no 'cypress tree in the courtyard'. Even though the cypress tree is a physical object, Jōshū said, "I am not pointing it out to you by using a physical object," and his disciple said, "Venerable Monk, pray, do not use some physical object to point it out to a person like me." The monk was not like some old ancestral tomb.[15] And because he was not an old tomb to begin with, he was able to bring It forth from where It had been entombed. And because It had been brought forth from where It had been entombed, this was comparable to Jōshū's saying to his disciple, "Come on, return my efforts!" And because he was saying, in effect, "Come on, show me It!" he said, "I am not pointing it out to you by using a physical object, so, come on, show It to me!"

---

13. 'A mutual encounter' not only refers to a disciple meeting a Master who recognizes him as a worthy vessel for the Dharma, but it also refers to the mutual recognition of each other's Buddha Nature, that is, 'Buddha recognizes Buddha, and Buddha bows to Buddha'.

14. That is, a disciple who is a genuine vessel for the Dharma will persist in making mistakes through misunderstanding what the Master is pointing to until he sees where he is wrong, which he can only do by being willing to make mistakes in the first place.

15. That is, the monk was not spiritually dead to begin with.

Well, what will the monk use to point it out with? It could be by his responding, "I am also like this."

> There was a monk who asked Great Master Jōshū, "Does a cypress tree also have Buddha Nature?"
>
> The Great Master replied, "Yes, he has."
>
> The monk then asked, "When does such a tree realize Buddhahood?"
>
> The Great Master replied, "He waits for the Empty Sky to come down to earth."
>
> The monk then asked, "And when does the Empty Sky come down to earth?"
>
> The Great Master said, "It waits for a cypress tree to realize Buddhahood."

Listen to what the Great Master is saying now, and do not disregard what that monk is asking. The Great Master's phrases, "when the Empty Sky comes down to earth" and "when a cypress tree realizes Buddhahood," do not express their mutually waiting for each other. It is the monk's asking about a cypress tree, about Buddha Nature, about 'the time when', about the Empty Sky, and about coming down to earth.

Now, by the Great Master's responding to the monk, "Yes, he has," he means that the Buddha Nature of a cypress tree does exist. By penetrating into what he is saying, you will penetrate into the meaning of the bloodline of the Buddhas and Ancestors. Saying that Buddha Nature exists in a so-called 'cypress tree' is saying something that cannot be expressed with conventional ways of speaking, nor had it ever yet been so expressed. A cypress tree already has Buddha Nature, so we need to clarify this state of affairs. Since he has Buddha Nature, we should inquire into how high a cypress tree is, how long his lifespan, what the measurements of his body are, and we should hear about his species and his lineage. Further, are the hundreds of thousands of cypress trees all of the same species or are they of different bloodlines? Can there be cypress trees that realize Buddhahood, and cypress trees that are doing the training and practice, and cypress trees that have awakened to the enlightened

Mind? Though a cypress tree may have realized Buddhahood, will he not be equipped with such things as training and practice or will he not have an awakening to the enlightened Mind? And, pray, what are the causes and coexisting conditions that connect a cypress tree and the Empty Sky? If a cypress tree's becoming Buddha is indeed the time when "I am awaiting Your coming down to earth," is the merit of a cypress tree invariably synonymous with the Empty Sky? In regard to the status of a cypress tree, we need to do our utmost to explore in detail whether Empty Space is the tree's initial position or his ultimate status. Let me put it to you, dear old Jōshū, is it because you too were a withered cypress tree that you could breathe such life into these matters?

In summary, a cypress tree's having Buddha Nature is beyond the realm of non-Buddhists or those of the two Lower Courses,[*] and the like, and is something that academic teachers of Scripture and those who compose scholarly commentaries have not encountered or heard about. And how much less could it be presented by the flowery speech of some dead tree or some heap of cold ashes! Simply, it is only those of Jōshū's species who explore the Matter thoroughly through their training.

Now, as to a cypress tree having Buddha Nature, which Jōshū expressed, is a cypress tree limited by being called 'a cypress tree', and is Buddha Nature limited by being called 'Buddha Nature'? This expression of Jōshū's is not something that a single Buddha or even two Buddhas have thoroughly exhausted. Even someone with the countenance of a Buddha would not necessarily be able to thoroughly exhaust what he expressed. Even among Buddhas, there may be Buddhas who express it and there may be Buddhas who cannot express it.

The phrase 'waiting for the Empty Sky to come down to earth' does not describe something that cannot happen, since every time a cypress tree realizes Buddhahood, the Empty Sky comes down to earth. Its coming down to earth is not concealed, but rather it is louder than even a hundred thousand rolls of thunder. When a cypress tree realizes Buddhahood, it will not only be within the twenty-four hours of some day, but it will also be within the time that surpasses any day's twenty-four hours.[16] The Empty Sky that comes down to earth is not only the empty sky that is seen by ordinary people or saintly ones. There is an Empty Sky in addition to the empty sky. It is something that others do not see, but which Jōshū himself encountered. The Earth which the Empty Sky comes down to is also not the earth that ordinary people or saintly ones inhabit, for there is also an Earth apart from that. It is not something that darkness or light reaches, and it was reached by Jōshū all alone. At the time when the Empty Sky comes down to Earth, even the Sun and Moon, even the Mountains and Rivers will have been waiting for It. Who says that Buddha Nature must invariably realize Buddhahood? Buddha Nature is a splendorous decoration that comes after realizing Buddhahood. Thus, a cypress tree and Buddha Nature are not different notes in the same tune.[17] In other words, They are indefinable, so we need to explore Them by asking, "What are They like?"

Delivered to the assembly during the season of the Japanese iris, on the twenty-first day of the fifth lunar month in the third year of the Ninji era (June 20, 1242), while residing at Kannondōri Temple in the Uji district of Yamashiro Province.

Copied by me on the third day of the seventh lunar month in the first year of the Kangen era (July 21, 1243).

Ejō

---

16. That is, it not only occurs within time (the twenty-four hours of a day) but goes beyond time (in the original text, this was expressed as 'the twenty-six hours of a day').

17. That is, they are not different words for the same thing.

35

On the Brightness of the Light

(Kōmyō)

Translator's Introduction: The word *'kōmyō'* has various meanings in this discourse. It refers to a sort of light, or 'glow', which can be seen in someone for whom the clouds of spiritual ignorance have dispersed. However, it also refers to that which underlies this manifestation: the shining forth of one's Buddha Nature both spiritually and physically. It also refers to the functioning of one's innate wise discernment. Hence, in this translation it is rendered in a variety of ways, depending on the immediate context: (physical) brightness, luminosity, glow, (spiritual) Brightness, and the Light.

Certain sections of this discourse may prove puzzling to some readers. Confusion may arise because Dōgen moves easily back and forth between referring to the brightness as a physical manifestation and the Brightness as a spiritual manifestation. Sometimes he means them both simultaneously. This is particularly evident in his discussion of the Eastern Quarter. A similar and more complex situation arises in regard to the kōan story of Meditation Master Ummon, where the practice of monks is likened to monastery buildings.

Great Master Chōsa Keishin of Hunan Province in Great Sung China, while addressing his assembly during a Dharma talk, once said:

> *The whole universe in all ten directions is a mendicant monk's Eye.*
>
> *The whole universe in all ten directions is a mendicant monk's everyday speech.*
>
> *The whole universe in all ten directions is a mendicant monk's whole body.*
>
> *The whole universe in all ten directions is the brightness of one's own being.*
>
> *The whole universe in all ten directions resides within the brightness of one's own being.*

> *In the whole universe in all ten directions there is*
> *not even one person who is not his, or*
> *her, own being.*

Our exploration of the words and ways of Buddhas through our practice with a Master must, by all means, be done with diligence. We must not become more and more casual and neglect it, for it is due to just such neglectfulness that teachers in the past who gained an understanding of what spiritual Brightness is were rare indeed.

Emperor Kao-ming of the Later Han dynasty in China—his forbidden name was Chuang and his name at entombment was Emperor Hsein-tsung[1]—was the fourth princely son of Emperor Kuang-wu. In the tenth year of the Eihei era (67 C.E.), during the reign of Emperor Kao-ming, two Indian monks, Kashapamātanga and Dharmaraksha by name, were the first to introduce Buddhist Teachings into China. In front of a platform that had been set up as a place to burn their copies of the Sutras if they lost, the two monks defeated the heretical followers of the Taoists through argument, thereby exhibiting the spiritual powers of Buddhas.

Later, in the Chinese P'u-tung era (520-527), during the reign of Emperor Wu of the Liang dynasty, our First Ancestor, Bodhidharma himself, traveled from India to Kuangchou Province in South China. He was the legitimate heir to the genuine Transmission of the Treasure House of the Eye of the True Teaching. He was the twenty-eighth Dharma descendant from Shakyamuni Buddha. Subsequently, he was permitted to hang up his traveling staff at Shōrin-ji Monastery on a remote mountain peak at the foot of Mount Sūzan. He authentically Transmitted the Dharma to the Second Ancestor, our Great Ancestral Meditation Master Eka, who personally experienced the brightness of the Buddhas and Ancestors. Before that time, there was no one who had personally seen, or even heard of, the Brightness of the Buddhas and Ancestors. Much less did any of them recognize their own brightness. Even if they had encountered that brightness, bringing it forth from the crown of their own head, they did not explore it with their own Eye. As a result, they did not clarify whether the

---

1. In ancient China, emperors had a name that was for their use alone and, while the emperor was alive, no one, under penalty of death, was permitted to use that name as part of their own.

brightness was long or short, square or round, nor did they clarify whether the brightness was curling up or spreading out, tightening or loosening. Because they felt uncomfortable about encountering the Brightness, their brightness became more and more estranged from Brightness. Even though this estrangement was itself an aspect of the Brightness, it was obstructed by the estrangement.

Stinking skin bags* who have become more and more estranged from their Brightness—and their brightness—hold views and theories like the following, "A Buddha's light, as well as our own brightness, must be red, white, blue, or yellow, like the light from a fire or light shimmering upon water, or like the luster of a pearl or the sparkle of a jewel, or like the light from a dragon or a celestial being, or like the light of sun and moon." Although folks such as these may sometimes be following a spiritually good teacher or what the Scriptures say, when they hear words of Teaching concerning brightness, they imagine it to be like the light of a firefly. This cannot be considered as exploring the Matter* with a Master by means of using their own heads and eyes. From the Han dynasty through the Sui, T'ang, and Sung dynasties down to the present day, such outpourings of opinions have been many indeed. This is why you should not study under scholastic Dharma teachers or pay attention to the questionable theories put forth by such teachers of meditation.

What is called 'the Brightness of the Buddhas and Ancestors' is the whole universe in all ten directions; It is the whole of Buddhas and the whole of Ancestors; It is each Buddha on His own, as well as all Buddhas; It is the light of Buddha; It is the Buddha illumined. Buddhas and Ancestors treat Buddhas and Ancestors as Brightness. Training with and awakening to this Brightness, They become Buddha, They sit as Buddha, and They realize Buddhahood. This is why it is said that this Light has illumined eighteen thousand Buddha lands in the Eastern Quarter.[2]

---

*   See Glossary.

2.   The Eastern Quarter is the spiritual realm of Akshobya Buddha.

This is the Light that is talked about in kōan* stories. This Light is the Light of Buddha. What illumines the Eastern Quarter is the luminosity of the eastern quarter. The Eastern Quarter is something other than what conventional people discuss as some 'here' or 'there'. It is the very heart of the Dharma Realm and the very middle of the Fist. Even though the phrase 'the eastern quarter' puts limitations on the Eastern Quarter, it is a veritable half-pound of brightness. Through your training, you need to explore the point that the Eastern Quarter exists in this land of ours, that the Eastern Quarter exists in other lands, and that the Eastern Quarter exists in the eastern quarter. In the term 'eighteen thousand', 'ten thousand' means 'half a Fist' and 'half of this very heart and mind of ours'.[3] It does not always mean 'ten units of one thousand', nor does it mean, say, 'ten thousand units of ten thousand' or 'a hundred units of ten thousand'. 'Buddha lands' refers to what is inside our eyes.[4] When we see or hear the phrase 'what illumines the Eastern Quarter', if we study it as if it were some white band of cloth extending in just one direction across the eastern sky, this will not be a case of our exploring the Way through our training. The whole universe in all ten directions is, simply, the Eastern Quarter, so we call the Eastern Quarter 'the whole universe in all ten directions'. On this basis, the whole universe in all ten directions exists. When the phrase 'the whole universe in all ten directions' is uttered, we hear the phrase 'eighteen thousand Buddha lands' being voiced.

---

3. In the Chinese and Japanese counting systems, 'eighteen thousand' is written with three characters that could be read as '(one unit of) ten thousand and eight units of one thousand'. Thus, since 'eighteen thousand' represents the whole of the Fist and the whole of our being, the phrase '(one unit of) ten thousand', as half of the whole expression, represents half the Fist and half of this very heart and mind of ours. In other words, half of the whole is half of the Whole.

4. That is, it refers to our own being when we look within ourselves.

Emperor Hsien-tsung of the T'ang dynasty was the imperial father of two emperors, Mu-tsung and Hsüan-tsung, and was the grandfather of three emperors, Ching-tsung, Wen-tsung, and Wu-tsung. Once, when he requested that the ashes of the Buddha be brought to him so that he could make an alms offering to them, they gave off a light that illumined the night. The emperor was overjoyed. Early the next morning, his retainers and ministers all presented congratulatory letters which said, "It is the Saintly responding to His Majesty's saintly virtue."

> At that time there was a minister, Han Yu Wen-kung by name—he was also called Tui-chih. He was in the habit of exploring the Matter whilst sitting in the back row of the Buddhist Ancestors. Wen-kung alone did not offer a congratulatory letter. Emperor Hsien-tsung asked him, "All the other retainers and ministers have offered our royal presence a congratulatory letter. Why have you not done so?"
>
> Wen-kung replied, "Your humble servant has seen in Buddhist writings that the Light of Buddha is not something blue or yellow or red or white, so the present light must simply be the glow from some guardian dragon."
>
> The emperor then asked, "Then what, pray tell, is the Buddha's light like?"
>
> Wen-kung did not reply.

Now, even though this Wen-kung is said to have been just an ordinary fellow in lay life, nevertheless he had the spirit of a stout-hearted trainee in the Way who had the ability to set the heavens and the earth a-spinning. Should any people undertake to explore the Matter through their training, this is the beginning attitude of mind that they should have. If they do not approach their study in this manner, they are apart from the Way. Even if flowers were to rain down upon them from the heavens when they were lecturing on the Scriptures, still their efforts would be in vain if they had not yet arrived at this principle in training. Even if they were among the 'thrice wise and ten times saintly',[*] if they were to keep their long tongues in their mouths the same as Wen-kung did his, that would be evidence of their giving rise to the desire to realize the Truth and of their giving rise to training and enlightenment.[5]

Be that as it may, there is something in Buddhist writings that you, Han Wen-kung, have still not encountered or heard about. How have you understood the saying, "The Light of Buddha is not something blue or yellow or red or white?" If you had the ability to grasp the fact that, when someone looks at a light that is blue, yellow, red, or white, it is not the Light of Buddha, then, when you see the Light of Buddha, you must refrain from considering It from the perspective of Its being something blue, yellow, red, or white. If Emperor Hsien-tsung had been a Buddhist Ancestor, he would have pursued the Matter in this way.

In short, the Light that is ever so clear is the luminosity of all the hundreds of things that sprout up like blades of grass, without anything being added to, or taken away from, their roots, stems, branches, leaves, fruit, glow, or color. There is the luminosity of the five paths, and there is the luminosity of the six paths.[6] Since these are the very places where the What exists, would that explain what light is and what brightness is? Surely, it must be describing how the great earth with its mountains and rivers suddenly came into existence. We need to explore in detail the saying by Master Chōsa that the whole universe in all ten quarters is our own brightness. We need to explore that Self which is the Brightness as being the whole universe in all ten quarters.

The coming and going of birth and death is the coming and going of one's brightness; going beyond the mundane and transcending the holy are the indigo and vermilion of that Brightness; becoming a Buddha and becoming an Ancestor are the black and yellow of that Brightness. Training and enlightenment are not apart from It, for they are what color the Brightness is. Grasses and trees, walls and fences, as well as skin, flesh, bones, and marrow are the scarlet and white of the Brightness. Smoke

---

5.   Long tongues are representative of the ability to eloquently voice the Dharma.

6.   'The five paths' refers to the five worlds of existence: namely, that of celestial beings, humans, animals, hungry ghosts, and hells. The six paths are the five paths plus existence in the world of asuras.

and mist, water and stones, as well as the path of birds and the hidden road, are the twists and turns of the Brightness. Experiencing one's own Brightness is the mutual encounter of meeting and recognizing a Buddha. The whole universe in all ten directions is one's true Self, and one's true Self is the whole universe in all ten directions—there is no place to escape to. Were there some way to escape this, it could only be by getting outside of our own physical body. Our present-day seven feet of skull and bones is precisely the form and image of the whole universe in all ten directions. Indeed, the whole universe in all ten directions which trains and enlightens us in the Buddha's Way is our skull and bones, our physical body with its skin, flesh, bones, and marrow.

Great Master Ummon Bun'en was a descendant of the thirty-ninth generation from the World-honored Tathagata. He was the Dharma heir of Great Master Seppō Shinkaku. Even though he was a latecomer to training among the Buddha's followers, he is a hero within our Ancestral lineage. Who could assert that a luminous Buddha had never emerged on Mount Ummon?

> There was a time when Ummon entered the Dharma Hall and addressed his assembly, saying, "All human beings, without exception, have the Light within themselves. But when they look for It, they do not see It, for It is shrouded in the darkness of ignorance. Just what is this Light that everyone has within themselves?" There was no one in his assembly who gave a reply. Putting himself in their place, he said, "The Monks' Hall, the Buddha Hall, the Temple Kitchen, and the Gate to the Mountain."[7]

The present statement of the Great Master that all human beings, without exception, have the Light within themselves is not saying that It is something that will manifest at some time in the future, or that It was something that existed in some past

---

7.   'The Gate to the Mountain' is a common term for the entrance to a monastery. The whole of Ummon's statement could also be translated as "the Monks' Hall, the Buddha Hall, and the Temple Kitchen as the gateways to the monastery."

generation, or that It is something that is fully manifesting Itself in front of some onlooker now. We need to clearly hear and remember his statement that all human beings, without exception, have the Light within themselves. This Light amasses hundreds of thousands of Ummons, helping them train together and say the same thing as with one voice. Ummon is not dragging this statement out from himself: it is the brightness of all human beings that takes up the Light and speaks these words for the sake of everyone. "All human beings, without exception, have the Light within themselves" is equivalent to saying, "The whole of humanity itself is what has the Brightness." The Brightness is what all human beings are. Taking hold of this Brightness, they turn It into external conditions and internal tendencies. Thus, we can say, "The Brightness is what totally possesses all human beings," or "Each Light is each and every human being," or "All human beings, by nature, have within themselves each and every human being," or "Each moment of Light, by nature, contains every moment of Light," or "Each instance of possession totally possesses every instance of possession," or "Each moment of totality contains every moment of totality." So, be aware that the Brightness that each human being completely possesses is what every human being fully manifests, and the Brightness is each individual human being, which each individual brightness completely possesses.

Now, I would like to ask Ummon, "What is it that you are calling 'each and every human being'? What is this thing you call 'Light?'" Ummon himself had said, "Just what is this Light that everyone has within themselves?" This question is the very brightness itself, and any doubt will kill the conversation. Even so, when such a matter is being raised, every human being that is present will be an individual instance of Light.

At the time, there was no one in his assembly who gave a reply. Even though they all had hundreds of thousands of answers, they spoke by means of not making a reply. This condition is the Wondrous Heart of Nirvana, which is the Treasure House of the Eye of the True Teaching, and which all the Buddhas and Ancestors authentically Transmit.

> Ummon, putting himself in the place of his assembly, said,
> "The Monks' Hall, the Buddha Hall, the Temple Kitchen, and the
> Three Gates."[8]

The present statement, "putting himself in the place of," means putting himself in the place of Ummon, putting himself in the place of his great assembly, putting himself in the place of the brightness, and putting himself in the place of the Monks' Hall, the Buddha Hall, the Temple Kitchen, and the Gate to the Monastery. But what did Ummon mean by referring to the Three Gates of the Monks' Hall, the Buddha Hall, and the Temple Kitchen? We ought not to call a great assembly, along with every human being in it, the Three Gates of the Monks' Hall, the Buddha Hall, and the Temple Kitchen. After all, how many Three Gates of the Monks' Hall, Buddha Hall, and Temple Kitchen are there? Should we regard them all as Ummon? Or as the Seven Buddhas?* Or as the twenty-eight Indian Ancestors? Or as the first six Chinese Ancestors? Or as the Fist? Or as the Nose? Even though the Three Gates of the Monks' Hall, Buddha Hall, and Temple Kitchen are, so to speak, any Buddha or Ancestor, Buddhas and Ancestors are persons who do not escape from being human beings. And they go beyond just being 'a human being'. Once they have become 'such a one',* there are instances where there are Buddha Halls that have no Buddha and where there are no Buddha Halls that lack Buddha. There are Buddhas who have luminosity and there are Buddhas who do not have luminosity. There is a luminosity without Buddha and there is a luminosity with Buddha.

---

8. From this point on in the discourse, Dōgen cites the Gate to the Mountain by an alternative name: the Three Gates (both names are read as sammon in Japanese). This shift in names carries an implication that each person who undertakes the training (enters the Gate to the Monastery) encounters the three principle areas of life in a monastery: the Monks' Hall (where one does meditation), the Buddha Hall (where one hears the Teaching), and the Temple Kitchen (where one carries out the ordinary tasks of everyday life). Since these areas of activity are also going on within the trainee, to that extent the trainee is the Monastery. In this sense what Ummon is saying could be translated as "The Monks' Hall, the Buddha Hall, and the Temple Kitchen are the Three Gates."

Great Master Seppō once addressed his assembly, saying, "I have fully recognized you all before the Monks' Hall." This was said at a time when Seppō's whole being, through and through, was his Eye. It was an occasion when Seppō caught a glimpse of the true Seppō. It was a Monks' Hall recognizing a Monks' Hall.

Hōfuku, alluding to his Master's remark, asked Gako,[9] "Putting aside his 'before the Monks' Hall' for the moment, where is it that Bōshū Pavilion and Useki Peak recognize each other?"[10] Thereupon, Gako sped back to the Abbot's quarters, whereas Hōfuku straightaway entered the Monks' Hall. In the present instance, the one's returning to the Abbot's quarters and the other's entering the Monks' Hall are both ways of expressing their having left self behind. It is a principle based on mutual recognition. It is two Monks' Halls mutually recognizing each other.[11]

Great Master Jizō Keichin once said, "The Chief Cook has entered the Kitchen Hall." This expression of his has put the Matter before the Seven Buddhas.

Delivered to the assembly at Kannondōri Kōshōhōrin-ji Temple on a summer night during the fourth period of the third watch of the second day of the sixth lunar month in the third year of the Ninji era (about 2:00 A.M., July 1, 1242). At that time during the wet season, the rain was pouring down, the drops gushing off the eaves. Where was the brightness to be found then? My great assembly has still not escaped from having been pierced to the heart by what Ummon said.

---

9.   Hōfuku and Gako were two of Seppō's disciples.

10.   Bōshū Pavilion and Useki Peak are two scenic places on Mount Seppō that were used as meditation sites.

11.   That is, both having awakened to the Truth and having recognized this awakening in each other, the one goes to the Abbot's quarters (a symbolic Bōshū Pavilion) for spiritual confirmation and instruction, and the other goes to the Monks' Hall (a symbolic Useki Peak) to continue his training through meditation.

Copied by me in the office of the Abbot's assistant at Daibutsu-ji Temple in Echizen Province
    on the third day of the twelfth lunar month in the second year of the Kangen era
    (January 1, 1245).

                                                                                      Ejō

36

On Learning the Way Through Body and Mind

(Shinjin Gakudō)

Translator's Introduction: In this discourse, the Japanese word *shin* is most often rendered as 'mind'. However, there are places where the reference is clearly to 'heart' or to 'intention' (what one has in mind), and it has been translated accordingly.

You cannot realize the Buddha's Way if you do not aim to practice the Way, and It will be ever more distant from you if you do not aim to study It. Meditation Master Nangaku Ejō once said, "It is not that your training and enlightenment are absent, but they must not be tainted with anything." If we do not study the Buddha's Way, then we will lapse into the ways of non-Buddhists or those who are immoral. This is why former Buddhas and later Buddhas all invariably trained in, and practiced, the Buddha's Way.

There are provisionally two ways to learn what the Buddha's Way is: namely, to learn by means of our mind and to learn by means of our body. To learn by means of the mind is to learn by all sorts of minds. Those minds include the discriminative mind, the mind of feelings and emotions, and the mind that sees the oneness of all things, among others. Also, after we have established a spiritual rapport with a Master and have given rise to the mind that would realize full enlightenment, we take refuge in the Great Way of the Buddhas and Ancestors and explore the daily functioning of the mind that seeks full enlightenment. Even if we have not yet given rise to the mind that truly aspires to realize full enlightenment, we should imitate the methods of the Buddhas and Ancestors of the past who gave rise to the mind that seeks enlightenment. This mind is the mind that has resolved to realize enlightenment; it is the manifestation of a sincere heart moment by moment, the mind of previous Buddhas, our everyday mind, and the three worlds of desire, form, and beyond form. All of these are the products of our mind alone.

Sometimes we learn the Way by casting aside these various minds, and sometimes we learn the Way by taking them up. Thus, we learn the Way by thinking about these minds, and we learn the Way by not thinking about them. Sometimes a kesa[*] of gold brocade is forthwith Transmitted and duly accepted.[1] Sometimes there is Bodhidharma's saying, "You have gotten what my marrow is," followed by standing in place after making three full prostrations.[2] There is learning Mind by means of mind, which is the Transmitting of a kesa to the one who pounded rice.[3] To shave one's head and dye one's robes is nothing other than to turn one's heart around and illumine one's mind. To scale the castle walls and enter the mountains is to leave one frame of mind behind and enter another.[4] That a mountain monastery is being entered means that whatever one is thinking about is based on not deliberately thinking about some particular thing.[5] That the worldly life is being abandoned means that what one is specifically thinking about is not the point. To fix one's gaze upon these thoughts is comparable to two or three rounded heaps: to play around with these thoughts in spiritual ignorance is comparable to myriad thousands of sharp edges. When we learn in this manner what the Way is, appreciation will naturally come from our making efforts, but efforts do not necessarily proceed from already having appreciation. Even so, to borrow unseen the Nostrils of an Ancestor of the Buddha and let them expel one's Breath, and to use the hooves of a donkey or a horse and let

---

[*]   See Glossary.

1.   This is an allusion to a Zen Buddhist traditional account that Shakyamuni, when dying, gave His gold brocade kesa to Makakashō as proof of Transmission.

2.   This is a reference to the Mind-to-Mind Transmission from Bodhidharma to his disciple Taiso Eka.

3.   A reference to the Mind-to-Mind Transmission from Daiman Kōnin to Daikan Enō, which was accompanied by passing on the kesa that Bodhidharma had originally brought with him to China.

4.   An allusion to Prince Siddhārtha's leaving his life in his father's palace behind and entering the mountains to seek the Way.

5.   An allusion to a kōan story concerning Meditation Master Yakusan, recounted by Dōgen in Discourse 26: On Wanshi's 'Kindly Advice for Doing Seated Meditation' (*Zazen Shin*), pp. 335–338.

them stamp the seal[*] of one's awakening, these have been signposts of the Way for tens of thousands in the past.[6]

In short, the great earth with its mountains and rivers, along with the sun, moon, and stars, are the very stuff of our mind. So, right at this very moment, what sort of thing is appearing before our very eyes? When we speak of the great earth with its mountains and rivers, the mountains and rivers, for instance, will refer to some mountain and some flowing water: but 'the great earth' is not limited to just this place where we are now.

Mountains are also of many types. There are great Mount Sumerus and there are small Mount Sumerus. There are those that lie horizontally and there are those that rise vertically. There are those within three thousand worlds and there are those in innumerable countries. There are those that depend on their form and there are those that depend on empty space.

Rivers likewise are of many types. There are celestial rivers and there are earthly rivers. There are the four great rivers and there is Lake Anavatapta from which they flow. There are the four Anavatapta lakes in the northern continent of Uttarakuru, and there are oceans, and there are ponds.[7]

'The earth' does not necessarily refer to land, and land does not necessarily refer to 'the earth'. The earth can refer to the land, and it can refer to the ground of our mind, and it can refer to earth that is treasured, such as a monastery. Though we say that earth is what all things are, this will not negate the concept of 'earth', for there may be worlds in which space is viewed as 'earth'.

---

6.   'Nostrils' refers to one's Buddha Nature, which is as plain as the nose on one's face. 'The hooves of a donkey' refers to one's commitment to plodding on, doing one's daily training to clean up one's karma. 'The hooves of a horse' refers to one's commitment to galloping on, going wherever necessary to help all sentient beings realize the Truth.

7.   Lake Anavatapta is traditionally said to be in Tibet, and is considered the source of the four major rivers of India. In Indian cosmology, there are four continents surrounding Mount Sumeru, which is considered the center of the universe. Uttarakuru is the northern continent.

There are differences in the way that the sun, moon, and stars are viewed by humans and celestial beings, since all their various viewpoints are not the same. Because this is the way things are, the perspectives of our whole mind function as one. These perspectives are already what our mind is. So, should we treat the great earth with its mountains and rivers, the sun, the moon and the stars as being within us or outside us, as arising or as departing? When we are born, is one speck of something added to us? At death, does one mote of something depart from us? Where are we to find this birth-and-death, along with our views about it? Up to the present, they have been just one moment of the mind and then a second moment of the mind. One moment of the mind and then a second moment of the mind is one great earth with its mountains and rivers and then a second great earth with its mountains and rivers. Since such things as the great earth with its mountains and rivers are beyond a matter of existing or not existing, they are beyond being large or small, beyond being acquirable or not acquirable, beyond being directly knowable or not being directly knowable, beyond being penetrable or not being penetrable, and they do not change in accordance with our having awakened or not.

You should definitely accept as true that what we call 'learning the Way through mind' is the mind, as it has just been described, accustoming itself to learning the Way. This truth goes beyond anything's 'being large or small' or 'existing or not existing'. Our learning of the Way is described in one Scripture as, "Knowing that a home is not our Home, we abandon our home, leaving home life behind in order to become a monk." This is beyond any measure of size, beyond any measure of proximity. It is beyond all the Ancestors from first to last, and it is even beyond a Master who has gone beyond Buddhahood by helping others to realize Buddhahood. There is verbally expounding upon the Matter[*] as being 'seven feet or eight feet'.[8] And there is actually embarking for the Other Shore, which is done for the sake of both oneself and others. This is what learning the Way is. Because learning the Way is as this, the tiles[*] and stones of our walls and fences constitute our very mind.

---

8.   That is, after having awakened to the Truth, one employs skillful means, which are adjusted to whatever situation arises, without becoming fixed to only one way of responding.

Further, our learning the Way is beyond such sayings as "The three worlds of desire, form, and beyond form, and these alone, are what constitute the mind," or "The whole universe, and this alone, is what constitutes the mind. It is the tiles and stones of our walls and fences." What was nurtured in the years before the Chinese Hsien-tung era (860-873) broke down in the years after the Chinese Hsien-tung era.[9] To learn the Way is our 'slogging through the mud and being drenched in the water'[10] and our 'binding ourselves without a rope'.[11] It is our having the ability to draw forth the Pearl and the skill to enter the Water for It. There will be the day when this Pearl dissolves, and there will be times when It is smashed to pieces, and there will be times when It is crushed to bits. We do not consider ourselves as being equal with those who are the pillars* of the temple, nor do consider ourselves to stand shoulder-to-shoulder with those who are as stone lanterns.* Because things are as they are, we learn the Way by running barefoot and we learn the Way by doing somersaults.[12] And who among you will fix your eyes upon It and look? For each and every one of us, there is our going forth in accordance with whatever circumstances arise. At such a time, because our walls are falling down, this helps us to learn that the ten directions are open to us, and because there are no gates, this helps us to learn that we are not kept from going anywhere.

As to the phrase, 'the mind that has resolved to realize enlightenment', this mind sometimes arises in a life-and-death situation, sometimes in the serenity of nirvana, and sometimes under other conditions. It does not depend on any place, and

---

9. An allusion to a remark made by the tenth-century Meditation Master Sōzan Honjaku who, along with his Master Tōzan Ryōkai, is credited with founding the Sōtō Zen lineage. The remark refers to his level of understanding early in his training as being superficial and to his understanding later as having gone beyond understanding.

10. A common Zen Buddhist phrase describing a monk's willingness to help others no matter what he or she may need to go through.

11. An allusion to keeping to the Precepts without feeling bound up by them.

12. This sentence describes how we learn, namely, by being willing to stumble on, stepping on all manner of things, and by being willing to be tossed head over heels, physically, mentally, and spiritually.

it is not obstructed by any place where it arises. The intention to seek enlightenment does not arise from any particular set of conditions and it does not arise from the intellect. It arises from the intention to seek enlightenment. In fact, it is the intention that seeks enlightenment. The intention that gives rise to seeking enlightenment is beyond existing or not existing, beyond the judgmental realm of 'good or evil', and beyond moral indifference. It is not something that arises as an effect from some previous life, nor is it something that beings in lofty worlds can always realize. It is simply the arising of the intention to realize enlightenment at that moment in time. Because it is not concerned with external circumstances, at the very moment when this intention to seek enlightenment arises, the whole universe, through and through, also gives rise to the intention to seek enlightenment. Though it is said that this arising seems to turn external circumstances around, the intention to seek enlightenment is something that these circumstances do not recognize. The arising of this intention is like both self and other stretching out their hands to each other. And we ourselves stretch out our hands as go forth amidst beings who are alien to us. We give rise to the intention to realize enlightenment even within the worlds of the hells, the hungry ghosts,* the animals, and the asuras.*

As to the phrase, 'the manifestation of a sincere heart moment by moment', at all moments we manifest a sincere heart. And we do it not for one or two moments, but moment by moment.

> The leaves of a lotus are round in their
> roundness
> And their roundness resembles a mirror:
> The spines of a water chestnut are sharp
> in their sharpness
> And their sharpness resembles an awl.

We speak of the leaves resembling a mirror, but they are so just moment by moment; we speak of the spines resembling an awl, but they are so just moment by moment.

As to the phrase 'the mind of previous Buddhas':

> A monk of long ago once asked National Teacher Echū, "Just what is the mind of previous Buddhas?"
>
> The National Teacher responded, "The tiles and stones of our walls and fences."

Since this is so, you need to realize that the mind of previous Buddhas is beyond the tiles and stones of Their walls and fences, and 'the tiles and stones of Their walls and fences' goes beyond what is called 'the mind of previous Buddhas'. This is how we learn what the mind of previous Buddhas is.

When we want to understand what 'mind' is, be it in this world or some other world, it is simply our everyday mind. Yesterday departs from this place and today comes from this place. When yesterday departs, the whole of the heavens departs, and when today comes, every bit of the earth comes: this is our everyday mind. Our everyday mind opens and closes within these confines. Because a thousand gates and ten thousand doors open or close at any one time, they are what 'everyday' is.

Now, 'the whole of the heavens' and 'every bit of the earth' are like forgotten phrases, like some voice gushing up out of the ground. The phrases are equal, the minds are equal, and the Teachings are equal. Our living and our dying die out in every moment, but we are ever ignorant of what preceded this latest body of ours. Though we are ignorant, if we give rise to the intention to seek enlightenment, we are undoubtedly advancing along the road to enlightenment. Already we have established this place, and there is no doubt about it. <u>And</u> we already have doubts about it, which is what being 'everyday' is.

The phrase, 'learning the Way through the body', means that we learn the Way by means of the body, that we learn the Way by means of our living flesh. Our Body comes from our learning the Way, and what has come from our learning the Way is our body along with our Body. The whole universe in all ten quarters is synonymous with our one real physical body, and the coming and going of birth and death is also synonymous with our real physical body. We train with this body when we part company with the ten evils, hold to the eight Precepts, take refuge in the Three

Treasures, and give up our homes, leaving home life behind to become a monk—this is to truly learn the Way. Thus we speak of this as 'our true human body'. By all means, those of us learning in these later times must not hold to the same opinions as those non-Buddhists who deny causality.

Meditation Master Hyakujō Daichi once said, "If you hold to the opinion that we are Buddhas by nature and are already in the Way of Meditation because we are innately immaculate and innately enlightened, then you belong among those non-Buddhists who deny causality." Unlike broken tools in a vacant house, these words of his are the product of his merits and virtues accumulated through his learning the Way. Having leapt beyond the opposites, he is brilliantly clear in all aspects; having let everything drop away, he is like wisteria that no longer depends on a tree for its support.

Sometimes those who learn the Way manifest in their own bodily form in order to help rescue others by giving voice to the Dharma, and sometimes they manifest in another bodily form in order to help rescue others by giving voice to the Dharma, and sometimes they do not manifest in their own bodily form in order to help rescue others by giving voice to the Dharma, and sometimes they do not manifest in another bodily form in order to help rescue others by giving voice to the Dharma, and so on, going so far as to not give voice to the Dharma in order to help rescue others. At the same time, when someone gives up their body and then raises their voice to proclaim the Dharma, there is something that silences all other voices. And by putting one's life on the line, there is something that will get to the Marrow when one opens one's hara.[13] Even if you had taken your first steps in learning the Way before the time of the Lords of Awe-inspiring Voices in the ever so distant past, you would have developed even further if you had been Hyakujō's own children and grandchildren.

---

13. 'Opening the hara to get to the Marrow' refers to a certain spiritual experience that may occur when someone's meditative mind is focused on the hara, which is the area just above the navel. This is sometimes represented by a picture of a monk—or an arhat—pulling open the hara to reveal within Something that is variously described as a Golden Buddha, the Child of the Lord, or the Embryo of Buddha (Skt. *Tathāgatagarbha*).

'The whole universe in all ten quarters' means that each of the ten quarters is the whole universe. East, west, north, south, plus northeast, southeast, northwest, and southwest, along with the zenith and the nadir, are what we call the ten quarters. We need to consider the occasions when their front and back, length and width, are thoroughly whole.[14] What we call 'considering' means clearly seeing and determining that, even though it is said that our human body is restricted by 'self and other', nevertheless it is the whole of the ten quarters. We hear in this expression something that has not been heard before, due to its implications that the ten quarters are equal to each other and that the universe is equal to itself.

A human body is composed of four elements* and five skandhas.* Its four elements and its six sense organs, all together, are not something thoroughly understood by ordinary, worldly people, but they are something that saintly people have thoroughly explored through their training. Further, we need to clearly see the ten quarters within a single dust mote, and it is not that the ten quarters are all packed up in one sack.[15] Sometimes, the Monks' Hall and the Buddha Hall are erected within a single mote of dust, and sometimes the whole universe is erected in the Monks' Hall and the Buddha Hall, for it is from these Halls that the universe has been built. The principle of this is that the universe in all ten quarters is our real Body. Do not follow erroneous views that deny causality. Since the universe is beyond measure, it is beyond being wide or narrow. The universe in all ten quarters is the eighty-four thousand skandhas that give expression to the Dharma, the eighty-four thousand meditative states, and the eighty-four thousand invocations. The eighty-four thousand skandhas that give expression to the Dharma are the turning of the Wheel of the Dharma, and the place where the Wheel of the Dharma turns spans the whole universe and spans all time. It is not a place without directions or boundaries: it is our real Body. You and I, right now, are human beings who are the real Body of the whole universe in all ten quarters. We learn the Way without ever making a mistake about

---

14. In other words, front and back, and length and width are not separate from each other, nor are they separate from the whole universe. Just as you cannot have a front without a back, so you cannot have anything that is somehow independent of the whole universe.

15. That is, there is no inside or outside of them.

such things. We go on, discarding one body and receiving another, for three great asamkhyeya eons, or thirteen great asamkhyeya eons, or immeasurable asamkhyeya eons,[16] during which time, without fail, we learn the Way. We learn the Way by now stepping forward, now stepping back. Our respectfully bowing, with hands in gasshō,[*] is our everyday behavior of walking and standing still. In our painting a picture of a withered tree, or in our polishing a tile made of dead ashes, there is not the slightest break. Though our days, as they say, are short and swift in their passing, our learning the Way is profound and far-reaching. So, even though the demeanor of those who have abandoned their homes and left home life behind to become monks may seem bleak, do not confuse them with woodcutters. And even though their lives may seem a struggle, they are not the same as farmers working in rice fields. So, do not compare them by discussing whether they are deluded or enlightened, or good or bad; do not pursue such questions as "Are they false or true?" or "Are they genuine or fake?"

When people speak of living and dying, coming and going, as being what the real human body is, they use the words 'living and dying' to describe the wandering of ordinary, worldly people lost in samsara as well as to describe what the great saintly ones have escaped from. But this does not mean that going beyond the ordinary and transcending the holy are simply to be considered as 'our real Body', for life and death come in two kinds and in seven kinds.[17] At the same time, because each and every one of these kinds, when thoroughly understood, is totally life-and-death, there is nothing that we need fear. And the reason why we need not fear life and death is that even before we have abandoned this life, we are already encountering death in the present. And even before we have abandoned death, we are already encountering life in the present. Life is not something that stands in the way of death, and death is not something that stands in the way of life. Neither life nor death are understood by ordinary, worldly people. Life may be likened to an oak tree in its growing; death may be likened to an iron man in its immobility. Though oak trees are restricted to being

---

16. 'Asamkhyeya' is a Sanskrit term of measurement for something that is experienced as being interminably long, but which simply takes as long as it takes.

17. There are various listings of the two and seven kinds of life and death, all of which describe different perspectives on how life and death function.

oak trees, life is never restricted by death, which is why we take up learning the Way. Life is not one sort of thing, and death is not another, second sort of thing. Never does death stand against life: never does life stand against death.

Meditation Master Engo once said:

> *Life fully manifests its function*
> *And death fully manifests its function as well,*
> *All within the limits of Great Unbounded Space,*
> *For they are both the moment-by-moment*
> *manifestations of a sincere heart.*

We need to do our utmost to tranquilly consider these words of his. Although Meditation Master Engo spoke these words, he still had not recognized that life and death are beyond the scope of their functions. When exploring 'coming and going' through our training, there is life-and-death in going, and there is life-and-death in coming. There is coming-and-going in life, and there is coming-and-going in death. With the whole universe in all ten directions as its two or three wings, coming-and-going flies off and flies back, and with the whole universe in all ten directions as its three or five feet, coming-and-going steps forward and steps back. With life-and-death as Its head and tail, the real Body, which is the whole universe in all ten directions, can reverse Itself and turn Its head around.[18] In reversing Itself and turning Its head around, It may look the size of a penny, or It may resemble the inside of a tiny mote of dust. The flat level ground is a precipitous cliff rising a thousand feet high. And the precipitous cliff rising a thousand feet high is the flat level ground. This is why there is the look of the southern continent and the look of the northern continent; by examining these, we learn the Way.[19] There is the Bones and Marrow of 'being beyond

---

18.   That is, just as our physical body can turn itself around and go a different way, so our minds can also turn away from delusion and toward enlightenment.

19.   The southern continent of Jambudvipa is associated with the world of human beings who are capable of learning because they are aware of their suffering, whereas the northern

deliberately trying to think about something and being beyond deliberately trying not to think about anything'. Only by our resisting the tendency to deliberately manipulate our thinking do we learn the Way.

Delivered to the assembly at Kōshōhōrin-ji Temple on the double good fortune day (the ninth day of the ninth lunar month) in the third year of the Ninji era (October 3, 1242).

Copied by me on the second day of the beginning of mid-spring in the fourth year of the Ninji era (February 22, 1243).

Ejō

---

continent of Uttarakuru is associated with the world of celestial beings who see no need to train because they are, at the moment, enjoying a constantly easy and blissful existence.

37

On a Vision Within a Vision
and a Dream Within a Dream

(Muchū Setsumu)

Translator's Introduction: The Chinese character *'mu'* in the title of this discourse is read in Japanese as *'yume'*. When translated into English, this single character encompasses the meaning of both 'dream' and 'vision', the former term denoting an experience that occurs while sleeping and the latter referring to an experience that occurs while being awake. The Japanese employ only the single word *yume* for both experiences. Also, in Buddhism, the whole of life and all that exists in the universe is viewed as being as insubstantial and impermanent as a dream or a vision. According to Dōgen, this dream-vision is also a manifestation of the Truth, which we either see or do not see depending on whether we are spiritually awake or still spiritually asleep.

Because the Truth, which all the Buddhas and all the Ancestors have manifested in this world, is something that existed before any thoughts or things had sprouted up, It is beyond anything that those with false and empty notions argue over. Accordingly, within the bounds of the Buddhas and Ancestors there has been the meritorious activity of That which goes above and beyond Buddhahood. Because this meritorious activity is independent of any specific occasion, it will far outlast the life span of any living being —be it for a shorter or longer time—for it never ceases, and it will be far beyond any way of measuring to be found in the realm of ordinary folk.

Further, the turning of the Wheel of the Dharma is the standard for That which has existed since before any thoughts or things had ever sprouted up. Since the great merit of Its turning is beyond praise, It has served as a signpost and model in thousands of times past. Buddhas speak of this Wheel of the Dharma as being a vision from within a vision. Because They see what enlightenment is from within Their enlightenment, They give expression to Their vision from within Their vision.

The place from whence They are giving expression to Their vision from within Their vision is the domain of Buddhas and Ancestors: it is the assembly of Buddhas and Ancestors. The domain and assembly of Buddhas, as well as the pathways and Dharma assemblies of the Ancestors, are based on Their innate enlightenment giving rise to Their experience of enlightenment and on Their subsequently giving expression to the vision that They are experiencing within Their vision. In encountering these sayings and expressions of Theirs, do not treat them as something apart from the Buddha's assembly, for They are Buddhas turning the Wheel of the Dharma. Because this Wheel of the Dharma encompasses everything in all directions, the Great Ocean, Mount Sumeru, all lands, and all thoughts and things have fully manifested themselves. This is the vision expressed within the vision, which existed prior to any dreams. All that manifests within the whole universe is but a dream. This dream consists of all the hundreds of things that sprout up ever so clearly. It is the very moment when we are about to give rise to doubt, the very moment when we are confused. This moment is, say, a sprouting up of the dream, a sprouting up within the dream, and a sprouting up that gives expression to the dream. In exploring this through our training, we find that the roots and stalks with their branches and leaves, and the blossoms and fruits with their lustrous colors and forms altogether comprise the great dream. And you must not confuse it with dreaminess.

Accordingly, when persons who have doubts about learning the Buddha's Way encounter the phrase 'a vision being expressed within a vision', they vainly imagine that it probably refers to dreaming up things that actually do not exist, or they suppose that it may be like piling delusion upon delusion. But this is not so. Even though one says that there is also delusion within delusion, by all means we need to thoroughly explore, with utmost effort, the path that penetrates through this expression to the comprehension of what is really meant by 'piling delusion upon delusion'.

'A vision expressed within a vision' is what all Buddhas are, and all Buddhas are 'wind and rain, water and fire'.[1] They accept and keep in mind the latter epithet and They accept and keep in mind the former epithet. 'A vision expressed from within

---

1.   That is, because Buddhas are beyond a personal self, They are a vision expressed within a vision, and when They express that vision, what They give voice to pours forth from Them like wind and rain, water and fire.

a vision' is what the Buddha of old was. Riding within His treasured Vehicle,[2] He forthwith arrived at His sitting place, where He realized the Truth. 'Arriving at His sitting place, where He realized the Truth' is synonymous with 'His riding within His treasured Vehicle'. "No matter whether the vision of trainees is distorted or correct, the Master either grabs hold of their deluded certainty or lets them go on in their own way, as he himself gives free rein to his elegantly skillful means."[3] At such moments, the Wheel of the Dharma sometimes sets into motion the realm of the great Dharma Wheel, which is beyond measure and beyond bounds. And sometimes It sets this realm in motion within a single dust mote, for even within a mote of dust, Its movement never ceases. The principle here is that no matter how the Dharma's being set in motion may bring about the experience of That Which Is, even the hostile will smile and nod. And because this setting of the Dharma in motion has brought about an experience of That Which Is, regardless of where this may occur, it is synonymous with setting elegantly skillful means in motion. As a result, all at once the whole earth is a limitless Dharma Wheel and the universe throughout is undisguised cause and effect. For Buddhas, these two realms are the ultimate. Keep in mind that the provisional instructions of Buddhas and the heaping up of Their voicings of the Dharma have established limitless ways of teaching by provisional means and have made limitless places in which the Dharma can abide. Do not look for limits to Their comings and goings. Completely relying on the Dharma, They come; completely relying on the Dharma, They go. Thus, Their planting kudzu and wisteria and Their letting the kudzu and wisteria entwine is the nature and form of supreme enlightenment.[4] Just as enlightenment is limitless, so sentient beings are limitless and supreme. Notwithstanding the fact that enticements and snares are limitless, letting

---

2. A reference to the One Vehicle, which derives from the *Lotus Scripture*. Dōgen discusses its meaning in detail in his Discourse 16: On 'The Flowering of the Dharma Sets the Dharma's Flowering in Motion' *(Hokke Ten Hokke)*, pp. 175-178.

3. A quotation from Dōgen's Master, Tendō Nyojō.

4. 'Planting kudzu and wisteria and letting them entwine' is descriptive of setting up a Master-disciple relationship and then letting the interdependence of Master and disciple grow.

them go is also limitless. When your spiritual question appears, it will yield thirty blows for you, which is the manifesting of a vision that is being expressed within a vision.

Thus, a rootless tree, an earth without opposites, and a valley that does not echo a shout are all manifest visions that are being expressed within a vision. This is not within the realm of ordinary people or those in lofty positions, nor is it what worldly folks take note of. The vision is enlightenment, so who could doubt it?—for it is not what is governed by doubt. And who could believe it?—for belief does not set it in motion. Because this supreme enlightenment is supreme enlightenment, we speak of it as a vision within a vision. There is the vision within and there is giving expression to the vision; there is the vision being expressed and there is one's being within the vision. Without being within a vision there is no expressing a vision, and without expressing a vision, there is no being within a vision. Without expressing a vision, there are no Buddhas, and without being within a vision, the Buddhas do not emerge into the world to turn the wondrous Wheel of the Dharma. That Dharma Wheel refers to each Buddha on His own, just as it refers to all Buddhas and to the vision that is expressed from within a vision. It is only in that vision which is expressed from within a vision that Buddhas and Ancestors exist as a supremely enlightened multitude. Further, the experience of what lies beyond the Dharma Body is a vision that is expressed from within a vision. Herein is there homage for each Buddha alone, together with all Buddhas. They have no attachment to head or eye, marrow or brain, body or flesh, hand or foot. And because They have no such attachments, as an ancient one once said, "The one who is a seller of gold will be a buyer of gold." We call this 'the Profound of the profound' and 'the Wondrous of the wondrous' and 'the Enlightened of the enlightened' and 'the Head that rests upon the head'. This is nothing other than the everyday behavior of the Buddhas and Ancestors.

In exploring this Matter* through your training, some of you may think that what is being referred to as a 'Head' is merely something extraneous atop the crown of a person's head. But it may not have occurred to you that what is really atop the crown is Vairochana* Buddha. And even less may you think that It is the Head from

---

*   See Glossary.

which all the hundreds of things ever so obviously sprout up, to say nothing of knowing what the word 'Head' is pointing to. From ancient times, the phrase 'placing a Head upon a head' has habitually been handed down. Foolish people, on hearing this, think that this is merely a saying that warns against anything that is superfluous or excessive. They treat it as an everyday maxim by saying, "Why put a head atop a head?" to express that there is no need for something. Surely, this is a mistake. For, when giving expression to a vision from within a vision, there is no difference in how both worldly and saintly persons misuse the phrase 'placing a Head upon a head'. Thus, for both worldly and saintly persons, their giving expression to a vision from within a vision must have occurred in the past and must still extend to the present day. You need to realize that when it comes to their having expressed a vision from within a vision in the past, they customarily believed that they were expressing a dream from within a dream. And when it comes to their expressing of a vision from within a vision today, they still treat it as their expressing a dream from within a dream. This, accordingly, is what the joy in meeting a Buddha is all about. Even though the vision that the Buddhas and Ancestors have of all the hundreds of things which sprout up ever so clearly is more obvious than a hundred thousand suns and moons, how sad that those who are spiritually blind do not see It. What a pity![5]

The 'Head' in the phrase 'the Head that rests upon the head' is the Head of a hundred sproutings, the Head of a thousand kinds of things, the Head of ten thousand varieties of things, the Head of one's whole being, the Head that is the whole universe which has never been hidden, the Head that is the whole universe in all ten quarters, the Head that matches a phrase of Scripture, the Head that is the top of a hundred-foot

---

5.   To paraphrase this complex passage, in the same way that people do not understand the spiritual meaning of the phrase 'placing a Head upon a head', they also misunderstand the nature of their everyday experience. Rather than seeing the Buddha Nature within all the myriad things that exist, they only see the insubstantiality of all things. By viewing things in this one-sided way, they sadly miss the joy of meeting Buddha, until and unless they encounter 'such a one' who can explain the deeper spiritual significance of all that exists.

pole. You should explore through your training, and do it thoroughly, that both 'what is resting' and 'what is upon' is the very Head of heads.

Thus it is that the saying from the *Diamond-cutting Scripture* that "Buddhas and the supreme, fully perfected enlightenment of Buddhas all come forth from this Teaching of Mine" is also expressing a vision from within the vision wherein the Head habitually rests upon the head. When this Teaching gives expression to a vision from within the vision, supreme enlightenment causes all Buddhas to come forth. And what is more, all Buddhas, being enlightened, give voice to this Scripture, which is, beyond doubt, Their expressing a vision from within the vision. Since the cause of the vision is not obscured, the result of the vision is not hidden from sight. It is simply a matter of one strike of a clapper making a thousand hits or ten thousand hits, or of a thousand strikes or ten thousand strikes making one hit or half a hit. Accordingly, you need to know that there is such a thing as giving expression to a vision from within the vision—one that involves the experiencing of That Which Is—and there are times when the one who gives expression to a vision from within the vision is 'such a person'.* And there is the giving expression to a dream from within a dream—one that does not involve the experiencing of That Which Is—and there are times when the one who gives expression to a dream from within a dream is not 'such a person'. And you need to know that the principle being recognized here is dazzlingly clear, namely, that giving expression all day long to a vision from within the vision is simply giving expression to a vision from within the vision. This is why a former Buddha once said, "For your sakes, I am now giving expression to the vision from within the vision. The Buddhas of the three periods of time—past, present, and future—all expressed the vision from within the vision and the first six Chinese Ancestral Masters also expressed the vision from within the vision." You should clearly study these words.

'Holding the flower aloft, with eyes atwinkle' is giving expression to the vision from within the vision, and 'respectful bowing securing for you the very Marrow of the Way' is also giving expression to the vision from within the vision.[6]

---

6.   'Holding the flower aloft, with eyes atwinkle' is a reference to the Transmission of the Dharma from Shakyamuni Buddha to his disciple Makakashō. Dōgen explores the

In sum, 'gaining the Way through a single verse of Scripture', as well as "I do not understand," and "I do not personally know that One," are all ways of expressing the vision from within the vision.[7] Because the Bodhisattva* of Great Compassion's making use of His ever so many hands and eyes is the same, His meritorious functions of 'seeing colors and seeing sounds' and of 'hearing colors and hearing sounds' are sufficient. Sometimes, one gives expression to the vision from within the vision by manifesting oneself in various forms to aid deluded beings. Sometimes, one gives expression to the vision from within the vision by giving voice to the Dharma over and over again. It is giving expression to the vision from within the vision when a Master grabs hold of the deluded certainty of his trainees or lets them go on in their own way. 'Pointing directly' is giving expression to the vision, just as 'hitting the target' is giving expression to the vision. Whether grabbing hold of the deluded certainty of one's trainees or letting them go on in their own way, you need to learn how to use an ordinary weighing scale. When you have learned this, then, beyond question, your ability to spot the difference between a pound and an ounce will emerge, and you will have your way of expressing the vision from within the vision.

If you have not yet reached equilibrium and are still arguing over how many ounces to a pound, you will not manifest balance. When you have achieved equilibrium, then you will see what balance really is. When you have completely achieved equilibrium, you will not depend on what is being weighed, or upon some scale, or upon the way a scale functions. You need to thoroughly explore that, even though you may rely on That which is as unbounded space, if you have not attained equilibrium, you will not see what balance is. When you yourself are relying on That

---

reference to 'respectful bowing' in his Discourse 10: On 'Respectful Bowing Will Secure for You the Very Marrow of the Way' *(Raihai Tokuzui).*

7.   'Gaining the Way...' is an allusion to the Sixth Chinese Ancestor Daikan Enō, who awoke to the Truth upon hearing someone recite a single verse from the *Diamond-cutting Scripture.* "I do not understand [the Buddha's Teaching]" is also an allusion to Daikan Enō, whose understanding went beyond an intellectual understanding of Scripture. "I do not personally know that One" was Bodhidharma's reply to Emperor Wu's question, "And who, pray, is this one who is confronting my royal presence?"

which is as unbounded space, letting the objects you encounter float freely in space, it will be your giving expression to the vision from within the vision, and within that space you will physically manifest equilibrium. Balance is the great truth of a scale, whereon we weigh space and we weigh things. Whether it is space or an object being weighed, when you reach equilibrium, you will express the vision from within the vision.

There is nothing that is not a liberated expression of the vision from within the vision. 'Vision' is synonymous with the whole of the great earth, and the whole of the great earth is synonymous with equilibrium. Therefore, our endlessly turning our head and setting our brains in motion are nothing other than our accepting in trust and acting in devotion, by means of which we realize the vision within our dreams.

Shakyamuni Buddha once said in verse,

> *The Buddha with His body all in gold*
> *Was adorned with the marks of a hundred*
> > *blessings.*
> *His very existence was like a pleasant dream*
> *In which He heard the Dharma and voiced It for*
> > *the sake of all.*

> *And in His dream He became a nation's king,*
> *One who forsook palace and household,*
> *As well as all desires for finer things,*
> *To find, instead, a place to train for Truth.*

> *Beneath the Bodhi tree*
> *He took His place upon the Lion's seat* *
> *And sought the Truth for seven days*
> *Before He reached the wisdom that He sought.*

> *Having fully reached the Supreme Way,*
> *He arose and turned the Dharma's Wheel,*

Expressing Truth for the sake of all
As hundreds of thousands of millions of kalpas*
passed Him by.

Beyond delusion is His wondrous Dharma
That helps all beings reach the Other Shore.
Then the day came when He entered nirvana
Like a lamp going out, its fuel spent.

If any in later times
Should express His peerless Dharma,
They too will reap great benefits
Like the meritorious virtues herein described.

By exploring through your training what the Buddha is saying in the present instance, you will fully realize what the assembly of all Buddhas is, for what He is saying is not a metaphor. The wondrous Dharma of Buddhas is simply that of each Buddha on His own, just as it is for all the Buddhas. Therefore, all things, both in a dream state and in an awakened one, are manifestations of the Truth. Within the awakened state, there is a turning of the heart, practice and training, enlightenment, and nirvana, and within the dreaming state there is likewise a turning of the heart, practice and training, enlightenment, and nirvana. The dream state and the awakened state—each is a manifestation of the Truth. They are beyond large and small, beyond superior and inferior.

At the same time, seeing or hearing a phrase like "And in His dream He became a nation's king," people in the past and present have mistakenly understood it to mean that, due to the influence of this foremost Dharma having been voiced, their own nighttime dreams will come true. Their understanding the phrase in this way means that they have not yet fully understood what the Buddha was Teaching. Dreaming and being awake have always been as one and the same, for they are both manifestations of the Truth. And even if the Buddha's Teaching were a metaphor, it would still be a manifestation of the Truth. And, as already stated, It is not a metaphor. What we create in a dream <u>is</u> the reality of the Buddha's Teaching. Shakyamuni

Buddha, as well as all the Buddhas and Ancestors, have turned Their hearts around and done the training and practice, and They have alike achieved a genuine awakening, and all within a dream. Because this is so, what the Buddha said as Teaching for the present-day mundane world is nothing other than 'what we create within a dream'.

Seven days expresses a measure for how long it takes to attain the wisdom of a Buddha. Turning the Wheel of the Dharma to help sentient beings reach the Other Shore has already been described as the passing of hundreds of thousands of millions of kalpas, for we should not speculate on the speed with which time passes within a dream.[8]

> *The Buddha with His body all in gold*
> *Was adorned with the marks of a hundred blessings.*
> *His very existence was like a pleasant dream*
> *In which He heard the Dharma and voiced It for the*
> *sake of all.*

Clearly you must have realized from this that 'a pleasant dream' is what the Buddha is. There is the Tathagata's phrase "His very existence," for He was not just some hundred-year long dream. "Voicing It for the sake of all" was His manifesting Himself in various forms. "Hearing the Dharma" was the sound that was heard by His Eye, the sound that was heard by His Heart, the sound that was heard by the old habits that He abandoned like an empty nest, and the sound that was heard before time began.

> *The Buddha with His body all in gold*
> *Was adorned with the marks of a hundred blessings.*

This is saying that 'a pleasant dream' is the bodily existence of the Buddha, which is His forthwith having arrived at the Now and having doubts no more. Even though the instructions of the Buddha do not cease for someone who has awakened, the principle

---

8.   That is, time is how we experience it rather than how it is measured by a clock. Therefore, the seeming length of a 'day' and the length of a 'kalpa' are variable.

of the Buddhas' and Ancestors' complete manifesting is, of necessity, Their manifesting a vision from within a vision. Through your training, you need to explore what it means not to vilify the Buddha's Dharma. When you explore through your training what not vilifying the Buddha's Dharma means, the present words of the Tathagata will immediately come forth.

Given to the assembly on the twenty-first day of the ninth lunar month in the third year of the Ninji era (October 16, 1242) in Yamashiro Province, Uji District, at Kannondōri in Kōshōhōrin-ji Temple.

Copying finished by me on the third day of the third lunar month in the first year of the Kangen era (March 24, 1243).

The Abbot's Assistant Ejō

38

On Expressing What One Has Realized

(Dōtoku)

Translator's Introduction: While *'dōtoku'*, the key term in this discourse, can be translated in various ways, all point to the same matter, namely, the way in which someone expresses, often through words, what has been realized spiritually. This is different from experiencing a psychological insight or having an intellectual comprehension.

All the Buddhas and all the Ancestors express what They have realized. This is why the Buddhas and Ancestors, when singling out an Ancestor of the Buddha, invariably ask, "Can that person express their realization or not?" They ask this question with Their heart and mind, with Their body, with Their traveling staff and ceremonial hossu, and as a pillar of Their temple and as a stone lantern.[1] For those who are not Buddhas or Ancestors, the question does not arise. The matter of their expressing what they have realized does not arise because such a state does not exist for them.

Expressing what one has realized is an ability that is not to be had by keeping in step with other people, nor is it some innate talent; simply, whenever trainees thoroughly practice the Way of the Buddhas and Ancestors, then they will be able to express what Buddhas and Ancestors have realized. While expressing Their realization for others, the Buddhas and Ancestors of the past continued Their training and practice, and thereby thoroughly awoke to the Way. In the present, we should also do our meditation wholeheartedly and do our utmost to practice the Way. When Ancestors of the Buddha wholeheartedly do the meditation of Buddhas and Ancestors and undertake to put into practice the Truth that the Buddhas and Ancestors have expressed, Their expression of what They have realized represents the effort of three years, or eight years, or thirty or forty years, as They express what They have realized with all Their might.

---

1. Please see the *Glossary* for the symbolic meanings of the last four terms in this sentence.

Within these time spans, however many decades long they may have been, there has been no disparity in how 'such a one' [*] has expressed what he or she has realized. Thus, when you become fully awake, what you will realize through your direct encounter with It will be the Truth. Because this encounter confirms as true the direct encounters of former times, when we now express what we have realized, it is beyond doubt. Thus, our expressing what we have realized in the present is supported by That which we directly met with in former times, and we support That which we directly met with in former times by expressing our realization today. This is why we can now express what we have realized, for we have personally met with It through our own experience. The expression of our realization in the present and our direct seeing in the past are as a single iron bar whose ends are ten thousand miles apart.[2] Our present efforts are directed by what we have realized of the Way and by what we have personally encountered.

We pile up long months and many years of keeping to these efforts, and what is more, we cease to cling to our past efforts over the months and years. When we attempt to let go, our skin, flesh, bones, and marrow alike strive to let go. And along with them, the land we live in with its mountains and rivers also strives to let go. At this time, while we are striving to let go so that we may arrive at the Ultimate Treasured Place, our effort to arrive fully comes forth, and, as a result, at the very moment of letting go, we will spontaneously express our realization as it immediately manifests before our very eyes. Even though it is said to be beyond the power of our body and mind, we will, nevertheless, spontaneously express what we have realized. Once our realization has occurred, we see that it is not something curious or strange.

Be that as it may, when you use words to express what you have realized, you will leave unsaid whatever is inexpressible through words. Even if you can see that you have indeed expressed what you have realized, if you have not realized that not all things can be verbally expressed, then you will lack the look of the Buddhas and Ancestors, and you will lack the Bones and Marrow of the Buddhas and

---

[*]   See Glossary.

2.   That is, they are fundamentally one and the same, while appearing as if they were totally separate.

Ancestors. As a consequence, how could Eka's expressing his realization by doing three prostrations before Bodhidharma and then standing silently in his place possibly be equaled by that bunch who are stuck on 'skin, flesh, bones and marrow'?[3] Furthermore, the understanding of that bunch who are stuck on 'skin, flesh, bones and marrow' does not even come close to Eka's understanding, as expressed by his doing three prostrations before Bodhidharma and then standing in his place, much less were any of that bunch equipped with what Eka had. Those whom we encounter right now as we do our practice amidst different kinds of sentient beings are just like those whom Eka encountered in the past as he did his practice amidst different kinds of sentient beings.[4] For us, there is a basis for our verbally expressing what we have realized and a basis for our not verbally expressing what we have realized. And for Eka, there was a basis for his verbally expressing what he had realized and a basis for his not verbally expressing what he had realized. And for that bunch, there is a 'self and other' in what they say and a 'self and other' in what they do not say.

Great Master Jōshū Shinsai, in instructing his assembly, once said, "If you were to spend your whole life not leaving the monastery, sitting as still as a mountain and not saying a word for five or ten years, no one would call you a mute, and later

---

3. The allusion here is to what occurred with the four disciples of Bodhidharma, three of whom expressed their understanding of their Master's Teaching verbally, whereas Eka, the fourth, bowed to the Master whilst remaining silent. Each disciple, in turn, was described by Bodhidharma as having realized one of four attributes: the Master's Skin, the Master's Flesh, the Master's Bones, and the Master's Marrow. In the present context, Dōgen is alluding to the literal-minded who are stuck with the notion that 'Skin, Flesh, Bones, and Marrow' represent four spiritual states in ascending order of superiority, rather than recognizing that each of the four disciples had obtained the substance of Bodhidharma's Teaching.

4. 'Doing one's practice amidst sentient beings" is a Zen Buddhist phrase referring to helping sentient beings reach the Other Shore, particularly those sentient beings whose perception of things is alien to the Buddhist Way.

on, not even the Buddhas would be your equal!"[5] Accordingly, when you reside in a monastery for five or ten years as the frosts of winter and the flowers of summer, time and again, pass you by, and when you esteem doing your utmost to practice the Way whilst spending your whole life without leaving the monastery even once, then your sitting as still as a mountain, which severs the roots of your dualistic thinking, will, before long, be an expression of your realization. Your walking, sitting, and reclining whilst not leaving the monastery will be instances of no one calling you a mute. Even though we do not know what our whole life will be like, if we make our lifetime one of not physically leaving the monastery, this will be our way of 'not leaving the monastery'. And what path through the trackless sky could one traverse in order to go beyond such terms as 'our whole life' and 'a monastery'? So, simply strive to sit as still as a mountain, and do not speak of 'not expressing It through words'. 'Not expressing It through words' is a way of expressing It that is correct from beginning to end.

Sitting as still as a mountain is for a whole lifetime, or for two whole lifetimes: it is not just for one or two occasions. When you have spent five or ten years in sitting as still as a mountain without saying a word, even the Buddhas will not think lightly of you. Truly, when you are sitting as still as a mountain without saying a word, even the Eyes of Buddhas will be unable to catch a glimpse of you, and even the strength of a Buddha will be unable to make you sway. At such a time, even the Buddhas will be unable to equal you.

Jōshū said that the expression 'sitting as still as a mountain' is beyond anything that even the Buddhas would call 'being a mute', and it is also beyond anything that They would call 'not being a mute'. Accordingly, a whole life spent without leaving the monastery is a life spent wholly expressing what one has realized.

---

5. Throughout this text, the word 'monastery' can be understood literally as referring to the physical place where trainees come in order to train together and figuratively as one's place of training, which is wherever one does the practice.

   In the present context, the Zen Buddhist term *'akan'*, translated here as 'a mute', refers to a thoroughly inexperienced trainee who is unable to say even a word in response to a Master's question.

Sitting as still as a mountain without saying a word for five or ten years is synonymous with expressing what one has realized for five or ten years. It is a whole life spent without departing from 'not verbally expressing' what one has realized, and it is a whole lifetime of five or ten years, and it is hundreds and thousands of Buddhas sitting to cut off Their dualistic thinking, and it is hundreds and thousands of Buddhas sitting to cut Themselves free from a 'self'.

Thus, the basis of the Buddhas' and Ancestors' expressing Their realization is Their spending Their whole life in not leaving the monastery. Even if you were a mute, you would still have this as a basis for expressing what you have realized, so do not draw the conclusion that a mute cannot have a way of expressing what he has realized. The person who has a way of expressing what he has realized is not necessarily someone who is not a mute, since a mute, too, has his way of expressing what he has realized. You need to be able to hear His mute voice: you need to listen to His mute words. If you are not mute, how can you possibly meet with a Mute, or converse with a Mute? Given that That Person is as silent as a mute, how are we to meet with Him or converse with Him? Exploring the Matter* in this way, you should thoroughly put into practice being as silent as a mute.

There was a monk in the assembly of Great Master Seppō Shinkaku who went just outside the mountain monastery and built himself a hermit's thatched hut. Though the years accumulated, he did not shave his head. Who can know what kind of life went on within that hut? As a rule, life within the mountains was depressing indeed.

He had fashioned a dipper out of wood and would go to the nearby ravine to get water for drinking. Truly, he must have been the sort who drinks from ravines. Consequently, as the days came and the nights passed, word of his customary habits leaked out, so that one day a monk came and asked him, "Why was it that the Ancestral Master Bodhidharma came here from the West?" The hermit replied, "Since the ravine is so deep, the handle of my dipper is long."

The inquiring monk was so dumbfounded that he left without bowing or asking the hermit for elucidation. Climbing back up the mountain, he recounted the event to Seppō. When Seppō heard the account, he said, "How wondrously strange! Even if it is as you say, this old monk will go and see for himself. By testing him, I'll get to the bottom of this, right off."

The heart of what Seppō said is that the merit of the hermit's remark was excellent, right up to the point of being wondrous, and even so, the old monk Seppō needed to go and see for himself. So, one day Seppō suddenly set off, asking his personal attendant to come along with a razor. He straightway arrived at the hermit's hut. No sooner had he spotted the hermit than he asked him, "If you can say what you have realized, should I not shave your head?"

We need to get to the heart of this question. "If you can say what you have realized, should I not shave your head?" can also be understood as "My not shaving your head means that you have a way of expressing the Matter," right? If the hermit's way of expressing what he has realized really did express the Matter, Seppō, in the last analysis, would not shave him. Those who have the capacity to hear this expression of the Matter need to listen, and should also clearly expound it for the sake of others who have the capacity to listen.

The hermit then washed his head and came before Seppō. Had he come as his way of expressing what he had realized or had he come as his way of not expressing what he had realized? Whichever the case, Seppō, accordingly, shaved the hermit's head.

This one episode is like the blossoming of an udumbara flower;[6] not only is it something rarely met with, it is rarely even heard about. It goes beyond the realm of the seven times saintly or the ten times saintly: it goes beyond what is glimpsed by the thrice wise or the seven times wise.* Those who are academic teachers of Scripture and writers of erudite commentaries, along with that bunch who crave mystical or magical powers, cannot fathom it at all. When we speak of encountering the emergence of a Buddha into the world, we are speaking of hearing a story like this one.

---

6.   The udumbara flower is said to blossom only once in every three thousand years.

Now, what could Seppō's remark, "If you can say what you have realized, should I not shave your head" really mean? When people who have not yet given expression to the Truth hear this story, those who are capable may be startled and doubt their ability, whereas those who are not yet capable may be completely bewildered. Seppō did not ask the hermit about 'Buddha', nor did he speak of 'the Way': he did not ask him about deep meditative states, nor did he speak of invocations.[7] Even though his inquiring as he did resembles asking a question, it is actually analogous to an assertion. You should explore this in detail through your training.

The hermit, though, had the look of the Genuine about him, so he could not help but give expression to the Dharma for the sake of others by his way of expressing what he had realized, and, as a result, he was not bewildered by Seppō's remark. He did not seek to go back into seclusion, as was his customary way, but washed his head and came forth. This is an expression of Buddha Dharma whose boundaries not even the wisdom of the Buddha Himself can reach. Expressing It can take the form of manifesting the Body, or giving voice to the Dharma, or rescuing sentient beings from their suffering, or washing one's head and coming forth.

Now then, if Seppō had not been the spiritually Real Person that he was, he would probably have thrown down the razor and burst out into gales of laughter. But Seppō had the essential spiritual strength and was that kind of Real Person, so he shaved the hermit's head. Truly, if Seppō and the hermit had not been 'Buddhas on Their own, together with all Buddhas', it could not have been like this; if they had not been 'one and the same Buddha, and also two Buddhas', it could not have been like this; if they had not been one dragon meeting another, it could not have been like this. The Black Dragon vigilantly guards the black pearl that He prizes so highly, and yet it naturally rolls into the hands of one who knows how to receive it.

---

7.   Discussing 'Buddha' and 'the Way' refers to the intellectualizing of Buddhism by scholarly commentators and academic teachers of Scriptural texts, whereas deep meditative states and invocations are areas that those seeking magical powers are apt to get into. An invocation is a phrase having spiritual significance, which is sometimes chanted as part of a trainee's ceremonial practice.

Keep in mind that when Seppō tested the hermit, the hermit saw who Seppō really was. In expressing what was realized without saying what was realized, the one was shaved and the other did the shaving. Accordingly, there are pathways whereby good spiritual friends who express the Truth unexpectedly meet each other. And among friends who claim that they have not realized anything, there have been occasions when they have recognized the True Self, even though they had no expectations of doing so. When you undertake through your training to recognize the True Self, you will express what you have realized when It manifests before your very eyes.

Written down at Kannondōri in Kōshōhōrin-ji Temple and given to the assembly on the fifth day of the tenth lunar month in the third year of the Ninji era (October 30, 1242). Composed and proofread by this mendicant monk.

Copied on the second day of the eleventh lunar month in the third year of the same era (November 25, 1242).

Ejō

39

On 'A Picture of a Rice Cake'

(Gabyō)

Translator's Introduction: In this discourse, Dōgen begins by exploring, from a literal perspective, the saying by Meditation Master Kyōgen Chikan that "A picture of a rice cake cannot satisfy one's hunger." In other words, a mental construct is no substitute for the direct experience of That Which Is. Also, knowing that suffering exists does not allay suffering. He then subtly turns this perspective around and shows how what we call a direct experience is shaped by how our mind depicts things.

Because all Buddhas are enlightened, all worldly beings are enlightened. Even so, Buddhas and worldly beings are not of one and the same nature or of one and the same frame of mind. Nevertheless, at the time when both manifest their enlightenment, the enlightenment of one does not inhibit the enlightenment of others. At the time when both manifest their enlightenment, they will manifest it without the two coming in contact with each other's manifesting it. This is the forthright Teaching that is characteristic of our Ancestors. So do not hold up some measure of sameness or difference as the gauge of someone's capacity to train. This is why it is said, "When we just barely comprehend what a single thing is, we comprehend what myriad things are." What is spoken of here as 'comprehending what a single thing is' does not mean that we deny the appearance that some thing previously had, nor does it mean that we make one thing stand against another, nor does it mean that we treat some thing as absolute and unique. Treating some thing as absolute and unique is synonymous with treating it as an obstruction and then being obstructed by it. When our comprehension is freed from the obstruction of 'I comprehend', one instance of comprehension is equivalent to myriad instances of comprehension. One instance of comprehension is equivalent to a single thought or thing, and the comprehension of one thought or thing is synonymous with the comprehension of myriad thoughts and things.

A Buddha of old once said, "A picture of a rice cake never satisfies hunger." Patch-robed novices who are seeking for a Master with whom to explore this saying, as well as bodhisattvas* and shravakas* who have come hither from all directions, are not all uniform in reputation and rank. And this includes those having the head of a celestial being or the face of a demon, all of whom come hither from all directions, their hides thick or thin. Although they may say that they are studying what Buddhas of the past and present have said, they are actually spending their lives living under some tree or in a hermit's thatched hut. As a consequence, when they are at the point of passing on the traditions of our monastic family, some may refer to this statement about a rice cake by saying, "He said what He did because engaging in the study of the Scriptures and commentaries will not instill true wisdom." And there are others who may say, "He spoke this way because He was trying to say that studying the Scriptural texts on the three provisional vehicles* and the one True Vehicle* is, moreover, not the path to enlightenment." In both instances, this is their engaging in judgmental thinking.

Speaking more broadly, those who assert that provisional Teachings are completely useless are greatly mistaken. They have not had the meritorious behavior of Ancestors in our tradition genuinely Transmitted to them, so they are in the dark about the sayings of Buddhas and Ancestors. Since they have not clarified what this one saying is about, who could affirm that they had thoroughly explored the sayings of other Buddhas?

For instance, the saying "A picture of a rice cake never satisfies hunger" is like the saying from the *Āgama Scripture*, "Refrain from all evil whatsoever, and uphold and practice all that is good."[1] And it is like Daikan Enō's query, "What is It that has come about like this?" And it is like Tōzan Ryōkai's statement, "I am always

---

*   See Glossary.

1.   That is, the Precepts (refraining from evil, etc.) will alleviate suffering (hunger), but only
        so long as one is living by them and not just mouthing them.

eager here in this place." For the time being, you need to explore these statements in a similar manner through your training.

Folks who have encountered the expression 'a picture of a rice cake' are few, and none of them have fully delved into what it means. How do I know this? In my testing one or two smelly skin bags[*] in the past, they had reached neither the level of certainty nor even the level of uncertainty: they simply seemed indifferent, as if they were refusing to lend an ear to some neighbor's chitchat. You need to realize that what is called 'a picture of a rice cake' includes the appearance of what is born of "father" and "mother", as well as the appearance of what has not yet been born of "father" and "mother".[2] At the very moment when a rice cake is actually made by using rice or wheat flour, without doubt, it is the moment when the reality of it manifests and the term for it is fulfilled. Do not explore through your training that a picture of a rice cake is something as trifling as our perception of the comings and goings of things. The 'colors' we use in 'painting a rice cake' will find their equivalents in the colors we use in painting a landscape. That is, in painting a landscape we use cerulean blue and earthen red pigments, and in painting a picture of a rice cake we use rice and wheat flour. Since, in both cases, the projects and the planning are equivalent, the materials we are using are also equivalent.

As a consequence, 'a picture of a rice cake' may refer to such things as a rice dumpling, a bean cake, a cake of tofu, a baked wheat cake, a fried rice cake—all of which arise from a picture we have drawn in our minds. You need to recognize that there are such things as pictures, cakes, and thoughts and things. Therefore, the cakes that are appearing in the here and now are all together 'pictures of rice cakes'. Should we seek for 'a picture of a rice cake' apart from this, ultimately we will never encounter it, for such a thing has never been thought up. Although a picture of a rice cake manifests at some one time, it does not manifest at some other time. Nevertheless, it lacks the characteristics of being old or young, and it leaves no traces of its coming and going. At the same time, nations and lands as 'pictured cakes' come forth and materialize here and now.

---

2.   Not yet born of "father" and "mother" refers to the time before duality arises, whereas what is born of "father" and "mother" refers to the arising of dualistic thinking.

In the phrase 'will never satisfy hunger', 'hunger' does not refer to something that is under the sway of the twenty-four hours of a day. And, at the same time, when one encounters a picture of a rice cake, it is not some convenient thing, for even were we to sample a picture of a rice cake, ultimately it would fail to satisfy our hunger. There is no rice cake that depends on our being hungry. And because there is no rice cake that depends on there being rice cakes, the vigorous way of living fails to be transmitted, and the traditional ways of training are not passed on. Hunger is a monk's traveling staff.* Whether borne horizontally or vertically, it undergoes thousands of changes and myriad transformations. A rice cake is also one manifestation of body and mind, be it blue, yellow, red, or white, or long, short, square, or round.

Now, when we paint a picture of a landscape, we use cerulean blue, verdant green, and earthen red colors to depict awesome cliffs and strangely shaped rocks, as well as making use of the seven treasures and the four treasures.[3] Managing the painting of a rice cake is also like this. When painting a human, we make use of the four elements* and the five skandhas;* when painting the Buddha, we not only make use of a clod of earth or mud, we also make use of His thirty-three auspicious characteristics, of a blade of grass, and of innumerable kalpas* of training and practice. Because depicting the Buddha in a scroll painting has always been like this, all Buddhas are depicted Buddhas and all depicted Buddhas are Buddhas. We need to investigate what a painted Buddha is and what a painted rice cake is. We need to explore in detail and with the utmost effort what a black turtle of stone is and what a monk's traveling staff of iron is, what a physical thing is and what a mental thing is. When we make such an effort, life and death, as well as coming and going, are simply

---

3.   In a mundane sense, 'the seven treasures' refers to various precious and semi-precious stones, as well to the seven treasures of a universal monarch, whereas 'the four treasures' refers to the four basic tools of a painter, namely, brush, ink, inkstone, and paper. On a spiritual level, 'the seven treasures' refers to the seven types of jewel trees that are to be found in the Pure Land, whereas 'the four treasures' refers to four divisions of the Scriptures: the Buddha's Teachings for all (the *Sutras*), His instructions for monastics (the *Vinaya*), the commentaries on the Buddha's Teachings (the *Shastras*), and the prayer-like invocations (the *Dharanis*).

drawings of a picture, as is, in a word, supreme enlightenment. In sum, neither the Dharma realms nor empty space are other than painted images.

A Buddha of old once said in verse:

> *When I finally realized the Way,*
> *The white snow, which had blanketed all in a*
> *thousand layers, departed*
> *And, in my making a picture of this,*
> *Blue-tinged mountains emerged on scroll after*
> *scroll.*

This is talk about the great realization. It is His way of expressing that His having done His utmost to practice the Way had come to full fruition. As a consequence, at the very moment of His having realized the Way, He has created a picture, wherein He calls blue-tinged mountains and white snow 'scroll upon scroll'. Notwithstanding that, there is not a movement or a moment of stillness that is not part of His making a picture. Our own efforts to do our utmost at the present time are simply obtained from our own pictures. The ten epithets of the Buddha and the three insights are 'scroll paintings'.[4] The five spiritual agents, the five spiritual powers, the seven characteristics of enlightenment, and the Noble Eightfold Path comprise 'scroll paintings'.[5] Were you to say that such pictures are not real, then all thoughts and things

---

4.   The ten epithets of the Buddha are 'The One Who Comes Thus', 'The One Worthy of Respect', 'The Self-enlightened One', 'The One of Perfect Conduct', 'The One Who is Well-gone', 'The Knower of the World', 'The Unsurpassed One', 'The Supreme Trainer of Those Who Can be Trained', 'The Teacher of Gods and Humans', and 'The Awakened One Who is the Refuge of the World'. The three insights are the recognition of impermanence, the recognition of no fixed, unchanging self, and the recognition of suffering.

5.   The five spiritual agents are trust, zeal, reflection, contemplation, and wise discernment. The five spiritual powers destroy doubt by trust, negligence by zeal, falsity by reflection,

are also unreal. If thoughts and things are not real, then the Buddha Dharma is unreal. If the Buddha Dharma is real, then it follows that a picture of a rice cake must be real as well.

> Ummon Bun'en was once asked by a monk, "What would you call talk that goes beyond 'Buddha' and transcends 'Ancestor?'"
>
> The Master replied, "A rice dumpling."[6]

We need to take our time to investigate this saying of his. Once a 'rice dumpling' has been brought into existence, there will be an ancestral Master who will speak out about "talk that goes beyond 'Buddha' and transcends 'Ancestor.'" And there are the 'trainees of iron will' who may not listen to him.[7] And there are novices who will listen because the Master has brought forth an expression of Dharma.

Now, Ummon's displaying the Matter* and hitting the bull's-eye by saying "a rice dumpling" are, to be sure, a couple of slices of a painted rice cake. And they contain talk about going beyond 'Buddha' and transcending 'Ancestor', and they contain a pathway for entering Buddhahood or for entering demonhood.[8]

---

confused or wandering thoughts by contemplation, and all illusions and delusions by wise discernment. The seven characteristics of enlightenment are being able to distinguish the true from the false, being undeflected from one's training and practice, being joyful, being rid of heaviness of mind, being at ease, being able to keep the mind focused, and not being thrown off by whatever arises.

6.   The term 'a rice dumpling' is being used in Dōgen's discussion as a metaphor for a question that the intellect 'cooks up' to chat about.

7.   Here, 'trainees of iron will' refers to those senior monks who hear the Dharma being voiced by a Master but have ceased to listen.

8.   That is, Ummon's reply is fine as far as it goes, but if the disciple remains attached to concepts like 'Buddha' or 'Ancestor' or 'transcendence', then he has entered the path to demonhood rather than the one to Buddhahood, where all such concepts are dropped off.

My former Master once said, "Tall bamboo and plantain enter into the making of a picture."[9] This expression is one by which those who have gone beyond long and short have explored 'making a picture' through their training.

'Tall bamboo' is the Chinese name for what we in Japan call 'long-stemmed bamboo'. Although people say that bamboo is the result of an interplay of yin and yang, it is we who are setting 'yin and yang' in motion. Even so, there is the time of a tall bamboo, but that time cannot be measured in terms of yin and yang.[10] Even though great saintly ones may catch a glimpse of yin and yang, they cannot fathom what yin and yang really are. Because yin and yang together constitute the impartiality of thoughts and things, the impartiality of weights and measures, and the impartiality of words and ways, it is something beyond the yin and yang that the minds and eyes of non-Buddhists and those of the two Lesser Courses* depend on. It is the yin and yang of tall bamboo; it is the reckoning of the stages in the life of a tall bamboo; it is the world of tall bamboos. The Buddhas in all ten directions exist as the household of tall bamboos. You need to realize that the cosmos with its heavens and earths is the roots, stems, branches, and leaves of a tall bamboo. Therefore, it causes the cosmos with its heavens and earths to endure, and it causes Mount Sumeru within the Great Ocean, along with the whole universe in all ten directions, to have substantiality, and it causes a Master's traveling staff and lacquered bamboo bow to be both complete and not complete.[11]

---

9.   Bamboo and plantain have long been used as subjects for both Chinese and Japanese paintings. Both have also been used as metaphors and carry various meanings. On the basis of the present quotation by Dōgen's Master, Tendō Nyojō, as well as Dōgen's discussion of it, bamboo is descriptive of the Master and plantain is descriptive of the trainee.

10.   That is, the life of a Master cannot be measured by applying mundane, dualistic measures such as yin and yang.

11.   The lacquered bamboo bow was entwined with a wisteria vine and was sometimes used by Zen Masters ceremonially in pointing to the Master-disciple relationship.

Plantain has earth, water, fire, wind, and space, as well as mind, will, consciousness, and wisdom. These are its roots, stems, branches, and leaves, along with the brightness of its flowers and fruit. So, when the winds of autumn envelop it and tear it, there is not a single mote of dust that remains on it. It can doubtless be described as pure and clean, for there is no sinew or bone within its core, nor any glue or other sticky substance upon its form. Liberation is its goal. Further, since it is not clinging to immediacy, it is beyond discussion of such measures of time as minutes and seconds. Through this endeavor, earth, water, fire, and wind are brought to life, and mind, intent, consciousness, and wisdom are made to experience the Great Death. Thus, in this lineage of ours, we have habitually received the Precepts, employing spring and fall, winter and summer, as Their tools.

The present activities of tall bamboo and plantain are making a picture. Accordingly, those who may awaken upon hearing the sound of bamboo being struck will make a picture, whether they be dragons or garter snakes,[12] for they will not harbor any doubts about the sentimental concerns of the mundane or the saintly.

> *That cane can be long, this way,*
> *And this cane can be short, this way,*
> *This cane can be long, this way,*
> *And that cane can be short, this way.*[13]

Because these are all images in a picture, they are, of necessity, in accord with each other. When there are long pictures, short pictures will not be lacking. Clearly, you need to thoroughly explore this principle. Because the whole universe and all thoughts

---

12.   Here, 'dragons' refers to monks of marked spiritual achievement combined with singular intellectual prowess, whereas 'garter snakes' refers to monks whose abilities are less pronounced. In either case, both are quite capable of distinguishing between the genuine and the mundane in spiritual matters.

13.   To paraphrase what this poem is pointing to, those of mundane thinking may discriminate among Masters, particularly on the basis of how long such a one has been functioning as a Master, but from a spiritual perspective, someone who is a Master is so because he or she is 'this way', that is, 'such a person', one who has fully realized the Truth.

within it are the act of drawing a picture, every human thought and thing emerges from a picture, and Buddhas and Ancestors come forth from pictures as well. Thus, beyond the image of a rice cake there is no medicine to satisfy our hungers, beyond the image of hunger there is no mutual encountering among humans, and beyond the image of fulfillment there is no capability.

In sum, to be satisfied with being hungry, to be satisfied with not being hungry, not to satisfy one's hunger, and not to satisfy one's not being hungry—all these would be impossible and inexpressible were it not for an image of hunger. You need to explore through your training that the concrete here and now at this very moment is a picture of a rice cake. When you explore the fundamental point of this through your body and mind, you will begin to master the meritorious function of ever so slightly setting things in motion and of your being set in motion by things. Prior to this meritorious function manifesting itself before your very eyes, your ability to learn the Way has not yet manifested fully. When you make this meritorious function fully manifest, you will fully realize just what a picture is.

Given to the assembly on the fifth day of the eleventh lunar month in the third year of the Ninji era (November 28, 1242) at Kannondōri in Kōshōhōrin-ji Temple.

Copied by me on the seventh day of the eleventh lunar month in the third year of the Ninji era (November 30, 1242) in the Kōshōhōrin-ji Guest Office.

Ejō

40

On Functioning Fully

(Zenki)

Translator's Introduction: As the postscript at the end of this discourse indicates, this talk was given by Dōgen not only for the benefit of his monastic community but also for the benefit of his lay followers, including his major lay patron, the Governor of Izumi Province. The discourse has an underlying assumption which may not be immediately evident to Western readers, namely that all humans have Buddha Nature, and indeed, <u>are</u> Buddha Nature, and that Buddha Nature is our True Self. Thus, even though we may not yet have recognized that this is the case, nevertheless our Buddha Nature is constantly functioning as Buddha Nature at all times, in life and in death, never ceasing or disappearing or lying dormant, ever displaying Itself right before our very eyes.

When we thoroughly explore what the Great Way of the Buddhas is, we find that It is liberation from delusion and letting our True Self manifest to the full. For some, this liberation from delusion means that life liberates us from life, and death liberates us from death. Therefore, both our getting out of birth-and-death and our entering into birth-and-death are the Great Way. Both our laying birth-and-death aside and our going beyond birth-and-death to the Other Shore are also the Great Way. Our True Self revealing Itself to the full is what life is, and life is our True Self revealing Itself to the full. At the time when our True Self reveals Itself, we can say that there is nothing that is not a full displaying of life, and there is nothing that is not a full displaying of death.

It is the operating of this True Self that causes life to come about and causes death to come about. At the very moment when we fully manifest this functioning of our True Self, It will not necessarily be something great or something small, or the whole universe or some limited bit of it, or something drawn out or something short and quick. Our life at this very moment is the True Self in operation, and the operating of our True Self is our life at this very moment.

Life is not something that comes and life is not something that goes; life is not something that reveals itself and life is not something that is accomplished. Rather, life is a displaying of one's Buddha Nature to the full, and death is also a displaying of one's Buddha Nature to the full. You need to realize that both life and death occur in the immeasurable thoughts and things within ourselves.

Also, calmly reflect upon whether this life of the present moment, as well as the various thoughts and things that co-exist with this life, are a part of life or are not a part of life. There is nothing—not a single moment, not a single thought or thing— that is not a part of life. There is nothing—not a single matter, not a single state of mind—that is not also a part of life. For instance, life is like a time when I am on board a boat. While I'm on this boat, I manipulate the sails, I handle the rudder, I push the punting pole. At the same time, the boat is carrying me along, and there is no 'I' that is outside this boat. My sailing in a boat is what makes this boat be a boat. You need to do your utmost to explore through your training what is going on at this very moment, for at this very moment there is nothing other than the world of the boat. The sky, the water, the shore—all have become this moment of the boat, which is completely different from occasions when I am not on a boat. Thus, life is what I am making life to be, and I am what life is making me to be. While being carried on a boat, my body and mind, with their inner causes and outer conditions, are, all together, a part of the way a boat functions. The whole of the great earth and the whole of the expanse of space are, likewise, a part of the way a boat functions. What this metaphor is saying is that life is what 'I' is, and 'I' is what life is.

The venerable monk Meditation Master Engo Kokugon once said, "Life is a manifestation of one's entire being, and death is a manifestation of one's entire being." We need to thoroughly explore this saying and clarify what it means. In the present instance, what 'thoroughly exploring this saying' refers to is the principle that life is a manifestation of one's entire being and is not concerned with beginnings and endings, for life is the whole of the great earth and the whole of unbounded space. At the same time, not only does this principle not stand against life's being a manifestation of one's entire being, but it also does not stand against death's being a manifestation of one's entire being. When death is also a manifestation of one's entire being, it is the whole of the great earth and the whole of unbounded space. And at the same time, not only does this principle not stand against death's being a manifestation of one's entire being, but it also does not get in the way of life's being a manifestation of one's entire being. Hence, life does not get in the way of death, and death does not get in the way of life. Both the whole of the great earth and the whole of unbounded space exist within life, and they exist within death as well.

Even so, it is not that the whole of the great earth is one thing and the whole of unbounded space is another thing; both operate to the full in life and both operate to the full in death. Therefore, even though it is not a matter of their being one single thing, it is also not a matter of their being different things. And even though it is not a matter of their being different things, it is also not a matter of their being identical things. And even though it is not a matter of their being identical things, it is also not a matter of their being many things. Hence, there are the various thoughts and things that are manifestations of one's entire being in life, and there are also the various thoughts and things that are manifestations of one's entire being in death, and there are the manifestations of one's entire being that are beyond 'life' and beyond 'death'. Both life and death exist within the manifestation of one's entire being.

Thus, all functions in life-and-death will be present, like a strong-armed man flexing his muscles or like someone at night reaching behind himself to grope for his pillow. They come forth whenever there is abundant luminosity from one's marvelous innate spiritual abilities. At the very moment of their coming forth, because the person is functioning fully within their coming forth, such a one may think that before they fully appeared in front of him, they had not appeared at all. Yet, before this full manifestation, there were previous manifestations of that person's True Nature. Even though such a person may say that he had some previous manifestation of his True Nature, it has not inhibited the present appearance of his True Nature. Thus it is that discriminatory opinions may arise before one's very eyes.[1]

---

1.   Such as the opinion that the manifestation of one's True Nature is a one-time thing.

Delivered to the assembly in the Kyoto office of the Governor of Izumi Province on the seventeenth day of the twelfth lunar month in the third year of the Ninji era (January 10, 1243).[2]

Copied by me on the nineteenth day of the first month in the fourth year of the same era (February 9, 1243).[3]

Ejō

---

2.   The governor, Yoshishige Hatano, was one of Dōgen's principle supporters.

3.   The seeming contradiction that both the third and the fourth years of the Ninji era occurred in 1243 is due to the fact that, in the lunar calendar, the last day of the third year fell on January 21, 1243, according to the Western solar calendar. The new lunar year, by our reckoning, then began on January 22.

41

On Expressing One's True Nature
by Expressing One's Intent

(Sesshin Sesshō)

Translator's Introduction: This title contains an ambiguity that is lost in translation. The term *sesshin* can be rendered either as 'expressing one's intent' or as 'expressing one's mind'. However, Dōgen refers to the phrase 'expressing one's mind' as a misinterpretation, especially if 'expressing' is taken to mean 'talking about', implying an intellectual discussion about the nature of mind. *Sesshō*, 'expressing one's intent', refers specifically to actively expressing one's spiritual intention to help all sentient beings reach the Other Shore. This is the way in which someone expresses his or her True Nature, which Dōgen identifies as one's Buddha Nature. And the expression of one's True Nature takes the form of expressing one's spiritual intent.

Once when Meditation Master Shinzan Sōmitsu was out on a walk with Great Master Tōzan Ryokai, the latter pointed to a nearby temple and said, "Within that temple, there is one who is expressing his True Nature by expressing his intention."

Shinzan, his elder brother in the Sangha, asked, "And who is that one?"

Tōzan replied, "With your asking this one question, my elder brother in the Sangha, that one has forthwith succeeded in completely passing away into death."

His elder brother Shinzan then asked, "Then who is it that is expressing his intention and expressing his True Nature?"

Tōzan replied, "He has revived from within death."[1]

The statement "To express one's intention is to express one's True Nature" is the foundation of the Buddha's Way from which Buddha after Buddha and Ancestor after

---

1.   This dialogue has a deeper meaning which Dōgen will reveal later. In the meantime, this dialogue can be understood as a reference to the dropping off of the illusory self.

Ancestor have emerged. Were it not for Their expressing Their True Nature by expressing Their intent, the wondrous Wheel of the Dharma would never have turned, the intention to realize Buddhahood would never have arisen, and training and practice would never have manifested. And the Truth would never have been realized simultaneously with the great earth and its sentient beings, for there has never been any sentient being who lacked Buddha Nature. Shakyamuni's raising of the flower, His eyes atwinkle, was His way of expressing His intention as an expression of His True Nature. Makakashō's face breaking out into a smile was his way of putting it. Our Second Chinese Ancestor Eka's respectfully bowing to Bodhidharma and then standing quietly in his place was his way of putting it. Our Ancestral Master Bodhidharma's entering China during the Liang dynasty was his way, and Daiman Kōnin's Transmitting the kesa* to Daikan Enō was his way. A certain Master's holding up his traveling staff* was his way, and another Master's laying down his ceremonial hossu* was his way of expressing his intention as an expression of his True Nature.

Generally speaking, every single meritorious action of Buddha after Buddha and Ancestor after Ancestor has been, through and through, Their expressing Their intention as an expression of Buddha Nature. There are ways of doing this in a normal, everyday manner, and there are ways of expressing it as 'the tiles* and stones of one's walls and fences'. And thus the principle described as "The arising of intentions is what gives rise to all the various thoughts and things" fully emerges, as does the principle described as "The dying away of intentions is the dying away of all the various thoughts and things." Nevertheless, one's intention is being expressed on such occasions, as is one's True Nature.

At the same time, run-of-the-mill folks have not penetrated into what intention means and they have not mastered what True Nature means, therefore they are in the dark as to what 'expressing intention' and 'expressing True Nature' really mean. Being ignorant of the profundity of what is being talked about and of the wonders that are being discussed, they say—and teach—that such things cannot possibly exist in the Way of the Buddhas and Ancestors. Because they do not know that 'expressing mind and expressing nature' means 'expressing one's intention and

---

*   See Glossary.

expressing one's True Nature', they think of it as 'talking about the mind and talking about the nature of things'. This is because they have not made an effort to critically examine whether they have indeed penetrated the Great Way.

A certain monk called Meditation Master Daie Sōkō,[2] once said:

> Folks today are fond of talking about mind and talking about nature, and because they are fond of talking about profundities and talking about wonders, they are slow to realize the Way. Since mind and nature form a duality, once these folks have discarded this duality, and have forgotten all about the profound and the wondrous as well, then dualities will no longer arise, and they will experience the Truth that the Buddha promised them.

These remarks of his show that he was still unaware of the silken thread that binds the Buddhas and Ancestors together, nor had he comprehended what the lifeline of the Buddhas and Ancestors is.[3] Accordingly, he only understood 'mind' to refer to discriminative thinking and consciousness, so he spoke this way because he had not learned that the various functions, such as discriminative thinking and consciousness, are what the <u>intellective</u> mind is. He wrongly viewed 'nature' to mean something that is abundantly clear and peacefully inactive, and did not understand whether Buddha Nature and the nature of all thoughts and things existed or did not exist. And because he had not seen his True Nature as It is, not even in his dreams, he had a false view of what Buddha Dharma is. The 'mind' that the Buddhas and Ancestors spoke of is the

---

2.   Daie was in the Rinzai Zen tradition, and is credited with having instituted the practice of focusing on deliberate penetration into classic kōan stories, rather than keeping to themeless meditation. Dōgen, in a rare criticism of specific monks, held Daie responsible for what he considered a perversion and betrayal of the pre-Daie Rinzai tradition.

3.   The particular silken thread that is mentioned here was used to bind Scriptural texts together and, as a metaphor, refers to the 'thread of Transmission' that runs through, and binds together, the Buddhas and Ancestors.

very Skin and Flesh, Bones and Marrow. And the 'nature' that the Buddhas and Ancestors have preserved is a monk's traveling staff and the shaft of a bamboo arrow.[4] The Buddhas and Ancestors have profoundly realized the Buddhahood promised Them by the Buddha, and this is what is meant by being a pillar[*] of the temple or a stone lantern.[*] How wondrous it is that the Buddhas and Ancestors hold up and offer to us Their wise discernment and understanding!

From the first, the Buddhas and Ancestors who are really Buddhas and Ancestors have always learned that this 'mind' and this 'nature' refer to 'intention' and 'Buddha Nature', and have given expression to them, and have put them into practice, and have awakened to them. They have preserved and kept to this profound and wondrous Teaching, exploring It through their training with their Master. We call those who are like this the Buddha's descendents who are truly studying the Buddhas and Ancestors. Those who are not like this are not really studying the Way.

Thus, Daie, your 'attaining the Way' does not attain the Way, and when it is time to go beyond attaining the Way, you are unable to do so. You stumble your way through both the times of attaining and the times of going beyond attaining. As you would have it, Daie, since mind and nature form a duality, we ought to discard them. This is your little attempt to explain 'mind', an effort that can only explain one-hundred-thousand-millionth of it! To say that the profound and the wondrous are both to be discarded is but one small aspect of it, and yet it is the only aspect that you bring up for discussion when talking about them. Without learning what the key point to all of this is, you foolishly speak of forgetting all about them, having considered them to be things that have left your own hands and departed from your own being. You have not yet discarded the narrow views of the Lesser Course,[*] so how could you possibly penetrate the inner depths of the Greater Course,[*] to say nothing about understanding the key point of what is above and beyond Buddhahood! It is difficult to say that you have ever tasted the tea and rice of the Buddhas and Ancestors.

Simply, to earnestly explore this Matter[*] under a Master is to thoroughly experience, at this very moment of our existence, the expressing of our intention as

---

4.   A monk's traveling staff and the shaft of a bamboo arrow are common metaphors for what a Zen Master uses to point a disciple to the truth.

the expression of our True Nature. This is how it was in the past and will be in the future. We should thoroughly explore this Matter for ourselves, since there is nothing that stands second or third to this.[5]

There was that time when our First Chinese Ancestor Bodhidharma gave instruction to his disciple Eka, saying, "If you simply bring to a halt all entanglements with things outside yourself and do not let your mind pant after things, then, with your very mind that is like walls and fences, you will thereby be able to enter the Way."

Eka tried in various ways to express his intention as well as his True Nature, but he did not succeed in realizing the Buddhahood that the Buddha had promised. Then, one day, he suddenly realized the Truth.

As a result, he said to our First Ancestor, "This time, for the first time, your disciple has brought his entanglements to a halt."

Our First Ancestor, already knowing what Eka had become aware of, did not probe further into the nature of his disciple's experience.

He simply asked him, "You haven't realized total cessation of these entanglements, have you?"

Eka replied, "No."

The First Ancestor then asked, "What is it like, then, for you?"

Eka replied, "As I am constantly recognizing It, I realize that words do not come near It."

The First Ancestor then remarked, "That is precisely the substance of Mind which has been Transmitted by all the Buddhas

---

5.   That is, it is unique and not simply one thing among many.

and all the Ancestors of the past. Since you now have It, you yourself must guard It well."

There are those who have doubts about this story, and there are those who take it up and expound upon it. Well, this is just one story among a number of stories on how Eka trained under Bodhidharma and served him. Eka repeatedly tried expressing his intent and his True Nature. At first he did not succeed in realizing what the Buddha had promised, but, little by little, he accumulated merits and piled up virtues until he finally realized the Way that our First Ancestor had spoken of. Those who are slow of wit have considered this to mean, "When Eka first attempted to express his intention and his True Nature, he had not yet awakened to what the Buddha had promised. The fault lay in his trying to express his intention and his True Nature, but later he let go of 'expressing my intention and expressing my True Nature', and thereby realized what the Buddha had promised."[6] They are speaking in this way because they have not yet penetrated the saying, "With your very mind that is like walls and fences, you will thereby be able to enter the Way." They are especially in the dark about how to go about studying the Way. And, should you ask why this is so, well, from the time when you first give rise to the intention to spiritually awaken and incline your steps towards training and practice of the Buddha's Way, you will be heartily putting into practice a difficult course of training. And, though you put it into practice, you may not hit the bull's-eye even once in a hundred tries. Even so, you will ultimately hit the target, sometimes by following the advice of your spiritual friend and sometimes by following Scriptural texts. The one hit today is due to the strength of a hundred misses in the past. It is the fulfillment of those hundred misses. Your listening to what is taught, training in the Way, and awakening to the Truth—none of these are any different from this. Although yesterday's efforts to express your intention and your True Nature were equivalent to a hundred misses, yesterday's hundred misses become today's suddenly hitting the bull's-eye. When you first begin to practice the Buddha's Way, it may be said that you have not yet thoroughly

---

6. That is, they viewed Eka as treating his intention and his True Nature as a duality, whereas they are really two aspects of the same thing.

penetrated the Truth due to lingering attachments. You cannot attain the Buddha's Way by abandoning It in favor of other ways. Folks who have not yet penetrated the training and practice of the Buddha's Way from start to finish find it difficult to clarify what this principle of penetration is.

The Buddha's Way is the Buddha's Way even when one first gives rise to the intention to train, <u>and</u> It is the Buddha's Way even when one fully realizes the Truth: It is the Buddha's Way—beginning, middle, and end. It is comparable to someone's walking for thousands of miles. When walking ten thousand miles, all that one can do is to take one step at a time, and within ten thousand miles are tens of thousands of steps. Even though the first step and the ten-thousandth step are different, all of it is still simply the act of walking ten thousand miles. At the same time, folks who have reached the height of folly believe that during the time when one is studying the Buddha's Way, one has not yet reached the Buddha's Way, for only when one has gone beyond Buddhahood is It really the Buddha's Way. They are like this because they do not know that the <u>whole</u> Way is our expressing the Way, that the <u>whole</u> Way is our practicing the Way, and that the <u>whole</u> Way is our realizing the Way. Those folks talk the way they do because they have been taught that only deluded people experience the great realization through their training and practice of the Buddha's Way. As a result, they do not realize that non-deluded people also experience the great realization through their training and practice of the Buddha's Way.

Even before we have realized what the Buddha promised, expressing our Buddha Nature by expressing our intent is already the Way of Buddhas. At the same time, it is through our expressing our True Nature by expressing our intent that we realize what the Buddha promised. We must not explore through our training that 'realizing what the Buddha promised' is restricted to the first great realization of a deluded person. The deluded have their great realization, and the enlightened have their great realization, and the unenlightened have their great realization, and the undeluded have their great realization, and all those who have realized what the Buddha promised have actually realized what the Buddha promised.

Consequently, expressing one's intention as an expression of one's True Nature is being straight and true within the Buddha's Way. Not having thoroughly comprehended this principle, Daie advises us that we should express neither our intention nor our True Nature, but this is <u>not</u> a principle of the Buddha Dharma. And, alas, things are so bad today in Great Sung China that there is no one who can even come up to gentleman Daie's low level of understanding.

Our Founding Ancestor, Great Master Tōzan Ryokai, who was uniquely venerated among our Ancestors, had thoroughly penetrated the principle that 'expressing one's mind' and 'expressing one's nature' are comparable, on a deeper level, to expressing one's intention as an expression of one's True Nature. An Ancestral Master who has not thoroughly penetrated this principle cannot have an expression comparable to the one Tōzan made in the account I told at the beginning of this discourse.

> Once when Meditation Master Shinzan Sōmitsu was out
> on a walk with Great Master Tōzan Ryokai, the latter pointed to a
> nearby temple and said, "Within that temple, there is One who is
> expressing His True Nature by expressing His intention."[7]

From the time when our Founding Ancestor set up his temple, his Dharma descendants have, without exception, correctly Transmitted our Ancestral tradition. It is something that those in other traditions have not even dreamed of. How much less could they know, even in a dream, how to understand it! Only his authentic heirs have correctly Transmitted it. Had they not correctly Transmitted this principle, how could anyone penetrate to what is fundamental in the Buddha's Way? The principle that we are now talking about, whether we plumb its depths or merely scratch its surface, is that of some human being expressing his or her intent and True Nature. The mind expressing itself, both on the outer surface and deeply within, is the True Nature expressing Itself both on the outer surface and deeply within. You need to do your utmost to thoroughly explore this. There is no expression that lacks True Nature, and there is no intention that lacks an expression.

---

7. This change in rendering the dialogue that Dōgen presented in the opening of this discourse presents a deeper, spiritual meaning behind this exchange.

What we call 'Buddha Nature' means that all things are expressing It, and what we call 'lacking a Buddha Nature' also means that all things are expressing It. Though we may explore through our training that Buddha Nature is what is meant by 'nature', if we should fail to explore through our training that we have Buddha Nature, it would not be the way to study the Way. And if we should fail to explore through our training that we lack a Buddha Nature, it would also not be the way to explore the Matter through our training.[8] When we explore the Teaching that expressing our intention through our training is synonymous with our True Nature, we become a Dharma heir of an Ancestor of the Buddha; when we trust that our True Nature is expressing Itself, we become an Ancestor of the Buddha for our Dharma heirs.

To state that "One's mind is ever restless, whereas one's nature is steady" is an assertion of non-Buddhists. To state that "The innate nature of things is profoundly clear, whereas their forms are ever shifting" is also an assertion of non-Buddhists. The way that Buddhists study 'mind' and 'nature' is not the way those folks study it. The way that Buddhists put their intentions into practice so as to put their Nature into practice is in no way like the behavior of non-Buddhists. The way that Buddhists clarify what Mind and Nature are finds no equivalent in what non-Buddhists teach.

In the Buddha's Way, there is an expression of intention that is personal and an expression of True Nature that is also personal, and there is an expression of both of them that goes beyond the personal. Also, there is a way of not expressing them that is personal, and there is a way of not expressing them that goes beyond the personal. When we have not yet studied the expressing of intention that goes beyond the personal, then this will be an expressing of intention which has not yet reached fertile ground. When we have not yet studied the expressing of intention that is personal, this too will be an expressing of intention that has not yet reached fertile ground. We study the expressing of intent that goes beyond any person, we study That which goes beyond the personal in expressing Its intent, we study a personal expressing of intention, and we study that there is someone who expresses his intention.

---

8. The meaning of 'lacking a Buddha Nature' is thoroughly explored by Dōgen in his Discourse 21: On Buddha Nature *(Busshō)*.

The strongest way that Rinzai phrased it was merely as 'a real person who is beyond rank'; he still had not phrased it as 'a real person who has a rank'. He had not yet displayed any other ways of exploring this through his training or any other ways of putting it. Thus, we must say that he had not yet reached the field of the Ultimate. Because expressing one's intention and expressing one's Nature is synonymous with expressing Buddha and expressing Ancestor, we and our Master may encounter each other through hearing, and we may encounter each other through seeing.

> Shinzan, Tōzan's elder brother in the Sangha, said, "And It is Who."

Elder brother Shinzan, in letting this way of expressing It emerge, could have put it this way earlier and he could put it this way later as well. 'It is Who' is his expressing his intention and his Buddha Nature right there at that moment.[9] Accordingly, at the time when it is put as "Who is It?" and at the time when it is put as "It is Who," this will be Its expressing Its intention and Its expressing Its True Nature. This expressing of Its intention and of Its True Nature is something that folks throughout the ten quarters have never known. Because they have lost sight of their Child and take It to be a thief, they likewise judge a thief to be their child.

> Tōzan replied, "With your asking this one question, my elder brother in the Sangha, that One has forthwith succeeded in completely passing away into death."

Many who are middling in their training, upon hearing these words, think, "Someone who is expressing his mind and expressing his nature is saying, 'Who is it?' and must be able forthwith to completely pass away into death." As a consequence, they are not conscious of its other meaning—'it is Who'—and never succeed in having an encounter with a Master, so it must be for them a dead and meaningless phrase. It isn't necessarily dead and meaningless. Those who have penetrated what this 'expressing True Nature by expressing intent' means must surely be few. To completely pass into death does not mean just being ten or twenty percent dead, for it means passing into

---

9.   Shinzan's response can be taken both as a question and as an answer: "Who is It that resides within?" and "It is Who (one's Buddha Nature) that resides within."

death one hundred percent.[10] At that very moment, who can say that this is not some limiting of the heavens and some covering up of the earth? It will be our letting go of trying to shed light upon our past, our present, our future, and, indeed, it will be our letting go of trying to shed light upon this very moment of now.

His elder brother Shinzan then said, "And It is Who that expresses His intention and expresses His True Nature."

Although the name referred to by the previous "Who is it?" and the present "And It is Who" is a veritable 'third son of a Mr. Chang', the One being referred to is actually 'the fourth son of a Mr. Lee'.[11]

Tōzan replied, "He has revived from within death."[12]

This phrase, 'within death,' points to having been able to pass directly into death. And Shinzan's saying "It is Who," which was not a casual remark, points directly to the condition of expressing his Nature by expressing his intent. This 'Who' directs the person who is expressing His intention and expressing His True Nature. Something to explore through your training is the assertion that we do not necessarily anticipate a one hundred percent passing away into death. The Great Master's statement, "He has revived from within death," refers to the manifesting of sounds and forms before one's very eyes, which expresses both intent and True Nature. And yet, even this will only be some ten or twenty percent of the entirety of passing away into death. Life, even though it is the totality of life, is not something wherein death

---

10. 'Passing into death one hundred percent' refers to completely and absolutely letting go of the false self.

11. That is, in both cases these two phrases seem to be exactly the same, but they are actually completely different in meaning.

12. Whereas Dōgen begins by discussing this dialogue from the standpoint of the dropping off of self, he now discusses it from the point of view of dropping off 'dropping off'. In other words, since the concept of self is an illusion, there is nothing to be dropped off. However, we cannot know this until the time when the false ego has been let go of. At that time, we discover that 'That Which Is' is the One who has actually done the dropping off, for It has ever been the only true reality.

is transformed and manifests as life. It is simply our letting go, from start to finish, of the notion of our 'possessing' life.

In sum, in the words and ways of the Buddhas and Ancestors, there is an expressing of one's intent and of one's True Nature like that described above, which is to be thoroughly explored through one's training. And to take this further, when we die a one hundred percent death, we have lived our life to the full.

You need to realize that from the T'ang dynasty to today, there have been many pitiable creatures who have not clarified that expressing intention and expressing one's True Nature is what the Buddha's Way is about. Further, they have been going around in the dark about the Teachings, practice, and direct experience, and have therefore made reckless remarks and unfounded assertions. We need to help them overcome what they have been and to realize what they can be. For their sake, we say that expressing Their True Nature by expressing Their intent has been the essential function of the Seven Buddhas* along with our ancestral Masters.

Delivered to the assembly in the first year of the Kangen era (1243) in Japan, at Kippō-ji Temple in the Yoshida Prefecture of Echizen Province.

Copied by me on the eleventh day of the first lunar month in the second year of the same era (February 20, 1244) while at the office of the Abbot's assistant.

Ejō

42

On Invocations:
What We Offer to the Buddhas and Ancestors

(Darani)

Translator's Introduction: Traditionally, a *darani* (Skt. *dhāraĭi)* is a prayer-like invocation used to pay homage to Buddhas and Bodhisattvas, and it may include some form of supplication. Dōgen expands upon the use of this verbal form to include other manners of expressing homage and supplication, such as making respectful bows to one's Master.

When someone's eye for exploring the essential Matter[*] through training with a Master is clear, the Eye of the True Teaching will be clear. And because the Eye of the True Teaching is clear, that person's eye for exploring the essential Matter through training with a Master can be clear. Whenever someone receives the authentic Transmission of this key point, it is inevitably due to the strength of that person's showing respect for a great spiritual friend. This is the great relationship: this is the Great Invocation. 'The great spiritual friend' refers to an Ancestor of the Buddha, one to whom a trainee should dutifully serve towel and water pitcher.[1] Thus, to bring tea to your Master or to make tea for your Master is to manifest the very heart and essence of the Teaching. It is to manifest the utmost marvelous spiritual ability.[2] To bring wash-up water to your Master and to pour it out for him is to leave coexisting

---

[*]   See Glossary.

1.   One of the first everyday tasks for an Abbot's Assistant was to bring the Abbot a towel and a pitcher of warm water for him to use in performing his morning ablutions.

2.   The marvelous spiritual ability is spontaneously doing our everyday activities whilst remaining free of a false self; it is our anticipating what needs to be done and then just doing it. Dōgen discusses this ability in Discourse 24: On the Marvelous Spiritual Abilities *(Jinzū).*

conditions undisturbed and to discern what is going on from the next room.[3] It is not only exploring through your training the very heart and essence of the Teaching of the Buddhas and Ancestors, it is your mutual encounter with one or two Ancestors of the Buddha within the very heart and essence of the Teaching. It is not only your receiving and making use of the marvelous spiritual ability of the Buddhas and Ancestors, it is your having found seven or eight Ancestors of the Buddha within your marvelous spiritual ability. Accordingly, the marvelous spiritual ability of each and every Buddha and Ancestor has been fully realized in this one bouquet of activities; the very heart and essence of the Teaching of each and every Buddha and Ancestor has been fully expressed in one picking of this bouquet. Because of this, in showing your respect for the Ancestors of the Buddha, there is nothing wrong in doing so by offering incomparable flowers and incense. Even so, to raise up the invocation of your meditative state and respectfully make an alms offering of it is to be an offspring of the Buddhas and Ancestors.

What is called 'the Great Invocation' refers to paying our respects, and because paying our respects is the Great Invocation, to pay our respects is to mutually encounter the Buddhas and Ancestors within our paying respect to Them. The term 'paying our respects' is patterned on a Chinese way of speaking and has been in social usage for ever so long. Be that as it may, it was not passed on to us from the Brahmanical Heaven or from India, but was correctly Transmitted from the Ancestors of the Buddha. It is beyond the physical realm of sights and sounds, so do not discuss whether it is something that comes before or after the Lords of Awe-inspiring Voices.

This paying of our respects is our lighting incense and respectfully making prostrations before our Master. Sometimes our Master is the one who ordained us upon our leaving home life behind and sometimes our Master is the one who Transmitted the Dharma to us. And there are cases where the Master who Transmitted the Dharma to us may also be the very Master who ordained us upon our leaving home life behind. To continually depend upon and show respect to these Masters is our prayer for seeking out a Master to put one's spiritual question to. As it is said, we

---

3.   It was customary for an Abbot's Assistant to anticipate the Master's needs whilst waiting in the assistant's room, which adjoined that of the Master.

should do our training under them and give them our support, without letting any moment be wasted.

At the beginning and end of our summer retreat, at the time of the winter solstice, and at the beginning and middle of each month, without fail, you should light incense and respectfully make prostrations to your Master. The following procedures should be used when paying your respects. A customary time for doing this is just before or just after taking your breakfast gruel. Dressed in a respectful way, pay your visit to the Master's quarters. 'Dressed in a respectful way' means wearing your kesa,* carrying your bowing mat, arranging your indoor sandals and white socks, and carrying a stick of some incense, such as aloes or sandalwood. When you come before your Master, you make monjin.* The attendant monk then prepares the incense burner and sets up a candle. If the Master is already seated, you should forthwith light the incense, or if the Master is behind the curtain, you should forthwith light your incense.[4] If the Master is lying down or eating, then you should forthwith light your incense. If the Master is standing up, you should ask the venerable monk to be seated and then make monjin to him, or ask him to make himself comfortable: there are various conventional ways of asking him to be seated. After you have let the venerable monk get seated in a chair, you make monjin to him. It should be a deep bow, as prescribed. After you have finished making monjin, you walk up to the incense stand and place the incense stick that you have been carrying into the incense burner in an upright position. Prior to being lit, the incense is sometimes carried by sticking it between the back of your robe and your neckband, or sometimes you carry it tucked in the bosom or the sleeve of your robe, as you wish. After making monjin, you take this incense stick out and, if it is wrapped in paper, turn your shoulder to the left and remove the wrapping paper. Then, holding the lit incense stick aloft with both hands, place it in the incense burner. You should set the incense straight. Do not let it lean to the side. When you have finished setting up the incense stick, you walk to the right with hands held in shashu.* When you arrive in front of your Master, facing the venerable monk you make a deep bow, doing monjin in the prescribed manner. Once you have finished, you spread your bowing mat and respectfully do your prostrations.

---

4.   This curtain is made of a thin, semi-transparent cloth and is often used as a room divider.

You do either nine prostrations or twelve. When your prostrations are over, fold up your bowing mat and make monjin. And there are times when you just spread out your mat and do three prostrations, and then offer the compliments of the season. With the present nine bows, you do not offer the compliments of the season, but should just spread your mat and make three prostrations three times. This custom has been passed on from the Seven Buddhas[*] in the distant past. We use this custom since it directly Transmits the fundamental principle of our tradition. Whenever we encounter a time for respectfully doing our prostrations, we should not fail to do them in this manner. In addition to this, whenever we have the opportunity to receive the benefits of a Dharma talk, we respectfully make our bows, and we respectfully bow when asking our Master for an explanation of some story about the Chinese Zen Masters. In the past, whenever the Second Chinese Ancestor asked the First Ancestor for his viewpoints, Eka always respectfully made three bows just like this. Whenever Bodhidharma expounded his perspective on the Treasure House of the Eye of the True Teaching, the Second Ancestor would respectfully make three bows.

You need to realize that respectfully bowing is the Treasure House of the Eye of the True Teaching, and that the Treasure House of the Eye of the True Teaching is the Great Invocation. In requesting a Master for an explanation, there are many in recent times who employ one prostration during which they thump their head on the ground, but the traditional manner is to do three prostrations. Prostrations done in gratitude for the benefit of the Dharma are not necessarily nine or twelve in number, but they may be three prostrations, or one less formal bow done respectfully, or six prostrations. All these are bows in which the forehead touches the mat.[5] In India, these were called the supreme bows of respect. Also, there are the six bows in which the forehead strikes the ground. (It has been said that when the forehead contacted the ground, it struck with such force that it would cause bleeding. For this reason too, the bowing mat was spread out.) Be it one bow, three bows, or six bows, in all cases the forehead comes in contact with the ground. Sometimes this is called 'kowtowing'.

---

5.   'The forehead touches the mat' is a rendering of a technical term for a form of prostration in which one raises one's hands, palms upward, once the head has lightly touched the mat. It is done as if to raise above one's head the feet of the person being bowed to.

This type of bowing also exists in secular society, where there are nine types of bows. When receiving the benefits of the Dharma there is also 'continuous bowing'. That is, we respectfully bow without ceasing, which can reach hundreds of thousands of bows. These are all bows which are habitually used within the assembly of an Ancestor of the Buddha.

Speaking generally about these bows, you should simply follow the directions of your venerable monk and do your bows in the prescribed manner. In sum, when respectful bowing abides in the world, the Buddha Dharma will abide in the world. Should respectful bowing pass away, then the Buddha Dharma will disappear.

In bowing respectfully to the Master who is Transmitting the Dharma to us, we do not choose only a specific time or argue over a specific place, we just bow. Sometimes we bow to him when he is lying down or eating, and sometimes we bow to him when he is occupied with relieving nature. Sometimes we are separated from him by a wall or a fence, and sometimes we are separated from him by a mountain or a river, but, looking from afar, we respectfully bow to him. Sometimes we respectfully bow to him even though we are separated from him by eons of time, and sometimes we respectfully bow to him even though we are separated from him by life and death, or by coming and going. And sometimes we respectfully bow to him even though we are separated from him by enlightenment and nirvana.

A disciple may do various bows like these, whereas the venerable monk who is your Master does not return your bow, but simply puts his hands in gasshō.* There may be occasions when he spontaneously makes use of a single bow, but customarily he does not employ that ceremony. At the time of your making such respectful bows, you do them while facing north. The venerable monk who is your Master is sitting upright, facing south. Standing on the ground, right before the venerable monk who is your Master, and facing north, you do your bow to him. This is the basic ceremony.[6] It has been correctly Transmitted that when genuine trust in the Master arises within

---

6.   The north-south positions were conventionally used in Chinese Buddhism to indicate who is the host (north) and who the guest (south) and did not necessarily correspond to geographical north and south.

someone, respectfully bowing while facing north is inevitably the first thing that occurs to that person.

This is why, in the days of the World-honored One, the human beings, celestial beings, and dragons who had taken refuge in the Buddha respectfully bowed whilst facing north out of reverence for Him. At first, after the Tathagata had realized the Truth, His five ascetic companions—Ajnyata Kaundinya, Ashvaji, Mahanama, Bhadrika, and Bashpa, who are known in Japan as Kōrin, Ahei, Makakōri, Batsudai, and Jūrikikashō —without giving it a thought, rose up and turned to face the Tathagata, offering Him their respectful bows whilst facing north. When non-Buddhists and bands of demons completely discarded their false views and took refuge in the Buddha, they invariably faced north and respectfully bowed, giving no heed to themselves or others.

Since then, for twenty-eight generations in India and the various generations in China, all those who have come to the assemblies of Ancestral Masters and have taken refuge in the True Dharma have respectfully bowed whilst facing north. This is an affirmation of the True Dharma and is beyond simply paying heed to the desires of Master or disciple. It is the Great Invocation.

> *There is the Great Invocation that, for our sake, is*
> *called 'fully perfected understanding',*
> *And there is the Great Invocation that, for our sake,*
> *is called 'paying our respects',*
> *And there is the Great Invocation that is the full*
> *manifestation of bowing respectfully,*
> *And there is the Great Invocation whose name is the*
> *kesa,*
> *And there is the Great Invocation whose name is the*
> *Treasure House of the Eye of the True*
> *Teaching.*

By reciting this invocation, we continually remain in stillness and thereby preserve the whole of the great earth. By continually remaining in stillness, we thereby fill the worlds in all the quarters. By continually remaining in stillness, we make manifest the whole sphere of time. By continually remaining in stillness, we cultivate the whole of the Buddha Realms. And by continually remaining in stillness, we realize what is within our hermit's hut and what is outside our hermit's hut. You need to thoroughly explore through your training that this is what the Great Invocation is really like. All invocations take this Invocation as their matrix. All invocations fully manifest as dependents of this Invocation. From the gateway of this Invocation, all Buddhas and Ancestors, bar none, derive Their giving rise to Their intention to realize the Truth and to earnestly follow the Way, right up to Their realization of the Truth and Their turning the Wheel of the Dharma. Since we are already the offspring of the Buddhas and Ancestors, we should thoroughly explore this Invocation in detail.

In sum, the robe that covered Shakyamuni Buddha has also covered all Ancestors of the Buddha in the ten quarters. And the robe that covered Shakyamuni Buddha is the kesa. The kesa is as a flag flown by Buddhists; it is the standard for their practice of the Buddha's Way. The chance to see the kesa and to undertake the practice is rarely encountered, rarely met with. You have received a human body in a remote land, which is rare enough, and, though some may say that you are foolish, the strength of your good roots from invocations performed in past lives is fully manifesting so that you now have the opportunity to encounter the Dharma of Shakyamuni Buddha. Though you are doing respectful bows to the Buddhas and Ancestors who have realized the Truth and are helping others to realize the Truth amidst the hundreds of thoughts and things that are sprouting up, this is Shakyamuni Buddha's fulfilling the Way; it is Shakyamuni Buddha's doing His utmost to practice the Way; it is Shakyamuni Buddha's wondrous transformation of the Great Invocation. Even though you may do respectful bows to former Buddhas of the past and present for billions of kalpas* beyond count, they will still simply be moments of being Shakyamuni Buddha.

To cover our body with a kesa even once is to have already obtained Shakyamuni Buddha's body and flesh, hands and feet, head and eyes, marrow and brains, and to shine forth, turning the Wheel of the Dharma. Such is the case when we wear the kesa, for this is our fully manifesting the merit of wearing the kesa. We preserve it and rely upon it, we love it and devote ourselves to it, and, over time, we protect it. We wear the kesa as we respectfully bow and make our offerings to

Shakyamuni Buddha. This is our doing our utmost to pursue the Way through our training and practice over incalculable eons of time.

Our respectfully bowing to Shakyamuni Buddha and making our offerings to Him means that we are respectfully bowing and making our offerings to the Master who has Transmitted the Dharma to us and to the Master who shaved our head. This is nothing other than our encountering Shakyamuni Buddha. It is our making a Dharma offering to Shakyamuni Buddha. It is our offering an invocation to Shakyamuni Buddha. In pointing this out, my former Master, the Old Buddha of Mount Tendō, said, "It is like Eka's coming over the snows to do his respectful bowing or like Enō's standing amidst the winnowed rice and doing his respectful bowing; these are excellent examples. They are the traces of former Ancestors. They are the Great Invocation."

Delivered to the assembly during the first year of the Kangen era (1243) at Kippō-ji Temple in Echizen Province.

Copied by me on the thirteenth day of the first month in the second year of the same era (February 22, 1244) in the quarters of the Abbot's assistant below the Kippō-ji hermitage in the same province.

Ejō

43

On the Moon as One's Excellent Nature

(Tsuki)

Translator's Introduction: Although the Chinese characters that Dōgen employs for the title of this discourse may be translated as 'one's excellent Nature', this term does not occur in the text itself. Rather, Dōgen appears to have used it to spell out with Chinese characters the Japanese word *tsuki*, 'the moon', which is a common Buddhist metaphor for one's innate Buddha Nature—the Moon of our Original Nature. And, at the same time, one's excellent Nature is synonymous with one's innate Buddha Nature.

Some readers may find this discourse less obscure if they substitute the words 'Buddha Nature' for the word 'Moon'.

Instances of Moons becoming full are not just 'three and three before that' and 'three and three after that'. And our innately fully perfected Moons are likewise not just 'three and three before that' and 'three and three after that'.[1] This is why Shakyamuni Buddha said:

> The true Dharma Body of the Buddha
> Is unbounded, like empty space.
> It reveals Its form by conforming to an object,
> Like water reflecting the moon.

The Ultimate Reality described as being 'like water reflecting the moon' may also be expressed as 'the Water and Its Moon', 'the real Water', 'the real Moon', 'being within Reality,' or 'the Reality within'. It goes beyond expressing what things appear to be like as Reality, for Reality is what is.

The real Dharma Body of the Buddha is just like unbounded space. And because this 'unbounded space' is the real Dharma Body of the Buddha, the whole

---

1. That is, instances of people fully realizing their Buddha Nature (that is, having a kenshō) are just as beyond count as the number of people who have Buddha Nature, which is everyone.

earth, the whole of all realms, all thoughts and things—that is, all things that manifest—are, in themselves, unbounded space. The hundreds of things that sprout up and the myriad forms that they take—all of which manifest before our very eyes— are just like the Dharma Body of the Buddha, <u>and</u> they are the real Dharma Body of the Buddha, <u>and</u> they are like the moon in water.[2] The time of the Moon's arising is not invariably at night, and the night is not necessarily the dark, so do not depend simply on narrow human ways of measuring things.[3] Even in places where there is no sun or moon, there will be day and night, for the sun and moon do not exist for the sake of day and night. And because the Sun and Moon are, both together, what is ultimately real, there is not just one or two Moons, nor just a thousand or myriad Moons. Even if some people say of themselves that their own Moon supports and relies upon their personal opinion of what the Moon is, such is their personal view of the Moon, and it is not necessarily an expression of the Buddha's Truth nor an instance of their wisely discerning what the Buddha's Truth is. Thus, even though we may say that there is a Moon tonight, the Moon tonight is not last night's Moon. You need to explore through your training that tonight's Moon through and through—beginning, middle, and end—is just tonight's Moon.[4] Because a Moon has inherited the Truth from a Moon, the Moon exists as such, but It is not something new or old.

Meditation Master Banzan Hōshaku once said:

---

2.   That is, the Dharma Body of the Buddha has two characteristics: It is like unbounded space and It <u>is</u> unbounded space. Further, all things that arise and manifest themselves have three characteristics: they are like the Dharma Body of the Buddha, they <u>are</u> the Dharma Body of the Buddha, and they are reflections of the Dharma Body of the Buddha.

3.   That is, a kenshō does not necessarily occur in the middle of the night.

4.   That is, how one's Buddha Nature may manifest today (like today's phase of the Moon) will be just for this day, and it will still be the whole of one's Buddha Nature.

> *The Moon of our heart and mind is solitary and at*
> *the full,*
> *Its light swallows up all forms that arise.*[5]
> *Its light is not something that illumines concrete*
> *objects,*
> *And concrete objects, in turn, are not things that truly*
> *exist.*[6]
> *When Its light and objects both vanish from sight,*
> *There is still That which is the What.*

What is now being expressed is that, without fail, the Ancestors of the Buddha, as disciples of the Buddha, possess the Moon of their heart and mind because they treat their Moon as their heart and mind. If It were not the Moon, It would not be their heart and mind, and without a heart and mind, there is no Moon. 'Solitary and at the full' means that It lacks for nothing. Whatever is more than 'two or three', we call 'all things'. When all things are in the Moon's Light, they are not seen as 'all things', hence Its Light swallows up all things. Since all things spontaneously absorb the Moon's light completely, Its Light swallows up the Moon's light, which means that Its Light swallows up all things. For instance, it will be the Moon swallowing up the Moon, and the Light swallowing up the Moon.[7] Accordingly, the Master expressed the Matter[*] as:

---

5. 'Swallows up', both here and throughout this discourse, is a metaphor meaning 'takes in and comprehends'.

6. That is, they do not have a permanent, unchangeable nature.

7. 'The Moon's light' refers to the reflected light of the Sun (that is, Buddha Nature), whereas 'the Moon's Light' refers to the Sun Itself.

[*] See Glossary.

> *Its light is not something that illumines concrete objects,*
> *And concrete objects, in turn, are not things that truly exist.*

Because Banzan had attained such a state, when people could be helped to reach the Other Shore by means of a Buddha Body, he would forthwith manifest his Buddha Body and give voice to the Dharma for their sake. And when people could be helped to reach the Other Shore by means of an ordinary physical body, he would forthwith manifest that customary physical body of his and give voice to the Dharma for their sake. It is said that he never failed to turn the Wheel of the Dharma from within his Moon. Even though the lunar yin energy and the solar yang energy illumine objects by means of the fire jewel—which is the Sun—and the water jewel—which is the Moon—he would forthwith manifest both. This heart and mind of his was nothing other than his Moon, and this Moon of his was, as a matter of course, his own heart and mind. This is how the Buddha's Ancestors, as disciples of the Buddha, master the principle of mind and the details of mind.

A Buddha of the past once said, "The whole of your mind contains everything, and everything contains the whole of your mind." Since this is so, your mind is everything, and everything is your mind. Because your heart and mind are your Moon, your Moon must be the Moon. Because everything, which is your heart and mind, is completely the Moon, the whole universe throughout is the whole Moon throughout. And being intimately acquainted with your self, through and through, is being intimately acquainted with your Moon, through and through. Even with the 'three and three before, or three and three after' over time immemorial, who among them is not a Moon? The Buddha with the Solar Face and the Buddha with the Lunar Face—which are our body and mind along with their internal propensities and external conditions at this present moment—will both be within our Moon.[8] Birth-and-death and coming-and-going will both be in our Moon, and the whole universe in all ten quarters will be the top, bottom, left, and right within our Moon. Whatever is going on right now in our daily life will be just some of the hundreds of things that sprout up in our mind ever so clearly within our Moon, and it will be what sprouts up in the minds of the Buddhas and Ancestors within Their Moon.

> Great Master Tōsu Daidō of Shuchou Province was once asked by a monk, "What is the Moon like when It is not yet full?"[9]
> The Master answered, "It swallows up three or four Moons."
> The monk then asked, "And after It is full, what is It like?"
> The Master replied, "It vomits out seven or eight Moons."[10]

What is being thoroughly explored here are the terms 'not yet full' and 'after becoming full'. Both of them are phases of the Moon. Within the three or four Moons that are in your Moon, there will be One that is not yet full; within the seven or eight Moons that are in your Moon, there will be One that is now at Its full. 'Swallowing up' is associated with 'three or four Moons'; such a moment as this is synonymous with a time when one's Moon is not yet full. 'Vomiting out' is associated with 'seven or eight Moons'; such a moment as this is synonymous with a time after one's Moon has

---

8. The Buddha with the Solar Face is said to have a lifespan of 1,800 years, whereas the lifespan of the Buddha with the Lunar Face is said to be one day. This reference was used by Meditation Master Baso to describe our original Buddha Nature as being beyond any temporal measure, such as 'long' or 'short'.

9. The topic of the discourse now shifts from the Moon as a reference to our Buddha Nature being 'what we are' to the Moon's phases, which is how our Buddha Nature manifests at different times.

10. 'Vomits out' is a metaphor for 'giving spiritual expression to'.

reached Its full. When the Moon swallows up Moons, It will involve three or four of Them.[11] There will be signs of the Moon's swallowing up and manifestations of the Moon's vomiting out. In the Moon's vomiting out phases, there will be seven or eight of Them. There will be a Moon that manifests in the vomiting out, for the Moon is also a manifestation of vomiting out. Therefore, It is our swallowing up completely and our vomiting out completely. The whole of the earth and the whole of the heavens is what we vomit out. The whole universe is what we swallow up. We need to swallow up self and swallow up other, and we need to vomit out self and vomit out other.

Once when Shakyamuni Buddha was giving Teaching to the Bodhisattva Vajragarbha,[12] He said:

> Just as the moving eye, for instance, can make still waters
> seem to pitch and roll, and just as the steady eye makes fire seem to
> spiral up, so too, when clouds are hastening by, the moon seems to
> move in the opposite way, and when one's boat is departing, the
> shore appears to drift in a counter direction.

We need to thoroughly explore and clarify just what it is that the Buddha has said concerning the hastening of clouds and the moving of the moon, as well as about the departing of one's boat and the drifting of the shore. Do not study this in haste or try to make it accord with the views of ordinary, worldly people. At the same time, it is a rare person who can recognize what this Buddha has voiced as the Voicing of a Buddha. When you can say that you are studying this statement as what a Buddha has voiced, then you will understand that full realization does not necessarily refer to

---

11. That is, when people are on the verge of having a spiritual experience, they will begin to show signs of its coming, which is often described as someone's 'beginning to ripen'.

12. Vajragarbha, 'He Who is a Veritable Treasure House for the Diamond of Wisdom', is a manifestation of Samantabhadra Bodhisattva, who represents patient, loving activity. Please see the *Glossary* for an explanation of the term 'Bodhisattva'.

'body and mind' or to 'enlightenment and nirvana', and 'enlightenment and nirvana' do not necessarily refer to 'full realization' or to 'body and mind'.

As to the hastening of clouds and the moving of the moon, as well as the departing of the boat and the drifting by of the shore of which the Tathagata spoke, at the time when the clouds hasten, the moon appears to move, and at the time when the boat sails off, the shore appears to drift by. This is saying that the clouds and the moon are simultaneously moving at the same pace, at the same time, and in the same manner, which is beyond one beginning as the other ends, and beyond one being before and the other after. Also, it is saying that the boat and the shore are simultaneously moving at the same pace, at the same time, and in the same manner, which is beyond one starting when the other stops and beyond the two moving in cycles. When we learn about how people behave, human behavior is beyond just a matter of starting and stopping, and the behavior of starting and stopping is beyond just being human. Do not compare or judge the behavior of humans by taking up 'starting and stopping'. The hastening of clouds and the moving of the moon, as well as the sailing off of a boat and the drifting off of the shore, are all like this. Do not foolishly take a narrow-minded view of this. Do not overlook the main point. The hastening of a cloud is not described by 'east, west, south, or north' and the moving of the moon is without cease, day and night, in both the past and present. The sailing off of the boat and the drifting of the shore are beyond the three temporal worlds of past, present, and future, and they can make use of the three temporal worlds. Therefore, having 'arrived' right away at this very moment, one is sated and no longer feels hungry.

At the same time, foolish people fancy that an unmoving moon appears to be moving due to the moving of the clouds, and that the drifting shore appears to be drifting due to one's sailing off on a boat. If it were as these foolish people say, how could it possibly be the Teaching of the Tathagata? The main point of the Buddha Dharma is beyond the small-minded views of ordinary human beings and those in lofty positions. Although It is beyond reckoning, there is still training and practice in accord with the trainee's abilities. Who among you would fail, time and again, to cast your line for boat and shore, and who among you would fail to quickly cast an eye to clouds and moon? What you need to understand is that the Tathagata was not using the clouds as a metaphor for something physical or mental, nor was He using the moon as a metaphor for something physical or mental, nor was He using the boat as a metaphor for something physical or mental, nor was He using the shore as a metaphor for something physical or mental.[13] You need to take your time to thoroughly and diligently explore this principle. One inch of the Moon's movement is equal to the full realization of the Tathagata, and the full realization of the Tathagata is but an inch of the Moon's movement. It is not a matter of moving or halting, nor is it a matter of progressing or retreating. Because the movement of the Moon goes beyond being merely a metaphor, Its essential nature and the way It appears are Its being 'solitary and at the full'.

Keep in mind that the pace of the Moon, even if it is at a gallop, is beyond having a beginning, middle, and end. This is why the first Moon has a second Moon. The first (which is Its Essential Nature) and the second (which is the way It appears) are, both alike, Moons. 'A good time for training and practice' is what the Moon is, and 'a good time for making offerings' is what the Moon is, and, with a swish of one's sleeves, taking one's leave to go to the Meditation Hall is what the Moon is.[14] Its roundness or squareness is beyond the turning of the wheel of coming and going. Whether making use of the turning wheel of coming and going or not making use of it, the Master grabs hold of the deluded certainty of his trainees or lets them go on in their own way as he gives free reign to his elegantly skillful means, and so it is with many Moons.

Written by me on the sixth day of the first lunar month in the fourth year of the Ninji era (January 27, 1243), whilst at Kannondōri in Kōshōhōrin-ji Temple.

The Mendicant Monk Dōgen

Copied by me on the day before of the end of the summer retreat in the first year of the Kangen era (July 22, 1243). *Ejō*

---

13. In other words, the reality of Buddha Nature is beyond our normal ways of thinking about body and mind.

14. This sentence presents the three responses to the question "How is the Moon right now?" which was put by Baso to his three disciples, Seidō Chizō, Hyakujō Ekai, and Nansen Fugan, who were watching the moon one night.

44

On the Flowering of the Unbounded

(Kūge)

Translator's Introduction: *Kūge*, the title of this discourse, has various meanings. The term is used in the *Shurangama Scripture* to refer to a physical disease in which one sees non-existent 'flowers' in the sky, and it is employed in the same Scripture as a metaphor for the effects of delusion, caused by one's being spiritually 'bleary-eyed'. Dōgen extends the meaning of *kūge* to refer to things as they really are: the flowerings of Buddha Nature (That Which Is as Unbounded as Space), as seen by one whose spiritual vision has become 'unfocused', due to his having left off hard-edged, dualistic thinking, which assumes that its mental constructs are real. The flowering that Dōgen speaks of refers to the whole universe as it is, which blossoms forth from within Buddha Nature, as well as to the blossoming of a kenshō, (that is, the seeing of one's True Nature) and the manifestation of Buddhas.

Our highest Founding Ancestor Bodhidharma once said in verse:

> *And when the Single Blossom opened Its five*
> *petals,*
> *The fruit thereof naturally came about of itself.*

You need to explore through your training the occasion for this opening of the One Blossom, along with exploring Its radiance and the form It takes. The One Blossom is comprised of five petals, one atop the other. The opening up of the five petals forms the One Blossom. When you have penetrated the principle of the one blossom, it will be in accord with Bodhidharma's statement:

> *From the first, I came to this land to Transmit the*
> *Dharma*
> *That I might rescue deluded beings.* [1]

---

1. These two lines are the opening lines of a quatrain by Bodhidharma, whose closing lines Dōgen quoted at the start of this text.

Seeking the radiance and form of this blossoming is what your investigation through your training should be all about. What Bodhidharma calls 'the resulting fruit' is something that one leaves to the fruit: he describes this as 'what naturally comes about of itself'. 'What naturally comes about of itself' is his term for mastering causes and being conscious of effects. There are the causes of the whole universe and there are the effects of the whole universe; there is our mastering the causes and effects of this whole universe and there is our being conscious of the causes and effects of this whole universe. One's natural self is oneself. This self, to be sure, is 'you', that is to say, it is the four elements* and the five skandhas* of which you are comprised. Because Bodhidharma is allowing for 'a true person devoid of any rank', he is not referring to a specific 'I' or to some 'other'. Therefore, that which is indefinable is what he is calling 'a self'. This natural state of 'being as it is' is what he is acknowledging.[2] The natural state of 'being as one is' is the time when the Single Blossom opens and Its fruit results: it is the occasion when the Dharma is Transmitted and one is rescued from one's delusions.

For instance, the moment when the blue lotus bursts into bloom is like being in the midst of a fire at the time of fire.[3] The fire's sparks and flames all converge at the point where the blue lotus bursts into bloom at the very moment when it bursts into bloom. If it were not the time and place of the blue lotus's blossoming, not even a single spark of fire would emerge, not even a single spark of fire would come to life. You need to know that there are hundreds of thousands of blue lotuses in a single spark of fire: they blossom forth throughout boundless space and throughout the earth. They blossomed forth in the past and they blossom forth in the present. When you witness the time and place of the fire emerging, you are witnessing the blossoming of the blue

---

*   See Glossary.

2.   What the translation does not make clear is that Dōgen is analyzing the word jinen in Bodhidharma's poem (rendered as 'naturally') as being comprised of two words: ji meaning 'self' and nen meaning 'being as it is'.

3.   The blue lotus refers to the blossoming of the spiritual flower of one's training and enlightenment, not to an actual plant.

lotus. Do not let the time and place of the blue lotus pass you by, but be a witness to its blossoming.

An enlightened one of long ago once said in a poem, "The blue lotus blooms amidst the fire." Thus it is that the blue lotus invariably blossoms forth in the midst of the fire. If you wish to know where 'being in the midst of the fire' is, it is the very place where the blue lotus blossoms forth. Do not neglect investigating 'being in the midst of the fire' through adopting the views of either ordinary people or those in lofty positions. Should you harbor any doubts, you might also doubt that the lotus arises within the water, and you might doubt that branches and twigs have any blossoms as well. Further, should you harbor such doubts, you might well doubt the existence of the outer, objective world. But this you do not doubt. If someone is not an Ancestor of the Buddha, such a person does not know that with the opening of the blossom, the whole world arises. 'The opening of the blossom' means 'three and three before that, as well as three and three after that'. In order to make the number of these more extensive, they have accumulated a luxurious growth, soaring ever higher.[4]

Letting this principle of blossoming come of its own accord, we need to consider whether it is spring or autumn. Blossoms and fruit do not only appear in spring and in autumn. There will invariably be other times when blossoms and fruit emerge. Every flowering and fruiting has endured while they have waited for their opportunity, and every opportunity has endured while it has waited for a flowering and a fruiting. Thus, all the hundreds of things that sprout up have their time of flowering and their fruiting, just as all manner of trees have their time of flowering and their fruiting. All manner of trees—such as those of gold, silver, copper, iron, coral, or crystal—have their flowering and their fruiting. Trees of earth, water, fire, wind, and boundless space have their flowering and fruiting. Human trees have their

---

4. To paraphrase, while the number of persons realizing the Truth is indefinite ('three and three before that, as well as three and three after that') it is decidedly more than just a few people. In fact, the number is staggering and ever increasing.

blossoming, human flowers have their blossoming, and withered trees have their blossoming.

It is within this context that the World-honored One spoke of the flowerings within Unbounded Space. On the other hand, those folks who pay attention to very little and see even less are unaware that petals and blossoms with their varied hues and brilliance are to be found within everything. These are 'the flowers of Unbounded Space', and such folk are only barely aware of a flowering of Unbounded Space. You need to be aware that the flowers of Unbounded Space are discussed within the words and ways of the Buddha, whereas non-Buddhists have no knowledge of such discussions about the flowers of Unbounded Space, much less do they have any understanding of them! Only the Buddhas and Ancestors have known about the blossoming and falling of the flowers of Unbounded Space as well as that of earthly flowers. Only They have known of such things as the blossoming and falling of the flowers within the human world. Only They have known that such things as the flowers in Unbounded Space, earthly flowers, and the flowers within the human world are all Scriptures; this is the standard by which we investigate what Buddha is. Because what has been taught by the Buddhas and Ancestors is this flowering of Unbounded Space, the realm of Buddha and the Teachings of Buddhas are therefore synonymous with the flowerings of Unbounded Space.

At the same time, when those who are commonplace and foolish hear about what the Tathagata said—namely, that what is seen by those with bleary-eyed vision are the flowerings in Unbounded Space—they assume that 'bleary-eyed vision' refers to topsy-turvy vision in human beings. Because their own diseased vision is already topsy-turvy, they believe that one experiences flowers in Unbounded Space as something floating in an absolute void. Being attached to this understanding, they have concluded that the three worlds of desire, form, and beyond form, the six worlds* of existence, the existence of Buddhahood, and the state of going beyond Buddhahood, are all really non-existent but are mistakenly seen as having existence. They go about making their living by asserting that, if we were to bring to a halt this bleary-eyed vision brought about by our delusions, we would no longer see these flowers in the void since, from the beginning, the void is devoid of flowers. How sad that folks like these do not know, from start to finish, the times of which the Tathagata spoke when flowers bloom in Unbounded Space. The principle of seeing flowers in Unbounded Space with 'bleary-eyed' vision—of which the Buddhas have spoken—is not understood by ordinary, everyday people and those who are non-Buddhists. The Buddhas and Tathagatas have trained with these flowers in Unbounded Space and They have put them into Their practice. By doing so, They have obtained Their robe, Their sitting place, and Their access to the Master's quarters, all of which is Their realizing the Way and attaining Its fruits. Holding aloft the blossom, with eyes twinkling,[5] is the raising of the spiritual question, which manifests our seeing flowers in Unbounded Space with bleary-eyed vision. That the Treasure House of the Eye of the True Teaching, which is the Wondrous Heart of Nirvana, has now been correctly Transmitted without a break is what we call seeing flowers in Unbounded space with bleary-eyed vision. Enlightenment, nirvana, giving rise to the intention to realize the Truth, one's own True Nature, and so forth, are two or three petals among the five which the blossoming of Unbounded Space opens up.

Shakyamuni Buddha once said in verse:

> *Further, it is like one with bleary-eyed vision*
> *Seeing blossoms in Boundless Space;*
> *When that bleary-eyed sickness is eradicated,*
> *The blossoms disappear into the Unbounded Space.*

There have never been any mundane academics or scholars who have understood this saying. Because they do not know what Unbounded Space is, they do not know what blossoms in Unbounded Space refers to, and because they do not know what blossoms in Unbounded Space refers to, they do not recognize 'one of bleary-eyed vision', nor are they themselves 'one of bleary-eyed vision', nor do they ever become 'one of bleary-eyed vision'. When those of unfocused vision mutually recognize each other, they will know what flowers in Unbounded Space are and they will see the flowering

---

5.   This is a reference to the Transmission of the Dharma from Shakyamuni Buddha to his disciple Makakashō. This occurred when the Buddha held aloft an udumbara blossom and Makakashō smiled in response.

of Unbounded Space. After they have seen the flowers in Unbounded Space, they will also see the flowers disappearing into Unbounded Space.[6] To think that once the flowers have disappeared into Unbounded Space they cannot return again is the view of those of the Lesser Course.* [7] When the flowers within Unbounded Space cannot be seen by such people, what can exist for them? By merely thinking that flowers within Unbounded Space are something to be dropped off, they do not recognize the Great Matter* that lies within the blossoming of Unbounded Space, nor do they know of the seeding, ripening, and falling away of That which blossoms within Unbounded Space.

Among the mundane academics and scholars of today, there are those who think that the yang-energy must govern empty space, and there are those who think that the sun, moon, and stars must be suspended in empty space. Accordingly, they consider what they expediently call 'flowers in empty space' to be something that takes on an appearance and form not unlike that of drifting clouds in the clear sky, or they think it must be like blossoms sent flying in the wind, hither and yon, up and down. They do not know that the four elements—which can create other things and which are, themselves, created—along with the various things of the outer world, as well as such things as one's innate enlightenment and Original Nature, are all called flowers in Unbounded Space. Further, they do not know that the four elements exist to do their creating in accordance with thoughts and things, nor do they know that, in accordance with thoughts and things, the outer world abides in its place. They simply recognize that there are thoughts and things that are in accord with the outer world. They only comprehend that there are flowers in empty space because of one's bleary-eyed vision, and do not comprehend the principle that there is an unfocusing of one's vision due to a blossoming in Unbounded Space.

You need to realize that what the Buddha called 'one with bleary-eyed vision' is one who is fundamentally enlightened, one who is wondrously enlightened, one who is at one with the Buddhas, one who is of the three worlds of existence, one who

---

6.   That is, they will see what 'going beyond Buddhahood' refers to.

7.   That is, they believe that one cannot have multiple experiences of realizing Truth, and that once one has realized Truth, the need to train is at an end.

has gone on beyond Buddhahood. So, do not, out of befuddlement, explore the foolish notion that being 'bleary-eyed' means being deluded and therefore go looking for some other way of progressing. Were you to do so, yours would be a meager view of the Matter. If the blossoming of bleary-eyed vision were a delusion, then that which attaches to the erroneous view that this is an erroneous view, as well as the attachment itself, would both be delusions. If both were delusions, then establishing what the underlying principle is would be impossible. If there were no underlying principle that could be established, then it would be impossible to establish that the blossoming seen by those of bleary-eyed vision is a delusion.

When enlightenment is seen as 'being bleary-eyed', then everything is within enlightenment and all things are bedecked with the quality of being out of focus. When delusion is seen as 'being bleary-eyed', then everything is within delusion and all things are bedecked with the quality of being out of focus. For the present, we can say that when one's bleary vision is impartial, the flowerings within Unbounded Space are impartial, that when bleary-eyed vision has not arisen, a flowering within Unbounded space has not arisen, and that when all thoughts and things have their True Form, bleary-eyed vision has its True Form. You should not get into discussions about past, present, and future, and do not hang onto 'beginning, middle, and end'. By not being hindered by 'arising and disappearing', you can make arisings and disappearings arise and disappear. They arise within Unbounded Space and they disappear within Unbounded Space; they arise within that which is out of focus and they disappear within that which is out of focus; they arise within flowering and they disappear within flowering, and so on, doing the same for all other times and places.

Learning about flowers within Unbounded Space may well take many forms. There is what is seen with bleary-eyed vision, and what is seen with wondrous eyes, and what is seen with the Eye of a Buddha, and what is seen with the eyes of an Ancestor, and what is seen with the vision of the Way, and what is seen with blind eyes, and what has been seen for three thousand years, and what has been seen for eight hundred years, and what has been seen for hundreds of kalpas,* and what has been seen for immeasurable kalpas.[8] Though it is said that all of these see a flowering in Unbounded Space, Unbounded Space is already of various kinds, and flowering, as well, is of all sorts.

By all means you need to realize that space is simply one form of sprouting. This space invariably produces its flowerings, just as the hundreds of sproutings of thoughts and things produce their flowerings. In asserting this principle, the Tathagata said that Unbounded Space originally had no flowering. Although It originally had no flowering, today It has Its flowerings, just as do the peach and damson trees and just as do the plum and willow trees.[9] It is as if the Tathagata had said, "Although yesterday the plum had no flowers, come the spring, the plum will have flowers." Well and good, for when its season arrives, it will produce flowers, since it will be the time for its flowering and the arriving of its flowering. The actual moment of its flowering is never arbitrary. The flowers of the plum and the willow invariably blossom on plum and willow trees. Upon seeing their flowers, we recognize them as those of the plum and the willow: upon seeing the plum and the willow, we discern what their flowers are. The flowers of the peach and the damson never bloom on plum or willow trees. The flowers of the plum and willow trees bloom on plum and willow trees, whereas the flowers of the peach and damson trees bloom on peach and damson trees. Likewise, the flowers of Unbounded Space bloom in Unbounded Space—they do not bloom on other things that sprout up or upon other trees. By looking at the various forms of the flowers of Unbounded Space, we can estimate that the flowers of Unbounded Space are boundless. By looking at the opening and falling of the flowers in Unbounded Space, you should investigate the spring and autumn of the flowers in Unbounded Space. The springtime for flowers in Unbounded Space and the springtime for other flowers will be alike. Just as the flowers of Unbounded Space are various, so will their springtimes be many. Thus there are the springs and autumns of

---

8. 'What has been seen for three thousand years…for immeasurable kalpas' refers to what has been experienced by Buddhas since before the time of Shakyamuni Buddha, by Bodhidharma, and by Ancestor after Ancestor at all times, past, present, and future.

9. The peach and damson trees are a common Chinese metaphor for disciples, whereas the plum and the willow represent the most beautiful of flowering trees.

past and present. Those who have been taught that the flowers of Unbounded Space are not real, though other flowers <u>are</u> real, are persons who have not encountered or heard what the Buddha taught. Upon hearing the Buddha's Teaching that Unbounded Space originally had no flowers, if one were to study this as meaning that there are now flowers of Unbounded Space where originally there were none, this would be narrow-minded and short-sighted. We need to step forward and take a more broadminded view.

Our Ancestral Master Eka once said, "The flowers, moreover, have never appeared." The main point of this is the principle, for example, that the flowers have never appeared, that they have never disappeared, that they have never been 'flowers', and that Unbounded Space has, moreover, never been 'space'. Do not look with suspicion upon what preceded or followed the time of their blossoming, or engage in idle discussions concerning their existence or nonexistence. Flowers invariably seem to be dyed with some color or other, but these various colors are not necessarily limited to flowers. In the various seasons, there are colors such as blue, yellow, red, and white. The spring ushers in flowers, and the flowers usher in spring.

The highly accomplished Mandarin scholar Ch'ang Cho was a lay disciple of Sekisō Keisho. Upon awakening to the Way, he composed a poem:

> *Its brilliant light serenely illumines everywhere*
> *amidst worlds as numerous as the sands of*
> *the Ganges.*[10]

This brilliant light has clearly illuminated the Monks' Hall, the Buddha Hall, the kitchen, and the mountain gate to the monastery. 'Everywhere amidst worlds as

---

10. This is the first line of an eight-line poem, which Dōgen quotes line by line. Each line is followed by his short commentary.

numerous as the sands of the Ganges' is where the brilliant light manifests and it <u>is</u> a manifestation of the brilliant light.

> *Sentient beings, both the ordinary and the saintly,*
> *are within my family.*

It is not that there are no ordinary, everyday people or that there are no wise and saintly ones, but in accord with this, be sure not to speak ill of either ordinary, everyday people or the wise and saintly.

> *When not a single thought arose, Its whole Body*
> *manifested Itself.*

Thought after thought is just one after the other; this is certainly 'non-arising'. This is Its whole body completely manifesting. This is why he said that not a single thought arose.

> *When my six sense organs moved even slightly,*
> *my mind was covered with clouds.*

Although the six sense organs are the eyes, ears, nose, tongue, body, and mind, they are not necessarily a matter of two times three; they can be some group of three, and then three before or after those three.[11] 'Moving' is like Mount Sumeru, like the great earth, like the six sense organs, like moving even slightly. Because moving is already like Mount Sumeru, not moving is also like Mount Sumeru.

> *Attempting to cut myself free from my defiling*
> *passions just added to my heap of*
> *spiritual diseases.*

It is not that he had never been sick before, for there was the disease of 'Buddha' and the disease of 'Ancestor'.[12] But now, using his perceptiveness to cut off his passions, he piled up his illnesses and increased his sickness. The very moment of cutting

---

11. That is, the sense organs are not necessarily just the standard six (two times three), but may manifest in countless ways.

12. That is, the spiritual greed to become a Buddha or an Ancestor.

oneself free is invariably synonymous with having a passion: they are simultaneous, and they are beyond being simultaneous. Passions are invariably bound up in the measures taken to cut oneself free from them.

To go after the Truth is also the wrong thing.

To turn one's back on Truth is wrong. To confront Truth is wrong. The Truth is the very confronting and the turning of one's back. Each and every instance of 'confronting' and 'turning one's back on' is what Truth is. And who knows that this 'wrong' is also what Truth is?

Submitting myself to worldly connections is not a
hindrance.

He submitted himself to one worldly connection after another, for submission after submission is what worldly connections are. This is called 'not being hindered'. As for being hindered or not being hindered, you should accustom yourself to letting your eyes be hindered.

Nirvana and birth-and-death are simply flowers
in Unbounded Space.

Nirvana is synonymous with supreme, fully perfected enlightenment. This is where the Buddhas and Ancestors reside, along with Their disciples. Birth-and-death is synonymous with one's True Body. Nirvana and birth-and-death exist in this manner and they are flowers in Unbounded Space. The roots and stems, the branches and leaves, the flowers and fruit, along with the brilliance and forms of the flowers of Unbounded Space, are all the blossoming forth of flowers in Unbounded Space. They are invariably connected with the fruits of Unbounded Space, which bestow the seeds of Unbounded Space. Because the three worlds of desire, form, and beyond form, which we are now experiencing, are the opening of the five petals, it is best to see these three worlds as the three worlds. You need to explore through your training that the three worlds are the true form of all thoughts and things, that they are the flowering of all thoughts and things. All thoughts and things beyond measure are the flowers of Unbounded Space and the fruits of Unbounded Space, and they are identical with the flowers of plum and willow, peach and damson.

When Meditation Master Fuyōzan Reikun in the Fuchou district of Great Sung China first came to train under Meditation Master Kisu Shishin, he asked his Master, "Just what is Buddha?"

Master Kisu replied, "If I tell you straight to your face, will you believe me?"

Reikun then said, "How would I dare not to believe your sincere words, O Venerable Monk?"

Master Kiso responded, "You yourself are precisely what It is."

Reikun then asked, "How am I to preserve and maintain It?"

Master Kiso answered, "When there is a single moment of your eyes being bleary, the flowers of Unbounded Space will come fluttering down."

The words that Master Kisu has just spoken, namely, "When there is a single moment of your eyes being bleary, the flowers of Unbounded Space will come fluttering down," express how Buddha is preserved and maintained. So, you need to realize that the fluttering down of the flowers of bleary-eyed vision is what all Buddhas manifest. By seeing the flowering and fruiting of Unbounded Space which Their Eye, all Buddhas preserve and maintain these flowers and fruit. By means of Their bleary-eyed vision, They cause the Eye to manifest. They have manifested the flowering of Unbounded Space within Their Eye and They have manifested Their Eye within the flowering of Unbounded Space. It is simply a matter of "When the flower of Unbounded Space is within Their Eye, a single moment of bleary-eyed vision flutters down, and when Their Eye is within Unbounded Space, all instances of bleary-eyed vision flutter down." Thus, bleary-eyed vision is a manifestation of all functions, and the Eye is also a manifestation of all functions, and Unbounded Space is also a manifestation of all functions, and flowering is also a manifestation of all functions. 'Fluttering down' is synonymous with 'thousands of Eyes' and with 'our whole body being covered with eyes'.[13] In short, at the time and place when the single Eye occurs, there will invariably be a blossoming in Unbounded Space along with the blossoming of that Eye. We call the blossoming of one's Eye 'flowers in Unbounded Space'. The expression 'the blossoming of one's Eye' is invariably synonymous with opening to the luminous, that is, to enlightenment.

This is why Great Master Rōya Ekaku said in a poem,

> *How wondrous the Buddhas in the ten quarters are!*
> *From the first, They have been flowers in your Eye.*
> *If you desire to make the acquaintance of the flowers*
> *in your Eye,*
> *They are, of course, the Buddhas in the ten quarters.*
>
> *If you desire to make the acquaintance of the Buddhas*
> *in the ten quarters, They will not be flowers*
> *in your eyes.*
> *If you desire to make the acquaintance of the flowers*
> *in your eyes, they will not be the Buddhas in*
> *the ten quarters.*
> *When you understand this clearly,*
> *The blame will lie with the Buddhas in the ten*
> *quarters.*
>
>
> *When this is not yet clearly understood,*
>
> *Shravakas are prone to dance*

---

13.   Dōgen explores these references to 'thousands of Eyes' and to 'being covered with eyes' in his Discourse 32: On Kannon, the Bodhisattva of Compassion *(Kannon).*

And pratyekabuddhas take to adorning themselves.[14]

Keep in mind that the Buddhas of the ten quarters are not unreal, but, from the first, They are flowers in our Eye. The place where the Buddhas of the ten quarters abide is within our Eye. If They were not within our Eye, then our Eye would not be the abiding place of Buddhas. The flowers in our Eye are neither non-existent nor existent, and they are beyond emptiness and reality: they are naturally what the Buddhas in the ten quarters are. If you earnestly desire to be acquainted with the Buddhas in the ten quarters, They are beyond being just 'flowers in your eyes', and if you earnestly desire to be acquainted with what the flowers in your eyes are, they will seem to be something other than the Buddhas in the ten quarters.

Because the Matter is like this, both your being clear and your not yet being clear are flowers in your Eye and they are also the Buddhas in the ten quarters. Your desire to be acquainted with what They are and what They are not is the Wondrous manifesting Itself, and It is a great wonder. The main point about the flowers of Unbounded Space and the flowers of the earth, of which Buddha after Buddha and Ancestor after Ancestor have spoken, is Their giving free rein to Their elegantly skillful means. Even though academic teachers of Scriptures and scholars who produce erudite commentaries thereon are able to hear the words 'flowers in Unbounded Space', there is no account of anyone, apart from an Ancestor of the Buddha, who has ever encountered, or even heard of, the Lifeblood of the flowers of the earth. And there are the sayings of the Buddha's Ancestors who have understood what the Lifeblood of the flowers of the earth really is.

---

14. To paraphrase the end part, when you understand clearly the difference between 'flowers in one's eyes' (delusion) and 'flowers in one's Eye' (enlightenment), it will be due to the Buddhas in the ten quarters (their 'fault'). As used here, the term shravakas refers to those who enjoy hearing the Teaching but are not necessarily interested in Its practical application, believing that they are already enlightened because they have an intellectual understanding of the Teaching, and therefore they jump for joy. On the other hand, pratyekabuddhas are those who are seeking enlightenment, but just for their own sake. When they believe that they have fully fathomed enlightenment, they wear their understanding as a badge of their achievement.

Meditation Master Etetsu of Mount Sekimon in Great Sung China was a venerable elder who had trained under Ryōzan Enkan. One day a certain monk asked him, "What is the Jewel in the Mountain?" The main point of asking this is the same as asking, "What <u>is</u> Buddha?" or like asking, "What is the Way?" The Master replied, "The flowers of Unbounded Space come forth from the earth, so, throughout the country, there is no way to buy them."

In all earnestness, you must not compare this saying with other expressions. Ordinary, mundane teachers, in discussing the flowers of Unbounded Space as 'flowers in the empty sky', speak only of their arising in the empty sky and disappearing into the empty sky. Since they have still not understood what 'reliance on Unbounded Space' means, how could they possibly understand what 'reliance on the earth' means? Only Sekimon knew this. 'Reliance on the earth' is ultimately relying on the earth through and through—beginning, middle, and end. His phrase 'coming forth' is synonymous with 'opening up'. That very moment is the flowers' coming forth from the whole of the great earth; it is their opening up over the whole of the great earth.

'Throughout the country there is no way to buy them' does not mean that there is nothing to buy throughout the country, but that there is no way to buy the Truth. There are the flowers of Unbounded Space which are based on coming forth from the earth, and there is the whole earth which is based on the opening of flowers. So, keep in mind this main point: the flowers of Unbounded Space cause both the opening up of the earth and the unfolding of Unbounded Space.

Given to the assembly on the tenth day of the third lunar month in the first year of the Kangen era (March 31, 1243) at Kannondōri in Kōshōhōrin-ji Temple.

Copied by me on the first day of the first lunar month in the second year of the same era (February 10, 1244), while in the quarters of the Abbot's assistant at Kippō-ji Temple in Echizen Province.

Ejō

45

On What the Mind of an Old Buddha Is

(Kobusshin)

Translator's Introduction: The Japanese term *'kobutsu'*, rendered herein as 'an Old Buddha', occurs often in Zen writings. It refers to one who has fully realized his or her True Nature and therefore has the Mind of an Old Buddha.

In the succession of the Dharma in our Ancestral tradition, there were forty Ancestors from the Seven Buddhas* down to Daikan Enō, and from Daikan Enō back to the Seven Buddhas there were forty Buddhas.[1] Because the Seven Buddhas equally had the merit of having realized enlightenment and of having turned back to help the world, the inherited Dharma extended forward to Enō and was traceable back to the Seven Buddhas. Because Enō had the merit of having realized enlightenment and of having turned back to help the world, It has been genuinely Transmitted from the Seven Buddhas, and It has been genuinely Transmitted from Enō, and It has been genuinely Transmitted to later Buddhas. It is not merely a question of who has preceded or has followed whom; the time of Shakyamuni Buddha is that of all the Buddhas in the ten quarters. During Seigen's time there was Nangaku, and during Nangaku's time there was Seigen. And during the time of Seigen's heir Sekitō, there was Nangaku's heir Baso. They did not stand against each other, nor was it a matter

---

*   See Glossary.

1.   Dōgen goes only as far as the Sixth Chinese Ancestor, Daikan Enō, because he was the first to have two Dharma heirs, Seigen Gyōshi and Nangaku Ejō. Dōgen's Sōtō lineage derives from Seigen, whereas the other Zen lineages, such as the Rinzai, trace their ancestry back to Nangaku.

677

of their not standing against each other. You need to thoroughly explore through your training that there was such meritorious behavior as this.[2]

Their having passed away long ago and Their not having completely passed away are both the meritorious deeds of Old Buddhas. Through our training with our Master, we explore the words and ways of Old Buddhas so that we may awaken to the Truth of Old Buddhas, for They are Old Buddhas for generation after generation. Even though the 'old' of 'Old Buddhas' is the same as that in 'new and old', such Buddhas have gone beyond what is past and what is present; They stand squarely in both the past and the present.

My late Master once said, "I had an encounter with the Old Buddha Wanshi."[3] Clearly recognize that there was an Old Buddha residing under Tendō's roof, and there was a Tendō residing under the roof of an Old Buddha.

Meditation Master Engo once said, "I fully prostrate myself before Daikan Enō, a true Old Buddha." You need to know that you too should do a full prostration to Daikan Enō, our Ancestor of the thirty-third generation from Shakyamuni Buddha, for he is indeed an Old Buddha. Because Meditation Master Engo had the splendorous brightness of an Old Buddha, he had an encounter with an Old Buddha, which is why he made such a respectful bow. Accordingly, you need to know that when he relied on Enō's being a Buddha from head-to-toe as spiritual 'fodder', this was the Old

---

2. That is, it goes beyond a matter of choosing between the pairs by thinking that one is right and the other wrong, or of not choosing between them by not committing oneself to one of the two traditions.

3. Wanshi, who was once the Abbot of Mount Tendō, had died five years before Dōgen's Master, Tendō Nyojō, who was also an Abbot of Mount Tendō, was born. 'To have an encounter' with a Master refers to the mutual recognition between two people that each is 'such a person', that is, someone who has spiritually awakened.

Buddha's way of getting hold of the water buffalo's nose ring, for anyone who has hold of this nose ring is an Old Buddha.[4]

Sozan once said,[5] "Atop Daiyū Peak there is an Old Buddha. The radiance that He emits illumines this place of ours." You need to realize that what Sozan is saying is that he had already had an encounter with an Old Buddha. He did not have to seek elsewhere, for the place where his Old Buddha resided was atop Daiyū Peak. Those who are not an Old Buddha cannot recognize the place where an Old Buddha resides. Those who know the place where an Old Buddha resides will be an Old Buddha themselves.

Seppō once exclaimed, "Jōshū, the Old Buddha!" Keep in mind that even though Jōshū was an Old Buddha, if Seppō had not also experienced the abilities of an Old Buddha for himself, it would have been difficult for him to fully comprehend how to pay homage to an Old Buddha. Well, Seppō was an Old Buddha himself. In his daily conduct, he depended upon his spiritual abilities as an Old Buddha while he did his explorations into 'an Old Buddha'. And in doing so, he did not need to go looking for answers from others nor did he engage in conversing about such things. In other words, that old fellow Seppō was just fine! The day-to-day customs of an Old Buddha and the everyday behavior of an Old Buddha do not resemble those of someone who is not an Old Buddha, for the latter are simply not first class. As a consequence, you should explore through your training from start to finish just what sort of conduct Jōshū found to be good, and you should explore through your training what the lifetime of an Old Buddha is.

---

4. 'Getting hold of the water buffalo's nose ring' is a reference to getting a handle on one's spiritual question, and is an image found in the classic Zen Buddhist *Ten Ox-herding Pictures*.

5. Sozan Kōnin, not to be confused with Sōzan Honjaku, both of whom were disciples of Tōzan Ryōkai.

The National Teacher Echū of Kōtaku-ji Temple in the Western Capital was a Dharma heir of Daikan Enō.[6] He was respected and esteemed by both worldly and celestial emperors alike. Even in China, to encounter or hear of the likes of such a one was truly rare. Not only was he the teacher of four imperial generations, but the emperors themselves pulled his carriage to the imperial court with their own hands. And what is more, having been invited to the celestial palace of Lord Indra, he ascended far into the Trayastrimsha Heavens where he gave voice to the Dharma for the sake of the celestial emperor and others of the celestial multitudes.

The National Teacher was once asked by a monk, "Just what is an Old Buddha?"

He replied, "The tiles* and stones of His walls and fences."

In other words, the question is stating, in effect, "I am 'such a one'* and you are 'such a one.'" The monk has taken this statement of the Truth and turned it into a question. And this question has become an assertion of the Truth far and wide, in both the past and present.[7]

Consequently, a response such as, "The myriad trees and the hundreds of sproutings are blossomings of the Flower" is an assertion of the Truth by an Old Buddha. And the response, "The nine mountains and eight oceans that are the arising of our world" is the face of the Sun and the face of the Moon for an Old Buddha, just as Bodhidharma's response, "You have my Skin, Flesh, Bones, and Marrow," is also the countenance of the Sun and Moon for an Old Buddha. Moreover, there will be 'the Mind of Old', which is a Buddha doing His practice, and there will be 'the Mind of Old', which is His realizing Buddhahood, and there will be the 'oldness' of a Buddha,

---

6.   Although National Teacher Echū was a Dharma heir of Daikan Enō and had two Dharma heirs of his own, his line ultimately died out.

7.   That is, what the monk said could be understood not merely as a question but also as an statement: it is the 'What' that is what an Old Buddha is. This double use of the word 'what' has already occurred in several kōan stories that Dōgen presented earlier.

which is what is in His mind.[8] We call it 'the Mind of Old' because of the 'oldness' of the Mind. Because Mind and Buddha are positively 'old', the Mind of Old is synonymous with a chair, as well as with bamboo and trees.[9] It is synonymous with the saying, "It is impossible to find anyone who understands one bit of the Buddha Dharma, even though one may search the whole of the great earth." And it is synonymous with a Master calling It 'the What' in response to a monk asking, "What is It?" The causes and conditions of this very moment, as well as the various lands and empty space, are nothing other than the Mind of Old, for they maintain and depend on the Mind of Old, and they maintain and depend on Buddhas of old. They maintain and depend upon two heads having one countenance and on having two heads in one picture.[10]

The National Teacher replied to the monk, "The tiles and stones of his walls and fences."

In other words, his main point is that there is a way of proceeding that is expressed as 'the tiles and stones of one's walls and fences', and there is a way of proceeding that is the tiles and stones of one's walls and fences. And there will be yet another way of putting forth the Truth. And there is a way of pulling back whereby the tiles and stones of the walls and fences speak from within the tiles and stones of our walls and fences. In the full perfection and completeness from which these ways of expressing the Matter* fully manifest before our very eyes, there are walls rising up a thousand or ten thousand feet, and there are fences rising up that encircle the earth and encircle the heavens, and there is the covering up of the tiles all the way or

---

8.   What is in the mind of an Old Buddha is His or Her accumulated wisdom based on spiritual experience.

9.   In Dōgen's day and even earlier in China, the only chair in a Zen monastery or temple was that which served as the Dharma seat from which the Master gave the Teaching. Bamboo and various trees are also often used as metaphors for the Buddha Mind.

10. Two heads having one countenance refers to a picture of Shakyamuni Buddha which depicts Him as being seated in meditation with another head appearing atop His own. The second head represents That upon which Shakyamuni Buddha is meditating, that is, it represents Vairochana Buddha.

half the way, and there are the sharp edges of the stones, both big and small. What exists like this is not only our minds but also our bodies, including both our innate tendencies and our external conditions.

Thus, you should ask, "What, pray, are the tiles and stones of <u>my</u> walls and fences?" and you should also state what they are. And if you should enter into a colloquy with your Master about this question, the reply should be "The Mind of an Old Buddha." In maintaining and depending on the Matter in this way, you should also thoroughly explore through your training with your Master just what your walls and fences are, what you acknowledge your walls and fences to be, and just what forms and stages they are taking now. The following questions also need to be thoroughly explored, and in detail. Do you produce your walls and fences by building them up, or do your walls and fences bring forth their own building up? Are they deliberately built up or not? Do you treat them as something sentient, or as something non-sentient? Do they manifest before your very eyes or not? When you make an effort to explore the Matter through training in this way, the Mind of the Old Buddha—whether It exists in the celestial worlds above or among humankind, or has manifested Itself in this land or in other lands—will be the tiles and stones of your walls and fences. Not a single mote of dust has ever yet stuck out its head to taint It.

Great Master Zengen Chūkō was once asked by a monk, "Just what is the mind of an old Buddha?"

The Master responded, "His mind's world has caved in."

The monk then asked, "Why has his mind's world caved in?"

The Master replied, "Would you prefer that I put the Matter as 'he no longer has a self of his own?'"[11]

---

11.   What this kōan story and Dōgen's subsequent commentary point to is that becoming an Old Buddha means letting the 'world' that one's intellect (lower case 'mind') has created collapse, which includes letting go of the notion of a separate, unchanging, permanent 'self', as one lets go of a sense of being separate from one's Buddha Nature. In the story,

As to the 'world' of which he spoke, the ten directions all together comprise the world of a Buddha. And there has never yet been a world devoid of Buddha. As to the form and stages of caving in, you should explore the whole of this world in all ten quarters. Do not study 'the world's caving in' as being yourself, because in the course of training you do not explore it as your self.[12]

As to the very moment of your caving in, will you experience it as one thing or two things, or as three, four, or five things? It is inexhaustible things! Whatever these things may be, the Matter will be one that Zengen preferred to put as 'not having a self of one's own'. A 'self' is what an Old Buddha prefers not holding on to. Do not selfishly begrudge this very moment and fail to transform your own self into the Mind of an Old Buddha.

Truly, prior to the Seven Buddhas, the Mind of the Old Buddha stood erect as a wall; after the Seven Buddhas, the Mind of the Old Buddha put forth sprouts. Prior to all the Buddhas, the Mind of the Old Buddha blossomed; after all the Buddhas, the Mind of the Old Buddha bore fruit. Prior to the Mind of the Old Buddha arising, 'the mind of an old Buddha' has dropped off.

Delivered to the assembly on the twenty-ninth day of the fourth lunar month in the first year of the Kangen era (May 19, 1243) at the Temple of the Six Paramitas.[13]

Copied by me on the twelfth day of the fifth lunar month in the second year of the Kangen era (June 18, 1244) in the office of the Abbot's assistant in the hermitage below Kippō Peak.

Ejō

---

the monk is apparently a novice who has not yet clarified the difference between mind (intellect) and Mind (one's Buddha Nature) or between an old Buddha (a long-dead historical figure) and an Old Buddha (one who has realized Truth).

12. That is, to explore it as your 'self' is simply a matter of the intellect exploring the concept of a self, a concept which the intellect has created in the first place.

13. This temple is in Kyōto near the government office of one of Dōgen's chief supporters.

47

On the Four Exemplary Acts of a Bodhisattva

(Bodaisatta Shishōbō)

Translator's Introduction: The four exemplary acts are also known as the four wisdoms: charity, tenderness, benevolence, and sympathy.

> *The first is offering alms.*
> *The second is using kindly speech.*
> *The third is showing benevolence.*
> *The fourth is manifesting sympathy.*

Offering alms means not being covetous. Not being covetous means not being greedy. Not being greedy, to put it in worldly terms, includes not currying favors by groveling or flattery. If we want to bestow the Teaching of the Genuine Way, even if it were upon someone who rules over the four continents, we must do it without wanting anything in return. Offering alms, for example, is like bestowing upon strangers wealth that we freely part with. Were we to offer to the Tathagata flowers from a far-off mountain or give to some sentient being a treasure coming from a previous life— be it Dharma or something material—in either case, the act would be endowed with the merit that accords with the offering of alms. There is the principle that even though such things are not something that we personally own, it does not hinder our offering them as alms.[1] And the humbleness of such offerings is not to be despised, for it is the sincerity of these meritorious deeds that counts.

When we leave the Way to the Way, we realize the Way. When we realize the Way, the Way will invariably continue to be left to the Way. When treasures are left to being treasures, such treasures will invariably end up as alms offerings. We bestow 'self' on ourselves, and we bestow 'other' on others. The influence of this offering of

---

1. This refers to the giving of something that does not have any owner, such as the Dharma, or the grains of sand on a beach which a child once offered. These types of offering are beyond the concept of 'ownership'.

alms not only penetrates far into the realms of those in lofty positions and of those who are ordinary people, but also permeates the realms of the wise and the saintly. This is because when people have become capable of accepting an offering of alms, they have therefore already formed a link with the donor.

The Buddha once remarked, "When a donor comes into a monastic assembly, others admire that person right from the start. You should realize that they have tacitly understood the heart of that person." As a consequence, should we offer only one sentence or one verse of the Dharma as alms, it will become a good seed in this life and in future lives. Should we offer the gift of even a single coin or a single blade of grass as alms, it will sprout good roots in this generation and in future generations. Dharma can be wealth and wealth can be Dharma—which it is depends on our wish and our pleasure.

Truly, bestowing one's beard on another once put someone's mind in order, and an offering of a few grains of sand once gained someone the rank of king.[2] These people did not covet some reward, but simply shared what they had. Providing a ferry or building a bridge as an alms offering creates a way to the Other Shore. When we have learned well what the offering of alms means, then we can see that accepting oneself and letting go of oneself are both offerings of alms. Earning a living and doing productive work have never been anything other than an offering of alms. Leaving flowers to float upon the wind and leaving birds to sing in their season will also be meritorious training in almsgiving. Upon his deathbed, the great King Ashoka offered half of a mango to several hundred monks as alms. As persons who are capable of accepting alms, we need to explore well the principle that this great alms gift points to. Not only should we make physical efforts to give alms, but we should also not overlook opportunities to do so. Truly, because we have inherited the merit from having given alms in past lives, we have obtained the human body that we now have.

---

2.   During the T'ang dynasty, when an officer in the court of Emperor T'ai-tsung fell ill and needed the ashes from a beard for medicine, the emperor burnt his own beard and offered the ashes to the officer. Once when the Buddha was on an alms round, a child who was playing in the sand put a few grains in the Buddha's alms bowl as an offering, and, due to this act, the child was later reborn as King Ashoka.

"Even if you give alms to yourselves, there can be merit, and how much more so were you to give alms to your parents, spouse, or children!" As a consequence of this statement, I have realized that even giving to oneself is a part of almsgiving, and giving to one's parents, spouse, or children will be almsgiving as well. Should we let go of a single dust mote of defiling passion as an alms offering, even though it is done for our own sake, we will feel a quiet, heartfelt gratitude because we will have had one of the meritorious deeds of Buddhas genuinely Transmitted to us, and because, for the first time, we will be practicing one of the methods of bodhisattvas.[*]

What is truly hard to turn around is the heart and mind of sentient beings. By making one offering, we begin to turn their mental state around, after which we hope to keep turning it around until they realize the Way. From this beginning, we should by all means continue to assist them by making alms offerings. This is why the first of the Six Paramitas is the Almsgiving Paramita.[3] The size of any mind is beyond measure: the size of any thing is also beyond measure. Be that as it may, there are times when the mind turns things around and there is also the practice of almsgiving, whereby things turn the mind around.

Kindly speech means that when we encounter sentient beings, we first of all give rise to feelings of genuine affection for them and offer them words that express our pleasure in knowing them. To put it more broadly, we do not use language that is harsh or rude. Even in secular society there are respectful customs for asking others how they are; in Buddhism there is the Master's phrase, "May you take good care of yourself," and there is the disciple's greeting, "I have been wondering how you've been doing." To speak with a feeling of genuine affection for sentient beings, as if they were still new-born babes, is what kindly speech is. We should praise those who have virtue and pity those who do not.

---

[*]   See Glossary.

3.   A paramita is a practice that Buddhas and bodhisattvas employ to help sentient beings reach the Other Shore. The six are almsgiving, observance of the Precepts, patient forbearance, diligence, being well-seated in one's meditation, and wise discernment.

Through our having fondness for kindly speech, kindly speech gradually increases. Thus, even kindly speech that goes unrecognized or unnoticed will still manifest itself right before us. While our present life persists, we should become fond of speaking kindly, so that we do not regress or turn away from it for generation after generation and for life after life. Kindly speech is the foundation for overcoming those who are angry and hostile, as well as for promoting harmony among others. When we hear kindly speech that is spoken directly to us, it brightens our countenance and delights our heart. When we hear of kind speech having been spoken about us in our absence, this makes a deep impression on our heart and our spirit. Keep in mind that kindly speech arises from a loving heart, and a loving heart makes compassion its seed. You should explore the idea that kindly speech can have the power to turn the very heavens around, <u>and</u> it is not merely a matter of praising someone's abilities.

Showing benevolence means working out skillful methods by which to benefit sentient beings, be they of high or low station. One may do this, for instance, by looking at someone's future prospects, both immediate and far-ranging, and then practicing skillful means to help that person. Someone once took pity on a stricken turtle and another once tended to a sick sparrow.[4] Neither of these people was seeking a reward; they simply acted from a feeling of benevolence.

---

4.   There is a classic Chinese story in which a man rescued a trapped turtle. As the turtle swam off, it looked back over its shoulder to its benefactor, as if to acknowledge its indebtedness. Later, the man rose to a high official position, and, when the seal of his office was cast, it miraculously appeared in the form of a turtle looking over its back. No matter how many times the seal was recast to remove the form, it would nevertheless reappear on the seal. Finally, the man realized that somehow the turtle had played a part in his having received his appointment, so he kept the strange seal out of gratitude.

   In another classic Chinese story, there was a boy who helped a sick sparrow recover and to whom the sparrow gave four silver rings as recompense, which ultimately led to the boy's being appointed to three high government positions.

Some people may foolishly think that if they were to put the welfare of others first, their own benefits would be reduced. This is not so. Benevolence is all-encompassing, universally benefiting both self and others. A person long ago bound up his hair three times during the course of his taking a single bath, and thrice spat out what he had in his mouth during the course of a single meal. And he did so solely from a heart that would benefit others. He was not reluctant to instruct his son to do so, if his son should encounter guests from a foreign land.[5] So, we should act to benefit equally both those who are hostile and those who are friendly, and act for the benefit of both self and other alike. When we attain such an attitude of mind, our showing of benevolence will neither retreat nor turn away from anything, and this benevolence will be shown even towards grass and trees, wind and water. And, in all humility, we should engage ourselves in helping those who are given to foolishness.

Manifesting sympathy means not making differences, not treating yourself as different and not treating others as different. For instance, the Tathagata was a human being just like other human beings. From His being the same as those in the human world, we know that He must have been the same as those in any other world. When we really understand what manifesting sympathy means, we will see that self and other are one and the same. Music, poetry, and wine have been companions for ordinary people, companions for those in lofty positions, and companions for the hosts of celestial beings. And there is the principle that ordinary people have been companions for music, poetry, and wine. And music, poetry, and wine have been companions for music, poetry, and wine. And ordinary people have been companions for ordinary people. And those in lofty positions have been companions for those in lofty positions. And celestial beings have been companions for celestial beings. This is what studying 'manifesting sympathy' means.

---

5.   A Chinese ruler once advised his son that if three guests were to come calling in
      succession while he was bathing, he should bind up his hair each time and go to greet
      them, and if three guests were to come calling in succession while he was dining, he
      should stop eating each time in order to greet them.

In particular, what the 'manifesting' in manifesting sympathy refers to is our ways of behaving, our everyday actions, and our attitudes of mind. In this manifesting, there will be the principle of letting people identify with us and of letting ourselves identify with others. Depending on the occasion, there are no boundaries between self and other.

It says in the *Kuan-tsu*,[6] "A sea does not reject water, and therefore is able to bring about its vastness. A mountain does not reject soil, and therefore can bring about its height. An enlightened ruler does not despise ordinary people, and therefore can bring about a large populace." You need to realize that a sea's not rejecting water is its being in sympathy with water. Further, you need to realize that the water has the complete virtue of not refusing the sea. For that reason, it is possible for waters to come together and form a sea, and for earth to pile up and form a mountain. And you certainly know for yourself that because one sea does not reject another sea, it forms an ocean, which is something much bigger. And because one mountain does not reject another mountain, it forms a larger mountain, which is something much higher. And because an enlightened ruler does not despise ordinary people, he creates a large populace. A large populace means a nation. An enlightened ruler means an emperor. An emperor does not despise people. And even though he does not despise people, it does not mean that there are no rewards and punishments. And even though there are rewards and punishments, they do not come about because he despises people. Long ago, when people were submissive, nations were without rewards or punishments— at least to the extent that rewards and punishments then were not the same as those of today. Even today, there may be people who seek the Way without expecting any reward, but this is beyond what foolish people concern themselves with. Because an enlightened ruler is clear-minded, he does not despise people. Although people invariably form nations and try to seek out an enlightened leader, nevertheless those who completely understand the principle of what makes an enlightened ruler 'enlightened' are rare. As a result, even though they are happy enough about not being despised by an enlightened ruler, they do not comprehend that they mutually should not despise their enlightened ruler. As a consequence, there is the principle of

6.   A multi-volumed Chinese Taoist work.

manifesting sympathy which is for both enlightened rulers and unenlightened people. This is why bodhisattvas vow to practice manifesting sympathy. And to do so, they need but face all things with a gentle demeanor.

Because each of these four exemplary acts completely encompasses all four exemplary acts, there will be, all told, sixteen exemplary acts.

Written down on the day of the Tango Festival in the fourth year of the Ninji era (May 24, 1243).

> *Written by the mendicant monk Dōgen*
> *who entered Sung China and received*
> *the Transmission of the Dharma*

On the Vines That Entangle: the Vines That Embrace
(Kattō)

Translator's Introduction: The term '*kattō*' literally means 'the kudzu and the wisteria', and it refers to two vines that grow by wrapping themselves around, say, a tree or a post. While the term serves as a common metaphor in both secular and Buddhist writings with the negative connotation of 'complications', 'difficulties', and 'that which we get entangled with', Dōgen extends its meaning in this discourse to describe, in a positive sense, the complex and complicated intertwining of the Master-disciple relationship.

Shakyamuni Buddha, who experienced the great, unsurpassed enlightenment, passed on the Treasure House of the Eye of the True Teaching only to Great Master Makakashō from amongst all of the assembly on the Divine Vulture Peak. Successor after successor experienced this genuine realization of the Truth, and It ultimately came down to the Venerable Bodhidharma in the twenty-eight generation. Following the example of the Ancestors, whilst Bodhidharma was in China he passed on the Treasure House of the Eye of the True Teaching to our Great Ancestor Eka, the fully awakened Great Master of the genuine lineage, thereby making him the Second Chinese Ancestor. The Twenty-eighth Ancestor, who was the first in China to act in accord with the behavior of the Ancestors, is called the First Chinese Ancestor, whereas Eka, as the Ancestor of the twenty-ninth generation, is called the Second Chinese Ancestor, as is the custom in the lands east of India.

After Bodhidharma had spiritually awakened, he received the Transmission of the very Marrow of the Buddha's instructions from the Venerable Hannyatara. Bodhidharma subsequently came to recognize the roots of his delusions because of these very roots, which he had previously used as the foundation for the proliferation of his delusions.

Generally speaking, the saintly all devise some method of training whereby they sever the roots of whatever vines are entangling them. But they might not explore how to cut off entangling vines by using the very vines themselves, for they may not have used these embracing vines as the means to understand their being entangled. So how could they possibly understand the inheriting of vines and the succession of vines by means of these embracing vines? It is rare for any to recognize that the inheritance of the Dharma is synonymous with embracing vines, and, since none of them have heard about it, none have yet expressed it this way. Surely, there could not possibly be many who have experienced it!

My former Master, an Old Buddha, once said, "The vines of the bottle gourd embrace the bottle gourd itself." This teaching that he gave to his assembly is something that had never been encountered or heard of anywhere in the past or present. The vines of the bottle gourd intertwining with the vines of the bottle gourd is the Buddhas and Ancestors thoroughly exploring what Buddhas and Ancestors are. It is the Buddhas and Ancestors realizing that there is no difference between the awakening of a Buddha and the awakening of an Ancestor. It has been referred to as the direct Transmission of the Dharma from Mind to Mind.

In speaking to his disciples, our Twenty-eighth Ancestor Bodhidharma said, "It seems that my time is near at hand, so why don't you express what you have realized?"

His disciple Dōfuku then said, "As I now see things, I am not attached to words nor have I given up words. I just make use of them."

The Ancestor replied, "You have realized what my Skin is."

The female monk Sōji said, "As I now understand things, it is like Ananda's catching sight of Akshobya's Buddha Land. Once seen, it is not seen again."

The Ancestor replied, "You have realized what my Flesh is."

Dōiku said, "The four elements,* from the first, are empty of any permanent self-nature, and the five skandhas* lack permanent existence. So, from my perspective, there is not one single thing to be realized."

The Ancestor replied, "You have realized what my Bones are."

Finally, Eka respectfully made three prostrations before the Ancestor and then silently stood in his place.

The Ancestor said, "You have realized what my Marrow is." As might be expected, he made Eka the Second Chinese Ancestor, Transmitting to him the Dharma and the kesa.*

What you need to explore through your training is that our First Chinese Ancestor's statement, "You have realized my Skin, Flesh, Bones, and Marrow," is what the Ancestor said. Each of his four disciples, respectively, expressed what they had realized; each demonstrated what they had learned. What they all had realized is the Skin and Flesh, Bones and Marrow which sprang forth from their own body and mind. It is the Skin and Flesh, Bones and Marrow of 'dropping off body and mind'. This is beyond anything that someone can gather from an Ancestral Master by means of intellectual understanding based on observation, which is simply comparable to one move in a game of *Go*. Likewise, it is not something that fully manifests before one's eyes as subject and object, or as this and that. At the same time, folks who have not experienced the genuine Transmission fancy that there were relative degrees of intimacy in what each of the four disciples comprehended, so that what the Ancestor was saying was that skin, flesh, bones, and marrow are not the same in their profundity. They think that skin and flesh are coarser than bones and marrow, and they say that the discerning thought of the Second Ancestor had surpassed that of the others, so that he alone obtained the certification of knowing what the marrow was. Those who talk like this have still not explored through their training what the

---

* See Glossary.

Buddhas and Ancestors are, nor have they experienced the genuine Transmission of which the Ancestors speak.

You need to recognize that the Skin, Flesh, Bones, and Marrow of which the Ancestor spoke are beyond being characterized as shallow or deep. Even though people's intellectual abilities may be superior or inferior, what the Ancestor said is simply a matter of the disciple's having realized 'what I truly am'. The fundamental principle here is that, in his saying to one disciple "You have realized what my Marrow is" while saying to another "You have realized what my Bones are," these statements are both beyond a matter of adequacy or inadequacy when it comes to giving spiritual guidance to people, or when 'pulling up one's weeds and then letting go of them'. For instance, it is like the Buddha's raising the flower or passing on His kesa.[1] What was uttered for the sake of the four disciples was, to begin with, essentially one and the same thing. And even though what the Ancestor said to each was essentially one and the same thing, this does not necessarily mean that their four understandings were essentially one and the same. Even though their four understandings were individually distinct, what the Ancestor said is simply what the Ancestor said.

Generally speaking, what is said and what is understood may not necessarily be identical. For instance, in expressing the Matter* to his four disciples, the Ancestral Master was asserting, "You have realized me as 'Me in the flesh.'" Even if there were a hundred thousand disciples after the Second Ancestor, there would be a hundred thousand ways of stating It, for the ways are inexhaustible. Since there were only four disciples to hear what he said, there were, for the moment, just the four expressions of 'Skin', 'Flesh', 'Bones', and 'Marrow', but there remain ways that were not yet expressed, for there are many ways to express the Matter.

You need to realize that even though Bodhidharma expressed the Dharma in the way he did for the sake of the Second Ancestor, he could also have expressed It as

1. The first reference is to the Transmission of Makakashō, wherein the Buddha raised a flower and Makakashō, realizing the deeper meaning behind the gesture, broke into a smile, which set the Buddha's eyes to twinkling in recognition. The second reference is to the Buddha's passing on His kesa to Makakashō when confirming him as His Dharma heir.

"You have realized what my Skin is." Even if he had said to Eka, "You have realized what my Skin is," the First Ancestor would have been Transmitting the Treasure House of the Eye of the True Teaching to him as the Second Ancestor, since 'realizing what the Skin is' and 'realizing what the Marrow is' are not based on either being superior or inferior.

Also, in expressing the Dharma in the way he did for the sake of Dōfuku, Dōiku, Sōji, or anyone else, he could have stated, "You have realized what my Marrow is." Even though he may say 'what my Skin is' to them, he will still be Transmitting the Teaching to them. The Body and Mind of the Ancestral Master is the Ancestral Master along with his skin, flesh, bones, and marrow. This is beyond considering the marrow to be an intimate part of him while viewing the skin as something distant from him.

Now, when someone who has an eye for exploring the Matter through training with a Master receives the certification of "You have realized what my Skin is," it is the result of that person's taking their training to the utmost, which 'gets' him or her the Ancestral Master. There are Ancestral Masters whose whole being is Skin, and Ancestral Masters whose whole being is Flesh, and Ancestral Masters whose whole being is Bones, and Ancestral Masters whose whole being is Marrow. And there are Ancestral Masters whose whole being is Mind, and Ancestral Masters whose whole being is Body, and Ancestral Masters whose whole mind is Mind, and Ancestral Masters who are Ancestral Masters through and through, and Ancestral Masters whose whole being 'has realized my You', and so on.[2] If there were a time when these Ancestral Masters appeared simultaneously and expressed the Dharma for the sake of a hundred thousand disciples, they might voice It as "You have realized my Skin." Even if their hundred thousand ways of voicing It were 'Skin, Flesh, Bones, and Marrow', bystanders and onlookers will vainly assume that these Masters are literally talking about skin, flesh, bones, and marrow. If an Ancestral Master were to have six

---

2.   The phrase 'has realized my You' expresses the oneness of Master and disciple from the perspective of the Master, just as "you have realized what my Skin is" expresses it from the perspective of the disciple towards the Master. Both expressions refer to the transcendence of 'self and other'.

or seven disciples within his assembly, he might employ some expression such as "You have realized what my Mind is" or "You have realized what my Body is." Or he might employ an expression like "You have realized what my Buddha Dharma is," or "You have realized what my Eye is," or "You have realized what my realization is." There are times when this so-called 'you' is the Ancestor and times when it is Eka. Thoroughly explore in detail the principle underlying the words 'you have realized'.

You need to realize that there will be a 'you having realized Me', and a 'me having realized You', and a 'realizing me being You', and a 'realizing you being Me'. In delving into the Body and Mind of the Ancestral Master, if you say that what lies within him and what lies outside him cannot be all of a oneness or that his whole Body cannot be his whole being, you are not in the land where Buddhas and Ancestors manifest. To have realized what the Skin is means to have realized what Bones, Flesh, and Marrow are. To have realized what Bones, Flesh, and Marrow are is to have realized what Skin, Flesh, and Countenance are. How could such a state as this be anything other than an understanding, as clear as a full dawning, of Master Chōsa Keishin's saying, "The whole universe in all directions is our Real, True Body?" Moreover, It is skin and flesh, bones and marrow. Consequently, It is 'realizing what my kesa is' and 'your having realized what the Dharma is'. Accordingly, even saying the words is a series of instances of 'springing out from delusion': Master and disciple harmonize and are equal. Even hearing the words is a series of instances of 'springing out from delusion': Master and disciple harmonize and are equal. The thorough harmonizing and equalizing of Master and disciple is the complicated, embracing kudzu and wisteria vines of the Buddhas and Ancestors. Shakyamuni's raising aloft the flower, His eyes atwinkle, is none other than the vines of kudzu and wisteria: Makakashō's breaking out into a smile is none other than Skin and Flesh, Bones and Marrow.

Moreover, you should thoroughly explore through your training that, just as the offspring of entangling vines have the capacity to drop off self, so also do branches and leaves, flowers and fruit appear, which all follow along with kudzu and wisteria vines. And because the offspring may be seen as dependent and, at the same time, independent of the vines, Buddhas and Ancestors manifest and our spiritual question appears before our very eyes.

Great Master Jōshū Shinsai, in instructing his assembly, once said, "Makakashō gave the Transmission to Ananda. Right now, say to what person did Bodhidharma give the Transmission?"

Thereupon, a monk asked him, "Well, what about the Second Ancestor, didn't he get the marrow?"

The Master replied, "Do not engage in slandering the Second Ancestor."

The Master said further, "Remember what Bodhidharma also said, that someone who is located on the outside realizes what the Skin is, whereas someone who is located on the inside realizes what the Bones are. Right now, say what someone who is located even further within realizes!"

A monk asked, "What is this 'realizing what the marrow is' really about anyway?"

The Master replied, "Just keep your focus on the Skin. For an old monk like me, the question of marrow doesn't even arise."

The monk asked, "But what is the marrow?"

The Master replied, "If that's the way things are for you, then you're still groping about for the Skin."

Accordingly, keep in mind that when you are still groping about for the Skin, you are still groping about for the Marrow, and in realizing what the Skin is through your groping, you also realize what the Marrow is. You should work diligently on the principle of "If that's the way things are for you, then you're still groping about for the Skin." In the monk's skeptically asking, "What is this 'realizing what the marrow is' <u>really</u> about anyway?" there emerged Jōshū's response of "Just keep your focus on the Skin. For an old monk like me, the question of marrow doesn't even arise." When someone focuses on the Skin, the marrow's not even coming up is what 'having realized what the Marrow is' really is. The doubting question of, "What about the Second Ancestor, didn't he realize what the marrow is?" arose because the monk was not focusing on the Skin. When we simply look at the occasion when Makakashō gave the Transmission to Ananda, it involved Ananda 'concealing His Body' in Makakashō and Makakashō 'concealing His Body' in Ananda.[3] Even so, at the time when the two 'see' each other within the giving of Transmission, they do not escape from their everyday behavior, which alters their countenance and their skin, flesh, bones, and marrow. This is why Jōshū made the remark, "Right now, say It! Bodhidharma gave the Transmission to a person of What!"[4] At the time when Bodhidharma gave the Transmission, he was Bodhidharma, and when the Second Chinese Ancestor realized the Marrow, he was Bodhidharma. As we thoroughly explore this principle, we see that the Buddha Dharma, right up to this very day, is still the Buddha Dharma. If this were not so, the Buddha Dharma would not have come down to us today. Through exploring this principle carefully and diligently, we should learn how to express it ourselves and we should teach others how to express it.

Jōshū also said that Bodhidharma remarked, "Someone who is located on the outside realizes what the Skin is, whereas someone who is located on the inside realizes what the Bones are. Right now, say what someone who is located even further within realizes!" The essential meaning of the 'outside' and 'inside' spoken of here is extremely straightforward. When we discuss 'outside', then Skin and Flesh, Bones and Marrow have their outside: when we discuss 'inside', then Skin and Flesh, Bones and Marrow have their inside. Accordingly, his four disciple Bodhidharmas, all together, had thoroughly explored, instance by instance, hundreds of thousands of myriad spiritually awakened states of Skin, Flesh, Bones, and Marrow. Do not imagine that there cannot be states above and beyond that of Marrow, for there are three or maybe even five states above and beyond that.

---

3.   'To conceal His Body in someone else' is a Zen Buddhist expression for someone's recognizing the Buddhahood of another.

4.   Jōshū's remark contains a play on words often found in Zen kōan stories. The phrase *jūmo no hito*, rendered earlier in its conventional meaning as 'what person' (thus making Jōshū's remark a question), is understood in a Zen context as 'a person of What', that is, a person whose state is beyond the ability of words to convey. This latter meaning changes Jōshū's remark into an assertion for his disciple to respond to.

The Old Buddha Jōshū was pointing out to his assembly just precisely what the Way of the Buddha is. This is beyond what others like Rinzai, Tokusan, Isan, and Ummon attained. It is something that they had never even dreamt of, much less expressed. It is something that present-day monastic 'old-timers' who are given to wild talk do not know even exists, and if we were to explain it to them, they would be startled and grow fearful.

Meditation Master Setchō Jukēn once said, "The two Masters—Jōshū and Bokushū—are examples of what it means to be an Old Buddha." Accordingly, the words of Old Buddhas are Their awakened experience of Buddha Dharma and Their own personal ways of putting the Matter which They uttered in the past. Great Master Seppō Shinkaku once exclaimed, "Jōshū, the Old Buddha!" A previous Ancestor of the Buddha also praised Jōshū by eulogizing him as an Old Buddha, and a later Ancestor of the Buddha eulogized him as an Old Buddha as well. Obviously, they are saying that he is an Old Buddha who has gone beyond any spiritually awakened state attained by others of the past or present.

Consequently, the fundamental principle is that Skin and Flesh, Bones and Marrow embrace us like the vines of kudzu and wisteria. This is the standard of the statement "You have realized what I truly am," which Old Buddhas point out to Their assembly. Explore this criterion thoroughly and diligently.

Also, some say that the First Ancestor returned to the West, but through our training we learn that is inaccurate. Undoubtedly, what the monk Sōun saw could not have been literally real.[5] How could Sōun possibly have encountered the goings and comings of the Ancestral Master? Simply take as the correct study that after the parinirvana of the First Chinese Ancestor, his ashes were consigned to Bear's Ear Mountain.

---

5.   The monk Sōun, upon his return to China from an imperially supported visit to India for the purpose of collecting Buddhist writings, claimed to have met Bodhidharma upon the Silk Road. This event occurred three years after Bodhidharma's death. Crown Prince Shōtoku spoke of a similar encounter with Bodhidharma in Japan. These encounters may have occurred in some sense other than a literal one.

Delivered to the assembly on the seventh day of the seventh lunar month in the first year of the Kangen era (July 25, 1243) at Kannondōri in Kōshōhōrin-ji Temple, Uji Prefecture, Yamashiro Province.

Copied by me on the third day of the third lunar month in the second year of the Kangen era (April 11, 1244) in the office of the Abbot's chief assistant at Kippō-ji Temple, Yoshida Prefecture, Echizen Province.

Ejō

48

On 'The Threefold World Is Simply Your Mind'

(Sangai Yuishin)

Translator's Introduction: The title of this discourse comes from the first line of a verse passage in the *Avatamsaka Scripture*, which Dōgen takes as his theme. The threefold world is comprised of three spiritual states, the names of which are often rendered in English translations as those of desire, form, and beyond form. The world of desire is associated with the six worlds of existence: human, hellish, animal, hungry ghost, fighting spirits, plus the six lowest of the celestial realms. The world of form is associated with four higher celestial realms in which carnal appetites have dropped off. The world beyond form is associated with the four uppermost celestial realms wherein there is only the enjoyment of meditative states. The main theme of this discourse is that these three 'worlds', all together, comprise the whole of existence, with nothing beyond them, and that they are all constructs of our own mind.

Our Great Master Shakyamuni once said in verse:

> *The threefold world is simply our one, whole Mind,*
> *For there is nothing apart from the Mind.*
> *Our mind, Buddha, and all sentient beings—*
> *These three are indistinguishable from each other.*

What He expressed in this single verse is the whole effort of His lifetime, and this whole effort of His lifetime was the whole of all His efforts. While these efforts were actions that were done deliberately, they must have been actions that were the free functioning of His words and deeds. Therefore the statement, "The three worlds are simply our one, whole Mind," which the Tathagata voiced, is the full manifestation of the whole Tathagata, and the whole of His lifetime is the whole of this one verse. The three worlds constitute our whole world and, at the same time, we do not say that the three worlds are what our mind is. That is why the three worlds are still a threefold world however much they may resemble the brilliance of a crystal jewel which pervades all directions.[1]

Although some may make the mistake of thinking that the mind is beyond the three worlds, this is totally impossible. The spaces of inside, outside, and in between, as well as the times of beginning, middle, and end—all are encompassed by the threefold world. The threefold world is just what is seen as the threefold world. And what is viewed as something beyond the threefold world is a misperception of the threefold world. The threefold world is viewed by some as 'an old nesting place' whereas others may see it as 'a new item'.[2] 'Old nests' and 'new items' are but different views of the same threefold world. This is why our Great Master Shakyamuni Buddha once said, "It is best to see the threefold world as the threefold world." What is looked at in this way is what the threefold world really is, and this threefold world is just as we perceive it to be. The threefold world is not one's fundamental being, nor is it our present existence, nor is it something that newly arises, nor is it something born from causes and conditions, and it is beyond anything that has a beginning, a middle, or an end. There is the threefold world that is left behind and there is the threefold world of the here and now. This is the mutual meeting of a marionette with a marionette.[3] It is the bringing forth and nurturing of kudzu and wisteria vines.[4] The threefold world of the here and now is what we see as the threefold world. 'What we see' means our seeing the threefold world as a threefold world. 'Seeing it as a threefold world' refers to the threefold world as it manifests right before us, as we manifest it right before us, and as our spiritual question manifests right before our very eyes. We

---

1.   This particular reference to a jewel-like brilliance occurs in Zen texts to describe the penetrating brilliance and clarity of the original state of one's mind.

2.   'An old nesting place' is a common Zen metaphor for a habitual, erroneous viewpoint, whereas 'a new item' refers to seeing things anew with enlightened eyes.

3.   A marionette, or wooden figure, is sometimes used metaphorically in Zen texts to refer to someone who has awakened to his True Nature and is no longer 'pulling the strings'.

4.   'Kudzu and wisteria vines' here refers to the Master-disciple relationship. Dōgen explores this metaphor in Discourse 47: On the Vines That Entangle: the Vines That Embrace (*Kattō*).

all innately have the ability to make the threefold world be the vehicle for the arising of our spiritual intention, our practice and training, our realizing enlightenment, and our experiencing nirvana. This is why our Great Master Shakyamuni once said in verse:

> *These three worlds, right now,*
> *Are what we all innately have,*
> *And all sentient beings within them,*
> *Without exception, are My children.*

Because these three worlds here and now are what the Tathagata innately had, the whole universe was His threefold world, because the threefold world <u>is</u> the whole universe. 'Here and now' encompasses the past, present, and future. The occurring of past, present, and future does not obstruct the here and now, but the occurring of the here and now does obstruct past, present, and future from arising.

That which 'we innately have' refers to the whole universe in all ten directions being our real, true Body. It refers to the whole universe in all ten directions being a mendicant monk's Eye. 'Sentient beings' are real, true bodies of the whole universe in all ten directions. Because each and every sentient being is born sentient, they are called 'sentient beings'.

'Without exception, they are My children' means that children are also manifestations of the ceaseless operation of Buddha Nature. Even so, of necessity, children receive their bodies, along with their hair and skin, all unharmed and unbroken, from a compassionate parent. Parents regard this as the child's fully manifesting. Yet, at this present moment, since there is no parent who is before and no child who is after, nor a child who is before and a parent who is after, nor a parent and child being lined up beside each other, we call this the principle of 'My children'. Although the body is not something that is given, we receive it; although it is not something that we snatch, we acquire it. It is beyond the characteristics of coming and going, beyond the measure of large and small, beyond discussions of old and young. We should hold to it like the 'old' and 'young' of the Buddhas and Ancestors. Sometimes there is a parent who is 'young' and a child who is 'old', or a parent who is 'old' and a child who is 'young', or a parent who is 'old' and a child who is 'old', or a parent who is 'young' and a child who is 'young'. One who makes a study of his parent's 'agedness' would not be a child; one who has not seen through the 'youthfulness' of his child would not be a parent. The 'age' and 'youth' of a child, as well as the 'age' and 'youth' of a parent, must be fully explored, in detail, and without haste.

There are parents and children for whom the parent-child relationship emerges at the same time, and there are those for whom the parent-child relationship disappears at the same time, and there are those for whom the parent-child relationship emerges at different times, and there are those for whom the parent-child relationship disappears at different times. Without standing against the compassionate parent, one has brought forth 'my child', and without standing against 'my child', one has brought forth the compassionate parent. There are sentient beings who are mindful, and there are sentient beings who are not mindful; there is my child who is mindful, and there is my child who is not mindful. In this manner, my child and I —and I am also a child—are both the true heirs of our Compassionate Parent Shakyamuni. All beings of the past, present, and future in the whole universe—every last one of them—are the Buddhas of past, present, and future in the whole universe. The children of all Buddhas are sentient beings, and the Compassionate Parents of all sentient beings are Buddhas. Consequently, the flowering and fruiting of the hundreds of things that arise are what all Buddhas have as Their own, and the rocks and stones, large and small, are what all Buddhas have as Their own as well. Their peaceful places are the forests and fields, for They are already free of attachment to forests and fields. Be that as it may, the main point of what the Tathagata said was simply the phrase 'My children'. You need to thoroughly explore that He never spoke of His being their parent.

Shakyamuni Buddha once said:

> Even the three Bodies of all Buddhas do not extend beyond the threefold world.[5] Since no sentient being exists outside the threefold world, why would there be some other place where the Buddha would transform Himself for their sake? Therefore, I say that the assertion that there is another world of sentient beings outside of the threefold world is a teaching from the non-Buddhist *Scripture on the Greater Existence,* and it is not what has been voiced by the Seven Buddhas.*

You should clarify through your thorough exploration with your Master that the three Bodies of all Buddhas are these three worlds. Nothing exists outside of these three worlds. For example, just as nothing exists outside the Tathagata, so too nothing exists outside of our walls and fences. And just as nothing exists outside of training, so too nothing exists outside of being a sentient being. Were there no sentient beings, who is it that could be converted by a Buddha? What is being converted by a Buddha is always a sentient being. Keep in mind that the saying, "Outside the threefold world, there is another world of sentient beings," is a product of the non-Buddhist *Scripture on the Greater Existence.*

The one, whole Mind is beyond being just one or two things. It is beyond the threefold world and beyond departing from the threefold world. It is beyond 'making mistakes'. It has the knowledge obtained from one's discriminating and It is not bound by that knowledge. It is the tiles* and stones of our walls and fences and It is the great earth with its mountains and rivers. Mind is synonymous with Skin and Flesh, Bones

---

5   These three Bodies of the Buddha (Skt. *Trikaya*) are: 1) The Truth Body (Skt. *Dharmakaya*), which represents Absolute Truth or Buddha Mind Itself. 2) The Reward Body (Skt. *Sambhogakaya*), which represents the blissful reward of Buddhist training. 3) The Transformation Body (Skt. *Nirmanakaya*), which is the physical body of the Buddha as It appears in the world.

*   See Glossary.

and Marrow; Mind is synonymous with holding the flower aloft and breaking into a smile.[6] There is the mind of attachment and the mind free from attachments. There is the embodied mind and there is the Mind beyond body. There is the mind that comes before the body, and there is the mind that comes after the body. When a body is born, it will be from a womb, from an egg, from moisture, or from some transformation. When a mind emerges, it will be from a womb, from an egg, from moisture, or from some transformation. Blue, yellow, red, and white are what the Mind is. Long and short, square and round are what the Mind is. Birth and death, coming and going, are what the Mind is. Years, months, days, and hours are what the Mind is. Dreams, visions, and flowers in the sky are what the Mind is. Water bubbles, foam, and flame are what the Mind is. The spring flowers and the autumn moon are what the Mind is. Our day-to-day moments are what the Mind is. Even so, It cannot be destroyed. For this reason, the Mind is the real appearance of all thoughts and things. The Mind is each Buddha on His own, along with all other Buddhas.

Great Master Gensha Shibi once asked his disciple Jizō Keichin, "Just how do you understand the saying 'The threefold world is simply your mind?'"

Pointing to a chair, Keichin said, "When naming that thing, Venerable Monk, what do you take it to be?"

The Great Master said, "A chair."

Keichin then said, "Venerable Monk, you do not understand 'The threefold world is simply your mind.'"[7]

---

6   This is a reference to the Transmission of the Dharma from Shakyamuni Buddha, who held aloft an udumbara blossom, to his smiling disciple Makakashō.

7.   Despite this remark's implication that the Master is lacking in some way, it actually has a positive meaning, namely, that the Master's understanding goes beyond a merely intellectual one.

> The Great Master replied, "When giving a name to that thing, I see it as bamboo and wood. When you name it, what do you take it to be?"
>
> Keichin responded, "When I name it, I also take it to be bamboo and wood."
>
> The Great Master then said, "Were we to search the whole of the great earth for somebody who understood Buddha Dharma, we would not be able to find a single one." [8]

Now, let us look at the Great Master's question, "Just how do you understand the saying 'The threefold world is simply your mind?'" Whether one has a way of understanding this saying or not, both states are synonymous with the threefold world being simply one's own mind. This is why the threefold world may not yet be 'simply one's mind'. [9] And this is why Keichin pointed to a chair and said, "When naming that thing, Venerable Monk, what do you take it to be?" You need to understand that "What do you take it to be?" means "How do you go about naming it?"

As to the 'chair' that the Great Master spoke of, we should also add, "Did he understand the term 'the threefold world' or not?" and "Is the chair synonymous with the term 'the threefold world' or does it go beyond it?" and "Was the term 'the threefold world' referring to the word 'chair' or to what the Great Master said?" You need to thoroughly investigate expressions like this so that you may learn to express the Matter yourself. By asking questions like this, you come to your own

---

8. One of the ways by which a Chinese Zen Master would test the spiritual level of a disciple was by asking him or her, "How do you understand such-and-such a saying?" It is evident from the context that the discussion centers on the principle of the difference and non-difference between component parts, such as bamboo and wood pieces (one's 'tiles and stones'), and the ordering of those pieces to form a functionally useful object, such as a chair (one's 'walls and fences'). Dōgen, apparently deliberately, does not say how this particular kōan story is to be understood, but s leaves the reader to decide how he or she would respond to Shibi's question.

9. That is, because one may not yet understand that the threefold world is simply one's mind, such a person will not recognize that this is so.

understanding of the Matter. And by investigating the experience of others, you can come to have your own experience of the Truth.

> Keichin then said, "Venerable Monk, you do not understand 'The threefold world is simply your mind.'"

This statement is, for example, equivalent to 'the East Gate and the South Gate' whereby Jōshū expressed what a Jōshū is—and he was also the West Gate and the North Gate. And furthermore there is an East Jōshū district and a South Jōshū district in China.[10] Even if you have an understanding of what 'the threefold world is simply your mind' means, you need to thoroughly explore what Keichin meant by his statement, "You do not understand 'The threefold world is simply your mind.'" Moreover, the statement that "The 'threefold world is simply your mind'" goes beyond 'understanding' and 'not understanding'.

> The Great Master replied, "When giving a name to that thing, I see it as bamboo and wood."

We certainly need to shed light upon the details of this most excellent expression, which goes beyond any discriminative concept. As to the Great Master's statement, "When giving a name to that thing, I see it as be bamboo and wood," what did he call it prior to his naming it as bamboo and wood in the present instance? In its jewel-like brilliance up to that moment, had it always been—beginning, middle, and end— bamboo and wood? In his calling it bamboo and wood at this time, is he saying that this is synonymous with the threefold world simply being one's mind? Or is he not saying that this is synonymous with the threefold world simply being one's mind? Keep in mind that, in his saying of a morning that the threefold world is simply one's mind, he may express it as 'a chair', or as 'simply the mind', or as 'the threefold world'. Even so, in his saying of an evening that the threefold world is simply one's mind, he may express it as, "When giving a name to that thing, I see it as bamboo and wood."

---

10. In other words, the name that we give to something is relative, not absolute. Thus, the East Jōshū district is east in relationship to the South Jōshū district, and vice versa.

You need to recognize that Keichin's saying "When I name it, I also take it to be bamboo and wood" may be part of a face-to-face interchange between Master and disciple, and then again it may be that they are both right from start to finish in exploring the Matter together. Be that as it may, you need to thoroughly explore through your training whether the Great Master's saying, "When giving a name to that thing, I see it as bamboo and wood," and Keichin's saying, "When I name it, I also take it to be bamboo and wood," are actually both saying the same thing and whether or not they are both correct.

> The Great Master then said, "Were we to search the whole
> of the great earth for somebody who understood Buddha Dharma,
> we would not be able to find a single one."

This expression also needs the closest scrutiny. Keep in mind that the Great Master, in naming it, simply took it to be bamboo and wood, as Keichin did also. Further, they had not understood "The threefold world is simply one's mind," nor had they failed to understand "The threefold world is simply one's mind," nor had they asserted that the threefold world is simply one's mind, nor had they failed to assert that the threefold world is simply one's mind. Even so, I should like to ask Great Master Shibi, "You assert that, were we to search the whole of the great earth for somebody who understood Buddha Dharma, we would not be able to find a single person, but see if you can answer me this: what do you take 'the whole earth' to be?" In sum, we need to thoroughly explore the Matter* in this way.

Given to the assembly on the first day of the seventh intercalary lunar month in the first year of the Kangen era (August 17, 1243) on Yamashi Peak in Echizen Province.[11]

---

11.   In the Chinese and Japanese lunar calendar, there are twelve months of either twenty-eight or thirty days. Since this creates a discrepancy with the 365-day solar calendar, every two or three years a thirteenth lunar month is inserted (intercalated) in the calendar at some point. In the present instance, it was inserted between the seventh and eighth lunar months. This is technically known as an intercalary lunar month. An analogy can be found with our inserting the day of February 29 every four years to even out the annual solar calendar, and that day is technically called an intercalary day.

Copied by me on the twenty-fifth day of the same month and year (September 10, 1243) whilst in the quarters of the acting Head Monk.

Ejō

49

On the Real Form of All Thoughts and Things

(Shohō Jissō)

Translator's Introduction: The title of this discourse implies that how we perceive things to be may not actually be their real form. In such contexts the term 'form' means 'the way things appear to us, how they look, and the form they take'. Also, the phrase 'each and every Buddha' is saying that everyone who has realized Buddhahood is unique in regards to the way in which They have fully and directly realized the Truth, and, at the same time, They are exactly like all other Buddhas as to what It is that They have realized. Because what is real is That Which is Real, wherever the term 'real form' occurs, it implies that all thoughts and things are inseparable from their True Nature. Hence, where Dōgen refers to 'real form', he is also referring to 'Real Form'.

    All Buddhas and Ancestors fully manifest Their thorough realization of what is real. What is real are all Their thoughts and the things around Them.[1] All Their thoughts and the things around Them comprise Their form just as it is, Their True Nature just as it is, Their body just as it is, Their mind just as it is, Their world just as it is, Their 'clouds and rain' just as they are,[2] Their daily activities—walking, standing, sitting, and reclining—just as they are, Their moving or being still within Their joys and sorrows just as they are, Their traveling staff* and Their ceremonial hossu* just as they are, Their flower raised aloft and Their face breaking into a smile just as they are,[3] Their inheriting the Dharma and Their prophesying Buddhahood just as they are,

---

1.   'All Their thoughts and things' are what They experience directly, whether it be what appears to arise from within as 'thoughts' or what appears to arise externally as 'things'.

2.   'Clouds and rain' is a common Chinese metaphor for sexual thoughts and feelings that arise.

*   See Glossary.

3   This is a reference to the Transmission of the Dharma from Shakyamuni Buddha, who held aloft an udumbara blossom, to his smiling disciple Makakashō.

Their training under a Master and Their doing the practice just as they are, and Their pine-like fidelity and Their bamboo-like integrity just as they are.

Shakyamuni Buddha once said:

> Only a Buddha is directly able to fully realize the real form
> of all thoughts and things, just as all Buddhas have done. What is
> called 'all thoughts and things' is form just as it is, True Nature just
> as It is, physical body just as it is, spiritual abilities just as they are,
> as well as actions just as they are, causes just as they are, conditions
> just as they are, effects just as they are, and consequences just as
> they are, for all things are Ultimate Reality, from beginning to end,
> just as they are.

The Tathagata's phrase 'Ultimate Reality from beginning to end' was His own way of expressing the reality of all thoughts and things. It is the way our Master Shakyamuni personally expressed it. It was His exploring through His training that all things are equal, because when we explore the Matter[*] through our training, all things are seen to be equal.

Each and every Buddha is the real form of the True Dharma, and the real form of the True Dharma is each and every Buddha. Each Buddha is 'the real form', and every Buddha comprises 'all thoughts and things'. Hearing the phrase 'all thoughts and things', we should not explore it as being the One, nor should we explore it as being the many. Upon hearing the phrase 'the Real Form', we should not understand it as something beyond emptiness, nor should we understand it as something beyond one's True Nature. 'Real' refers to each Buddha and 'form' refers to every Buddha. Being 'directly able' refers to each Buddha and 'fully realizing' refers to every Buddha. 'All thoughts and things' refers to what each Buddha is, whereas 'the Real Form' refers to what every Buddha is. 'All thoughts and things are undoubtedly all thoughts and things' is realized by each Buddha, and 'all thoughts and things are reality' is realized by every Buddha.

Hence, there are forms just as they are and there is the True Nature just as It is, wherein all thoughts and things exist as thoughts and things of their own accord. And forms are, precisely, forms: there are their forms just as they are and there is their True Nature just as It is. When Shakyamuni manifested in the world as Buddha, He expounded, practiced, and realized the Real Form of all thoughts and things just as all Buddhas have done. What He expounded is synonymous with His being directly able to realize the Truth to Its fullest. Though we say that what He experienced was a full realization, He had to be able to directly realize It. Because such a realization was beyond having a beginning, middle, or end, it was His form just as it was and His True Nature just as It was.

His being directly able to fully realize It is synonymous with the Real Form of all His thoughts and things. The Real Form of all His thoughts and things is synonymous with their forms just as they were. Their forms just as they were is synonymous with His being directly able to realize His True Nature just as It was. His True Nature just as It was is synonymous with His being directly able to realize His True Body just as It was. His True Body just as It was is synonymous with His being directly able to realize His spiritual abilities just as they were. His spiritual abilities just as they were is synonymous with His being directly able to realize His actions just as they were. His actions just as they were is synonymous with His being directly able to recognize their causes just as they were. Their causes just as they were is synonymous with His being directly able to recognize their conditions just as they were. Their conditions just as they were is synonymous with His being directly able to recognize their effects just as they were. Their effects just as they were is synonymous with His being directly able to recognize their consequences just as they were. Their consequences just as they were is synonymous with His being directly able to recognize that all things are equally manifestations of Ultimate Reality, from beginning to end, just as they are.

His assertion that all things are equally manifestations of Ultimate Reality, from beginning to end, is their being just as they are as they manifest before us. Hence, if the effect called 'nirvana' is not the result of some cause, then it follows that the effect called 'cause and effect' must be the result of nirvana. To the extent that these effects—namely, those of form, innate nature, physical body, and spiritual abilities—

mutually limit each other, the forms, innate natures, physical bodies, and abilities of all thoughts and things—however immeasurable and unbounded they may be—are their real forms. And to the extent that these effects—namely, those of form, innate nature, physical body, and spiritual ability—do not limit each other, they are their Real Form together with their being such things as form, innate nature, physical body, and spiritual ability. When we entrust the task of defining form, innate nature, physical body, and spiritual ability to such things as effects, consequences, causes, and conditions, there will be an expression that is eighty or ninety percent of a full realization. When we do not entrust the task of defining form, innate nature, physical body, and spiritual ability to such things as effects, consequences, causes, and conditions, there will be an expression that is a one hundred percent full realization.

What has been called 'form just as it is' is not one single form nor is it one uniform thing just as it is: it is That which is beyond measure and bounds, which is inexpressible and unfathomable, and which is just as It is. You should not consider a measurement in hundreds or thousands to be Its measure, but you should measure It by using the yardstick of 'all thoughts and things', by using the yardstick of 'Its Real Form'. Thus, each and every Buddha is able to fully realize the Real Form and the Real Nature of all thoughts and things. And each and every Buddha is directly able to fully realize the Real Physical Body and the real potential of all thoughts and things. And each and every Buddha is directly able to fully realize the real activities and the real causes of all thoughts and things. And each and every Buddha is directly able to fully realize the real conditions and the real effects of all thoughts and things. And each and every Buddha is directly able to fully realize the consequences of all thoughts and things. Each and every Buddha is directly able to fully realize that all thoughts and things are equally manifestations of Truth—that is, of Ultimate Reality—from beginning to end, just as all Buddha's have done.

For reasons like these, the Buddha lands in all ten directions are simply each and every Buddha. Further, there is not a single one, not even half a one, that is not 'each and every Buddha'. 'Each and every' refers to, for example, a Physical Body being provided with a physical body, or a form bearing witness to Form. And it is also like the innate nature of a physical body retaining its innate Nature. This is why the

Buddha said, "Only I and all the Buddhas in the ten directions can directly know these things."

Thus, the very moment of being able to fully realize these things and the very moment of being able to know them are, both alike, instances of 'for the time being'. If we ourselves were different from the Buddhas in the ten directions, how could we possibly realize what the Buddhas in all the ten quarters have taught? Because right here in this place there are no 'ten directions', the ten directions are this very place right here.[4] As a result, when Real Form encounters all thoughts and things, the Spring dwells within Its flowers, human beings encounter the Spring, the Moon illumines the moon, people come face-to-face with their True Self and see It reflected in Water, and all of these alike are the principle of a mutual encountering.[5]

This is why we learn through our training with a Master what Real Form is by means of <u>his</u> real form, and why the Buddhas and Ancestors have inherited from Buddhas and Ancestors the kesa,* which is the mantle of Truth. This is why Buddhahood is predicted for every single thing by means of every single thing. The Dharma was Transmitted for the sake of each and every Buddha, and the Dharma was inherited for the sake of each and every Buddha. This is why birth-and-death and coming-and-going exist. It is why the intention to train, training and practice, the attaining of Wisdom, and nirvana exist. By making use of the intention to train, training and practice, the attaining of Wisdom, and nirvana, we thoroughly explore that the human body really is birth-and-death and coming-and-going, and, in protecting what we have received, we now hold firm and we now let go. With this as our bloodline, the flower opens and bears its fruit; with this as their bones and marrow, Makakashō and Ananda existed.[6] The forms, just as they are, of wind, rain, water, and fire are what Makakashō and Ananda fully realized, and the innate natures, just as they are, of blue, yellow, red, and white, are what they fully realized as well. By relying

---

4.   That is, the ten directions are everywhere at every instant and not in just one place at one time.

5.   That is, of self encountering Self.

6.   Ananda was Makakashō's Dharma heir, making him the Second Indian Ancestor.

upon our physical body and spiritual abilities, we turn the mundane into the sacred, and by relying upon their effects and consequences, we surpass Buddha and transcend Ancestor. By relying on these causes and conditions, we take hold of dirt and transmute it into gold. By relying upon effects and consequences, we receive the Transmission of the Dharma along with the robe.

The Tathagata then said that this gives expression to the real seal[*] of the Ancestors. Let me express this another way. This was His putting into action, hearkening to, and bearing witness to the seal of Real Form. We need to truly investigate the Matter in this manner. What this is basically pointing to is, for instance, like a pearl whirling around in a bowl or a bowl whirling around a pearl.

The Buddha Who Is Radiantly Bright as Sun and Moon once said in verse:

> *The meaning of 'all thoughts and things are the*
> *Real Form'*
> *Has already been voiced both for your sake and*
> *for the sake of others.*[7]

In exploring this saying through your training with your Master, you should thoroughly investigate that the Buddhas and Ancestors have invariably taken the meaning of 'all thoughts and things are the Real Form' to be synonymous with the one great Matter. The Buddhas and Ancestors have proclaimed what the 'Real Form' of the eighteen realms of the senses actually is.[8] Throughout the time before the existence of Their body and mind, the time after the existence of Their body and mind, and the time during the existence of Their body and mind, They gave expression to

---

7. A quote from the *Lotus Scripture*. All references to 'this discourse' that follow in this text refer to the *Lotus Scripture*.

8. The eighteen realms of the senses are the six sense organs of eye, ear, nose, tongue, body, and mind, along with the six sense objects of form, sound, smell, taste, sensation, and thought, and the six sense consciousnesses (that is, the awareness of each organ that allows perception to occur.)

such things as the Real Form, Its Nature, Its physical embodiment, and Its spiritual abilities. Those who have not fully realized what Real Form is, those who have not given expression to It, those who do not understand It, and those who have not gone beyond their present understanding of real form are not Ancestors of the Buddha, but rather demons or beasts.

Shakyamuni Buddha once said, "The fully perfected enlightenment of all bodhisattvas[*] is encompassed within this discourse of Mine. This discourse of Mine opens up the Gate of Skillful Means and points to the genuine Real Form of all things."

'All bodhisattvas' means all Buddhas. Buddhas and bodhisattvas are not different species, nor are they different in maturity or in excellence. This bodhisattva and that bodhisattva are not two separate persons, nor are they self and other, nor are they some person of past, present, or future. Rather, training to become Buddha is their means in the Dharma of putting the Bodhisattva Way into practice. They became a Buddha with the first arising of their intention to realize Buddhahood, and they will become a Buddha in the final stage of Bodhisattvahood. And there are bodhisattvas who have become Buddhas countless hundreds and thousands and millions of times. There are those who say that after bodhisattvas become Buddhas, they discontinue practice because there is nothing left for them to do. Such people are mundane persons who have no direct knowledge of the Way of the Buddhas and Ancestors.

Those called 'all bodhisattvas' are the original Ancestors of all Buddhas, and all Buddhas are the original Teachers of all bodhisattvas. Whether all these Buddhas did Their practice in the past and awoke to the Truth, do it in the present, or will do it in the future, whether They do the practice first with Their body in order to awaken to the Truth, or ultimately do the practice with Their mind, all these will be in accord with this discourse of the Buddha—beginning, middle, and end. Whatever else can be encompassed or included will also be in accord with this discourse, and, at this very moment, this discourse of His awakens us to all manner of enlightenment.

A Buddha's discourse is beyond the sentient and the non-sentient; it is beyond the relative and the absolute. Even so, when He became aware of bodhisattvas, of ordinary humans, of the Real Form of things, and of this discourse, He opened the

Gate of Skillful Means. The Gate of Skillful Means is the unsurpassed meritorious functioning of the fruits of Buddhahood. It is the Dharma that resides in the place of Dharma and It is the form of the world as it constantly manifests. The Gate of Skillful Means does not refer to some momentary skill. Trainees take up the Real Form of all thoughts and things, and explore It thoroughly through their training with a Master. Although this Gate of Skillful Means manifests Itself in such a way as to cover the whole universe with the whole of the universe, those who are not among 'all bodhisattvas' are not within Its realm.

Seppō once said, "The whole of the great earth is the gateway to liberation, but people are afraid to enter the gate even if they are dragged through it." So, keep in mind that even though the whole earth and all the worlds are gateways to liberation, it will not be easy to go in and out of any of them, and those who have tried to pass through one are not many. When people are dragged, they neither get in nor get out. If they are not dragged, they neither get in nor get out. The one who advances his step will stumble, and the one who retreats will be delayed. So, what further is to be said? If we try to force a person either to go in or out of the gate, the gate will become more and more distant. If we take the gate and get it to enter a person, there will be a chance of their going in or out of it.

'To open the Gate of Skillful Means' means to point to the genuine Real Form of things. Even though we chop time up into moments of beginning, middle, and end, pointing to the genuine Real Form of things covers the whole of time. The underlying principle of momentarily opening the Gate of Skillful Means involves opening It by opening the whole universe. At the very moment when you catch sight of the opening of the whole universe, it will be something that you have never encountered before. By our grasping once or twice at an intellectual concept of what opening of whole universe is and then grasping at it for a third or fourth time as something real, we cause the Gate of Skillful Means to open. Accordingly, it may seem that the whole universe is identical with opening the Gate of Skillful Means, but it appears to me that an immeasurable number of whole universes have each taken a small piece from the opening of the Gate of Skillful Means and have made that small piece into the form that each universe displays. But their grandeur is due entirely to their being encompassed within the present discourse.

'To point out the authentic Real Form' means to keep hearing the phrase 'the Real Form of all thoughts and things' throughout all worlds and to realize enlightenment throughout all worlds. It is to help all humanity understand the underlying principle that Real Form is what all thoughts and things are and to help manifest the whole of the Dharma.

Accordingly, the unsurpassed, enlightened Wisdom of the forty Buddhas and forty Ancestors is completely included within this present discourse;[9] It is encompassed within this discourse, and this discourse is encompassed within It. The meditation cushion and the meditation board are Supreme Wisdom and, as such, they are encompassed within this discourse.[10] Shakyamuni's holding the udumbara blossom aloft and Makakashō's breaking into a smile, as well as respectful bowing which secures the very marrow of the Way, are all encompassed within this discourse.[11] To open the Gate of Skillful Means is to point to the authentic Real Form.

Even so, an untrustworthy bunch in present-day Great Sung China, not knowing what to think, do not see where the Treasure is housed and act as if the phrase 'Real Form' were devoid of meaning. So they study the sayings of Lao-tzu and Chuang-tzu, asserting that their teachings are equal to the Great Way of the Buddhas and Ancestors. They also say that the Three Teachings—Buddhism, Taoism, and Confucianism—are in agreement with each other. Or they say that the Three Teachings are like the three legs of a tripod that would overturn if even one leg were absent. I am completely unable to come up with any simile for their excessive foolishness.

---

9. The forty Buddhas is an allusion to the Buddhas from the Seven Buddhas down to the Thirty-third Chinese Ancestor Daikan Enō. The forty Ancestors refers to the Ancestors from Daikan Enō up through the Seven Buddhas.

10. The meditation board is a plank that was used, particularly by the aged or the infirm, to rest one's chin upon or to lean against while doing long sessions of seated meditation.

11. Dōgen explored this reference to respectful bowing in great detail in Discourse 10: On 'Respectful Bowing Will Secure for You the Very Marrow of the Way' *(Raihai Tokuzui).*

We cannot acknowledge that people who talk like this have ever heard the Dharma of the Buddha. And why? Because the Dharma of the Buddha had its origin in India where, during the eighty years of His life, the Buddha spent fifty years of His prime giving voice to the Dharma in order to transform both ordinary people and those in lofty positions. By transforming sentient beings, He helped them to enter the Buddha's Way. After that, twenty-eight Indian Ancestors experienced the genuine Transmission, which is considered to be the ultimate, the subtlest, the finest, and the most esteemed. All those who were outside the Way or who were demons in lofty positions were ultimately defeated. We do not know the number of ordinary people and those in lofty positions who realized Buddhahood and became Ancestors. Even so, none of them ever said that the Buddha's Dharma was insufficient for them, so they never paid a call on Confucianism or Taoism in China. If one were to agree that the Three Teachings were in accord, then at the time when the Buddha's Dharma emerged, such teachings as Confucianism and Taoism should have emerged concurrently in India. But the Teaching of the Buddha's Dharma is encapsulated in the saying, "In the heavens above and the earth below, I alone am the sole Honored One." [12] We should think back to the events of that time and we should not make a mistake by forgetting them. Talking about the Three Teachings being in accord does not equal even the babbling sounds of a little baby. It is a statement made by that bunch who are out to destroy the Buddha's Dharma. Folks like that are all too many. It is provoking to see that people like these have become guiding teachers for ordinary humans and those in lofty places, while others have even become teachers and masters to emperors and kings. Alas, the Buddha Dharma is degenerating in present-day Great Sung China! My former Master, who was an Old Buddha, strongly cautioned me about this.

People like these are seeds that produce the two Lesser Courses* and the non-Buddhists. They have already wasted two or three centuries without even

---

12. This quotation is attributed to the Buddha. Immediately following His Birth, He is purported to have taken seven steps and then pointed up towards the heavens with His right hand and down towards the earth with His left, whilst uttering the words quoted above.

knowing that Real Form exists. They speak only of exploring the True Teaching so that they might escape from the continual cycle of birth-and-death. Many are those who do not even know what it means to explore the True Teaching of the Buddhas and Ancestors, for they fancy that just living in a monastery is what practice is. How pitiful that the words and ways of the Ancestral Masters are now dying out! It is what the venerable monks of long-standing who hold to the true words and ways of the Buddha greatly lament. Do not give ear to the words and phrases that emerge from the likes of that bunch spoken of earlier. Rather, we should pity them.

Meditation Master Engo once said, "Birth-and-death and coming-and-going are a person's true Real Body." By exploring this expression, we will come to know ourselves and we will give our consideration to the Buddha Dharma.

Chōsa once said, "The whole universe in all ten directions is a person's true Real Body. The whole universe in all ten directions lies within the radiant brightness of one's own True Self." But, in general, even veteran trainees in present-day Sung China still do not know that they need to explore a saying like this through their training.[13] Much less do they know how to put it into practice! Were we to quote this saying to them, they would simply go red in the face and be left speechless.

My former Master, the Old Buddha, once said:

> Veteran trainees all over Sung China have still not illumined either the past or the present. They have not yet grasped the underlying principle of the Buddha Dharma. Although the whole universe in all ten directions, among other things, is

---

13.   'Veteran trainees' is a common term for monks who have been in monastic life for a long time but have made little or no progress spiritually.

constantly presenting itself in this manner, how could they possibly know it? Outside of Great Sung China, it is as if they had never even heard of it.

After hearing this, I questioned veteran trainees throughout Sung China about this underlying principle, and to tell the truth, few had even heard of it. How sad that they dishonor the offices they occupy with such pointless talk!

Meditation Master Ōan Donge once addressed Tokki Daitoku, saying:

> If you wish to understand the Matter easily, then throughout the whole twenty-four hours of each day, just keep your focus on the arising of mind and the moving of thoughts. As you approach the moving thoughts, you may suddenly experience the Ungraspable, That Which Is the Here and Now. It will be like vast, unbounded space, and there will be no forms or delimitations within that space. Outside and inside will be one and the same; self and other will both become extinct, and the unfathomable and the clear will both disappear. The three periods of time—past, present, and future—will be equal. Those who arrive at this state are called 'people at ease in the Way who are unattached to anything and have nothing more to accomplish.'

These are the words spoken by the elder Ōan who used his full strength to express the essence of the Dharma. But this is simply his chasing after shadows, as if he did not know how to stop pursuing words. Can the Buddha Dharma not exist when inside and outside are not one and the same? What is this 'inside and outside'? Also, the assertion of the Buddhas and Ancestors is that there <u>are</u> forms and delimitations within space. And what does he mean by 'space'? When we think about it, Ōan did not yet know what space is, nor had he seen what space is, nor had he taken hold of space, nor had he struck space.

Ōan speaks of mind arising and thoughts moving, and yet there is the fundamental principle that the Mind never moves, so how could there possibly be an arising of mind within the twenty-four hours of a day? No mind can come and enter into the twenty-four hours of a day, nor can the twenty-four hours of the day come into the twenty-four hours of the Mind. Much less can there be an arising of Mind! And what, pray, is the moving of one's thoughts? Do thoughts move or do they not move? Or are they beyond moving and not moving? What is this 'moving' of his? Moreover, what is 'not moving'? What is he calling 'thoughts'? Do thoughts occur within the twenty-four hours of a day? Or do the twenty-four hours of a day occur within one's thoughts? Or can there be a time beyond these two?

He says that if you wish to understand the Matter easily, then throughout the whole twenty-four hours of each day, just keep your focus on the arising of mind and the moving of thoughts. But what is this Matter that can be understood easily? Is 'easily understood' something he is saying about the Teaching of the Buddhas and Ancestors? If so, then he needs to know that the Buddha's Teaching is beyond easy to understand or difficult to understand, which is why Nangaku and Baso followed their respective Masters for ever so long in their practice of the Way.[14]

Ōan speaks of suddenly experiencing the Ungraspable, That Which Is the Here and Now. But he has never encountered the Way of the Buddhas and Ancestors even in his dreams. How can one of such limited ability as his possibly be up to 'wishing to understand easily'? Understand clearly that he had not yet thoroughly explored the Great Teaching of the Buddhas and Ancestors. If the Buddha's Dharma was like what he said, how could It possibly have come down to us today?

Now, this is the case with Ōan himself. Yet, were we to seek for ever so long among the veteran monks in mountain monasteries of the present day for someone who was like Ōan, we would not encounter him. And were we to search until our eyes grew dim, we would not encounter a veteran monk who was the equal of Ōan. There are many in recent times who acknowledge Ōan, but even so, it would be difficult for me to acknowledge that he had realized the Buddha Dharma. I would simply say that he deserves a seat among the juniors in a monastery and that he is of average

---

14. Nangaku's Master was Enō and Baso's Master was Nangaku.

experience. And why? Because Ōan did at least have enough spirit to spot 'such a person'.* Folks today cannot recognize 'such a person' because they do not even know themselves. Although I say that Ōan had not yet fully arrived, he did have experience of the Way, experience that such folks as the veteran monks of today do not have. Though I would say that Ōan had heard good words, they had not penetrated his ears, much less had he 'seen them' with his ears. They had not penetrated his eyes, much less had he 'heard them' with his eyes. Though this is the way that Ōan was, today he would naturally have awakened to something. Veteran monks in the mountain monasteries of Great Sung China today have not even caught a glimpse of what Ōan's 'inside and outside' means; nothing that comes out of their mouths or that shows on their faces are in the same realm as him. Folks like this cannot tell whether the Real Form that the Buddhas and Ancestors have expressed is embodied within the words and ways of the Buddhas and Ancestors. This is why, for the past two or three centuries, none of the folks who speak wildly, like these old veteran monks, have been able to speak of or to see Real Form.

In giving informal instruction in the Abbot's private quarters, my late Master, the Old Buddha of Tendō, said in verse one night:

> *Tonight, Tendō Mountain is blessed with calves,*
> *And a golden-faced Gautama holds aloft the Real Form.*
> *"If buying is your wish, how will you afford Its priceless price?"*
> *So cries the night bird from above the solitary cloud on high.*

When the situation is as described above, venerable senior monks who are accomplished in the Buddha's Way speak of Real Form. Those who do not know the Buddha Dharma and who do not explore the Buddha's Way do not speak of Real Form.

The preceding poem came about in the following manner. It was nearing the fourth watch of a night in the third lunar month in the spring of the second year of the great Sung era of Hōkyō (1226), when three beats from the summoning drum sounded from above.[15] Putting on my kesa and taking my bowing mat, I left the Cloud Hall through the front entrance. The sign to go enter the Master's room for a spiritual interview had been hung up. First off, I followed the crowd of monks up to the Dharma Hall. Going past the west wall of the Dharma Hall, I climbed the west stairway to the Ancestral Shrine. Passing by the west wall of the Ancestral Shrine, I climbed the west stairway of the Hall of Great Brightness. The Hall of Great Brightness is where the Abbot's quarters are. Going by the southern end of a screen along the west side, I reached the incense stand and, after offering incense, I did my prostrations. I had expected that lines would have formed here for entry into the Master's room, but I did not see even one monk. The Abbot's main room had been screened off from me by bamboo blinds. I could hear, but barely, the sound of the Teaching being given by this Great Monk who was the Head of our temple.

At that moment, the monk who was Precentor, Sokon by name, from Szechwan Province, arrived. After he too had offered incense and made his prostrations, we quietly approached the main room, which was packed with monks who were seated regardless of east or west.[16] The Abbot's informal talk was in progress, so we quietly entered behind the assembly and listened to it while continuing to stand.

He was giving an account of Meditation Master Daibai Hōjō's living in the mountains. At the part where he described Hōjō's wearing clothes made from lotus leaves and harvesting pine trees for food, many in the community began to weep.[17] During his detailed recounting of the story of Shakyamuni Buddha's retreat on Vulture Peak, again, many who heard it were moved to tears.

The Master ended his Dharma talk by saying, "The retreat on Mount Tendō draws near. Since it is springlike now, it is neither cold nor hot. It will be a fine time

---

15. The Abbot's quarters were in the highest building on the mountain.

16. That is, the monks were mixed together regardless of whether they were juniors or seniors.

17. There are various accounts of Chinese hermit monks living off of or supplementing their diet with parts of pine trees. Sprigs of new growth were eaten, as well as pine nuts.

to do seated meditation, so why would any junior or senior not wish to sit in meditation?" He then recited his poem quoted above.

When the poem was finished, he struck the right arm of his meditation seat with his right hand and said, "Enter my room for your spiritual interview." His topic for the spiritual interview was "The night bird cries out and the bamboo on the mountain splits open." These were his very words for the spiritual interview. He offered no commentary. Even though our monastic family was large, many had no response, as they were simply overawed.

This method of conducting a spiritual interview was not done anywhere else; only my late Master, the Old Buddha of Tendō, used it. During such informal teaching, my Master's seat was surrounded by screens which the community crowded around. While the monks remained standing, the interviews took place with whichever monk was prepared to enter the Abbot's presence. When a monk had finished his interview, he departed through the door of the Abbot's quarters in the customary manner. Those who remained, still standing as they were before, could see and hear everything, not only the dignified manner of stepping forward and then halting by the one entering for his interview, but also the deportment of the Abbot and his command for the next monk to enter. This ceremony never existed in other places, and it may be that other veteran Abbots were unable to do it. During interviews with other Masters, monks wanted to enter the Abbot's interview room before the others did, whereas in entering my Master's room, the monks wished to enter after the others. We should not forget that there are differences in people's minds and ways of behaving.

From that time until this first year of the Japanese Kangen era (1243), eighteen years have passed quickly within the changing scenery. I cannot remember how many mountains and bodies of water there have been between Mount Tendō and this mountain, but the Real Form of those beautiful words and wondrous phrases of my Master has been engraved on my body and mind, on my bones and marrow. I believe it would be difficult for monks in that monastic assembly to ever forget hearing the Dharma talk and entering for a spiritual interview on that occasion. On that night, the light of the new moon shone from behind the temple buildings and though, from time to time, a night bird would sing out, it was a night tranquil and still.

Great Master Gensha Shibi was once giving an informal talk when, upon hearing the chirping of some swallow chicks, he said, "How profoundly they discuss Real Form! How skillfully they expound the essence of the Dharma!" Thereupon, he stepped down from his Dharma seat.

    Then, a novice monk who was behind him, chasing after instruction, said, "I don't get it."

    The Master said, "Oh, be off with you! There's no one who'd believe you."

Having heard Shibi's statement, "How profoundly they discuss Real Form," one might well take it to mean that swallow chicks alone profoundly discuss Real Form, but this is not so. During his informal talk, Shibi heard the chirping of some swallow chicks. It was not that the swallow chicks were profoundly discussing Real Form, and it was not that Shibi was profoundly discussing Real Form, and it was not a cross between the two, but it was that at that very moment itself, there was a profound discussion of Real Form.

    We should take a moment to thoroughly explore this story. There is the informal instruction, hearing the swallow chicks' chirping, and the assertion, "How profoundly they discuss Real Form! How skillfully they expound the essence of the Dharma!" And there is Shibi's stepping down from his Dharma seat, the novice monk chasing behind him for instruction saying, "I don't get it," and the Master's response, "Oh, be off with you! There's no one who'd believe you." Although the statement, "I don't get it," need not necessarily be a request for instruction on Real Form, it is nevertheless the lifeblood of the Buddhas and Ancestors, and the very Bones and Marrow of the Treasure House of the Eye of the True Teaching.[18]

    You need to comprehend that even if this monk, in seeking instruction, asserted either that he did or that he did not understand, Shibi should say to him, "Oh,

---

18.   That is, the remark is customarily understood by Buddhas and Ancestors to mean "I don't get It."

be off with you! There's no one who'd believe you." Shibi said what he did not because the novice monk had said that he did not understand, but because the monk had already understood.[19] Truly, even though it could have been someone other than this monk, say, any third son of Mr. Chang or fourth son of Mr. Li, and even though all thoughts and things are Real Form, at the time and place when one penetrates directly into the Lifeblood of the Buddhas and Ancestors, one's exploring Real Form through one's training manifests just like this. This had already manifested by the time of Seigen's assembly.[20]

Keep in mind that Real Form is the genuine Lifeblood which has been passed on from rightful heir to rightful heir, that all thoughts and things are what each and every Buddha has completely and thoroughly explored, and that each and every Buddha manifests His characteristic marks, just as they are.[21]

Given to the assembly during a day in the ninth lunar month of the first year of the Kangen era (October or November, 1243) at Kippō-ji Temple in Echizen Province, Japan.

---

19. That is, the monk was trying to inveigle Shibi into discussing and intellectualizing what he had said.

20. That is, the exploration of Real Form had already begun generations earlier in the assembly of Seigen Gyōshi. Shibi was in Seigen's lineage, as was Dōgen.

21. That is, all Buddhas exhibit the characteristic marks and distinguishing signs of a Buddha, no matter how unique each Buddha may be.

50

On Buddhist Scriptures

(Bukkyō)

Translator's Introduction: In this discourse, Dōgen uses the word 'Scripture' to refer not only to the Scriptural writings of Buddhism but also to individual persons, as well as to all things in the universe, since each in its own way embodies the Dharma.

Dōgen proceeds to launch a highly charged attack on the founding Ancestors of two of the five traditions of Chinese Zen Buddhism, namely, those founded by Rinzai and Ummon, though he spares the tradition established by Ōbaku, who was Rinzai's Master. One can only speculate that the emotional tone of this attack arose from his desire to keep his disciples from trying to incorporate the practices of those traditions into their own practice and training.

Dōgen then extends his attack by taking on the so-called Chinese tripod theory, which was current in his day. According to this theory, Chinese culture and civilization are like a sacred vessel which gains its stability by being supported by three 'legs', namely, Taoism, Confucianism, and Buddhism. The theory was originally put forth by some Buddhists in an attempt to counter the argument that only Taoism and Confucianism were truly Chinese since these teachings were indigenous to China, whereas Buddhism was a foreign religion and therefore something superimposed on the Chinese culture. Dōgen argues against this by saying that if Taoism and Confucianism needed Buddhism to maintain cultural stability, then it would follow that Chinese Buddhism would also need Taoism and Confucianism because it likewise could not stand on its own. Therefore, those Buddhists who wanted to introduce Taoist or Confucianist elements into their training were not strengthening it, but diluting it with elements irrelevant to Buddhist practice.

Within the Buddhist Scriptures, there are methods for teaching bodhisattvas[*] and there are methods for teaching Buddhas. Both of these methods are tools of the Great Truth. These tools comply with their Owner, and the Owner uses His tools. Accordingly, the Buddhas and Ancestors in both the western land of India and in the eastern land of China were persons who, of necessity, followed some good spiritual friend or followed what the Scriptures taught, with never a gap in Their giving rise to

---

[*]   See Glossary.

the intention to realize Buddhahood, Their doing Their training and practice, and Their realizing the fruits thereof. In giving rise to Their intention to realize Buddhahood, They relied on Scriptural texts and spiritual friends, and in Their doing the training and practice, They relied on Scriptural texts and spiritual friends, and in Their realizing the fruits of Their practice, They also relied on Scriptural texts and spiritual friends. Our giving rise to our first spiritual intention and then later encountering the words of the Scriptures is likewise in harmony with Scriptural texts and spiritual friends. And if, amidst our giving rise to our intention, Scriptural verses arise within us, this too is in harmony with Scriptural texts and spiritual friends.

Spiritual friends, of necessity, have thoroughly penetrated the Scriptural texts. 'Thoroughly penetrated' means that they have made the Scriptures their homeland, and they have made Them their body and mind. They have set up the Scriptures for the sake of others and have made the Scriptures their parents and their offspring. Because spiritual friends have made the Scriptures into what they practice and understand, they have thoroughly explored Them. And a spiritual friend's washing his face and drinking his tea is also an ancient Scripture. And the saying, "Scriptures give birth to spiritual friends," describes, for instance, Ōbaku's bringing about the birth of a monastic offspring by giving him thirty blows with his staff. It also describes the three strikes that Daiman Kōnin gave which brought about the Transmission of the kesa* along with the Dharma.[1] And these two are not the only cases. There is the monk who awoke to the Truth upon seeing peach blossoms, and the monk who awoke to the Truth upon hearkening to bamboo being struck by a stone, and the One who awoke upon seeing the morning star—all are good examples of Scriptures giving birth to spiritual friends. And there have been 'skin bags and fisted ones' who, having first opened their Eye, benefited much from Scriptural texts. And

---

1. The most notable Dharma heir of Ōbaku was Rinzai, the 'monastic offspring' referred to here. Daiman Kōnin Transmitted to Daikan Enō the bowl and kesa believed to have belonged to Shakyamuni Buddha.

there are also 'wooden ladles and jet-black buckets' who, having learned a great deal from Scriptural texts, then opened their Eye.[2]

What we call Scriptures is precisely the whole universe in all directions. There is no time or place that is not a Scripture. Some Scriptures make use of the language of Ultimate Reality, whereas others make use of the language of secular reality. Some make use of the language of celestial beings, whereas others make use of the language of human beings. Some make use of the language that animals speak, whereas others make use of the language that asuras[*] speak. Some make use of the words that sprout up like hundreds of grasses in a field, whereas others make use of the words that flourish like the thousands of trees in a woodland. Thus it is that what is long or short, square or round, as well as what is blue, yellow, red, or white, all of which are arrayed throughout the whole universe like ever so many trees in a forest, are the words of a Scripture; they are what appears on the surface of a Scriptural text. They serve as the tools of the Great Truth, which comprise what a Scripture is in Buddhist traditions. Such a Scripture can spread out and cover the whole of time, and It can flow out and cover all lands. It opens the gateway to teaching human beings without forsaking anyone anywhere. It opens the gateway to Scriptural matters and rescues all manner of beings everywhere. In teaching Buddhas and bodhisattvas, it becomes the whole of the earth, indeed, the whole of the universe. It opens the gateway to skillful means and the gateway to abiding in one's True Place. And, without forsaking a single person, or even half a one, It points to the true Real Form. The great intention of each Buddha and bodhisattva right now is to obtain much benefit from these Scriptures, even though this may not be something done intentionally by means of one's discriminative thinking and conscious endeavor, or by means of one's going beyond discriminative thinking and conscious endeavor.

The time of positively procuring a Scripture is beyond 'past and present', because past and present are simply moments in the time of 'procuring a Scripture'.

---

2.   'Skin bags' is a metaphor for ordinary human beings. 'Fisted ones' is a metaphor for trainees whose Master raises a fist to show that the Ultimate is beyond words or concepts. 'Wooden ladles' refers to those who are trying to awaken to the Truth, and 'jet-black buckets' is a metaphor for monks who are ignorant of the essence of Buddhism.

What is manifesting right now before our very eyes is the whole universe in all ten directions. This is what 'procuring a Scripture' really means. In that such a Scripture has already been read, recited, and thoroughly penetrated, the Wisdom of Buddha, along with our natural innate wisdom and the wisdom acquired without a teacher, have already fully manifested before the arising of our own mind and body. At the moment when we encounter a Scripture, we do not doubt that we have entered a special state that is new to us. When this Scripture has been accepted by us and then passed on to others by our reading or reciting It, we can say that the Scripture has made full contact with us. This state of affairs quickly becomes a scattering of flowers and a making of garlands. At first we see only the words embedded within phrases, but there is 'something indescribable' to be found between the lines.

We call such Scriptures 'the Dharma'. They contain an accumulation of eighty-four thousand expressions of the Dharma. Within these Scriptures are such words as 'the Buddhas who have fully realized Universal Truth', 'the Buddhas who have appeared and are residing in the world right now,' and 'the Buddhas who have arrived and entered nirvana'. 'The One Who Comes in This Way' and 'The One Who Goes in That Way'—that is, the Tathagata—are both terms that appear in these Scriptures and are expressions of the Dharma within the Dharma. 'Raising aloft the flower, with eyes atwinkle' and 'his face breaking into a smile'[3] are old Scriptures that have been accurately Transmitted from the Seven Buddhas.* And 'standing in the snow and severing one's arm' as well as 'respectfully bowing and securing the very Marrow of the Way' are expressions which encapsulate old Scriptures about Master and disciple truly hearing each other.[4] Ultimately, the Transmitting of the Dharma and the kesa to Daikan Enō was nothing other than the arrival of the moment when all the

---

3. This is a reference to Shakyamuni Buddha's Transmitting the Dharma to His smiling disciple Makakashō by holding an udumbara flower aloft.

4. The reference to cutting off one's arm is to the Second Chinese Ancestor, Taiso Eka, who is said to have cut off his arm in order to find the Truth. This 'severing' may refer to giving up one's attachments rather than to a literal, physical act. Dōgen fully explores the reference to respectful bowing in Discourse 10: On 'Respectful Bowing Will Secure for You the Very Marrow of the Way' *(Raihai Tokuzui).*

Scriptures were spread out and entrusted to him. The three strikes on the mortar by Daiman Kōnin and the response of three siftings of rice in the winnowing basket by Daikan Enō brought about a Scripture holding out His hand to a Scripture, whereby a Scripture made a Scripture His legitimate heir.

In addition, Enō's saying, "Who is this One that comes thus?" is a thousand Scriptures for teaching Buddhas and tens of thousands of Scriptures for teaching bodhisattvas. And Nangaku's reply, "For me to explain what even one thing is would not hit the mark," does well to account for the accumulation of the eighty-four thousand expressions of the Dharma, as well as the twelve divisions of the Mahayana[*] canon. And even more, a Master's fist and heel, his traveling staff[*] and ceremonial hossu,[*] are ancient Scriptures and new Scriptures, as well as Scriptures on what has limits and Scriptures on That which is without limits. From the first, doing one's utmost in training within the Sangha and diligently doing seated meditation are Buddhist Scriptures, and they are Buddhist Scriptures right to the end. They are Scriptures written on leaves from the Bodhi tree; they are Scriptures written upon the vast expanse of sky.

In short, the one moment of movement and the two moments of stillness which the Buddhas and Ancestors have exhibited, as well as Their holding on and Their letting go are, naturally enough, the unrolling of Buddhist Scriptures. Because They have explored through Their training that the ultimate standard is that there is no absolute ultimate, They have inhaled and expelled the Scriptures through Their nostrils and They have absorbed and expelled the Scriptures through Their toes. 'Before "father" and "mother" had yet been born',[*] there was a taking in and expelling of Scriptures, and before the Lords of Awe-inspiring Voices appeared, there was a taking in and expelling of Scriptures. We receive Scriptures and give expression to Scriptures by means of the whole earth with its mountains and rivers, and we receive Scriptures and give expression to Scriptures by means of the sun, moon, and stars. Some Buddhas and Ancestors have held to the Scriptures by means of the Self that existed before the kalpa[*] of emptiness, and Some have held onto the Scriptures by means of the body and mind that They had before They had a countenance. Scriptures like these were brought into view by Their breaking open a dust mote or by Their breaking open the whole universe.

Our great Twenty-seventh Ancestor, the Venerable Hannyatara,[5] once said:

> In my humble way, what I breathe out does not conform
> itself to external conditions and events, and what I breathe in does
> not take up residence in the realm of my skandhas.* The Scriptures
> that I recite are always like this, for they are comprised of hundreds
> of thousands of millions of billions of scrolls, not just one or two
> scrolls.

Hearing what our Ancestral Master said in this way, we should explore through our training that she caused the Scriptures to revolve with her every exhalation and inhalation. To understand 'revolving the Scriptures' in this way is to know wherein the Scriptures reside. Because she could revolve Them and there was something to revolve, which was her revolving the Scriptures and the Scriptures revolving her, she must have totally understood and recognized what They are.[6]

My late Master was constantly saying:

> Here in my temple, you should simply sit in meditation
> without having recourse to burning incense, making bows, reciting
> the name of Buddha, confessing your shortcomings, or reciting
> Scriptures. Just do your utmost to practice the Way and drop off
> body and mind.

Few are the folks who understand a remark like this. And why? Because if they were to take the phrase 'reciting Scriptures' literally, they would be violating its

---

5.   There is a long-standing Indian tradition which holds that Hannyatara was a female monk renowned for her extraordinary spiritual prowess.

6.   Dōgen has an extensive commentary on Hannyatara's remarks in Discourse 20: On Reading Scriptures (*Kankin*).

intention, and if they were not to take the phrase 'reciting Scriptures' literally, they would be turning their back on his words. We cannot have words for It and we do not lack words for It. So, quick, quick! Speak, speak! You must explore this fundamental principle through your training! Because this principle exists, a Master of long ago said, "To read Scriptures, you will need to be equipped with an Eye for reading Scriptures." By all means you need to realize that if there had not been Scriptures in the past and in the present, there could not be such a statement as this. You need to explore through your training that there is the reading of a Scripture called 'dropping off' and there is the reading of a Scripture called 'without having recourse'. Since this is so, each person—or even half a person—who does the training will, without question, receive the Transmission and become a child of the Buddha, so do not foolishly study the false views of non-Buddhists. Because the Treasure House of the Eye of the True Teaching, which is now fully manifesting before your very eyes, is what the Buddhist Scriptures are, every Buddhist Scripture is the Treasure House of the Eye of the True Teaching. They are beyond being the same or different, beyond being self or other. Keep in mind that because the Treasure House of the Eye of the True Teaching is ever so abundant, none of you will be able to illumine It completely.[7] And even so, you will be able to expound upon the Treasure House of the Eye of the True Teaching without ever failing to trust in It. And so it will be with the Buddhist Scriptures. Though the Scriptures are ever so many, you need but trust and accept Them, and put into practice a single verse or phrase from Them. You need not fully comprehend all eighty-four thousand of Them. Just because you cannot be expert in all the Buddhist Scriptures, do not be rash and say that the Buddhist Scriptures are not the Buddha Dharma. Even though you may hear others call themselves the very bones and marrow of the Buddhas and Ancestors, when we look with straightforward eyes at those who speak this way, we see that they are simply present-day trainees who are stuck on words. While some of them may be as good as those who accept and keep to a single phrase or a single verse, there may also be those who do not measure up to them. Do not insult the Buddha's True Teaching by relying on this superficial understanding of theirs. Nothing in the world of sound and form is more spiritually

---

7.   That is, realizing enlightenment does not mean becoming omniscient.

meritorious than the Buddhist Scriptures. Sounds and forms may delude you if you are still greedily chasing after them. However, the Buddhist Scriptures will never delude you, so do not mistrust or slander Them.

Even so, over the last couple of centuries or so in Great Sung China, certain mistaken, smelly skin bags have said, "There's no need for you to keep the sayings of the Ancestral Masters in mind, much less is there any need for long study of Scriptural Teachings or for your trying to make use of Them. Simply, make your body and mind like a dead tree or cold ashes, like a broken wooden ladle or a bottomless tub." Folks like these have become a type of non-Buddhist or celestial demon, and to no good purpose. They seek to make use of things that are useless, and accordingly, they twist the Teachings of the Buddhas and Ancestors into wild and perverted teaching. What a pity! How terribly sad! Even 'broken ladles' and 'bottomless tubs' have been ancient Scriptures for some Ancestors of the Buddha. Rare has been the Ancestor of the Buddha who has completely tallied the number of texts of these Scriptures. Those who say that the Buddhist Scriptures are not the Buddha Dharma have not studied the occasions when Ancestors of the Buddha have made use of Scriptures, nor have they explored through their training the occasions when Ancestors of the Buddha have revealed their True Nature through their reliance on Scriptures, nor do they know how to gauge the level of intimacy between the Buddha's Ancestors and the Buddhist Scriptures. Careless folks like these are as common as rice and flax seeds, bamboo canes and reeds. They ascend the Lion Throne* and establish monasteries everywhere, passing themselves off as teachers of gods and humans. Because the inaccurate have studied with the inaccurate, their principles are likewise inaccurate, and because they are ignorant, they fail to seek what is reliable, but simply pass from darkness into darkness. How pitiful! And because they have not realized the Body and Mind of Buddha Dharma, they do not know what the deportment of body and the behavior of mind should be. Since they have not clarified what lies at the heart of either existence or emptiness, if someone should ask them a question about this, they may arbitrarily raise a fist, but they are really in the dark as to what it means to make such a gesture. Since they have not clarified which paths are genuine and which are false, if someone should ask them a question about this, they hold up a ceremonial hossu, but they are not clear as to the significance of holding it up. Or, in a misguided attempt to offer a helping hand for someone's sake, they may cite Rinzai's *Four Perspectives* or his *Four Relations Between Reflecting and Acting,* or quote Ummon's *Three Phrases* or Tōzan's *Three Paths* or his *Five Relative Positions* as standards for study of the Way.[8]

My late Master, the monk of Tendō, was always laughing at this and would say:

How could 'learning what Buddha is' possibly be like that? We have clothed both our body and our mind with the Great Truth that the Buddhas and Ancestors have authentically Transmitted. In exploring this through our training and in aiming at mastering it through and through, we have no time to spare. What free time do we have for including the dubious remarks of modern-day trainees? Truly, you need to realize that old senior monks all over Great Sung China are lacking in the Truth, and it is clear that they are not exploring through their training what the Body and Mind of the Buddha Dharma is.

This is how my late Master pointed out the Matter* to his assembly.

To tell the truth, in the case of Rinzai, he was a newcomer in Ōbaku's assembly. Ōbaku had already used his staff to inflict sixty blows on Rinzai before the latter left to make a formal call on Daigu, with whom he had a meeting to discuss the mind of a certain old woman. This Dharma conversation helped to illumine matters in his daily conduct and, as a consequence, he returned to Ōbaku. Because those who heard this account were deeply impressed by it, they believed that Rinzai and he alone

---

8.　Dōgen's apparently negative view of Tōzan's two treatises in the present context is clarified later in this discourse.

had received Ōbaku's Buddha Dharma, and, moreover, they even fancied that Rinzai had surpassed Ōbaku. But this is simply not so.

Although it must be said that Rinzai had barely entered Ōbaku's assembly and was as yet the juniormost monk at the time, nevertheless, when the venerable senior monk Chin prompted him to ask his spiritual question, Rinzai did not know what to say.[9] Even though someone has not yet clarified what the Great Matter is, how could anyone who is committed to exploring It through their training fail to rise to the occasion while listening to the Dharma and simply be dumbstruck like that? You should realize that such a one is not foremost in ability. Further, Rinzai never had the ardor of his celebrated Master, and we have yet to hear of any sayings of his that surpass those of his Master. Ōbaku, though, did have ways of putting things which evinced a greater wisdom than that of his own Master. And he could put into words Teachings that even the Buddha had not yet uttered, and he had an understanding of the Dharma that even the Ancestors had not yet fathomed. Ōbaku was an Old Buddha who transcended both past and present. He was more highly esteemed than Hyakujō and was of even greater genius than Baso. Rinzai lacked such an eminent spirit. And why? Because he never made any remark, not even in his dreams, which had not already been expressed in the past or present. It is as if he merely understood the many and overlooked the One, or grasped the One and overlooked the many. How can we possibly think that his *Four Perspectives* partake of the flavor of the Dharma or that it serves as a compass that points the correct way to explore the Teaching?

Ummon was a member of Seppō's community. Even though he functioned as a great teacher for all manner of people, it must be said that he was still one of those who are stuck on erudition. Should you attempt to find the Source by relying on people

---

9.   Chin was one of Ōbaku's Dharma heirs and succeeded him as Abbot upon Ōbaku's death. The situation described here probably refers to the question asked by the Abbot or a senior monk of someone who has come to a temple for the first time. It is usually ambiguous, thereby inviting the potential trainee to respond in a socially conventional way or to see the deeper, spiritual meaning embedded in the question, which calls for a spiritually focused response. Apparently, Rinzai was totally nonplussed and could not come up with a reply on either side, much less with a question.

like him, you would simply end up on some paltry tributary. In the times before Rinzai arrived and Ummon appeared, what, pray, did the Buddhas and Ancestors rely upon as Their standard for exploring the Way? Hence, you need to understand that within the houses of Rinzai and Ummon, the proper training of the Buddha's tradition was not passed on. Because they had nothing authoritative to rely upon, they recklessly put forth their own questionable teachings. Such fellows irresponsibly slandered the Buddhist Scriptures, so you people should not follow them in that. If the Scriptures are to be cast aside, then the teachings of Rinzai and Ummon should also be cast aside. If we cannot make use of the Scriptures, then we will have no water to drink, much less a ladle to scoop it up with.

Further, our founding Ancestor Tōzan's *Three Paths* and *Five Relative Positions*, which detail the Matter, are frankly beyond anything that the careless and inaccurate are able to understand. The underlying principle was accurately Transmitted to him and he forthwith pointed out what proper Buddhist conduct is. We should not presume to liken his teaching to that of other traditions.

Also, there are irresponsible people who say, "Although they are different to begin with, the teachings of Taoism, the teachings of Confucianism, and the Scriptures of Shakyamuni ultimately have the same goal. They are just different ways for entering the gate to Truth." Or they may say, "They are like the three legs of a tripod." This is at the heart of a hot debate among present-day monks in Great Sung China. When people speak like this, the Buddha Dharma has already been banished from the earth and perished for them. And we should also say that not even a smidgen of the Buddha's Teaching has ever come to them. People like this rashly attempt to express what Buddha Dharma is even though they are blocked from penetrating It. They erroneously say that the Buddhist Scriptures are of no use because there is a separate Transmission in the tradition of our ancestral Master Bodhidharma.[10] They are small-

---

10.   This view, which Dōgen considered to be erroneous, derives from a misinterpretation of a poem attributed to Bodhidharma, which has been interpreted by some as a rejection of Scriptural texts. Dōgen's view is that the Scriptural texts and the pointing to the heart are two aspects of what is Transmitted. Bodhidharma's poem is as follows:

The separate Transmission that is outside the Teachings

minded people who have not inquired into what the boundaries really are in the Way of the Buddhas. They say that one need not make use of Buddhist Scriptures, but what about our Master Bodhidharma's poem? Do they make use of it or do they feel that they do not need it? There are many instances of Teaching in what our Ancestor said that are just like what is in Buddhist Scriptures. Would they have us use his Teaching or discard It? Were they to say that our Ancestor's Truth is not the Buddha's Truth, who then would trust our Ancestor's Truth? Our Ancestral Master is an Ancestral Master because the Buddha's Truth was authentically Transmitted to him. If there were someone who had not received the authentic Transmission of the Buddha's Truth, who, pray, would call him 'my Ancestral Master'?

We venerate Bodhidharma as our First Chinese Ancestor because he was our Twenty-eighth Indian Ancestor. If we say that what our Ancestor said was apart from what the Buddha said, it would be difficult indeed to establish who our Tenth or our Twentieth Ancestor was! The reason that we revere our Ancestral Teachers who have received the Transmission in turn, heir after heir, is due to the importance of the Buddha's Truth. If there were one of our Ancestral Masters who had not had the Buddha's Truth authentically Transmitted to him, how would he be able to face either ordinary people or those in higher realms? And what would be more difficult still would be to turn aside from our most profound intention to realize Buddhahood in order to follow some teacher who had no connection with the Buddha's Way!

Untrustworthy crazies today vainly sneer at the Buddha's Truth because they are unable to determine which teaching is the Buddha's Truth. For them to compare, even for a moment, Taoist or Confucian doctrines with the Buddha's Teaching is not only pitiable folly, it is also the karmic* consequence of their wrongful deeds in past lives and signals the decline of their nation, because it belittles the Three Treasures of Buddha, Dharma, and Sangha. The paths of Confucius and Lao-tzu are in no way the same as the path of an arhat,* to say nothing of the paths of those in the two highest states of bodhisattvahood! Confucius and Lao-tzu were barely able to read the great

---

Does not depend on the written word;
It directly points us to our human heart,
So that we may see our True Nature and thereby become Buddha.

wonders of heaven and earth and see in them what the saintly saw and heard. It would have been hard for them to clarify in one lifetime, or even in many lifetimes, just what our Great Saintly Shakyamuni's law of causality is. They could just barely discern the sitting place of body and mind that is found within the activity of 'non-activity', but they were unable to clarify what the Universal Truth within the limitlessness of every moment truly is. In short, the Confucian and Taoist teachings are so inferior to the Teachings of the Buddha that the differences cannot even begin to be described by terms like 'the separation between heaven and earth'. To recklessly discuss them as all having one and the same principle is to slander the Buddha Dharma and to slander Confucianism and Taoism. Even though there are some accurate points in the teachings of those two, our present day veteran monks have not even clarified a fraction of those points, much less have they grabbed hold of the Great Handle even once in ten thousand tries! Although instruction and training can be found in the works of both of these, ordinary, run-of-the-mill scholars today cannot readily follow it. There is none in that bunch who could even try to do that training. They cannot even connect one bit of teaching with another. How much less could these present-day veteran monks possibly realize the profound subtleties of Buddhist Scriptures! Not having clarified what the other two are actually about, they just irresponsibly put forth their own questionable teachings.

In Great Sung China today, such fellows ascribe the title of master to themselves as proof that they are entitled to take up the profession. Without shame for past or present, and with a befuddled mind, they make a mishmash of what the Buddha said. It is difficult to acknowledge that they have received the Buddha Dharma. Monks like these all say, "The Buddhist Scriptures do not contain the original intention behind what the Buddha said. The Ancestral Transmission contains what His original intention was. In the Ancestral Transmission alone, that which is mysterious, unique, profound, and wondrous has been passed on."

Saying things like this is the extreme in silliness. It is what the deranged say. In the authentic Transmission of our Ancestral Masters, there is nothing mysterious or special that in any way differs in even one remark or half a verse from what is in the Buddhist Scriptures. The Buddhist Scriptures and the sayings of our Ancestors are both alike as to what has been authentically Transmitted, which has flowed out from

Shakyamuni Buddha. But the Ancestral Transmission has been Transmitted only from heir to heir. Given that, how could such heirs possibly not know Buddhist Scriptures, or fail to clarify them, or fail to recite them? An ancient worthy once said, "You are deluding yourself with the Scriptures: the Scriptures are not deluding you." There are many stories about ancient worthies reading Scriptures.

What I would like to say to those who are inaccurate is the following: "If it were as you say, then if you throw out Buddhist Scriptures, you will be throwing out the Buddha's Mind, as well as His Body. If you throw out His Body and Mind, then you will be throwing out His disciples. If you throw out His disciples, you will be throwing out the Way of the Buddhas. If you throw out the Way of the Buddhas, will you not be throwing out the Way of the Ancestors? Were you to throw out both the Way of the Buddhas and the Way of the Ancestors, you would be just one more shaven head among a hundred others. Who could then say that you did not deserve a good thwack! Not only would you be at the beck and call of every lord and his retainers, you will also be called to account by Old Yama, Lord of the Dead."

Old veteran monks in present-day China no sooner receive a note from some lord or retainer than they proclaim themselves to be the Abbot of a temple and, on that basis, go around mouthing wild words like those alluded to above. And there is no one to distinguish right from wrong. Only my late Master, and he alone, would break out into laughter over that bunch. None of the senior monks from other monasteries recognized what was going on.

As a rule, we should not think that just because monks come from foreign parts they must have a clearer understanding of the Way, or that because they are teachers of some emperor of a great nation they must invariably have penetrated the Matter. All foreigners do not necessarily have the makings of a monk: good people are good and wicked people are wicked. Within the three worlds of the universe, the potential of people will be the same.

Likewise, those who have realized the Truth are not necessarily the ones who are chosen to be teachers to emperors of great nations, since emperors also have difficulty in knowing who has realized the Way. They simply make their appointments on the basis of the advice they hear from their retainers. In past and present, there have been imperial teachers who have realized the Truth and imperial teachers who have not realized the Truth. It is the unenlightened person who gets appointed in corrupt times, just as it is the enlightened person who does not get appointed in those times. And why is that? Because there are times when 'such a person'* is recognized and times when 'such a person' is not recognized. We should not forget the age-old example of Jinshū.[11] Jinshū became an imperial teacher. He lectured on the Dharma while seated before the bamboo curtain of the emperor and he gave voice to the Dharma while seated before the gilded screen of the empress. And what is more, he held the highest seat among the seven hundred high-ranking monks of Kōnin's assembly. And at the same time, long ago on Mount Ōbai there was the temple laborer named Ro.[12] By changing his occupation from woodcutter to temple laborer, he freed himself from hauling firewood. Even so, he took up the occupation of pounding the temple's rice. Though some may feel sorry that he was of humble birth, he nevertheless left secular life behind him and even transcended monkhood, for he had realized the Dharma and had had the sacred robe passed on to him while still a lay person. This is something that was unheard of in the past, not even in India to the west, and it constitutes a remarkable precedent set in the eastern land of China. It is as if even the seven hundred high-ranking monks did not compare with him nor could the dragon elephants* of his whole nation follow in his footsteps. He is truly an heir of the Buddha who has taken his position as our Ancestor of the thirty-third generation after Shakyamuni. If our Fifth Chinese Ancestor Daiman Kōnin had not been a true spiritual friend and guide who was able to recognize 'such a person', how, pray, could this possibly have come about as it did? Quietly reflect on this principle and do not be hasty. We should desire to develop the ability to recognize 'such a one'. To fail to do so is a great sorrow for both oneself and others, a great sorrow for our whole nation. Broad knowledge and a superior view of things are not necessary. You need only to seek the Eye that recognizes 'such a person' and quickly develop your abilities to do

---

11.   Jinshū was the most outstanding monk in Daiman Kōnin's huge assembly on Mount Ōbai. Only Daikan Enō, who was a lay laborer in the monastery at that time, was able to demonstrate a deeper understanding of the Dharma, and he thereby became Kōnin's Dharma heir and the recipient of the bowl and robe of Bodhidharma.

12.   Ro was the family name of Daikan Enō.

so. Should you lack the ability to recognize 'such a one', you will sink into ages of darkness.

Hence, you need to realize that, beyond doubt, there are Buddhist Scriptures within the Way of the Buddha. You need to explore the extensive texts and the profound meaning of Their mountains and rivers, and you should make these Scriptures your standard for doing your utmost to train in the Way.[13]

Given to the assembly during the ninth lunar month of the first year of the Kangen era (October 1243) while residing at Kippō-ji Temple in the Yoshida district of Echizen Province.

---

13. In this context, 'mountains and rivers' can be seen as aspects of movement and stillness within meditation practice. It can also describe obstructions that are encountered in our daily experience, and hence to the Scriptures' Teachings on how to overcome those obstructions.

51

On the Buddha's Way

(Butsudō)

Translator's Introduction: In this discourse, Dōgen takes to task the common view that there are five Chinese Zen sects—namely, Sōtō, Rinzai, Hōgen, Igyō, and Ummon—which are different and have unique ways of training and teaching. Dōgen argues that there is only one way, the Buddha's Way, and that this Way is the same for all authentic expressions of Buddhism and is encapsulated in the phrase, 'the Transmission of the Treasure House of the Eye of the True Teaching, which is the Wondrous Heart of Nirvana'. He does, however, recognize that there are various lineages within Buddhism, but states that they all share the same underlying Truth of the Buddha's Way and do not constitute unrelated or unique ways of training.

The Old Buddha Enō once addressed his assembly, saying, "From me back to the Seven Buddhas,* there have been forty Ancestors." When we thoroughly explore this statement, we see that he means there are forty Buddhas coming down from the Seven Buddhas to Daikan Enō. When we count Buddha after Buddha and Ancestor after Ancestor, this is how we count Them. When we count Them like this, the Seven Buddhas are seven Ancestors and the thirty-three Ancestors are thirty-three Buddhas. This is the thrust of what Daikan Enō is saying. This is the Buddha's instruction for genuine Dharma heirs; only the inheritors of the genuine Transmission have had passed on to them the genuine method of counting.

From Shakyamuni Buddha down to Daikan Enō, there have been thirty-four Ancestors. This Transmission from Buddha to Ancestor—Buddha after Buddha and Ancestor after Ancestor—has been just like Makakashō's having a mutual encounter with the Tathagata and the Tathagata bringing out a smile from Makakashō.[1]

---

*   See Glossary.

1.   Makakashō was Shakyamuni Buddha's Dharma heir.

Just as Shakyamuni Buddha explored the Matter[*] through His training with Kāshyapa Buddha,[2] so it is with Master and disciple today. As a result, the Treasure House of the Eye of the True Teaching has been personally Transmitted from Dharma heir to Dharma heir. The true life of the Buddha Dharma is nothing other than this authentic Transmission. Because the Buddha Dharma has been authentically Transmitted in this manner, it has been passed along by Dharma heir after Dharma heir.

Hence, the meritorious behavior and the essential operation of the Way of the Buddhas have been inherent within each of them, without exception. The Way of the Buddhas has been passed on from India in the west to China in the east, a distance of some hundred and eight thousand miles, and It has been passed on from the time when the Buddha was in the world down to this very day, a span of some two thousand years. Those folks who have not explored this fundamental principle through training with a Master arbitrarily say such wild and mistaken things as calling the Treasure House of the Eye of the True Teaching, which is the Wondrous Heart of Nirvana, 'the Zen sect,' or they call our Ancestral Masters 'Zen Patriarchs', or they declare academic teachers to be Zen Masters, or call them 'Zen monks', or call themselves 'devotees of Zen'. These are all branches and leaves who take warped views to be the root. In India and China from ancient times down to the present day, no one has ever spoken of 'the Zen sect', which is the term by which these people arbitrarily refer to themselves. Such people are demons out to destroy the Buddha's Way. They are a malicious group who are enemies to the Ancestors of the Buddha.

It says in the *Forest Records*:[3]

Bodhidharma first went from the kingdom of Liang to the kingdom of Wei. He traveled to the foot of Mount Sūzan and rested

---

2.   During a previous life.

3.   *Sekimon*, a twelfth-century work by Kakuhan Ekō, a Rinzai monk, which he compiled while he was staying at Sekimon Temple.

his traveling staff at Shōrin-ji Temple. He simply sat in stillness, facing a wall: he was not engaged in learning how to meditate. For a long time no one could figure out why he was doing that and, consequently, interpreted it as his learning how to meditate.

Now, meditation in its narrow sense is simply one among various practices, so how could it suffice to say that this was all there was to the Saintly One? Yet, people of his time did just that. Those engaged in making chronicles followed suit and reported him as being among the ranks of those learning how to meditate and grouped him with people who are as dead trees or cold ashes.[4] Even so, the Saintly One's practice did not simply stop at doing meditation; he also did not act contrary to meditation. And even with the yin and yang described in the *Book of Changes*, he did not act contrary to yin and yang.

Bodhidharma's being called the Twenty-eighth Ancestor is based on the virtuous monk Makakashō's being called the First Ancestor. He is the Thirty-fifth Ancestor when counting from Bibashi Buddha.[5] And not all of the Seven Buddhas and those of the twenty-eight generations who followed Them were able to awaken to the Truth just by means of formal meditation practice. This is why the old Master of Sekimon said, "Meditation in its narrow sense is simply one among various practices, so how could it suffice to say that this was all there was to the Saintly One?"

This old Master had come to see a bit of what people are really like and had entered the inner meaning of the doctrines of our Ancestral tradition. This was why he spoke as he did. In recent times throughout Great Sung China, it would be difficult to find such a one as he, and we should be thankful to meet such a one. And even if

---

4. 'Dead trees and cold ashes' is a common Zen Buddhist figure of speech for someone who has dropped off self. In the present context, it implies that Bodhidharma had gone just so far in his practice, but no further.

5. Bibashi Buddha is the first of the Seven Buddhas, the last of whom is Shakyamuni Buddha.

formal meditation were the central practice, we should not name it 'the Zen sect'.[6] And what is more, formal meditation practice is not the whole essence of what the Buddha taught.[7]

Even so, folks who willfully call the great Way that has been genuinely Transmitted from Buddha to Buddha 'the Zen sect' have not yet encountered the Way of the Buddhas even in their dreams, nor heard of It in their dreams, nor had It Transmitted to them in their dreams. Do not even suggest that the Buddha Dharma may exist among that bunch who identify themselves as belonging to 'the Zen sect'. Who was it that invented the name 'the Zen sect'? Surely it was not called the Zen sect by any of the Buddhas, Ancestors, and Masters in our lineage. Keep in mind that the name 'the Zen sect' is one used by Mara, the lord of demons, and it is his band of devils that customarily use Mara's term: it is not the descendants of the Buddhas and Ancestors.

Once when the World-honored One held up an udumbara blossom before an assembly of millions on Vulture Peak, His eyes atwinkle, the whole assembly fell silent. Only the face of the honorable Makakashō broke into a smile. Thereupon, the World-honored One said, "I confer upon Makakashō my Treasure House of the Eye of the True Teaching, which is the Wondrous Heart of Nirvana, along with my sanghati robe."[8]

What the World-honored One conferred upon the virtuous monk Makakashō was His Treasure House of the Eye of the True Teaching, which is the Wondrous Heart of Nirvana. He did not add, "I confer upon Makakashō my Zen sect." He said, "along

---

6. Dōgen's term *zenshū* can be rendered not only as the Zen sect but also as the Zen school, the Zen Church, the Meditation School, etc.

7. That is, there is also living in accord with the Precepts and, for monastics, the monastic rules and procedures, as well as the Bodhisattva Vows.

8. The sanghati robe is one of the three types of robe that were allowed to Buddhist monks at that time. Dōgen gives a detailed explanation of each type of robe in Discourse 84: On the Spiritual Merits of the Kesa *(Kesa Kudoku)*.

with my sanghati robe." He did not say, "along with the Zen sect." Accordingly, the name 'Zen sect' was never heard whilst the World-honored One was in the world.

> Our First Chinese Ancestor, Bodhidharma, in pointing out the matter to our Second Ancestor, Eka, said, "The unsurpassed and wondrous Way of the Buddhas requires difficult and painful training, as well as the ability to bear what is difficult to bear, and all this over innumerable periods of time. Why would anyone desire the True Vehicle whilst having only little virtue and less wise discernment, or whilst having a belittling mind and a slothful attitude?" He also said, "The Dharma seal[*] of the Buddhas is not something to be obtained from worldly folk." And he also said, "The Tathagata conferred the Treasure House of the Eye of the True Teaching upon the virtuous monk Makakashō by means of the Treasure House of the Eye of the True Teaching."

What is now being pointed to is the unsurpassed and wondrous Way of the Buddhas, along with the Treasure House of the Eye of the True Teaching and the Buddha seal of the Buddhas. At that time there was no mention whatsoever of a 'Zen sect', nor was there any cause or condition for calling anything 'the Zen sect'. Now, the Treasure House of the Eye of the True Teaching had come to be Transmitted face-to-face by the raising of eyebrows and the twinkling of eyes. It has come to be bestowed with body and mind, bones and marrow. It has come to be accepted with body and mind, bones and marrow. It has been Transmitted and accepted from a previous Self to a later Self; it has been Transmitted and accepted above and beyond the ordinary mind. Within the assembly of the World-honored One and Makakashō the term 'Zen sect' was not heard; within the assemblies of our First and Second Chinese Ancestors, the term 'Zen sect' was not heard; within the assembly of our Fifth and Sixth Ancestors, the term 'Zen sect' was not heard; within the assembly of Seigen and Nangaku, the term 'Zen sect' was not heard. There is no indication of who it was that came to use the term or when it came about. Perhaps those scholars who should not be counted as real scholars, those whose ulterior motive was to destroy the Dharma or to plagiarize It, may have come to use the term. If present-day students of the Way carelessly use a term that the Buddhas and Ancestors had not permitted, they may well miss the gateway to our tradition.

Further, it makes it seem as if there is another method of training called 'the Zen sect', a method that is different from the one used by Buddha after Buddha and Ancestor after Ancestor. If there is a method that is different from the Way of the Buddhas and Ancestors, it will be a method of non-Buddhists. Since you are already the offspring of the Buddhas and Ancestors, you should explore through your training the Bones and Marrow, as well as the appearance, of the Buddhas and Ancestors. You have already embarked on the Way of the Buddhas and Ancestors, so do not depart from It and explore non-Buddhist ways. It is rare for us to have the opportunity to obtain and preserve the body and mind of a human being, and this present opportunity is due to the supporting merit from our doing our utmost to practice the Way in the past. Should you mistakenly support non-Buddhist ways after having received this benevolent gift, you will not be repaying your indebtedness to the Buddhas and Ancestors.

During recent generations in Great Sung China, there have been many common folk throughout the land who have heard this erroneous name of 'the Zen sect' and therefore speak of 'the Zen sect', or speak of 'the Bodhidharma sect', or speak of 'the Buddha Mind sect'. These wrong names are bruited about, competing with each other and corrupting the Buddha's Way. These names are the wild rantings of people who do not know the Great Way of the Buddhas and Ancestors and who have never encountered, or even heard about, the Treasure House of the Eye of the True Teaching. Much less do they believe that It exists! How could anyone who knows the Treasure House of the Eye of the True Teaching call the Buddha's Way by a wrong name?

This is why Sekitō Kisen, in ascending to the Dharma seat, addressed his great assembly saying, "The Dharma Gate that I have accepted has been Transmitted to me by a previous Buddha. It has been done without getting involved in discussions of contemplative meditation or of diligence in practice. It was given solely that I might master the wise perception of a Buddha."

You need to know that Ancestors of the Buddha who have received the authentic Transmission from the Seven Buddhas, as well as from all other Buddhas, express Themselves like this. The only words they speak are "The Dharma Gate that I have accepted has been Transmitted to me by a previous Buddha." Sekitō did not say, "The Zen sect that I have accepted has been Transmitted to me by a previous Buddha." He did not get into arguments about such topics as contemplative meditation or diligence in practice. What was given to him was given solely for the purpose that he might master the wise perception of a Buddha. It was solely the wise perception of a Buddha which he was to master—and without being averse to contemplative meditation and diligence in practice. This is equivalent to the statement, "I confer my Treasure House of the Eye of the True Teaching." 'My' means 'what I possess'. 'The Dharma Gate' means 'the True Teaching'. 'My', 'what I possess', and 'my Marrow' are what <u>you</u> receive through Transmission.

Great Master Sekitō Kisen was the sole Dharma heir of the Founding Ancestor Seigen Gyōshi and was the only one permitted to enter his Master's private quarters. And Seigen was a Dharma offspring of the Old Buddha Daikan Enō, who shaved his head.[9] Thus, the Old Buddha Daikan Enō was Seigen's Ancestor, as well as his monastic father, and the Founding Ancestor Seigen was Sekitō's elder brother in the Sangha, as well as his Master. As a hero in the Buddha's Way and in the stream of the Ancestors, Great Master Sekitō Kisen stands alone. Only Sekitō, and he alone, mastered the authentic Transmission in the Way of the Buddhas. All the instances of his bringing the Teaching to fruition which he manifested through words were the timeless acts of an Old Buddha manifesting His eternal presence. We should regard Sekitō as possessing the Eye of the Treasure House of the True Teaching; he is not to be compared with self or other. Ignorant people are wrong to compare him with Baso.[10]

---

9.   That is, he ordained Seigen as a monk.

10.   Better known as Baso Dōitsu, a contemporaneous monk in Rinzai's lineage.

So, you need to keep in mind that the Buddha's Way, which was Transmitted and received from a previous Buddha, was not called 'contemplative meditation', much less was it ever called, or discussed as, 'the Zen sect'! Clearly, you need to realize that calling It 'the Zen sect' is a mistake of enormous proportions. By thinking that religious practice must be part of either a concrete sect or an abstract sect, the inexperienced defame the Way, as if It were something not worth exploring if It were not called 'a sect'. The Buddha's Way cannot be like that, so be certain that It has never been called 'the Zen sect'.

At the same time, the mainstream of people in recent generations are befuddled and do not know the old customs. That bunch who have not received Transmission from a past Buddha mistakenly say, "Within the Buddha Dharma, there are the methods and customs of the five sects." This is the natural progression of a decline in the Teaching. There has not yet been one person, or even half a person, who is able to halt It.[11] My late Master Tendō, an Old Buddha, was the first to show concern for this situation, due to his mastery of the Dharma, and to our good fortune.

My late Master, an Old Buddha, once ascended the Dharma seat and addressed his assembly, saying, "People nowadays just talk of there being separate traditions and customs, such as those of Ummon, Hōgen, Igyō, Rinzai, and Sōtō, but this is not the Buddha's Teaching, nor is it what Ancestors and Masters say." The opportunity to hear someone addressing the assembly in this way has been difficult to encounter even in a thousand years. My late Master alone expressed it like this. It is hard to hear such Teaching anywhere throughout the ten quarters, and only those in his assembly were able to hear it. Even so, among a thousand monks, many are those whose ears do not truly hear and whose eyes do not truly see. Even less do they hear with their hearts, and less still do they hear with their whole being! Even if someone had listened with the whole of his own body and mind for millions of myriad eons, he

---

11. 'Person', here, refers to one who is fully enlightened, whereas 'half a person' is someone who is partially enlightened.

could never have made use of my late Master's awakened body and mind to listen to it, or awaken to it, or develop faith in it, or to drop body and mind off. Sad to say, everyone within the ten directions of Great Sung China considered the old veteran monks of other monasteries to be on a par with my late Master. Should we consider folks who thought like this to be equipped with eyes, or should we consider that they were not yet equipped with the Eye?

Further, there were some who viewed my late Master as standing shoulder-to-shoulder with Rinzai and Tokusan. We can surely say that these folks had likewise never encountered my late Master nor had they ever met up with Rinzai. Before I had done my respectful bows to my late Master,[12] an Old Buddha, I had already aimed at thoroughly exploring the so-called 'deeper principles of the five sects'. After I had done my respectful bows to my late Master, the Old Buddha, I clearly understood that 'the five sects' was just an arbitrary name.

Because this is so, there was no such term as 'the five sects' at the time when the Buddha's Teaching was flourishing in Great Sung China, nor did anyone of even more ancient times put forth the term 'the five sects'. Now that the Buddha's Teaching is beginning to decay, the term 'the five sects' emerges from time to time. This is because people are confused in their explorations of the Matter and are not committed to their pursuit of the Way. To all of you trainees who are sincerely seeking to thoroughly explore the Matter through your training, I loathe having to warn you that you must not hold onto these arbitrary terms for five sects. Do not take such terms to be representative of the traditions and customs of five separate families. How much less should you hold onto terms such as 'the three profundities and the three necessities' and 'the four perspectives and the four modes of reflection and action' associated with Rinzai's lineage, to say nothing of 'the three phrases' attributed to Rinzai, 'the five levels' of Tōzan and Sōzan, and 'the ten types of Truth, which are the same for all Masters' that is associated with Fun'yō!

What our Master Shakyamuni Buddha said was not as narrow in perspective as all this, and He did not value this type of thinking highly. This was not the sort of

---

12. That is, before Dōgen had committed himself to being Nyojō's disciple.

thing that was taught at Shōrin-ji Monastery or upon Mount Sōkei.[13] Sad to say, it is what the shaven-headed trainees of these degenerate days of the Dharma say, those who do not really hear the Teaching and whose body, mind, and eyes are still in the dark.

We who are the living children and potential heirs of the Buddhas and Ancestors must not speak in this manner. Among Masters who abide in, and keep to, the Teaching of the Buddhas and Ancestors, wild words such as these are never to be heard. Second-rate teachers of recent times, who have never heard the whole of what the Buddha Dharma is expressing, who are not totally devoted to what the Ancestors have said, and who are in the dark about their own Original Nature, have given rise to sectarian names like those mentioned earlier out of pride in their small bits of learning. Once these sectarian names became established, those who were young in their training did not learn the proper way to search for the Source and, as a consequence, vainly pursued superficialities. They did not have the spirit that venerates the old ways, but rather engaged in conduct that was mixed with secular customs. However, even the worldly-minded warn people that following worldly ways is ignoble.

Emperor Wen of the Chou dynasty asked his wise minister Taikung, "Why is it that our society is in ever-increasing turmoil, putting the nation in peril? Even though, as a ruler, I endeavor to employ wise counselors, I am not gaining any benefit from them."

Taikung responded, "You may hire the wise, but you will not benefit from them because you have only appeared to have received their sage advice, and therefore you gain nothing from getting their wise counsel."

Emperor Wen then asked, "Wherein does such a fault lie?"

---

13. Shōrin-ji Monastery is associated with Bodhidharma and Mount Sōkei is associated with Daikan Enō.

Taikung replied, "The fault lies in being fond of those who are praised by the worldly instead of finding those who are truly sagacious."

Emperor Wen then asked, "What do you mean by having a fondness for those who are praised by the worldly?"

Taikung said, "When people are fond of listening to what the worldly praise, some may take the unwise to be wise; some may take the slow-witted to be intelligent; some may take the disloyal to be loyal; some may take the untrustworthy to be trustworthy. If, on the basis of what the worldly praise, your lordship were to consider someone to be wise and intelligent, or consider someone to be incompetent, then the one who has many henchmen will be advanced, but the one who has few supporters will not. Thus, when a crowd of wicked ones band together and try to conceal the one who is wise, loyal retainers may be put to death on false charges, while false counselors skirmish for prestige and court rank. Thereby, society is in ever-increasing turmoil, and, as a consequence, the nation cannot avoid being put in peril."

Even the worldly grieve when their nation and their customs are in peril. When the Buddha Dharma and the Way of the Buddha are in peril, the disciples of the Buddha will inevitably feel grief. The reason for this peril is the irresponsible following of worldly ways. When people hearken to what is praised by the worldly, they do not find those who are genuinely wise. If you wish to find one who is genuinely wise, you will need to have the resourcefulness that illumines the past and looks forward to what lies ahead. What the worldly praise is not invariably wise, nor is it invariably saintly, and what the worldly slander is likewise not invariably wise, nor is it invariably saintly. Even so, by considering the matter three times over, you may avoid confusing the times when someone who is wise has invited censure with times when someone who is a fraud is being praised. If rulers should fail to make use of the truly wise, it will be a loss for their country, and if they should employ the slow-witted, it will be a source of national regret.

Now, the arising of the term 'the five sects' is an aberration of the secular world. Those who follow these worldly ways are many, but those who can recognize them as being worldly are few. You should regard those who mistake worldly ways for saintly ways, as well as those who follow them, to have reached the height of folly. How could those folks who follow worldly ways possibly recognize the Buddha's True Teaching? How could they possibly become Buddhas and Ancestors? The Dharma has been Transmitted to heir after heir of the Seven Buddhas. Those folks whose understanding is based merely on words and who speak of 'the five sects' do not realize that five different versions of the *Vinaya* were never established in India.[14]

So, you should recognize that our Ancestral Masters turned the true life of the Buddha's Teaching into their own true life. None of them ever said that there were five sects, each with their own traditions and practices. To learn that there are five Zen sects within the Buddha's Way is not the true inheritance from the Seven Buddhas.

My late Master once addressed his assembly, saying, "In recent years, the Way of our Ancestral Masters has degenerated. Bands of demons and beasts are many. They often go on about 'the traditions and practices of the five sects'. How distressing! How truly distressing!" Hence, we know all too well that none of the twenty-eight generations in India or the twenty-two Ancestors in China ever taught about any traditions or customs of five Zen sects. Our Ancestral Masters, who were all worthy of the title of Ancestral Master, have all been the same in this. Those who go about proclaiming that there are five Zen sects, each with its own unique tenets, are folks who are deceiving the public. They are a bunch who have heard little and whose understanding is shallow. If everyone in the Buddha's Way set up his own unique way, how could the Buddha's Way possibly have come down to us today? Makakashō would have set up his own way and Ananda would have set up his. If the principle of setting up one's own way was the authentic Way, the Buddha Dharma would have

---

14.   The *Vinaya* is a section of the Buddhist canon that contains rules of monastic discipline.

disappeared in India long ago. Who would honor principles that individual people had set up on their own? If each person sets up his own principles, who could determine which were true and which were false? What was true and what was false could never be determined. If the true and the false cannot be determined, who could recognize what was actually the Buddha Dharma? If its principles cannot be clarified, it would be difficult to call anything 'the Way of the Buddha'. The names of the so-called 'five Zen sects' did not arise during the lifetime of any of the five Ancestral Masters. After those who were called 'the Ancestral Masters of the five Zen sects' had entered nirvana, mediocre trainees within their families, those whose Eye had not yet become clear and whose feet did not know how to step forth, established these names without asking their Master's permission and contrary to the Teaching of the Ancestors. This is so evident that anyone can recognize it.

Meditation Master Isan Reiyū was a Dharma heir of Hyakujō Daichi. He lived as Abbot on Mount Isan while Hyakujō was still alive. He never said that the Buddha Dharma should be called the Igyō sect.[15] And Hyakujō never said, "From your time onwards, you should dwell on Mount Isan and call your sect the Igyō sect." Neither Master Isan nor his Ancestor Hyakujō ever used such a name, so you need to keep in mind that it is a fraudulent name. And even though people use his name as part of their name for a sect, we should not single out Kyōzan in this way.[16] If it were appropriate for Isan and Kyōzan to have used their own names, they would have used them, but because it is not appropriate to use one's own name, they did not use their personal names in the past and we should not use them in the present. People do not speak of an Enō sect, or of a Nangaku sect, or of a Baso sect, or of a Hyakujō sect. It is impossible that the Dharma of Isan could differ from that of Enō, or could surpass It, or could ever be a rival to It.

15.	The name Igyō derives from the first syllable of Isan's name and the first syllable of Kyōzan Ejaku's name. Kyōzan was one of Isan's Dharma heirs.

16.	Since Isan had four other Dharma heirs.

The words that Isan and Kyōzan spoke were undoubtedly not like one pole being carried by two men. If people wanted to establish a name for a sect, they should have called it the Isan sect or the Daii sect, since there is no reason for calling it the Igyō sect. If 'the Igyō sect' were an appropriate name, it would have been called this when the two venerable elders were still alive. What was there to prevent them from using a name that they could have used while they were still alive? To go counter to what their parental Ancestors said and use the name 'the Igyō sect', which neither used while they were alive, is to be children who are devoid of filial piety. This name does not represent the basic intention of Meditation Master Isan or the original purpose of our esteemed teacher Kyōzan. It has not been genuinely Transmitted by an authentic Master. It is clear that it is a fraudulent name used by fraudulent people. Do not let it be spread abroad anywhere in the whole universe.

After abandoning his position as an academic lecturer on Buddhist Scriptures, Rinzai became a disciple of Ōbaku. On three occasions he tasted Ōbaku's staff, for a total of sixty strokes, and he awoke to his Original Nature whilst exploring the Matter with Daigu.[17] Even though he had not yet fully penetrated Ōbakū's Mind, he took up residence at Rinzai-in Monastery in Chenchou Province. Nevertheless, he never spoke a single sentence to the effect that the Buddha Dharma that had been Transmitted to him should be called the Rinzai sect, nor did he even speak one phrase to that effect, nor did he ever express such a thing by raising a fist or by picking up a ceremonial hossu.* Even so, mediocre trainees within his monastic family failed to preserve their monastic parent's conduct, as well as the Buddha Dharma, and, soon afterwards, mistakenly gave rise to the name 'the Rinzai sect'. If this name had been contrived whilst Great Master Rinzai was still alive, he certainly would have had something to say about the matter, since it is counter to the Teachings of our First Chinese Ancestor.

---

17.   His awakening was aided by Daigu's helping him to realize why Ōbaku had beaten him.

As Rinzai was dying and was about to pass on the Dharma to Meditation Master Sanshō Enen, he said, "After my departure, do not let my Treasure House of the Eye of the True Teaching perish."

Enen replied, "My Venerable Monk, how would I dare to let your Treasure House of the Eye of the True Teaching perish?"

Rinzai then said, "If there were someone who questioned you about It in a peremptory manner, how would you respond?"

Enen immediately gave out with a loud yell that sounded like a donkey's braying.

Rinzai said, "Who would not believe that my Treasure House of the Eye of the True Teaching, which I am passing on to this blind jackass, would perish?"

The words spoken by Master and disciple were just like this.[18]

Rinzai never said, "Do not let my Zen sect perish," nor did he say, "Do not let my Rinzai sect perish," nor did he say, "Do not let my sect perish." What he did say, quite simply, was, "Do not let my Treasure House of the Eye of the True Teaching perish." Be very clear about this, for you should not call the Great Way that is authentically Transmitted by the Ancestors of the Buddha 'the Zen sect' or call it 'the Rinzai sect'. Indeed, you should not even dream of calling It 'the Zen sect'. Even though his term 'letting It perish' refers to that thread which runs through the Treasure House of the Eye of the True Teaching, as well as to the way in which It manifests, It is Transmitted in just the way that Rinzai did it. His 'letting It perish' by passing It on

---

18.   Rinzai's response is intended ironically and has the effect of adding some light-hearted humor to what was actually a very serious moment. This display of humor is demonstrative of the deep trust that existed between Master and disciple.

to this blind donkey is truly the 'Who knows' of Transmission.[19] In Rinzai's lineage, it was only Enen who received the Transmission in this way. You should not compare him to or equate him with any of his younger or older brothers in the Dharma.[20] Naturally, he was placed near a bright window.[21] The story of Rinzai and Enen is that of Buddha and Ancestor. Today, a Rinzai Transmission is just as the Vulture Peak Transmission of ancient times. So, the principle is clear that one should not speak of a Rinzai sect.

Great Master Ummon Bun'en first trained under the venerable elder Chin and may have been one of Ōbakū's offspring. He later became a Dharma heir of Seppō. This Master never said that one should refer to the Treasure House of the Eye of the True Teaching as 'the Ummon sect'. But later, some members of his monastic family, not realizing that the false names 'the Igyō sect' and 'the Rinzai sect' were inappropriate titles, set up the new name of 'the Ummon sect'. If it had been Great Master Ummon's underlying intention to give his name to a sect, it would be difficult to affirm that he possessed the Body and Mind of the Buddha Dharma. When people nowadays give his name to the name of a sect, it is as if they were calling an emperor the lowliest of commoners.

Meditation Master Hōgen of Seiryō-in Monastery was the authentic Dharma heir of Great Master Jizō Keichin. He was the Dharma grandchild of Gensha Shibi.

---

19. The phrase 'Who knows' has a double meaning in Zen texts. It can be taken as a question, meaning, "Who can possibly see what is passed on at Transmission?" and it can also be taken as an assertion, meaning "It is 'the Who'—that is, the Buddha Nature—that knows what is Transmitted."

20. Enen was one of Rinzai's seven Dharma heirs. The Rinzai lineage, however, passed on through another of Rinzai's heirs.

21. This is said of someone whose spiritual ripeness is so apparent upon his arrival at a monastery that he is given a place in the Trainees' Hall—traditionally described as 'a well-lit place'—where the Master can keep an eye on him.

He grasped the fundamental meaning without any error. Daihōgen was the Master's title bestowed upon him by the emperor and the name that he used for his signature. There is not a single word among his thousands of words, not one sentence among his thousands of sentences, by which he established the title of 'the Hōgen sect' by using his title as a name for the Treasure House of the Eye of the True Teaching.[22] Even so, those in his lineage have given rise to the name 'the Hōgen sect'. If Hōgen were alive today to spiritually lead others, he would not lead them down the path of using the term 'the Hōgen sect'. Since Meditation Master Hōgen has already passed away, there is no one to save us from this sickness. Even after thousands of myriad years, people who would be loyal to Meditation Master Hōgen must not take 'the Hōgen sect' for their name if they wish to remain faithful to his Teaching.

In summary, both Ummon and Hōgen were distant offspring of our Great Ancestor Seigen. The Bones of the Way were passed on to each of them, along with the Marrow of the Dharma.

Our Founding Ancestor, Great Master Tōzan Ryōkai, inherited the Dharma from Ungan. Ungan was the direct heir of Great Master Yakusan. Yakusan was the direct heir of Great Master Sekitō. Great Master Sekitō was the sole disciple of our Founding Ancestor Seigen. There were no others who stood head-and-shoulders with Seigen, so the conduct of the Way was authentically Transmitted to him and to him alone. That the true life of the Buddha's Way has still survived in China is due to Great Master Sekitō's having been authentically Transmitted in full.

Our Founding Ancestor Seigen lived at the same time as the Old Buddha Daikan Enō and he trained his disciples on Mount Seigen in the same way as Daikan Enō trained his. In that Master Enō helped Seigen to emerge as an enlightened Abbot within the world and that both of them served as Abbots during the same period of time, Seigen must have been a genuine Dharma heir above other genuine Dharma heirs, a Founding Ancestor among Founding Ancestors. It is not the case that exploring the Matter with one's Master is preferable to functioning as an Abbot. As

---

22. The Hōgen sect is better known by its Chinese name of the Fayen sect.

students of the Way, you should know that a monk who stood shoulder-to-shoulder with Daikan Enō during that time would be preeminent today.

On the occasion when the Old Buddha Daikan Enō was giving instruction on how one should enter parinirvana, Sekitō, who was seated in the back row, came forward and asked the Master whom he should depend on once the Master had passed on.[23] The Old Buddha Enō told him to pay a visit to Seigen Gyōshi; he did not tell him to pay a visit to Nangaku Ejō. Thus it is clear that the Old Buddha's Treasure House of the Eye of the True Teaching was authentically Transmitted to our Founding Ancestor Seigen and to him alone.[24] Even though we acknowledge that both Seigen and Nangaku were leading disciples who had realized the Way, only our Founding Ancestor Seigen walked on genuinely spiritual footsteps. The Old Buddha Daikan Enō had thus made his own offspring the offspring of Seigen, who, as the spiritual parent of the great-grandparent of Tōzan, was clearly someone who had realized Daikan Enō's Marrow and who was a genuine heir in the Ancestor's lineage.[25]

Great Master Tōzan, as the fourth generation Dharma heir of Seigen, received the genuine Transmission of the Treasure House of the Eye of the True Teaching, which opened his Eye to the Wondrous Heart of Nirvana. There is no separate Transmission, no separate sect, in addition to this. Our Great Master never showed his Fist or his twinkling Eye to his assembly, calling either 'the Sōtō sect'. Further, since there were no mediocre trainees mixed in with his family, how could there possibly be any in his family who spoke of a 'Sōtō sect'!

---

23. Sekitō was a teenager at the time. His sitting in the back row implies that he was a relatively new novice.

24. Daikan Enō had two preeminent disciples, Seigen and Nangaku. Dōgen's Sōtō lineage comes via Seigen, whereas all other extant lineages come via Nangaku.

25. That is, Sekitō was originally one of Daikan Enō's disciples. Because he was not yet named as a Dharma heir, he became Seigen's disciple and, subsequently, his Dharma heir. In turn, Sekitō became the spiritual parent to Yakusan, who became the spiritual parent of Ungō, who became the spiritual parent of Tōzan.

The name 'Sōtō sect' may have derived from someone adding Sōzan's name to Tōzan's. If this is so, then Ungo and Dōan should also have been included.[26] Ungo was a guiding Master among ordinary people, as well as among those in loftier positions, and was even more revered than Sōzan. When it comes to this name 'Sōtō', clearly some stinking skin bag* in an offshoot lineage who fancied himself the equal of Tōzan devised the name 'Sōtō sect'. Truly, even though the situation is as clear as the sun in broad daylight, it is as if the sun were being obscured by floating clouds.

My late Master once said, "Nowadays there are many who have ascended a Lion's Seat* and who act as though they were teachers of ordinary people and those in lofty positions. Even so, none of them has an understanding of the underlying principles of the Buddha Dharma." From this perspective, those who are striving to uphold one of the so-called 'five sects' and make the mistake of getting stuck on the words in some Master's saying are truly enemies of the Buddhas and Ancestors. And some, regarding themselves as belonging to a branch of followers of Meditation Master Ōryū Enan, are in the habit of calling themselves 'the Ōryū sect'. Perhaps their branch will not go on very far before they recognize their error. Speaking generally, while the World-honored One was in the world, he never spoke of 'the Buddha sect' or of 'the Vulture Peak sect'. He did not speak of 'the Jetavana sect', or of a 'My Mind sect', or of a 'Buddha Mind sect', so from what words of the Buddha did the name 'Buddha Mind sect' come? Why do people today speak of a 'Buddha Mind sect'? Why would the World-honored One feel the need to call His mind a sect? And why should a sect ever be connected to a mind? If there is to be a Buddha Mind sect, then there ought to be a Buddha Body sect. And we should have a Buddha Eye sect, and a Buddha Ear sect, or even a Buddha Nose and Tongue sect. There would have to be such things as a Buddha's Marrow Sect, a Buddha's Bones sect, a Buddha's Legs sect,

---

26. Ungo and Sōzan were both Dharma heirs of Tōzan. Sōzan's line ultimately died out, whereas Ungo's continued on with Dōan as his Dharma heir.

or a Buddha Nation sect. No such sects exist at present. Keep in mind that the name 'the Buddha Mind sect' is a phony name.

When Shakyamuni Buddha gave expression to the True Form of all thoughts and things throughout all Buddha lands and when He gave voice to all the Buddha lands throughout the universe, He did not speak of having set up some sect within any of these Buddha lands. If it were the practice of Buddhas and Ancestors to name sects, it would have been done in one of the Buddha lands, and if these names existed in one of the Buddha lands, it would have been something that a Buddha would have spoken of. The Buddha did not speak of it, so you should know for certain that it did not exist in the Buddha lands. It is not practiced in the Way of the Ancestors, so you should know for certain that it is not something that the Ancestors found useful. It is not only something that other people would laugh at, but it is also something that would be held in check by Buddhas. Therefore, it is something that you yourselves should laugh at. So, I beg you, do not create sectarian names, and do not say that there are five sects within the Buddha Dharma.

In more recent times, there was a childlike person named Chisō who collected a small spattering of sayings of Ancestral Masters along with what he called 'the sectarian lineages of the five families'. He named his work the *Eyes of Human and Celestial Beings*. People have not understood what this work really is. Bunches of novices and present-day trainees have fancied that it is accurate, and some of them even go about carrying a copy of it tucked within their robes. This work is not the eyes of human and celestial beings, but rather something that blinds the eyes of human and celestial beings. How could anyone possibly accrue any merit by disregarding the Treasure House of the Eye of the True Teaching?

This *Eyes of Human and Celestial Beings* was compiled and edited by a senior monk named Chisō in Mannen Temple on Mount Tendai around the twelfth lunar month in the sixth year of the Shunhsi era (1188). Even though it was compiled in more recent times, if its statements were accurate we could approve of it. But this work of his is utter madness and blind folly, for he lacked the Eye for exploring the Matter, nor did he have the Eye of one who has journeyed far in search of a Master, to say nothing of having the Eye for recognizing Buddhas and Ancestors! We should not use this work. He shouldn't have been called Chisō, which means 'He Who is Wise and Knowing', but Gumō, which means 'He Who is Blinded by Ignorance'. He is someone who does not know what 'such a person' * means and who has never met 'such a person', and, because of this, he has arbitrarily compiled sayings without picking out just the sayings of those who are 'such a person'. It is obvious that he does not know what 'such a person' is.

The reason why those folks who study Scriptures in China assign sectarian names to them is because they wish to compare the opinions of the various teachers of this and that. Now, the Treasure House of the Eye of the True Teaching of the Buddhas and Ancestors has been Transmitted from Dharma heir to Dharma heir. These heirs are incomparable, for they have no 'this or that' which can confuse others. Be that as it may, there are some trainees of long standing who are inaccurate and who employ sectarian names to no purpose. Because they are engaged in the hot pursuit of personal gain, they do not stand in proper awe of the Buddha's Way.

The Buddha's Way is not someone's personal 'Buddha's Way'. It is the Buddha's Way of the Buddhas and Ancestors. It is the Buddha's Way of the Buddha's Way. As Minister Taikung once said when talking with Emperor Wen, "The whole nation is not the nation of one person. It is the whole nation's whole nation." Thus, even an ordinary layman had wisely discerned this and had put it this way.

As children of the Buddhas and Ancestors, you must not permit those within the Great Way of the Buddhas and Ancestors to recklessly follow along with the foolish and the blind by setting up sects and giving them personal names. That is a great impropriety, and one who acts like this is not a person of the Buddha's Way. If it was right for us to go around naming sects, the World-honored One would have done so Himself. In that the World-honored One had not already given His name to a sect, why should His children use such names after His parinirvana? Who could be more spiritually skillful than the World-honored One? If someone lacks skill, no good can come of it. Again, if the Buddhas and the Ancestors have not acted contrary to the

Way in the past by setting up sects in Their own names, who of His children would name a sect after themselves?

You need to explore the Matter through your training by studying the past and examining the present, and do not be arbitrary about it. When Shakyamuni Buddha was in the world, His disciples were apprehensive lest they should differ from Him by even a hair, or lest they should miss even one jot within the hundreds of thousands of myriad points of His Teaching, for they wished to experience the joy of realizing the Truth which they had chosen as their inheritance, and they would not go against It. Thus, we should vow to seek and serve the Buddha and hear His Dharma over the course of many lives. Those who would deliberately go against the transforming Teaching that the World-honored One gave while He was in the world and give rise to sectarian names are not disciples of the Tathagata nor are they offspring of the Ancestral Masters. Their breaking of Precepts is more serious than the transgressions of others. They have rashly disregarded the importance of the unsurpassed wisdom of the Tathagata, and, by selfishly fostering their own sect, they have made light of or disregarded those who preceded them to such an extent that we can say they do not even know who their predecessors were. They did not trust in the meritorious behavior of the World-honored One during His time. The Buddha Dharma cannot exist within the dwelling places of such people.

So, if you wish to receive the authentic Transmission of the conduct of the Way, you must not look for or hearken to sectarian names. That which Buddha after Buddha and Ancestor after Ancestor has received and authentically Transmitted is the unsurpassed wisdom of the Treasure House of the Eye of the True Teaching. The Dharma that is possessed by the Buddhas and Ancestors has been wholly Transmitted by the Buddhas and Ancestors, and there is nothing new to be added to the Dharma. This principle is the very Bones of the Dharma and the very Marrow of the Way.

Given to the assembly at Kippō-ji Temple in the Yoshida district of Fukui Prefecture on the sixteenth day of the ninth lunar month in the first year of the Kangen era (October 30, 1243).

Copied by me during the third watch of the night on the twenty-third day of the tenth lunar month in the same year (November 6, 1243).

Ejō

52

On the Heart-to-Heart Language of Intimacy

(Mitsugo)

Translator's Introduction: The term *'mitsugo'* has a variety of meanings which come into play throughout this discourse. In its conventional, mundane sense, it refers to using a secret language. That is, someone is using language to conceal something, to hide its meaning from the uninitiated. It also refers to some unique or personal way in which a Buddha or Ancestor puts the Great Matter, a way that has a sense of immediacy in contrast to something discursive. And it refers to the way that Master and disciple communicate, which has inherent in it an element of intimacy or closeness that arises from their being of one Mind and of one Heart.

When your spiritual question fully breaks open and manifests the Great Truth that all Buddhas preserve within Their hearts, the sayings "You too are like this and I too am like this" and "We must guard well" express this awakening to Shakyamuni's prediction of Buddhahood.

One time when Great Master Ungo Dōyō was being offered alms by a high government official, he was asked, "They say that the World-honored One had a secret way of communicating and that Makakashō did not conceal it. What was the World-honored One's secret way of communicating?"

The Great Master called out to him, "O Minister!"

The man acknowledged the call with a "Yes?"

The Great Master said, "Do you get It?"

The official replied, "No, I don't get it."

The Great Master then said, "Were you not to get It, it would be because it is the World-honored One's 'secret' way of putting It. If you were to get It, it would be because Makakashō did not keep It to himself."

The Great Master was making fully apparent that he was a fifth-generation descendant of Seigen and a teacher of those in lofty positions, as well as of ordinary people, and that he was an excellent spiritual friend to those throughout the whole universe in all ten directions, who gave guidance to both the sentient and the nonsentient.[1] As the Forty-sixth Buddha among the Buddha's heirs, he voiced the Dharma for the sake of the Buddhas and Ancestors. Whilst residing in his hermitage on Three-peak Mountain, he was sent food from celestial kitchens as alms. At the time when the Dharma was transmitted to him and he realized the Truth, he transcended the realm of being sent such alms.[2]

What is quoted here now as "The World-honored One had a secret way of putting It and Makakashō did not conceal It" is what the Forty-sixth Buddha passed on to us as the Original Face of forty-six generations. It is not a matter of chasing after someone who has realized It, nor is It something that comes from outside oneself, nor is It something that Makakashō and he alone was originally endowed with, nor has It ever been some prize newly awarded to someone. It is the manifesting of an intimate and personal way of putting It; it is not a matter of the World-honored Shakyamuni having some secret language of His own. All Buddhas and Ancestors have Their own intimate way of putting It. Whoever has already become a World-honored One, without doubt, has an intimate way of putting It. And when someone has an intimate way of putting It, there is no doubt that there will be a Makakashō who will not conceal It. We must not forget to explore through our training the principle that when there are a hundred thousand World-honored Ones, there will be a hundred thousand Makakashō's. 'Exploring through our training' means not intentionally trying to understand everything all at once, but taking great pains in striving a hundred or even a thousand times, as if you were trying to cut through something hard. Do not fancy

---

1. The sentient are those who are sensitive to the Dharma and the nonsentient are those who have not yet learned how to listen to It.

2. While someone is seriously pursuing the path to enlightenment, that person receives celestial sustenance, and when someone realizes the Truth, the offering of celestial sustenance ceases, since there is no longer any need for it.

that when someone has something to relate to you, you should immediately understand what is being said.

In that he of Mount Ungō had already become a World-honored One, he was equipped with an intimate and personal way of putting It and he had Makakashō's way of not concealing It. In your explorations, do not pursue the idea that the calling out of "O Minister!" and the Minister's replying "Yes?" are some secret way of communicating.

In the narrative, the Great Master pointed out the Matter* to the high government official, saying, "Were you not to get It, it would be because it is the World-honored One's 'secret' way of putting It. If you were to get It, it would be because Makakashō did not keep It to himself." You should be determined to do your utmost for as many eons as it takes to pursue what is being said here. What he is saying is, "When you are in a state of not getting It, that is the World-honored One's intimate way of putting It." He is not saying that not getting It was due to the official's being dull-headed. This was his way of giving his support for the official to really listen to what is going on by calmly exploring the principle of 'were you not to get It'. The official needed to do his utmost in pursuing the Way. Also, his saying, "If you were to get It," goes beyond saying, "You have already comprehended it."[3]

There are many different ways to go in exploring the Buddha Dharma through one's training. Among them lies the essential matter of grasping what the Buddha Dharma is or of not grasping what the Buddha Dharma is. Those who have not yet encountered an authentic Master do not even know that such an essential matter exists. In wild confusion, they misunderstand, thinking that there is some kind of secret language, and thereby they recklessly shut off their eyes and ears from seeing and hearing. This goes beyond saying that your understanding is the condition upon which Its 'not being concealed' is based, for It is still not concealed even when you

---

*   See Glossary.

3.   That is, grasping the significance of what the Great Master is pointing to goes far beyond
      having a purely intellectual or speculative understanding.

do not understand It. Do not pursue through your training that not concealing It means that anybody can see or hear It. It is already in plain view right here and now. And when can we say for certain that nothing is hidden? At this very moment, we need to try to make a thorough examination of this point, since we are not to explore through our training that matters which are unknown to us are what is meant by 'intimate ways of putting It'. The very moment of not understanding the Buddha Dharma is one part of an intimate way of putting It. That part is what invariably belongs to the World-honored One; it is the World-honored One's existence.

Even so, people who have not heard the instructive teaching of a genuine Master may take to sitting upon the Buddha's Lion Seat,* but they have not yet encountered this underlying principle even in their dreams. They arbitrarily say such things as the following:

> The statement, "The World-honored One had a secret way of communicating," refers to His raising up a flower, His eyes atwinkle, whilst He stood before an assembly of hundreds of thousands upon Vulture Peak. And He did so because the words used in the Buddha's preaching are superficial, being concerned only with names and forms, whereas giving expression to It without recourse to words by His holding aloft a flower and twinkling His eyes is the occasion which established this secret way of communicating. The hundreds of thousands in the assembly did not comprehend this, because this was His secret way of communicating for the sake of that assembly. The statement, "Makakashō did not conceal It," refers to Makakashō's face breaking into a smile as if he already knew that the World-honored One would raise the flower and His eyes would twinkle. This is the true secret key to practicing the Way, and it is what has been passed on in case after case.

The folks who, hearing this, think it to be true are as common as rice and hemp seeds, bamboo canes and reeds. They are the sort of folks who populate monasteries in all nine divisions of China. How sad that this way of thinking has sent the Way of the

Buddhas and Ancestors into a decline! Someone whose eyes are bright and clear can surely get to the bottom of what is really going on here, point by point.

If the words the World-honored One used were really something superficial, then His holding the flower aloft, with His eyes atwinkle, would also be something superficial. Were anyone to consider what He said to be merely name and form, that person is not 'such a one' * who has learned what the Buddha Dharma really is. Those who consider what is spoken to be no more than names and forms have not yet comprehended that the World-honored One was beyond the use of language as merely 'names and forms'. They have not yet let go of the confused, emotional attitudes of ordinary, worldly people. What permeates the Body and Mind of Buddhas and Ancestors is the dropping off of self, Their giving expression to the Dharma, and Their using language to voice It, that is, Their turning the Wheel of the Dharma. There have been many indeed who, having witnessed and listened to It, have greatly profited from It. Those whose practice is based on faith, as well as those whose practice is based on understanding the Teaching, are cloaked in Its influence in places where there is an Ancestor of the Buddha, or partake of Its influence even in places where there is no Ancestor of the Buddha. How could any of the hundreds of thousands in that assembly possibly fail to have witnessed that His holding the flower aloft, His eyes atwinkle, was a holding aloft of a Flower, with His Eye atwinkle? Anyone in the assembly might have been shoulder-to-shoulder with Makakashō, or might have been living in the same way as the World-honored One. And anyone in the assembly might have been exploring the Matter in the same way as hundreds of thousands of others in the assembly were doing, or might, at the same time, have been giving rise to the intention to realize Buddhahood, for they were walking the same spiritual path in the same country. By relying on the wise discernment gained from direct experience, they may see the Buddha and hear His Teaching, or by relying on the wisdom gained from not knowing, they may see the Buddha and hear His Teaching. After having encountered a Buddha for the first time, one will subsequently recognize Buddhas as numerous as the grains of sand in the Ganges. In any particular assembly of a Buddha, there may be people numbering in the hundreds of thousands of millions, and we may see each Buddha in all the assemblies holding aloft the Flower, Eye atwinkle, at the same time. No observing eye is dim; every listening ear is keen. And there is the Eye of the Heart, and there are the eyes of the body. There is the Ear of the Heart, and there are the ears of the body.

How does that other bunch understand 'Makakashō's face breaking into a smile'? Let them try to put that into words. If it were as those folks say, they would have called that smile 'a secret communication'. But to call it 'his not concealing anything' would be piling foolishness atop foolishness. Later, the World-honored One said, "I have the Treasure House of the Eye of the True Teaching, which is the Wondrous Heart of Nirvana, and I have transmitted It to Makakashō." Is His speaking in this way using speech or not using speech? If the World-honored One had a dislike for spoken language and preferred holding a flower aloft, He surely would have also held up a flower on this occasion. And then, how could Makakashō fail to understand and how could the assembly fail to hear? Do not rely on the tales of those folks who talk this way.

To summarize, the World-honored One had His own way of talking, His own way of acting, and His own way of awakening to the Truth. Foolish people fancy that having one's own way of putting the Matter—that is, His having a 'secret' way—means that other people did not know what He Himself knew. Hence, there were those who were 'in on it' and those who were not 'in on it'. Those who had been voicing their opinions about a 'secret way' in India or the eastern lands from remote antiquity to the present day have not explored the Buddha's Way through their training. Among the uneducated in both secular life and in those who left secular life behind, secrets were many, whereas, among the educated, secrets have been few indeed. How could those of broad experience possibly have secrets? And how much less can there be secret talk or secret intentions when one is wholly equipped with sharp eyes and sharp ears, or with the Eye of wisdom and the Ear of wisdom, or with a Buddha's Eye and a Buddha's Ear? Associating such things as a secret language, secret intentions, or secret actions with the Buddha's Teaching is not in accord with this principle. When we encounter 'such a person', of course we hear his way of putting It, and we express our way of putting It. When we know our True Self, we know what another's way of demonstrating It is pointing to. Moreover, an Ancestor of the Buddha is capable of understanding the previously mentioned 'secret' intentions and 'secret' language. Keep in mind that, at the very moment of being an Ancestor of the Buddha, secret ways of saying It and secret ways of enacting It vie with each other to manifest. What we mean by 'secret' is the principle of intimacy, of closeness. It means that there is no gap. It embraces Buddha and Ancestor. It embraces you and it embraces me. It embraces our practice. It embraces those of our generation. It embraces our meritorious deeds. It embraces what is most intimate. Even when the Eye of a Buddha espies 'such a person' encountering intimate talk and intimate talk encountering 'such a person', He may not see it, even though He may try. The practice of intimacy is beyond anything known by self or other. Only the Intimate Self can know it, for it is beyond the ken of any other intimate person. Because Intimacy resides all around you, everything relies on Intimacy; each thing or even half a thing relies on Intimacy. You need to explore this principle, doing your utmost to clarify what it is.

In conclusion, whenever and wherever we are practicing the Way, it invariably involves an intimate way of expressing the Matter for the benefit of 'such a one'. This is the legitimate succession of Buddha after Buddha and Ancestor after Ancestor. Because this very moment of Now is such an occasion, we are intimate with our self, with the self of others, with the Buddhas and Ancestors, and with all the different species. As a result, it is an intimacy atop intimacy, ever anew. Because such Teaching, practice, and awakening are what a Buddha or Ancestor is, they comprise what Buddhas and Ancestors intimately pass on.

My Master's Master, Setchō, once said to his assembly in verse:

> *The World-honored One had an intimate*
> *way of speaking,*
> *Which Makakashō could not conceal,*
> *For in the night, flowers had rained down,*
> *Bathing the citadel in their perfume.*

Here and now, Setchō's expression, "For in the night, flowers had rained down, bathing the citadel in their perfume," is the very essence of what Intimacy is. Because Setchō proclaimed this, you should scrutinize the Eye and Nose of our Buddhist Ancestor. It was a place that neither Rinzai nor Tokusan were able to reach. You need to open up and explore the Nostrils that are in your Eye, and let the tip of your Nose sharpen up your Ear. And what is more, you need not go all that deeply into your Ear, Nose, or Eye to make Them your whole body and mind, and without making Them over again. We take this as the principle of "the raining down of flowers gives rise to the world."[4]

Setchō's expression, "Bathing the citadel in their perfume," is synonymous with the True Self being concealed while the outer form becomes ever more like a hermit training in his hut. Therefore, thoroughly explore and pass on to others that within the everyday life of the family of the Buddhas and Ancestors, the World-honored One will have His intimate words and Makakashō will not conceal them from us. Each of the Seven World-honored Buddhas,[*] in turn, explored the Matter through Their training just as you do now. Makakashō and Shakyamuni likewise probed deeply into the Matter so that They might understand It. I pray that you are now doing the same.

Given to the assembly on the twentieth day of the ninth lunar month in the first year of the Kangen era (November 3, 1243) at the old monastery of Kippō-ji in the Yoshida district of Echizen Province.

Copied while staying in the office of the Abbot of the same monastery on the sixteenth day of the tenth lunar month in the same year (November 29, 1243).

Ejō

---

4.   This quote is a line from a poem by Bodhidharma's Master, the Venerable Hannyatara. Dōgen modified it slightly to fit in the context of his discourse by substituting the words 'raining down of flowers' for Hannyatara's 'opening of a blossom'.

53

On the True Nature of All Things

(Hosshō)

Translator's Introduction: 'The True Nature of all things' (*hosshō*) refers not only to the way things are just as they are, but also to our Buddha Nature and to That Which Is.

If you are really doing your exploring through your training, whether by following the Scriptures or by following your spiritual friend, you will ultimately realize the Truth by yourself, independent of your Master. Realizing the Truth by oneself independent of one's Master is the functioning of one's True Nature. And even so, if you are inherently keen, you will still need to call upon a Master and inquire of the Way. And even if you are not inherently keen, you will still need to do your utmost in practicing the Way. But who among you is not inherently keen? Each one of you follows both the Scriptures and the advice of a good friend in order to arrive at the enlightenment which is the fruit of Buddhahood. Keep in mind that inherent keenness means that when you encounter the Scriptures or come face-to-face with a spiritual friend, you are encountering the meditative state of your True Nature, and that when you encounter the meditative state of your True Nature, you attain the meditative state of the True Nature of all things.[1] It is our tapping into the wisdom from our previous lives, attaining the three illuminations, and awakening to fully perfected enlightenment.[2] Coming face-to-face with our inherent keenness, we study it; coming face-to-face with the wisdom that goes beyond having a Master and that is inherent within us, we straightforwardly Transmit it. If we had no inherent keenness, then even

---

1. The 'meditative state of one's True Nature' refers to entering the realm where we can see the True Nature of all things.

2. The three illuminations are seeing what conditions result from the past lives of oneself and others, seeing what conditions are likely to arise for oneself and others in future times, and seeing what the miseries of present life conditions are in oneself and others, along with how to remove their root causes.

though we came face-to-face with the Scriptures and a spiritual friend, we could not hear what the True Nature of all things is, nor could we realize It. The Great Truth is not a principle like that of someone drinking water to know for himself whether it is warm or cool.[3]

All Buddhas, along with all Bodhisattvas[*] and all sentient beings, by the power of their inherent keenness, clarify what the Great Truth of the True Nature of all things is. They clarify what the Great Truth of this True Nature is by following the Scriptures and by following their spiritual friend. In this way, they come to understand their own True Nature. The Scriptures are what True Nature is: they are our true Self. And because True Nature is our true Self, It is not the self that non-Buddhists and devilish beings misunderstand It to be. Within True Nature there is no 'non-Buddhist' or 'devilish being'; it is simply a matter of "Come to breakfast! Come to dinner! Come to supper!"[4] Even so, when those who call themselves long-time trainees of twenty or thirty years encounter talk about the True Nature of all things, they stagger on through their lives in a daze. Styling themselves as being both long-disciplined and enlightened, they climb up upon a Master's wooden Dharma seat. Then, when they hear the Voice of their True Nature, or catch sight of the Form of their True Nature, their body and mind, and everything around them, simply bob up and down in a pit of confusion. In this unpleasant state of affairs, they mistakenly imagine that after the universe has fallen away, the True Nature will appear, and that this True Nature will no longer be comprised of the myriad forms that exist in the world. The principle of the True Nature of all things can never be like that. The myriad forms of all that exists in the world and the True Nature of all things lie far beyond discussions of being the same or being different, and they transcend any talk of being separate or being united. Because they are beyond past, present, and future, beyond being discontinuous or

---

3.   That is, the Great Truth is absolute, whereas the testing of the temperature of water through direct experience is relative.

*   See Glossary.

4.   That is, all beings are invited, for they are already included within this True Nature.

continuous, beyond physical form, sensation, thoughts, actions, and consciousness, they <u>are</u> what the True Nature of all things is.

Meditation Master Baso Dōitsu from Chiang-hsi in Hungchou Province once said:

> All sentient beings from countless eons past have never departed from the meditative state of the True Nature of all things, but rather they have always resided within It. Putting on clothes and eating meals, conversing and making respectful replies, using one's six sense organs: all such activities are totally what True Nature is.

The True Nature of all things that Baso spoke of is the True Nature expressed by True Nature. It harmonized with Baso and he harmonized with It. Once he had heard It, how could he have failed to speak out? The True Nature of all things rode astride Baso.[5]

Now, people absorb meals and meals absorb people. The True Nature of both of these, from the start, has never left the meditative state of the True Nature of all things. Their True Nature, after manifesting Itself, has never left the True Nature of all things. Their True Nature, before manifesting Itself, has never left the True Nature of all things. The True Nature of all things over countless eons of time is simply the meditative state of the True Nature of all things. So we describe this True Nature as being eons beyond measure. Accordingly, whatever is here at this very moment is the True Nature of all things, and the True Nature of all things is what exists at this very moment. When we put on our clothes and eat our meal, it is the meditative state of the True Nature of all things that is putting on the clothes and eating the meal. The True Nature of clothing is fully manifested; the True Nature of food is fully manifested. The True Nature of eating is fully manifested; the True Nature of dressing is fully

---

5.   There is a play on words here. Baso's name literally means 'our Ancestor who is a horse', the horse being a common Zen metaphor for someone who goes traveling near and far to help all sentient beings.

manifested. If we did not put on clothes and eat food, if we did not converse and make respectful replies, if we did not use our six sense organs, if we were not performing all our actions, then we would not be in the meditative state of the True Nature of all things, nor would we have entered into our own True Nature. What was just quoted here and now from Baso is what the Buddhas fully conferred to Shakyamuni Buddha, and it is what the Ancestors have accurately Transmitted to Baso. Authentically Transmitted and handed on by Buddha after Buddha and by Ancestor after Ancestor, It was authentically Transmitted through the meditative state of the True Nature of all things. Buddha after Buddha and Ancestor after Ancestor, without having to enter this meditative state, have set Their True Nature frolicking like a fish leaping about in the water. Even though teachers of doctrine who rely on the written word speak of 'true nature', it is not the True Nature of which Baso spoke. Now, there may be some merit in human beings, who have never yet departed from their True Nature, thinking that they must certainly be devoid of a True Nature, but this will just be a fresh instance of their True Nature manifesting Itself. Even were we to talk or converse as if we lacked True Nature, or were to work or act as if we lacked True Nature, this too would only be True Nature manifesting Itself.

The passing of days and months of immeasurable eons past has been the passing of the True Nature of all things. And it is just the same for the present and the future.

We may take the measure of our body and mind to be just the measure of our body and mind, not recognizing them as an aspect of our True Nature, but this way of thinking about them is also a function of our True Nature. Or we may take the measure of our body and mind not to be a true measure of our body and mind, while still not recognizing them as an aspect of our True Nature, but this way of thinking about them is likewise a function of our True Nature. Whatever we may consider or not consider them to be, in either case they are an aspect of our True Nature. To think that the 'Nature' in 'True Nature' means that water does not flow and that trees do not flourish and then wither away is a non-Buddhist view.[6]

---

6.   That is, it is non-Buddhist to think that because something has True Nature, it is absolutely unchanging.

Shakyamuni Buddha once said, "The appearance of each thought and thing is just as it is, and the nature of each thought and thing is likewise just as it is." Accordingly, flowers blooming and leaves falling are just True Nature as it is. Even so, foolish people fancy that within the realm of True Nature flowers do not bloom and leaves do not fall. Right now, without questioning anyone else, articulate your own doubts by forming a concept or image of them. Go over them thoroughly three times as if they were being expounded by someone else, and chances are that you will have already extricated yourself from them. It is not that these doubts are wicked thoughts, but they are simply thoughts arising at a time before you have clarified your doubts. When you are clarifying your doubts, do not think that you need to get rid of them. The blooming of flowers and the falling of leaves are, quite naturally, the blooming of flowers and the falling of leaves. The thinking which gives rise to the idea that there can be no blooming flowers or falling leaves within True Nature <u>is</u> True Nature Itself. True Nature manifests Itself when our thinking is freed from concepts or images, and is therefore in accord with the way that True Nature 'thinks'. The totality of Its thinking resembles a contemplation on the True Nature of all things.

Baso's phrase, 'totally what this True Nature is,' is truly eighty or ninety percent of expressing the Matter.*[7] And yet there are many things that Baso did not expound. He did not say that all true natures never depart from their True Nature. Nor did he say that all True Natures are totally what True Nature is. Nor did he say that no True Nature ever departs from being a sentient being. Nor did he say that the True Nature of all sentient beings is but a small bit of the True Nature of all things. Nor did he say that all sentient beings comprise the whole of the True Nature of all things. Nor did he say that the totality of True Nature is just a small bit of a sentient being. Nor

---

7. In Zen, to say that someone is expressing eighty or ninety percent of the Matter is a complimentary way of saying that someone has had a full realization that goes beyond anyone's ability to completely express.

did he say that half of a sentient being is half of someone's True Nature. Nor did he say that the absence of sentient beings is what the True Nature of all things is. Nor did he say that True Nature is not a sentient being. Nor did he say that the True Nature of all things frees Itself from 'being True Nature'. Nor did he say that sentient beings drop off 'being a sentient being'. He simply said that sentient beings do not depart from the meditative state of the True Nature of all things. He did not say that this True Nature cannot depart from the meditative state of sentient beings. Nor did he assert that the meditative state of True Nature departs from or enters the meditative state of sentient beings. Much less can we hear him say that the True Nature of all things is synonymous with realizing Buddhahood, or that sentient beings' awakening to their True Nature is their True Nature's awakening to True Nature. Nowhere does he assert that non-sentient beings do not depart from the True Nature of all things.

At this moment I would like to ask Baso, "What is it that you call 'sentient beings'? If what you call 'True Nature' refers to 'sentient beings', then It is That Which Comes in This Way. If what you call 'sentient beings' refers to beings that are sentient, then what you say resembles Nangaku Ejō's saying, "Were I to put It in words, they would not hit the bull's-eye." So, YOU! NOW! SAY WHAT IT IS! RIGHT RIGHT NOW!

Given to the assembly at the beginning of winter in the first year of the Kangen era (November 14, 1243) at Kippō-ji Temple in Echizen Province.

54

On the Dharma That Nonsentient Beings Express

(Mujō Seppō)

Translator's Introduction: As Dōgen's discourse makes clear, he understands 'sentient' and 'nonsentient' in a specific way. Sentient beings are those who are still wedded to their senses, which give rise to the duality of self and other, that is, they are those who are ordinary, worldly human beings. 'Nonsentient beings' refers to whatever exists just as it is, which includes not only such things in nature as trees, rivers, mountains, and stones, but also those beings who have dropped off the false self, who have escaped from the tyranny of their greeds, hatreds, and delusions, and who have freed themselves from slavery to their senses; that is, they have become 'such a person'.

Expressing the Dharma within the Dharma's ever-present expression is the manifest spiritual conundrum that Ancestors of the Buddha entrust to Ancestors of the Buddha. This expressing of the Dharma is the Dharma expressing Itself. It is beyond being sentient or nonsentient. It is beyond something intentional, beyond something unintentional, and beyond karmic* causes producing something intentional or unintentional. And it is beyond the methods of those who pursue causal conditions. Even so, it does not travel in the paths of birds.[1] When the Great Way is fully realized, the expressing of the Dharma is fully realized. And when the Treasure House of the Dharma is entrusted to an heir, the expressing of the Dharma is entrusted to that person as well. When the flower was held aloft, an expressing of the Dharma was held aloft.[2] And when the kesa* was Transmitted, an expressing of the Dharma was Transmitted. This is why, since before the time of the Lords of Awe-inspiring Voices, Buddhas and

---

*   See Glossary.

1.   That is, unlike birds in flight, the Dharma leaves traces.

2.   This refers to the Transmission of the Dharma from Shakyamuni Buddha to His disciple Makakashō. This occurred when the Buddha held a flower aloft and Makakashō, recognizing its significance, smiled in response.

Ancestors alike have paid homage to the expressing of the Dharma, and, since before the time of the Buddhas, They have customarily made expressing the Dharma Their fundamental practice. Do not explore through your training that expressing the Dharma is something that the Buddhas and Ancestors have customarily regulated, for it is They who have been regulated by the expressing of the Dharma. This expressing of the Dharma is not limited to the expounding of the eighty-four thousand gates that make up the whole of the Dharma; there are immeasurable, limitless gates that make up the whole of the expressions of the Dharma. So, do not explore through your training that expressions of Dharma by former Buddhas are what constitute expressions of Dharma by later Buddhas. Just as former Buddhas do not return to be later Buddhas, so it is with expressing the Dharma. The ways of expressing It that were used in the past are not the ways by which It is expressed later on. This is why Shakyamuni Buddha said, "In the same manner that any Buddha of past, present, or future expressed the Dharma, I too, likewise, give voice to a Dharma that is in no way separate from Theirs."

Thus, just as They made use of the expressions of Dharma of other Buddhas, so He made use of the expressions of Dharma of those other Buddhas. And just as He authentically Transmitted the expressing of Dharma, so those Buddhas authentically Transmitted the expressing of Dharma. There is the authentic Transmitting from my late Master back to the Seven Buddhas,[*] and there is the authentic Transmitting from the Seven Buddhas down to the present—and there is the Dharma that nonsentient beings express. And within this Dharma that nonsentient beings express there are Buddhas and there are Ancestors. Do not fix in your mind that the saying, "I am now expressing the Dharma," is something new that is not part of the authentic Transmission. And do not use it in an attempt to substantiate that the true Transmission of past and present is just an old nesting place in some demon's cave.[3]

---

3. An 'old nesting place' refers to habitual ways of thinking that are no longer valid. 'Some demon's cave' is a synonym for delusion.

National Teacher Echū of Kōtaku-ji Temple in the Western Capital of Great T'ang China was once asked by a monk, "Do even nonsentient beings voice the Dharma?"

The National Teacher replied, "They are always expressing It with ardor, and there is no interruption in their voicing of It."

The monk said, "Why then do I not hear It?"

The National Teacher replied, "Though you yourself do not hear It, that won't stand in the way of others hearing It."

The monk asked, "I'm still unclear. What kind of people could possibly hear It?"

The National Teacher said, "Saintly ones can hear It."

The monk then asked, "Venerable Monk, do you also hear It?"

The National Teacher answered, "I do not hear It."

The monk then asked, "Since you, Venerable Monk, do not hear It, how do you know that nonsentient beings voice the Dharma?"

The National Teacher replied, "Fortunately for you, I do not hear It. If I heard It, I would be on the level of the saints, and then you could not hear <u>my</u> voicing of the Dharma."

The monk then said, "If that is the case, then sentient beings play no part in the Dharma."

The National Teacher responded, "I express the Dharma for the sake of sentient beings, but I do not express It for the sake of saints."

The monk then asked, "What are sentient beings like after they hear It?"

The National Teacher answered, "They are beyond being 'sentient beings.'"

Novices, as well as those long in the practice, who may be exploring through their training what the statement "The nonsentient give expression to the Dharma" means, should straightaway be diligent in their study of this story of the National Teacher. "They are always expressing It with ardor, and there is no interruption in their voicing of It" is how he put it. 'Always' is one instant of time within all times. "There is no interruption in their voicing of It" implies that expressing It is already coming forth, and without interruption.

Do not explore the matter of 'the nonsentient' giving expression to the Dharma as if it were necessarily like that of sentient beings who are making vocal sounds to express the Dharma. To take voicings in the realm of sentient beings out of their context and then liken them to voicings in the realm of the nonsentient is not the Way of the Buddha. When the nonsentient give expression to the Dharma, it may not necessarily be with audible sounds, just as, for instance, a sentient being's giving expression to the Dharma may not involve audible sounds.

For the time being, you should diligently explore this through your training by asking yourself and others, "Just what is a sentient being? Just what is a nonsentient being?" Accordingly, you should pay the utmost attention to details in order to explore through your training just what this matter of nonsentient beings expressing the Dharma is about. According to the opinions of foolish people, the rustling of trees in the forest, the opening of flowers, and the falling of leaves are believed to be nonsentient things expressing the Dharma, but such people are not persons who have learned what the Buddha taught. If it were so, then who could not hear the Dharma that is expressed by the nonsentient? For the moment, you should reflect on whether or not there are grasses and trees and forests in the realm of the nonsentient, and whether or not the realm of the nonsentient is intersecting, or mingling with, that of the sentient. At the same time, to take such things as grasses and trees or tiles and stones to be nonsentient is to be less than fully educated. And to believe that being nonsentient means being grass and trees or tiles and stones is to tire of exploring the Matter.* Even if you were to believe that human beings view such things as grass and trees to be patterned after the nonsentient, such things as grass and trees are not something that the mental efforts of ordinary, worldly people actually take measure of. And the reason for this is that there are great differences between the celestial forests of those in lofty positions and the forests of ordinary human beings, and that what is produced in China is not equivalent to what is produced in its bordering lands, and that the vegetation which grows in the oceans and that which grows amidst the mountains are not the same. And what is more, there are forests that grow in the open sky and forests that grow in the clouds. And there are hundreds of grasses and thousands of trees that sprout up in wind and fire. In sum, there are those things that need to be explored as being sentient and there are those things that need to be explored as being nonsentient. And there are grasses and trees that resemble humans and animals when the differences between the sentient and the nonsentient have not yet been made clear. And what is more, when we see a Taoist mountain hermit's trees and rocks, flowers and fruits, and hot and cool springs with our own eyes, they are beyond doubting, but explaining them is difficult indeed! Having barely even seen the grasses and trees from a great country like China and observing only the grasses and trees of a small, single nation like Japan, do not imagine that they must be like those found throughout the whole universe.

The National Teacher said, "Saintly ones can hear It."

That is to say, in the assembly where a nonsentient one expresses the Dharma, all saintly ones stand up to listen. The saintly ones and the nonsentient ones bring about listening and they bring about expressing.[4] The nonsentient one is already expressing the Dharma for the sake of the saintly ones, but is It put in a saintly way or in an ordinary, everyday way? In other words, when you have completely clarified the manner in which the nonsentient express the Dharma, you will realize that what you hear is no different from what the saintly hear. When you have been able to realize this, you will clearly understand the realm of a saintly one. In addition, you should continue to explore through your training the daily conduct that traverses the path through the heavens, transcending both the mundane and the saintly.

---

4. That is, their response encourages others in the assembly to listen, and their attention to what they are hearing encourages the one who is speaking to give voice to the Dharma.

The National Teacher said, "I do not hear It."

Do not presume that these words are easy to understand. Does he not hear It because he has gone beyond the mundane and transcended the saintly? Or does he not hear It because he has torn asunder the old nest of 'the worldly versus the saintly'? By your making a diligent effort, you can realize what he is saying.

The National Teacher said, "Fortunately for you, I do not hear It. If I heard It, I would be on the level of the saints."

This statement is beyond being the best way of putting it and beyond being just another way of putting it. His saying "Fortunately for you, I..." is beyond the mundane and the saintly. Might his "Fortunately for you, I..." be that of an Ancestor of the Buddha? Because an Ancestor of the Buddha is beyond the mundane and has transcended the saintly, what he hears may not be the same as what the saintly hear.

Pursuing the chain of reasoning behind the National Teacher's statement "Then you could not hear my voicing of the Dharma," you should stew on what the enlightened state of Buddhas and saintly ones is. The National Teacher's underlying principle is, namely, "When the nonsentient express the Dharma, the saintly can hear It, and when the National Teacher expressed the Dharma, the monk could hear It." You should, day after day, deeply and at length, do your utmost to explore this chain of reasoning through your training. Now I would like to put it to the National Teacher—and I am not asking about sentient beings <u>after</u> they hear the Dharma—how is it with sentient beings at the very moment when they hear the Dharma being expressed?

Our Founding Ancestor, Great Master Tōzan Ryōkai, while training under the great monk, Abbot Ungan Donjō, once asked the Abbot, "What person can hear the Dharma expressed by a nonsentient being?"

Abbot Ungan answered, "The nonsentient can hear It."

Tōzan then asked, "O Venerable Monk, can you hear It or not?"

The Abbot replied, "If I heard It, you would be unable to hear my expressing of the Dharma."

Tōzan then said, "If that is the way things are, then Venerable Monk, I have not heard your expressing of the Dharma."

The Abbot responded, "Since you have not heard even what I have given voice to, how could you possibly hear the expressing of the Dharma by nonsentient beings!"

Thereupon, Tōzan composed the following verse, which he presented to the Abbot.

> *How wondrous! Oh, how wondrous!*
> *The Dharma voiced by the nonsentient boggles*
> *the mind.*
> *When we hear It with our ears, in the end It is*
> *hard to comprehend.*
> *When we hear It with our Eye, we can, by all*
> *means, understand It.*

You will need to do your utmost, not only in this life but also in many later ones, to examine in detail the principle underlying Tōzan's saying, "What person can hear the Dharma expressed by a nonsentient being?" This question is certainly equipped with the merit of also being a statement.[5] This remark of his has Skin and Flesh, Bones and Marrow. Not only is it a Transmitting of Mind by means of Mind,

---

5. That is, Tōzan's remark can be construed not only as a question but also as a statement: A 'person of What' can hear the Dharma expressed by a nonsentient being. 'A person of What', like 'such a person,' is a common way in Chinese Zen Buddhism to refer to one who has fully realized the Truth.

but it is also a transmitting of Mind by means of mind so that both new monks and novices who have been training for a long time may affirm It. It takes its place among the keys which unlock the doors to genuinely Transmitting both the kesa and the Dharma. How could anyone today possibly expect to realize It after an effort of three seasons or four months? Even though Tōzan had seen and heard the underlying principle that the National Teacher expressed as, "The Dharma that the nonsentient express can be heard by the saintly," nevertheless he now, once again, asked, "What person can hear the Dharma that the nonsentient express?" Does this confirm what the National Teacher said? Should we see what Tōzan said as a question or should we see it as a statement? If he was not agreeing with the National Teacher in general, how could he possibly have spoken as he did? If he was agreeing with the National Teacher in general, how could he possibly have failed to understand what the National Teacher was saying?

Abbot Ungan said, in effect, "The nonsentient can hear the Dharma that the nonsentient express."

In authentically Transmitting this bloodline of ours, we need to explore through our training the dropping off of body and mind. Saying that the nonsentient can hear the Dharma that the nonsentient express will be equivalent, in sum and substance, to saying that when Buddhas give voice to the Dharma, Buddhas can hear It. An assembly that is listening to the Dharma that the nonsentient express may be nonsentient, even though it is comprised of the sentient and the nonsentient, or of the worldly along with the wise and saintly. By relying on this Teaching in sum and substance, we can distinguish the true ones from the false in both the past and the present. Even though there are those who have come from India, if they are not true Ancestral Masters whose Transmission is authentic, you must not follow them. Even though they may have been part of a continuous succession who have studied for a thousand myriad years, if they are not in the succession of heir after heir who have received the genuine Transmission, we could hardly accept from them the mantle of the Dharma—that is, the kesa.

Now that the authentic Transmission has spread to Eastern lands, it should be easy to distinguish the functioning of the true from the false. Even if someone hears only the statement, "When a human being gives voice to the Dharma, human beings can hear It," that person may attain the Bones and Marrow of the Buddhas and Ancestors. If you make it a matter of life and death when you listen to what Abbot Ungan and National Teacher Echū are saying, you will understand that 'the saintly' spoken of in "The saintly can hear It" means 'the nonsentient', and 'the nonsentient' spoken of in "The nonsentient can hear It" means 'the saintly'. It is to say, "What is expressed by the nonsentient is the Nonsentient" because the Dharma expressed by the nonsentient is what the Nonsentient is. Hence, it is the Dharma that the Nonsentient expresses. It is the Nonsentient that expresses the Dharma.[6]

Our Founding Ancestor Tōzan said, "If that is the way
things are, then Venerable Monk, I have not heard your expressing
of the Dharma."

Here and now, his saying, "If that is the way things are…" takes up the principle underlying the statement, "When the nonsentient express the Dharma, the nonsentient can hear It." In accord with the principle behind "When the nonsentient express the Dharma, the nonsentient can hear It" is "Then Venerable Monk, I do not hear your expressing of the Dharma."[7] At this time, Tōzan is not only taking a back seat to the nonsentient's expressing of the Dharma, but he was also showing his eagerness to voice the Dharma for the sake of nonsentient beings with an ardor that pierced the very heavens. Not only had he thoroughly penetrated the nonsentient's expressing of the Dharma, but he had also thoroughly mastered, and gone beyond, 'hearing' versus

6.   That is, when the word 'nonsentient' is capitalized, it refers to Buddha Nature Itself.

7.   This statement was Tōzan's way of asserting that his True Self has not become enlightened because he recognized that this True Self (the 'I' here) is already enlightened and has always been so. At the same time, it is an expression of Tōzan's humility and his assertion that his Master's expression of the Dharma is within the realm of 'the saintly'.

'not hearing' the nonsentient express the Dharma. And, pushing on, in the matter of
the sentient giving voice to the Dharma, he had gone beyond 'expressing' versus 'not
expressing,' and he had thoroughly penetrated 'expressing by those in the past',
'expressing by those in the present', and 'expressing by those in the future'. And
moreover, in expressions of the Dharma that go beyond being heard or not being
heard, he had completely clarified the principle of 'this is sentient' and 'this is
nonsentient'.

To generalize, hearing the Dharma is not limited merely to the sphere of the
ear as a sense organ or to someone's being conscious of sounds. We hear the Dharma
with our whole vitality, with our whole mind, with our whole body, with our whole
being. We hear It from 'before the time when "father" and "mother" were born'* and
from before the time of the Lords of Awe-inspiring Voices until the limits of our future
and throughout the limitless future. The Dharma is heard before the body and after the
mind. There is much to be gained from these instances of hearing the Dharma, so do
not think that unless our mental consciousness is involved, there is nothing to be
gained from hearing the Dharma. Someone whose mind has gone astray or whose
body is sunk in a torpor can still profit from hearing the Dharma, just as someone who
is unaware of their body and mind can also profit from hearing the Dharma. All
Buddhas and all Ancestors invariably live through moments like these when They are
becoming a Buddha or an Ancestor. How can the intellectual efforts of ordinary,
worldly people possibly catch sight of how the mighty force of one's practice comes
to behold Body and Mind? They cannot fully clarify for themselves even what the
bounds of body and mind are. Once the meritorious seeds of hearing the Dharma have
been sown within the fertile fields of body and mind, they will know no season of
decay. Ultimately, they will sprout, and, with the passing of time, they will surely bear
fruit.

Foolish people think:

Though people may not be remiss in listening to the
Dharma, if they do not progress along the path to understanding and
if they do not have good enough memories, they will not be able to
acquire any benefits. What is vitally important—be it with the body
and mind of an ordinary person or of someone in a lofty position—

is to devote oneself to memorizing the Dharma extensively by listening to It many times. If people forget what they have heard while attending a Dharma talk and go blank once they have left their seat, what benefit do you think there would be in that? What learning could possibly be gained by that?

They speak this way because they do not have a genuine Master and have never encountered 'such a person'.* It is understood that someone who has not received the genuine Face-to-Face Transmission is not a genuine teacher, whereas someone who has received the genuine Transmission of Buddha after Buddha is a genuine teacher. Foolish people speak of their holding the Dharma consciously in mind and, at least temporarily, not forgetting It. Actually, the merit of hearing the Dharma envelops both the mind and the conscious memory. At this very moment, there is the meritorious functioning of the Dharma which envelops our body and which even envelops us prior to the body's arising, which envelops our mind and even envelops us prior to the mind's arising, which envelops us after the mind has arisen, which envelops our causes, conditions, results, actions, forms, True Nature, and physical substance, which envelops the Buddhas and envelops the Ancestors, which envelops self and envelops others, and which envelops our skin, flesh, bones, and marrow, among other things. Its meritorious functioning fully manifests, enveloping the words and ways of expressing It, and enveloping our everyday actions, such as sitting and reclining, as It heals and fills the universe.

Truly, the merit derived from hearing the Dharma is not easily recognized, but should you encounter the great assembly of an Ancestor of the Buddha and thoroughly explore Its Skin and Flesh, Bones and Marrow through training with him or her, there will be no time when the meritorious strength of their expressing the Dharma will not guide you, and there will be no place where you will not receive the strength derived from hearing the Dharma. In this fashion, by letting the waves of time pass either quickly or slowly in a natural way, you will see the coming forth of Its fruits. Even listening to It many times in order to memorize It extensively ought not to be discarded altogether, but you should not treat that one aspect as the primary tool.

Those who are exploring the Matter with a Master should know this, and our Founding Ancestor Tōzan had thoroughly explored It.

> Abbot Ungan said, "Since you have not heard even what I have given voice to, how could you possibly hear the expressing of the Dharma by nonsentient beings!"

Here, Abbot Ungan has loosened his collar in order to certify that our Founding Ancestor Tōzan has the Bones and Marrow of the Forefathers, which Tōzan had just then revealed by manifesting his awakening to both enlightenment and the promise of Buddhahood. Ungan is saying, in effect, "You are as if you did not hear my expressing It." This is not Ungan's affirmation of some run-of-the-mill person. He was making clear that, even though nonsentient expressions of the Dharma are multi-faceted, they do not exist for the sake of the intellect. Tōzan's succeeding as Ungan's heir at this time is truly an intimate matter. Those in the realms of the mundane and the saintly cannot easily reach it or catch a glimpse of it.

> Thereupon Tōzan composed the following verse, which he presented to the Abbot:

> *How wondrous! Oh, how wondrous!*
> *The Dharma voiced by the nonsentient boggles*
> *the mind.*

Thus the nonsentient, as well as the Dharma that the nonsentient express, are both difficult for the discriminating, deliberative mind to handle. What is this thing we call 'nonsentient'? You should explore through your training that it is not the mundane or the saintly, and that it is beyond being sentient or nonsentient. 'Mundane' and 'saintly', as well as 'sentient' and 'nonsentient', whether voiced or not voiced, will be on a level with the lunacies produced by discriminatory thinking. Now, since It is mind-boggling, It has been and will continue to be a great mystery. It cannot be reached by the wisdom and consciousness of the mundane or of the wise and holy, nor is It concerned with the plans and considerations of mortals or celestial hosts.

> *When we hear It with our ears, in the end It is*
> *hard to comprehend.*

Even if we had celestial ears, or ears attuned to the whole universe and to the whole of time, when we aim at listening with our ears, It is ultimately too difficult to understand. Even if we had an ear to the wall or an ear atop a pole, we could not understand the Dharma that the nonsentient express, because It is beyond sound. It is not that we cannot hear It with our ears, but even were we to do our utmost for a hundred thousand eons, ultimately It would be too difficult to understand. It has the everyday dignity of the One Way that is beyond sounds and forms: It does not reside in the nests and caves of the mundane and the saintly.

> *When we hear It with our Eye, we can, by all*
> *means, understand It.*

Certain people fancy this to mean, "What human beings in the present see as the coming and going of grasses and trees, and flowers and birds, is what may be described as 'hearing a sound with one's eyes.'" This point of view is completely mistaken and is not at all the Buddha Dharma, nor does the Buddha Dharma have any principle like this.

When we explore through our training our Founding Ancestor Tōzan's expression 'when we hear It with our Eye', the place where the Dharma expressed by the nonsentient resounds is in the Eye, and the place where the sound of the Dharma expressed by a sentient being manifests is in the eyes. You should thoroughly and broadly explore this Eye. Because hearing sound with the eyes must be comparable to hearing sound with the ears, hearing sound with the Eye must be unlike hearing sound with the ears. Do not explore this as "There are organs of hearing in the eyes," or as "Eyes are therefore ears," or as "Sounds are manifesting in the eyes."

A former Master, Chōsa Keishin, once said, "The whole universe in all ten directions is the solitary Eye of a mendicant monk." Do not be eager to get into discussions about hearing sounds through this Eye being a reference to Tōzan's saying "When we hear It with our Eye." Even though you may study the words that the ancient Master spoke, namely, "The whole universe in all ten directions is the solitary Eye," the whole universe in all ten directions <u>is</u> the solitary Eye, and further, there are the thousand hands of Avalokiteshvara, [*] each with its Eye. And there are the thousand Eyes of the True Teaching. And there are thousands of Eyes in one's ears. And there are thousands of Eyes on the tip of one's tongue. And there are thousands of Eyes from the point of view of one's heart. And there are thousands of Eyes that penetrate our mind. And there are thousands of Eyes that penetrate our body. And there are thousands of poles, each with an Eye at its tip. And there are thousands of Eyes before our body appears. And there are thousands of Eyes before our mind appears. And there are thousands of Eyes within death. And there are thousands of Eyes within life. And there are thousands of Eyes of self. And there are thousands of Eyes of other. And there are thousands of Eyes atop our eyes. And there are thousands of Eyes that do the training. And there are thousands of Eyes that are vertical. And there are thousands of Eyes that are horizontal.

So, even though you may learn that the totality of all Eyes is the totality of all realms, you have still not fully experienced the Eye. Simply make it a pressing need to thoroughly explore hearing the Dharma expressed by the Nonsentient with your Eye. Now, the main point in what our Founding Ancestor Tōzan was saying is that it is difficult to comprehend with the ears the Dharma that the Nonsentient is expressing, for it is your Eye that hears the sound. And, further, there is hearing the sound as it permeates one's body, and there is hearing the sound with one's whole being. Even if you fully experience hearing the sound with your Eye, you need to come to the realization that the Dharma that the nonsentient express can indeed be heard by the nonsentient, and then let it go.

Because this principle has been passed down, my late Master Tendō, an Old Buddha, said, "The vines of the bottle gourd embrace the bottle gourd's vines." This is a nonsentient being who is giving voice to the Dharma in which the awakened Eye of our Ancestor Ungan has been passed on, along with his Bones and Marrow. Based on the principle that all expressions of the Dharma are nonsentient, nonsentient beings express the Dharma, which is a traditional Teaching. It is for the sake of the nonsentient that the nonsentient give voice to the Dharma. What is it that we call 'the nonsentient'? You need to know that it is the one who hears the Dharma that the Nonsentient expresses. And what is it that we call 'expressing the Dharma'? You need to know that it is that which does not know 'I am nonsentient'.

Great Master Tōsu Daidō in Shuchou Province[8] was once asked by a monk, "Just what is this 'nonsentient beings express the Dharma' stuff all about?"

The Master responded, "Do not bad-mouth it."

What Tōsu is asserting here now is the very practice of the Dharma of an Old Buddha and it is the governing principle in our Ancestral tradition. Generally speaking, such statements as "Nonsentient beings express the Dharma," and "Expounding the Dharma is what a nonsentient being is," are instances of not bad-mouthing it. Keep in mind that the expounding of the Dharma by the nonsentient is precisely what the defining attribute of an Ancestor of the Buddha is. That bunch who have followed

---

8. There is an interpolation in the text at this point, whose authorship is uncertain. It reads: He was Dharma heir to Suibi Mugaku; in his lifetime he was called Daidō Myōkaku, as well as the Old Buddha Tōsu.

Rinzai and Tokusan don't know about it; only our Ancestors of the Buddha have explored it thoroughly through their training.

Given to the assembly at Kippō-ji Temple in the Yoshida district of Echizen Province on the second day of the tenth lunar month in the first year of the Kangen era (November 15, 1243).

Copied here on the fifteenth day of the tenth lunar month in the same year (November 28, 1243).

Ejō

55

On Washing Your Face

(Semmen)

Translator's Introduction: The importance that Dōgen placed on this discourse is signaled in the postscript by the fact that he gave it to his community on three occasions. The first occasion was in 1239 as a companion piece to Discourse 7: On Washing Yourself Clean (Senjō). It was repeated with the addition of a final paragraph in 1243, when he and his monks were staying in Kippō-ji Temple while Eihei-ji Temple was being built nearby. The third delivery, with some emendations, was given at Eihei-ji in 1250. This last version is the one presented here.

The title has a double meaning. On a literal level, 'face' refers to the physical part of the body; on a metaphorical level, it refers to the surface of the mind's mirror, which is also being cleansed by seeing the spiritual significance of the mundane act of cleaning the former. As the text makes abundantly clear, on the literal level the face includes not only the whole outer surface of the head but also, most importantly, the mouth, teeth, and tongue. An implement for brushing the teeth similar to that which Dōgen describes is still the preferred form of toothbrush with many Theravadin monks.

In the *Lotus Scripture* it says in verse:

> *Anoint your body with fragrant oil*
> *After having washed away all dust and dirt,*
> *And put on a fresh, clean robe,*
> *So that you are clean both within and*
> *without.*

This Teaching is one that the Tathagata voiced before the Lotus assembly for the sake of those who practice the four forms of conduct that ease the way of practice.[1] It is unequaled in His Teachings at other assemblies, and is surely unlike that found in

---

1. These four forms of conduct were also voiced by the Tathagata in the *Lotus Scripture*. One translation may be found in "The Scripture on the Conduct That Eases the Way" from *Buddhist Writings on Meditation and Daily Practice*, (Shasta Abbey Press, 1994), pp. 5-25.

other Scriptures. Since this is so, cleansing your body and mind and anointing yourself with fragrant oil after having removed the dust and dirt of life is foremost in the Buddha's Teaching. And putting on a fresh, clean robe is one of the methods for purifying yourself. By washing away the dust and dirt and by anointing yourself with fragrant oil, you will be clean both within and without. When both inside and outside are clean, the conditions around you and the conditions within you will be immaculate.

Even so, befuddled people who do not understand what the Buddha's Dharma is and who do not practice the Buddha's Way say, "Bathing merely cleanses the body's skin, but it does not cleanse the five vital organs or the six forms of entrails within the body. Since it does not cleanse each of these, one after the other, we cannot really become immaculate. Therefore, it follows that we cannot really cleanse our bodies." People who talk like this do not yet know the Buddha's Dharma, nor have they even heard It; they have not encountered a true teacher or met an offspring of the Buddhas and Ancestors. You should just cast aside the words of folks who hold to false views like these. Instead, explore and put into practice the True Teaching of the Buddhas and Ancestors. The limits of all thoughts and things have never been determined, and what lies within and outside the various elements, likewise, cannot be fully grasped. This is why what lies within our mind and outside our body is also beyond our grasp.

Be that as it may, when bodhisattvas[*] who are in their final body[2] are sitting in the Meditation Hall and are just on the verge of realizing the Way, even they wash their kesa[*] and then cleanse their body and mind. This is part of the ordinary, everyday behavior of all Buddhas in all times—past, present and future—everywhere in the ten directions.

Bodhisattvas who are in their final body are different from other types of beings in all matters. Their meritorious wise discernment and the splendor of their body and mind are most precious and unsurpassed. The same will also be true for their

---

*   See Glossary.

2.   A technical term for one who is about to realize Buddhahood. It is synonymous with a non-returner, which is the third of the four stages of arhathood. A brief explanation of these four stages can be found in the Glossary.

methods of washing and cleansing, not to mention the fact that everyone's body and mind, along with their limitations, differ according to the times. Within the time of one period of seated meditation, it is said, three thousand worlds have passed away. Even though such a period of time is like this, it is not some measure of self or other: it is the meritorious fruit of the Buddha Dharma. The measure of body and mind is beyond 'five feet' or 'six feet', because body and mind are beyond the five or six feet that we conventionally define as 'five feet' and 'six feet'.

The place where body and mind exist is also beyond both the limits and the limitlessness of the realms of self or other, or of the whole universe or immeasurable universes, because "Right here is where the What is, whether the Matter* is put clumsily or put delicately."[3] The dimensions of mind are beyond anything the discriminations of intellective thought can possibly know: they are beyond anything that the non-discriminations of not thinking can possibly fathom. Because this is the way the dimensions of body and mind are, it is also the way the dimensions of cleansing are. To grasp what these dimensions are and to train until one fully realizes them are precisely what Buddha after Buddha and Ancestor after Ancestor are concerned with and have held to. We should not take our estimate of ourselves to be foremost, nor should we take our estimate of ourselves to be real. Therefore, it follows that when we wash and cleanse ourselves in this manner, we fully fathom the dimensions of body and mind, and we make ourselves immaculate. Whether we see ourselves as comprised of six elements, or five skandhas,* or of That which is indestructible, through our cleansing we can make everything immaculate.

This does not mean that we are immaculate only after we have fetched water and washed ourselves with it. How can water be inherently pure or inherently impure? Even if it were inherently pure or inherently impure, we cannot assert that it makes the place we bring it to pure or impure. It is simply that, when we preserve the methods that the Buddhas and Ancestors have trained in and actualized, then a Buddha's

---

3. This quotation is a remark made by Meditation Master Fuke to Meditation Master Rinzai when both were novice monks. This kōan story, as recounted by Dōgen in his Chinese *Shinji Shōbōgenzō*, is given in the Addendum to Discourse 21: On Buddha Nature *(Busshō)*, p. 279.

methods for using water with which to wash the body and using the Water with which to cleanse the mind will have been handed down to us. Accordingly, in training to realize Buddhahood, we go beyond 'clean', we discard 'unclean', and we abandon 'not clean' and 'not unclean'.

Hence, even though we may not yet have soiled ourselves, we wash and cleanse ourselves, and even when we have reached Great Immaculacy, we still wash and cleanse ourselves. This process has been preserved solely in the Way of the Buddhas and Ancestors. It is beyond what those who are non-Buddhists understand. Were the situation as those befuddled persons say, even if we were to reduce the five vital organs and the six forms of entrails to particles of dust so minute that they were like empty space, and then completely use up the waters of the great ocean in washing them, unless we washed the inside of these particles, how could they possibly be immaculate? And unless we washed the inside of empty space, how could we possibly achieve complete immaculacy within and without?

Such befuddled people are also incapable of recognizing the process of cleansing emptiness. We make use of Emptiness to cleanse emptiness, and we make use of Emptiness to cleanse body and mind. Those who, with faith, accept cleansing as a form of the Dharma will be preserving what the Buddhas and Ancestors trained in and came to realize. That is to say, in the True Dharma of Buddha after Buddha, Ancestor after Ancestor, and Successor after Successor of the Buddhas and Ancestors, when we engage in cleansing ourselves, then body and mind—both inside and out— along with the five vital organs, the six forms of entrails, the outer world and the inner world, the inside, outside, and middle of the realms of thoughts and things, as well as unbounded space, are all instantly immaculate. When we make use of incense or flowers in purifying ourselves, then our deeds of past, present, and future, as well as their accompanying causes and conditions, are instantly immaculate.

The Buddha said, "By washing thrice and perfuming thrice, our body and mind become immaculate." Thus, the method for washing our body and cleansing our mind is to habitually do one perfuming with one washing, and by such a sequence to do three washings and three perfumings. We then pay homage to the Buddha, recite some bit of Scripture, and do seated meditation followed by walking meditation. Once our walking meditation is finished and before we endeavor to sit up straight in seated meditation again, it is said that we should always wash our feet. Even if our feet have not become sullied, this is still the method of the Buddhas and Ancestors.

In these three washings and three perfumings of which He spoke, washing once refers to taking a bath: it is bathing the whole body. And after having done so, we get dressed as usual, then we light incense in a small censer and cense inside the bosom of our upper robe, as well as censing our kesa, our meditation place, and so forth. After that, we bathe again and cense again. We do it like this three times. This is the ceremony that accords with the Dharma. At this time, even though the six sense organs and the six types of objects that stimulate them are still there, they will undoubtedly manifest the virtue of immaculacy before your very eyes. And, as the Buddha taught, even though we may not be rid of the three poisons of greed, hate, and delusion or of the four topsy-turvy beliefs,[4] the virtue of being immaculate will immediately manifest before our very eyes. Who can fathom It by using conventional ways of thinking? What person can spot It by using his ordinary eyes? For instance, when we wash aloes wood to cleanse it for making incense, we should not break it into bits and pieces before washing it, nor should we grind it into a powder before washing it; it attains immaculacy simply by our washing the whole piece, in a body.

The method for cleansing has been definitely set forth in the Buddha's Teaching. We wash our body, we wash our mind, we wash our feet, we wash our face, we wash our eyes, we wash our mouth, we wash our private parts, we wash our hands, we wash our alms bowl, we wash our kesa, and we wash our head. All of these are part of the True Teaching of all the Buddhas and Ancestors of the past, present, and future.

When we undertake to make an offering to Buddha, Dharma, and Sangha, we first wash our hands and face, rinse out our mouth, and put on a clean robe. We then bring some type of fragrant wood, and, taking fresh water in a clean bowl, we wash this incense. Once this is done, we offer it to the realm of Buddha, Dharma, and

---

4. Namely, believing that what is impermanent has permanence, that what causes suffering is pleasurable, that what is sullied is pure, and that what is without self has a self.

Sangha. May the offering we make to the Triple Treasure be as sandalwood incense from the Malaya Mountains that has been washed in Lake Anavatapta's water of eight virtues.[5]

Washing the face was passed down from India in the west and spread throughout China in the east. Although the procedure is made clear enough in various passages in the monastic regulations, it will still be something that Buddhas and Ancestors hold to and directly pass on to Their genuine successors. It is not merely something that Buddha after Buddha and Ancestor after Ancestor have come to practice over the centuries; it has flowed down through hundreds of thousands of millions of eons of the past, and will continue to do so in the future. It does not merely remove dirt and grime; it is the lifeblood of the Buddhas and Ancestors.

It is said that if we do not wash the face, both our receiving obeisances and our making obeisances to others will be stained.

> When we bow, and bow to others,
> If we can make our bow to That which is bowed to,
> Then our True Nature will be free and serene,
> For 'True Nature' too will have dropped away.

This is why we must, by all means, wash the face.

The time for washing our face may be during the pre-dawn fifth watch or it may be after the sun has risen. When I was staying with my late Master, Nyojō, he took the third period of the third watch (around 2:00 A.M.) to be the time for doing it. Putting on our skirt and undershirt, or a full under-robe, and carrying our hand towel,

---

5.   The Malaya Mountains in southern India are renowned for their highly prized sandalwood. Lake Anavatapta is considered by some as the source of the four major rivers of India, and by others as a lake on Mount Sumeru. Its eight virtues are its sweetness, its coolness, its softness, its lightness, its purity, its absence of odor, its harmlessness to the throat, and its harmlessness to the stomach.

we proceeded to a washstand. A hand towel is a piece of cloth twelve feet long. It should not be white in color since white is prohibited.

It says in the *Great Scripture on the Three Thousand Forms of Everyday Behavior for Monks*:

> There are five things to consider when using the hand towel. First, wipe with the top and bottom ends. Second, wipe your hands with one end and wipe your face with the other. Third, do not wipe your nose with it. Fourth, should it become soiled through using it to wipe up grease or dirt, by all means wash it right away. Fifth, do not wipe your body with it. When you wash, each of you should have your own towel.

When handling our hand towel, we should take care of it in the following way. We fold the hand towel in two and then drape it over our left forearm. We wipe our face with one half of the hand towel and our hands with the other half. The statement "Do not wipe your nose with it" means that we do not use it to wipe the insides of our nostrils or the mucus from them. We should not use the hand towel to wipe our sides, back, belly, navel, thighs, or lower legs. We should wash our hand towel if it becomes soiled with dirt or grime. When it gets wet, we dry it by the fire or hang it out in the sun to dry. We should not use a hand towel when taking a bath.

The washing place for those in the Cloud Hall is the rear washstand.[6] The rear washstand is to the west of the Illumination Hall.[7] This layout is what has been passed on to us. For retreat huts and private quarters, a washstand is put in a convenient place. The Abbot washes up in the abbatical quarters. In the residence for elderly monks, a washstand has been put in a convenient place. When the Abbot is residing in the Cloud Hall, he should use the rear washstand to wash up.

When going to the washstand, we hang the middle part of our hand towel over the nape of our neck. Bringing the two ends in front over our shoulders, we use

---

6. The Cloud Hall is the hall where the monks meditate. 'The rear washstand' refers specifically to the washstand behind the Cloud Hall.

7. The Illumination Hall is used when senior monks other than the Abbot give Dharma talks.

both hands to take the ends under our arms and to our back. Then, crossing the ends, we bring the left end around to the right and the right end around to the left, and tie the ends in front of our chest. When we do it in this fashion, the upper part of our robe is covered by the hand towel, and our sleeves are bound up by it above our elbows, while below our elbows, our arms and hands are left exposed. It is just as if we had tucked up our sleeves with a sash.[8]

Next, if we are at the rear washstand, taking a wash bucket in hand, we go to where the iron cauldron is and get a bucket of hot water. Then, returning, we put it atop the washstand. If we are somewhere else, we pour hot water from the hot water tub into a washbowl.

Next, we use our willow twig.[9] Nowadays, in various monasteries in Great Sung China, the method for chewing a willow twig has long been discarded and is not passed on, so there is no place for chewing a willow twig. But today at Eihei-ji Temple on Mount Kichijō there is a place for chewing a willow twig, which is our present way of looking at the matter. Accordingly, first we chew the willow twig. Then, holding the willow twig in our right hand, we recite the appropriate verse. I In the "Pure Deeds" chapter of the *Avatamsaka Scripture*, it says the following:

> *Taking this willow twig in hand,*
> *I pray that all sentient beings*
> *May realize in their hearts the True Dharma*
> *And thereby become naturally pure.*

After we have finished reciting this text and are about to chew the willow twig again, we should then recite the following:

---

8.   The sleeves worn by monastics during Dōgen's time were of a large, koromo style and therefore needed to be bound up.

9.   The willow twig was used as a toothbrush.

> *Chewing the willow twig this morning,*
> *I pray that all sentient beings*
> *May obtain the teeth for overcoming evil,*
> *So that they may chew up their defiling passions.*

Having finished reciting this text, we chew on our willow twig.

The length of a willow twig is the width of four, eight, twelve, or sixteen fingers. As it says in Article 34 of the *Code of Behavior for Members of the Greater Sangha*, "We use for our teeth a twig of suitable dimensions. The longest is the width of sixteen fingers, the shortest is the width of four fingers." We need to keep in mind that it should not be shorter than four fingers and that beyond sixteen fingers is not a suitable dimension. The thickness is that of our little finger. However, there is nothing to preclude it from being thinner than that. Its shape is that of the little finger: one end thick, one end thin. The thicker end is chewed into fine shreds. As it says in the *Great Scripture on the Three Thousand Forms of Everyday Behavior for Monks*, "Do not go beyond a third of an inch along the length of the willow twig." We must chew it well, then rub and clean the front and back of our teeth as if we were polishing them. We rub and polish, and then rinse out our mouth from time to time. We should thoroughly polish and clean the base of our teeth above the gums and thoroughly scrape between our teeth, and wash that area clean. When our mouth is rinsed out again and again, our teeth will be washed clean.

After we have done this, we need to clean our tongue. It says in the *Great Scripture on the Three Thousand Forms of Everyday Behavior for Monks*:

> There are five things to consider when scraping the tongue.
> First, do not go beyond three times. Second, if your tongue begins
> to bleed, by all means cease. Third, do not soil your sanghati robe
> or your feet by flailing your hands about.[10] Fourth, when discarding

---

10.   The sanghati robe is the largest of three basic types of kesa. Dōgen gives a detailed explanation of all three in Discourse 84: On the Spiritual Merits of the Kesa *(Kesa Kudoku)*.

your willow twig, do not put it where others walk. Fifth, always scrape your tongue in a screened off area.

In the phrase 'scrape your tongue three times', 'scraping your tongue' means putting some water into your mouth and scraping your tongue repeatedly. It does not mean scraping it just three times. Keep in mind the statement that if your tongue begins to bleed, by all means cease.

As to the remark that we should thoroughly scrape our tongue, it says in the *Great Scripture on the Three Thousand Forms of Everyday Behavior for Monks*, "Purifying your mouth means chewing a willow twig, rinsing your mouth out, and scraping your tongue." Hence, the willow twig is something that the Buddhas and Ancestors, along with Their successors, have come to preserve and hold to.

The Buddha was living in the Bamboo Grove Park at Rajagriha, along with twelve hundred and fifty monks. It was the first day of the twelfth month, and King Prasenajit was providing food for them on that day. At daybreak he personally offered the Buddha a willow twig. After the Buddha had taken and thoroughly chewed it, He discarded what remained. No sooner had it touched the ground than it came to life, with roots and sprouts gushing forth in great profusion, until it was five hundred yojanas* tall. Its leaves and branches spread out like a cloud to a circumference of the same magnitude. At length, it brought forth blossoms as large as cart wheels. Finally, it produced fruit the size of five-gallon jars. The roots and buds, branches and leaves, were entirely comprised of the seven treasures,* whose various colors glimmered with extraordinary beauty. In accord with their color, they gave off rays of light that eclipsed both sun and moon. When the fruit was eaten, it proved as delicious as nectar. Its fragrance filled the four quarters; whoever smelled it was truly filled with delight. As the fragrant breeze came blowing, the branches and leaves rubbed against each other so that they all gave forth melodious sounds, delightfully voicing the essence of the Dharma. Whoever heard this never tired of listening. The hearts of all the people who witnessed this transformation of the tree grew ever more pure and their reverence and trust deepened. The Buddha then gave voice to the Dharma according to their ability to grasp Its intent, so that all their hearts were opened to comprehend It. Those who sought what the Buddha intended attained their goal and were reborn in a heavenly state, their number being extremely great.[11]

The method for making an alms offering to the Buddha and the assembled monks was invariably to proffer willow twigs at daybreak. After that, various other offerings were prepared. There are many instances of willow twigs being given to the Buddha, and there are many instances of the Buddha using a willow twig, but, for the time being, I have presented the story of King Prasenajit's personally making the alms offering, along with the story of this great tree, because you should know about them.

Also on that day, six non-Buddhist teachers were all bested in debate by the Buddha. Being dismayed and frightened, they took to flight. Ultimately, as the Scripture recounts:

All six teachers together threw themselves into the river and drowned. The nine hundred million followers of these six teachers all came to the Buddha, seeking to be His disciples. Upon the Buddha's welcoming them as monks, their beards and hair naturally came off, and they had Dharma robes on their bodies, for they had all become mendicant monks. As the Buddha voiced the Dharma for their benefit, pointing out Its essence, they disentangled

---

11. This narrative is quoted from "The Defeat of the Six Teachers," which is the second chapter of the *Scripture on Accounts of the Wise and the Befuddled*.

themselves from their defiling passions and fully attained arhathood.[*]

Thus, because the Tathagata was already accustomed to using willow twigs, both ordinary people and those in lofty positions made alms offerings of them. It is clear that all Buddhas and Bodhisattvas, along with disciples of the Buddha, beyond doubt, hold to chewing a willow twig. Should anyone not use a willow twig, they will have forfeited the Teaching. And what a pity that would be!

It says in the Bodhisattva Precepts section of the *Scripture of Brahma's Net:*

> During the two retreat periods in winter and summer, as well as during the renewal period at the beginning of summer when pilgrimages are undertaken, as a disciple of the Buddha, you should always have for your personal use a tooth-cleaning willow twig, soap, your three monastic robes, a water jug, your alms bowl, your bowing mat, your mendicant's traveling staff, an incense burner, a clothes box, a water filter, a towel, a razor, something to light a fire with, tweezers, a hammock, a Scripture and *Vinaya* text, an image of the Buddha, and some image of a Bodhisattva. Whenever you go on a pilgrimage or travel for other spiritual reasons, be it for thirty miles or three hundred, you should always carry these eighteen objects with you. The retreat periods last from the fifteenth day of the first month to the fifteenth day of the third month and from the fifteenth day of the eighth month to the fifteenth day of the tenth month; during these two periods you should always carry these eighteen objects with you when you travel, just as a bird carries its two wings.

Not even one of these eighteen objects should be missing. If you lack any, you would be like a bird that had shed one wing. Even though one wing remained, the bird would be unable to fly, for its condition would not be the way birds are. Similarly for bodhisattvas: if they are not equipped with these eighteen 'wings', it will not be the way that bodhisattvas do their practice.

Among these eighteen articles, the willow twig already occupies the first position and should be the very first thing you supply yourself with. Folks who are clear about the use of the willow twig will be bodhisattvas who are clear about the Buddha Dharma. Those who have not yet clarified this matter have probably not encountered the Buddha Dharma even in their dreams.

Hence, to see the willow twig is to encounter the Buddhas and Ancestors. If someone should ask me, "What is its purpose?" I would reply, "How fortunate we are to have witnessed that old fellow Dōgen chewing on a willow twig."

All Buddhas and bodhisattvas of past, present, and future invariably accept and hold to this Bodhisattva Precept from the *Scripture of Brahma's Net.* Thus, they have likewise come to accept and hold to the willow twig in the three periods of time.

It says in the *Procedures for Cleanliness in a Zen Temple:*

> It is imperative that you read, recite aloud, and thoroughly comprehend both the Ten Great Precepts and the Forty-eight Less Grave Precepts in the Mahayana* *Scripture of Brahma's Net,* and thereby know well what keeps to them or breaks them, as well as what they permit or prohibit. But do so in accord with the sage words from the golden mouth of the Buddha. Do not indulge in following ordinary people in such matters.

By all means, you need to understand that Buddha after Buddha and Ancestor after Ancestor have correctly Transmitted the import of what this quotation is saying. Whatever deviates from this is not the Buddha's Way, nor is it the Buddha's Teaching, nor is it the Way of the Ancestors.

Be that as it may, in Great Sung China today the willow twig is never to be seen. In the fourth month of the eighteenth year of the Chinese Chia-ting Era (1223)

when I began to visit the various monasteries and temples in China, the willow twig was unknown to the monks, and it was likewise unknown in court and country both to ordinary people as well as to those in lofty positions. Because it was unknown to any in the monastic family, whenever I inquired about the method for using a willow twig, they would turn pale and lose their composure. What a pity that this spotless method has been lost. Folks who barely rinse out their mouths have fashioned a device by cutting more than an inch of hair from a horse's tail and then setting it, two inches deep, into a piece of ox horn about a third of an inch thick and six or seven inches long, so that it quite resembles a horse's mane. This is the only thing they use for cleaning their teeth. It is an inappropriate implement for monks to use. As it may well be an unclean utensil, it is not an instrument of the Buddha's Teaching. Pious common folk, who worship the emperor and other celestial beings, are bound to be repelled by it. Further, commoners and monks both use this instrument as a tool for brushing the dirt off their shoes, or use it for brushing their hair. Though some of these tools may be a bit larger or smaller, they are one and the same in their usage. And only one in ten thousand use even this inadequate device. As a result, the breath of monks and householders alike is foul smelling. When people two or three feet away speak, their bad breath comes forth and even a whiff of it is hard to take. Not even those praised as venerable senior monks who have realized the Way or those who are known as teachers and guides for ordinary people and those in lofty positions know that there is a method for rinsing the mouth, scraping the tongue, and chewing a willow twig. Based on this, we cannot begin to know in how many other ways we may now find the Great Way of the Buddhas and Ancestors in decay. Although I do not begrudge either committing my dewdrop existence to thousands of miles of blue waves, or my crossing foreign mountains and rivers in order to find the Way, yet I must regret this sad state of affairs. How many unstained methods have already disappeared there? How sad, how very sad!

Despite this, throughout the whole of Japan both monks and laity in court and country are all personally acquainted with the willow twig, which may be due to their personal experience of the Buddha's light of wisdom. Even so, their way of chewing a willow twig is not like the standard practice, and the method for scraping the tongue has not been introduced to them, probably due to their being in too big a hurry. Still, those who are aware that they should use a willow twig—in contrast with the people of Sung who are totally unaware of the willow twig—have naturally learned this method of the spiritually preeminent ones. Among the practices of mountain hermits, we find that they too use the willow twig. You need to realize that, as they say, it is the instrument whereby all may emerge from the dust; it is the tool of immaculacy.

It says in the *Great Scripture on the Three Thousand Forms of Everyday Behavior for Monks*:

> There are five things to consider when using a willow twig for chewing. First, cut it according to the proper length. Second, split it according to the proper method. Third, when chewing its head, do not go beyond one third of an inch. Fourth, in cleaning between the teeth, chew it three times. Fifth, make use of the sap to bathe your eyes.

Our present-day practice of washing our eyes by scooping up some water in our right hand from the water that we used for chewing the willow twig and rinsing out our mouth was originally a doctrine in the *Great Scripture on the Three Thousand Forms of Everyday Behavior for Monks*. Nowadays in Japan, it is a long-standing domestic custom. The method for scraping the tongue was transmitted by the exemplary monk Eisai.[12] Before disposing of your used willow twig, use both hands to split it in two, tearing it from the chewed end. Put the sharp edge of the split twig crosswise on your tongue and scrape it. That is, take up some water with your right hand, put it in your mouth and rinse it out, and then scrape your tongue. Again and again, rinse your mouth and scrape your tongue, scraping repeatedly with the edge of the split willow twig as if you were attempting to draw blood.

When you are rinsing your mouth, you should silently recite the following verse, as put forth in the *Avatamsaka Scripture*:

---

12. The Japanese monk who introduced the Rinzai tradition into Japan. He was the first Zen Master under whom Dōgen trained.

> *In cleansing my mouth and teeth,*
> *I pray that all sentient beings*
> *Will turn towards the Gate to Immaculacy*
> *And ultimately attain freedom.*

Repeatedly rinse your mouth out and use the ball of the first, second, or third finger of your right hand to cleanse the inside of your lips and under your tongue, as if you were licking them clean. When you have recently eaten something oily, you should use ground honey locust pods. When you have finished with the willow twig, you should then dispose of it out of sight. After you have disposed of your willow twig, you should snap your fingers three times. There is a container for disposing of willow twigs on the rear washstand. In other places, you should dispose of it in an unobtrusive place. You should spit out the water from rinsing your mouth somewhere other than in the washbowl.

Next, we need to wash our face. Scooping hot water from the washbowl in both hands, we wash all over, from the forehead to the eyebrows, the eyes, the nose, the inside of the ears, the crown of the head, and the cheeks. We should first douse them thoroughly with hot water and then scrub them. Take care not to let tears, spittle, or nasal mucus drip into the washbowl water. When washing in this manner, do not use excessive amounts of hot water, spilling or slopping it outside the washbowl, so that you run out of it too soon. Wash until the dirt and oil has been removed. Wash behind your ears, since water does not customarily reach there. Rinse your eyeballs, since they cannot be cleaned with sand. And washing even from your hairline up over the crown of your head is ordinary, everyday monastic behavior. After you have finished washing the face and have disposed of the water in your washbowl, snap your fingers three times.

Next, wipe and dry your face with one end of your hand towel. After that, take off the hand towel, fold it as it was before, and hang it over your left arm. At the rear washstand behind the Cloud Hall are face-wiping cloths for common use; long pieces of toweling have also been provided, and there are charcoal braziers. Members of the community need not worry about there not being sufficient toweling for drying their face. They can dry their heads and faces with those provided or use their own hand towel: both are proper methods.

When washing your face, do not make a sound by noisily clanging the ladle against your bowl. And do not let the surrounding area get wet by splashing hot or cold water about. Quietly reflect on the fact that, even though we were born in the final five hundred years of the Dharma and live on a remote island, the merit that we have accumulated from the past has not fallen into decay. We should rejoice in deepest gratitude that we have had correctly passed on to us the ordinary, everyday behavior of earlier Buddhas and that, without stain, we do our training to experience the Truth. In returning to the Cloud Hall, we should step lightly and speak with a low voice.

In the private quarters of aged and virtuous monks, without question there needs to be a washstand, since not washing the face is counter to the Dharma.

When washing the face, there are methods for using facial medicines.

In short, chewing a willow twig and washing the face are the True Teachings of Old Buddhas. Those who do their utmost to train with a heart that is fixed on the Way should train with and experience these Teachings. Using cold water when there is no hot water is an ancient custom, a long-established method. When there is neither hot nor cold water available, in the early morning wipe your face thoroughly dry, using a fragrant grass, powdered incense, or the like. Then, pay homage to the Buddha, recite a Scripture, light incense, and do seated meditation. To do our religious practices before we have washed our face is discourteous.

Delivered to the assembly on the twenty-third day of the tenth lunar month in the first year of the En'o era (November 21, 1239) at Kannondōri in Kōshōhōrin-ji Temple, Yamashiro Province.

In India and China, kings, princes, ministers of state, government officials, lay Buddhists, monks, men and women in court and country, all the people throughout wash their faces. Among their household goods is a washbasin, perhaps of gold, perhaps of tin. Every morning, some people perform the act of washing their face at a shrine to a celestial deity or at the gravesite of their ancestors. Others offer their face-washing at the stupa* of a Buddha or an Ancestor. After lay Buddhists and monks have washed their faces and straightened their clothing, they bow to those in heavenly states, and bow to the resident spirits, and bow to the Ancestors of their lineage, and bow to their parents. They bow to their teachers, and to the Triple Treasure, and to the myriad beings in the three worlds of desire, form, and beyond form, and they bow to the benevolent guardian spirits. There are none who forget to wash their face, not even farmers and rice growers, fishermen and woodcutters. Even so, they do not chew the willow twig. In Japan, amongst emperors and ministers of state, old and young, courtiers and gentry, householders and monks, both ordinary people and those in lofty positions all remember to chew a willow twig and rinse out their mouth, but they do not wash their face. In each country, it is a case of one strong point and one shortcoming. To preserve and hold to the practice of washing the face and chewing a willow twig corrects this deficiency and is the luminous manifestation of the Buddhas and Ancestors.

Delivered again to the assembly on the twentieth day of the tenth lunar month in the first year of the Kangen era (December 2, 1243) at Kippō-ji Temple in Yoshida Prefecture, Echizen Province.

Delivered to the monks on the eleventh day of the first lunar month in the second year of the Zenchō era (February 13, 1250) at Eihei-ji Temple on Mount Kichijō in Yoshida Prefecture, Echizen Province.

56

On the Model for Doing Meditation

(Zazengi)

To train under a Master is to do seated meditation. In doing seated meditation, a quiet place serves well. Spread out your meditation mat so that it lies thickly. Do not put it in a place that is windy or smoky, and do not expose it to rain or dew. Make the place where you sit secure for your body. There is the example from the past of Shakyamuni's sitting in a diamond-hard place under the Bodhi tree, seated upon a huge rock in the shape of a lotus, upon which He had spread out a thick cushion of dry grass. Your sitting place should be lit, without letting it be in the dark, day or night. Make 'warm in winter and cool in summer' your technique.

Set aside all involvements and give everything a rest. Do not think about what is good or what is bad. Do not exercise your discriminatory mind or weigh and judge your mind's remembrances, concepts, and reflections! Do not aim at becoming a Buddha, and drop off any concern with whether you are sitting or lying down. Eat and drink in moderation. Cherish the light of days and the dark of nights. Take to doing seated meditation as though you were extinguishing a fire upon your head. The Fifth Chinese Ancestor, Daiman Kōnin of Mount Ōbai, did not do anything particularly different: he just diligently did seated meditation.

When sitting in meditation, wear your kesa.[*] Spread out your mat and put your round cushion atop it. Do not sit in lotus position with the cushion supporting the whole of your legs, but put it well behind the back half of your legs. Consequently, the mat will be under your knees and thighs while the cushion will be under the base of your spine. This is the method for seated meditation that has been used by Buddha after Buddha and Ancestor after Ancestor.

Some people sit in the half lotus position and some sit in the full lotus position. When sitting in the full lotus position, we put the right foot atop the left thigh

---

[*]   See Glossary.

and the left foot atop the right thigh. The tips of our toes should line up uniformly on our thighs and not lie unevenly. When sitting in half lotus position, we simply place our left foot on our right thigh.[1]

We should drape our clothing in a loose-fitting manner, yet neatly. We place our right hand atop our left foot and our left hand atop our right hand. The tips of our two thumbs touch each other. Both hands are then held close to our body. The point at which the two thumbs touch should be placed opposite the navel.

You should sit with your body upright, that is, not leaning to the right, inclining to the left, bending forward, or arching back. You need to align your ears with your shoulders and your nose with your navel. Let your tongue rest in your mouth. Breathe through your nose. Your lips and teeth should be touching. Your eyes should remain open, but neither widely nor narrowly so.

With body and mind regulated in this manner, breathe out once. Sit with the stillness of a mountain, and let what you are thinking about be based on not deliberately trying to think about any particular thing. How can what anyone is thinking about be based on not deliberately thinking about <u>something</u>? Simply, by not making 'what I am thinking about' the point of your meditation. This, then, is the technique for doing seated meditation. Seated meditation is a practice and not something for intellectual study. It is the Dharma Gate to peace and joy. It is unstained training to realize the Truth.

Delivered to the monks at Kippō-ji Training Temple, Yoshida Prefecture, Echizen Province, in the eleventh lunar month of the first year of the Kangen era (December 1243).

Copied in the chief disciple Ejō's quarters at Kippō Hermitage, Echizen Province, on the twentieth day of the first lunar month in the second year of the same era (March 1, 1244).

---

1. Readers who choose to follow Dōgen's practice of sitting in full or half lotus are cautioned to alternate which leg is on top so as to avoid back problems that can develop over long-term practice. Also, to avoid putting injurious strain on the spine and knees, several other modes of sitting have developed in the Zen tradition, such as sitting in a chair or on a meditation bench. One may even meditate while lying down.

57

On the Plum Blossom
(Baika)

Translator's Introduction: The plum tree holds a particular place in Chinese culture, one that was transplanted into the culture of Japan. As the earliest blooming of all trees, it comes into flower in the latter part of winter and is therefore considered a harbinger of spring. In Buddhist contexts, it is used as a metaphor for Shakyamuni Buddha, who was considered the first to bring forth the blossoming of the Dharma, and whose blossoming has inspired others to seek and find the Way.

By extension, the plum tree is also seen as a reference to one's Master and, in his writings, Dōgen frequently refers to his Master as an 'Old Buddha'. Further, the plum blossom is used as a metaphor for the udumbara flower which Shakyamuni held aloft, His eyes atwinkle. Upon seeing this, His disciple Makakashō broke out into a smile in response to his spiritual recognition of True Nature.

Dōgen's commentaries in this discourse are based primarily on various poems that his late Master, Tendō Nyojō, had composed. The discourse begins with a poem that describes Nyojō's relationship with his own Master, Setchō Chikan. Dōgen uses this poem to comment on the Master-disciple relationship in general, as well as to explore various applications of the metaphor to the functioning of the non-personal Buddha Nature (the Plum Blossom) after the conventional body and mind have dropped off.

The perspective from which Dōgen speaks derives from just such a spiritual experience, which not all of his disciples would have had. How he puts things often bypasses customary modes of discourse wherein one's intellect functions as the final arbiter of meaning. To attempt to explain or 'rationalize' all the allusions in this text would require extensive annotation and would seem counter to Dōgen's intent in the first place. To put it simply, his process of 'boggling the mind' is intended, in part, to liberate his disciples from conventional modes of thinking and to help point them towards their True Nature.

My late Master Tendō, an Old Buddha, was the thirtieth Abbot and a most venerable monk of Keitoku-ji Temple on the renowned Mount Tendō in the Keigen district of Great Sung China. Once when speaking to the assembly he said, "Here at Tendō in midwinter have come forth the first lines of a verse." He then recited the following poem of his:

The thorn-like, spike-branched Old Plum Tree
Suddenly bursts forth, first with one or two blossoms,
Then with three, four, five, and finally blossoms beyond
count.
No perfume to take pride in, no fragrance to boast of.
In scattering, they evoke a springtime scene as they are
blown over grass and trees.
The patch-robed monks, to a one, have no sooner shaved
their heads
Than, suddenly, the weather shifts with howling winds
and squalling skies,
Until the whole earth is wrapped in swirling snow.
The Old Plum Tree's silhouette is barely to be seen,
As the freezing cold seizes their noses and rubs them raw.

The Old Plum Tree with which he began his talk was a silhouette barely to be seen when It suddenly burst into bloom and bore fruit. Sometimes It brought forth a springtime, sometimes It brought forth a winter. Sometimes It brought forth howling winds, sometimes It brought forth squalling skies. Sometimes It was simply the head of a patch-robed monk, sometimes It was the Eye of my Old Buddha. Sometimes It changed into grass and trees; sometimes It suddenly changed into a pure fragrance. Its sudden spiritual transformations and spiritually wondrous ways were inexhaustible, even up to the point where the great earth and the high heavens, along with the luminous sun and the pure moon, were functioning like trees, due to the arboreal merits of the Old Plum Tree, as they—Master and disciple—entwined around and supported each other, like the vines of kudzu and wisteria do.

At the time when the Old Plum Tree burst into bloom, Its flowering characterized the world. Whenever Its flowering characterizes the world, that is what we call 'the arrival of spring'. On that occasion, there is a single blossom of five petals that bursts forth. At the time of this single blossom, there can be three, or four, or five blossoms, or there can be a hundred, or a thousand, or myriad blossoms, right up to there being countless blossoms. These blossomings forth are nothing compared to the one or two or countless boughs that the Old Plum Tree can boast of. Flowers such as the udumbara and the blue lotus are like one or two branchings of the Old Plum Tree's blossoming.[1] All blossomings, in general, are beneficent gifts of the Old Plum Tree. There is the Old Plum Tree of common folk and the Old Plum Tree of those in loftier realms. And from within the Old Plum Tree, both the ordinary human realms and the realms of the more lofty manifest, due to the merits of the Tree. We call the hundreds and thousands of blossoms the flowering of ordinary people and of those in loftier realms; the thousands of millions of blossoms are the flowering of Buddhas and Ancestors. At this very moment in time the blossoms cry out, "A Buddha has appeared in the world!" and they cry out "From the first, the Ancestral Master Bodhidharma came to this very land of ours!"

My late Master, an Old Buddha, once addressed his assembly in verse:

> *When Gautama finally lost His deceiving eyes,*[2]
> *There appeared in the snow a single blossom on*
> *one bough of the Old Plum Tree.*
> *What has now arrived is the growing of thorn-like*
> *spurs,*
> *So that all the more I laugh at the spring winds*
> *which send all things flying in disarray.*

Now that this Old Buddha has turned the Wheel of the Dharma to Its full throughout the whole universe, it has created an opportunity for all ordinary folk, as well as those in lofty positions, to realize the Way. There is nothing that has not been covered with the benefits of the Dharma, even including clouds and rain, winds and water, plants

---

1. The udumbara flower is said to bloom only once every three thousand years. For this reason it is used in Buddhism as a metaphor for how difficult it is to come into contact with the True Teaching. The blue lotus is a metaphor for wise discernment and one's victory over slavery to the senses.

2. Gautama, Prince Siddhārtha's family name, is customarily used to refer to Shakyamuni Buddha before His enlightenment.

and insect life. The heavens and the earth, along with their domains, having been set
in motion by this Wheel of the Dharma, are like fish freely and vigorously swimming
about in water. When people say, "I am hearing words that I have not heard before,"
they are saying, "I am listening to the Dharma of the present moment." When they
say, "I am getting what I did not have before," they are giving a name to their realizing
the Dharma of the present moment. In short, His Wheel of the Dharma cannot be seen
or heard without there being at least a vague feeling of happiness and prosperity.

In and about the hundred and eighty provinces within Great Sung China
today, there are temples in the mountains and in populated areas whose number is
beyond reckoning. Within them, the number of trainees is great. But most of them
never met my late Master, the Old Buddha. Further, only a small percentage of those
who had met him actually heard what he had to say. And even more, how could there
possibly be many who had a one-to-one meeting with him and made their prostrations
to him?[3] And those permitted in his private quarters were fewer still, to say nothing
of those who were permitted to do prostrations to my late Master's Skin and Flesh,
Bones and Marrow, Countenance and Eye.

My late Master, the Old Buddha, did not readily allow new monks to stay in
the monastery. He would often say, "Those who are unfamiliar with the mind that
seeks the Way cannot dwell here with me," and then he'd send them on their way.
Once rid of them, he would say, "If they are not 'such a one',* what, pray, do they
want to achieve? Dogs like that are noisy beings. They are not permitted in the
monastery." I have actually witnessed this and personally heard him say that. In
private, I thought to myself, "What could they possibly have done wrong that even
though they are his countrymen, he would not allow them to dwell with him? By what
good fortune have I been permitted to enter his monastery, even though I am an alien
seed from a distant foreign land? And further, I have been allowed to have free access
to the Abbot's private quarters that I might do prostrations to his venerable body and
listen to his words of Dharma. Though I am foolish and ignorant, I have been able to
form a fruitful bond with him."

---

3.   That is, became his disciples.

At the time when my late Master was doing his part to transform the worldly ways of Sung China, there were people who were able to explore the Matter,* as well as those who were not able to do so. Now that my late Master, the Old Buddha, has departed from the world of Sung China, it has probably become even more dismal than a moonless night. And why is that? I would simply answer, "Because around the time of my late Master, an Old Buddha, there were no Old Buddhas like my late Master, the Old Buddha." Thus, when you trainees of today encounter and hear what he said in his poems, do not think that other countrymen of yours are able to encounter and heed the Wheel of the Dharma and thereby explore the Matter with a Master. The Plum Blossom in the snow is a single glimpse of the udumbara flower. How often does it happen in everyday life that, while looking respectfully at the Treasure House of the Eye of the True Teaching of the Buddha Tathagata, we vainly fail to break into a smile when His eyes twinkle? Right now, beyond doubt, we have already had authentically Transmitted to us—and affirmed for us—that the Plum Blossom in the snow is the very Eye of the Tathagata. Taking this up, some may take the Eye to mean a painted eye on a forehead or the pupil within an organ of sight. But when we get inside the Plum Blossom through our training and completely investigate It, such dubious explanations do not come forth any longer. This is the very Eye of the statement, "In the heavens above and the earth below, I alone am the Honored One."[4]

Thus it is that the celestial flowers in the world of the heavens and the celestial flowers in the world of humans—coral tree flowers and great coral tree flowers, as well as the red manjusha tree flowers and great red manjusha tree flowers—along with flowers that are kindred to innumerable lands within the ten quarters, are all the kith and kin of the Plum Blossom in the snow. Because they have received a portion of the beneficence of the Plum Blossom, millions of blossoms are the kin of the Plum Blossom and should, therefore, be called miniature plum blossoms. Illusory flowers in the sky, earthbound flowers, flowerings within the mind of

---

4.   This quotation is attributed to the Buddha who, upon His birth, is said to have taken seven steps and then uttered these words. However, as the discourse states, it was Gautama's Eye (Buddha Nature) that made the statement. That is, the 'I' in the quote does not refer to a personal self. It is Buddha Nature Itself that is making the claim.

meditation, and so on, are all large and small flowers that are kindred to the Plum Blossom. The flowers that have opened within the millions of domains within the Flower are all a portion of the beneficence of this Plum Blossom.[5] Apart from the beneficence of the Plum Blossom, there is not a single raindrop or dewdrop of beneficence. The bloodlines of all who have flowered have come forth from the Plum Blossom. Do not explore the statement "The whole earth was wrapped in swirls of snow" as something that occurred only at Shōrin-ji Monastery. That snow was the Eye of the Tathagata, which shone upon Eka's head and under his feet.[6] Do not merely explore it as what the snow of 'a snow-covered shrine in the snow-capped Himalayan Mountains' refers to. It was the Treasure House of the Eye of the True Teaching for Old Gautama,[7] for in that place He fully realized the opening of the five eyes.[8] The eyes of the Thousand-eyed One would have been completely fulfilled within these five eyes of His.[9]

Truly, there was not one smidgen of the Real Form of all thoughts and things that Old Gautama did not fully realize within the luminous brilliance of His body and mind. Even though the views of ordinary people and those in lofty positions have differences, and even though the feelings of the mundane and the saintly stand far apart, the vast expanse of snow is what the earth is, and the earth itself *is* a vast expanse

---

5.   'The Flower' is an allusion to the multi-petaled lotus that opens upon the crown of the Tathagata's head, in the center of which sits Vairochana Buddha, that is, the Cosmic Buddha.

6.   The reference here is to the Second Chinese Ancestor Eka, who stood all night in the deepening snow outside Bodhidharma's quarters while seeking to be Bodhidharma's disciple.

7.   A reference to Gautama doing His training in the Himalayan Mountains.

8.   'The five eyes' refers to Gautama's two physical eyes, which are the non-worldly eyes of someone who is in meditation, plus the Eye of wise discernment, the Eye of the Dharma, and the Eye of a Buddha.

9.   'The Thousand-eyed One' refers to the Bodhisattva Avalokiteshvara of the Thousand Eyes and the Thousand Hands, who is the embodiment of the compassion of Vairochana Buddha.

of snow. If there were no vast expanse of snow, there would be no Earth anywhere within the universe. The whole of this vast expanse of snow—inside and out—is synonymous with these eyes of Old Gautama.[10]

You need to realize that both the Flower and the Earth are completely beyond birth and death. The Flower is beyond birth and death, and because the Flower is beyond birth and death, the Earth is beyond birth and death. Because both Flower and Earth are completely beyond birth and death, the Eye is beyond birth and death. What is called 'beyond birth and death' is synonymous with supreme enlightenment. What is seen at that very instant of enlightenment is simply a Plum Blossom branch. What is expressed at that very moment is simply 'a Plum Blossom bough in the snow'. Both Earth and Flower are Life that transcends life.

Further, the phrase 'the vast expanse of snow' means the vast expanse of snow totally, inside and out. The whole universe is one's Original Mind. Because Original Mind is what the flowers in the whole universe feel, the whole universe is the Plum Blossom. Because the universe is the Plum Blossom, the whole universe is synonymous with the eyes of Gautama. What they perceive at the moment of understanding is the Great Earth with Its mountains and rivers. Arriving at the Matter, arriving at the Moment, is synonymous with Bodhidharma's poem, which is an expression of what has been arrived at:

> *From the first, I came to this land to Transmit the Dharma*
> *That I might rescue deluded beings,*
> *And when the Single Blossom opened Its five petals,*
> *The fruit thereof naturally came about of itself.*

Even though there was his coming from the West and his barely arriving in the East, nevertheless the Plum Blossom was 'the Now' of what arrived.

Bodhidharma's manifesting 'the Now' like this is called 'the growing of thorn-like spurs'. Now at this very moment, there are old branches and new branches on large limbs, which has resulted in places where old twigs and new twigs are on

---

10. That is, what one sees before spiritually awakening is the product of the intellect's interpretation of the data from the sense organs.

small branchings. You need to explore the places wherein these have arrived, and explore 'arrival' as meaning 'the Now'. 'What is within three, four, five, six blossoms' means 'what is within countless blossoms'. The Flower is equipped with internal meritorious functions that are profound and far-reaching, and It clearly opens up external meritorious functions that are far-reaching and great. Both this 'internal' and 'external' manifest in the blooming of one blossom. Because it is just one bough, there is no other, different one, since it is not one species among others. The One who calls the arrival of the one bough 'the Now' is our Old Fellow Gautama.

Because there is only One Bough, It is what is Transmitted from heir to heir. Hence, it is expressed as "My Treasure House of the Eye of the True Teaching is what I Transmit to Makakashō," and it is expressed as "You have got what my Marrow is." In this manner, because each heir is a greatly honored and valued life where an arrival has manifested, it is a matter of the five petals opening, for five petals comprise a plum blossom. Thus, there are the Seven Ancestral Buddhas,* and there are the twenty-eight Indian Ancestors and the six Chinese Ancestors up through Enō, plus nineteen other Ancestors.[11] All are the five petals opening on just One Bough; it is just One Bough of five-petaled blossoms. Once you have explored the One Bough and the five petals, you will encounter face-to-face the genuine 'Transmission of the Plum Blossom in the snow' being Transmitted to you. Once you have turned yourself around and turned your mind around within the way that the words 'only One Bough' relate to each other, 'clouds' and 'moon' are what are equal, whereas 'valleys' and 'mountains' are different from each other.

However, folks who have never had an Eye for exploring the Matter are wont to say, "What the five petals means is that there is the one flower which is comprised of the First Chinese Ancestor Bodhidharma plus the subsequent five generations of

---

11. As traditionally counted, the six Chinese Ancestors would be Bodhidharma down through Enō. As to the nineteen subsequent Ancestors, which are not specifically identified as being Chinese, some scholars understand the nineteenth to refer to Nyojō, but by actual count he would be the seventeenth. Dōgen's Dharma heir, Kōun Ejō, would be the nineteenth, which may be why Dōgen does not identify the nineteen as being specifically Chinese.

Chinese-born Ancestors, and because the line-up of the five transcends past and present, before and after, we speak of them as the five petals." These words are not even worth taking up and refuting. These folks, sad to say, are not sentient beings who explore the Matter with Buddhas or train with Ancestors. How could the saying 'one flower comprised of five petals' possibly be limited to just these five generations? Are those who have come after the Sixth Ancestor not to be spoken of? What such folks have to say does not even come up to the prattle of little children. It is something they don't see or hear about even in their dreams.

My late Master, the Old Buddha, once said as his salutary poem that followed his formal Dharma talk on a New Year's Day:

> *On this first day of the year I wish you happiness.*
> *All the myriad things arising are fresh and new.*
> *Upon reflection, my great assembly, I submit to you,*
> *The Plum Tree has blossomed early this spring.*

When I quietly reflect upon this poem, I realize that even if you dear old veteran monks in all ten quarters within the three periods of time have let go of your bodies, if you have no equivalent of "The Plum Tree has blossomed early this spring," who would say that you have expressed the Matter fully? My late Master alone, the Old Buddha, was the Old Buddha among Old Buddhas.

The fundamental meaning of what he said was that once the Plum has blossomed, a myriad springtimes are quick to follow its lead. The myriad springtimes are but one or two of the meritorious functions of the Plum Tree. Just one springtime can make the myriad things that arise into something fresh and new, and make our myriad thoughts and things into a New Year's Day.

His wish for our happiness denotes the authenticity of his Eye. 'The myriad things that arise' are not only of the past, present, and future, they are what existed before the Lords of Awe-inspiring Voices and what will come after the future. Because he is saying that the past, present, and future, which are immeasurable and inexhaustible, are ever fresh, this freshness has dropped off 'freshness'. Thus, what he reflected on and submitted was his wish for his great assembly, because what he wished was that each of them might be 'such a person'.

My late Master Tendō, the Old Buddha, during a Dharma talk for his assembly, once said in verse:

> *If a single word accords with the Truth,*
> *It will not change, though myriad generations pass:*
> *Thus, eye-shaped willow buds sprout forth from new branches,*
> *Whereas plum blossoms fill up the older boughs.*[12]

That is to say, pursuing the Way for hundreds of eons is, from beginning to end, equivalent to a single word according with the Truth, and the effort of one moment's thought is, from before to after, the same as its not changing, though myriad generations pass. The willow brings about a luxuriant growth of new branches and contrives 'eyes' to burst out upon them; even though the branches are new, it is 'eyes' that they bring forth. The principle is that the 'eyes' are nothing other than 'eyes', <u>and</u> we thoroughly explore these branches as being new. The 'new' should be explored through your training as meaning "Everything is all new." To say that plum blossoms fill up the older boughs means that Plum Blossoms are entirely old boughs, that They permeate old boughs, that the old boughs <u>are</u> Plum Blossoms. For example, plum boughs explore the Matter just as willow branches do; plum boughs come into being just as willow branches do; plum boughs are filled up, just as willow branches are. Because plum boughs are filled up with bloomings, just as willow branches are, this is the same as saying, "I have the True Teaching which I Transmit to Makakashō." The countenance of the One filled the countenance of the other with His raising the Flower aloft: the flowering of the one filled the flowering of the Other by his breaking into a smile.

---

12.   In this section of the discourse, 'willows' refers to those who are new to training, for whom all is new and who are 'all eyes', whereas the plum tree refers to a Master whose years of training, like old boughs, have brought forth a profusion of blossoms.

My late Master, the Old Buddha, in formally addressing his assembly, once said in verse:

> *The riverside willows look as though adorned*
> *with a minister's waist sash:*
> *The plum blossoms look as though clad in an*
> *archer's gauntlet.* [13]

This gauntlet is not like some fine brocade from Szechwan Province or like Pien-ho's priceless jewel:[14] it is simply the opening of a Plum Blossom. The opening of a Plum Blossom is equivalent to 'you whom my Marrow has gotten'.[15]

Once, when King Prasenajit invited the Venerable Pindola to a midday meal, the king asked him afterwards, "I have been given to understand that you, O Venerable One, have actually met the Buddha. Is this true?"[16]

The Venerable One pointed to the Matter by using his hand to raise his eyebrow.

Concerning this, my Late Master, the Old Buddha, composed a poem:

---

13. On a literal level, this verse describes the way the dark branches of the budding willow and the bright blossoming plum tree look.

14. Pien-ho was a person in ancient China who offered to three rulers a huge, unpolished jewel that he had found, but none of these rulers were able to perceive its intrinsic value, and they therefore summarily rejected the offering.

15. "You whom my Marrow has gotten" is Dōgen's reversal of the words Bodhidharma spoke to Eka when confirming him as a Dharma heir: "You have gotten what my Marrow is."

16. As used in the translation of this section of the discourse, 'to meet the Buddha' means having had a social contact with the historical Shakyamuni, whereas 'to encounter Buddha' means having seen one's own Buddha Nature.

> *Raising his own eyebrow as response to the question,*
>   *he laughed,*
> *Showing without guile that he had 'encountered*
>   *Buddha' in a familiar way.*
> *For which he deserves gratitude from the four quarters*
>   *up to this very day.*
> *The Spring occurs within the twigs of the Plum, which,*
>   *wrapped in snow, are ever so cold.*

This story is about King Prasenajit once asking a Venerable One whether he had or had not actually met the Buddha. 'Encountering Buddha' means becoming a Buddha, and 'becoming a Buddha' means using one's hand to raise an eyebrow. If the Venerable One had merely realized some fruit of arhathood and were not a full-fledged arhat,* he could not have encountered Buddha. If he had not encountered Buddha, he could not have become Buddha. If he had not become Buddha, he would probably not have used his hand to raise an eyebrow, signaling that he had realized Buddhahood.

Accordingly, you need to keep in mind that, as a disciple who had received the Face-to-Face Transmission of Shakyamuni Buddha and as one who had already experienced the fourth fruit of arhathood and was awaiting his rebirth in the world as a present-day Buddha,[17] how could the Venerable One possibly not have encountered Shakyamuni Buddha? 'Having met Shakyamuni Buddha' does not mean 'encountering Buddha'. As you explore this through your training, understand that to encounter Shakyamuni Buddha as Shakyamuni Buddha is 'encountering Buddha'. In that King Prasenajit was able to open his eyes to exploring, he had come in contact with one who skillfully used his hand to raise an eyebrow. You simply need to have the Eye of a Buddha to explore the principle underlying 'having encountered Buddha in a familiar way'. This Spring, of which my Master spoke, is beyond humankind, beyond the domains of a Buddha; It is within the twigs of the Plum Tree. How do we know this is so? Because the chill of the snow is the raising of an eyebrow.

---

17.   The fourth fruit of arhathood refers to the results experienced from attaining the fourth stage of arhathood. Please see the Glossary for an explanation of these four stages.

My late Master, the Old Buddha, once said in verse,

> *Our Original Countenance is beyond birth and death.*
> *The Spring is within the blossom of the Plum and has*
> *entered a picture.*

To paint a picture of Spring, you need not paint willows, or plum trees, or peach trees, or damson trees; you should just portray Spring. To picture willow, plum, peach, or damson is to picture a willow tree, a plum tree, a peach tree, or a damson tree; it is not yet portraying Spring. It is not that Spring should not be portrayed, but apart from my late Master, an Old Buddha, there is no one within India in the west and China to the east who has portrayed Spring. Only my late Master, the Old Buddha, and he alone, had sharp-tipped a brush to portray the Spring. The Spring he spoke about now is the Spring within the picture, because he has put It into the picture. Because he had no need to call upon other abilities, he could simply make a plum blossom be Spring by putting it or its tree into the picture—such were his skillful means.

Due to the clarity of my late Master, the Old Buddha, concerning the Treasure House of the Eye of the True Teaching, he Transmitted It to Buddhas and Ancestors who had assembled from all ten quarters over the past, present, and future. Thus it was that he penetrated what the Eye is and clarified what a Plum Blossom is.

On the sixth day of the eleventh lunar month in the first year of the Kangen era in Japan
(December 18, 1243), at Kippō-ji Temple in the Yoshida district in Echizen province,
where snow, some three feet deep, has wrapped the whole earth in swirling white.

If perchance some demon of self naturally arises and the Plum Blossom seems not to be the Eye of Gautama, then ponder on the question, "What physical thing can <u>you</u> see as the Eye that is more apt than the Plum Blossom?" And if at such a time, you search for the Eye somewhere else, then every moment will be your being face-to-face with It and failing to recognize It, because mutual recognition will not have occurred to you as possible. Today is not 'my today', it is the today of our whole tradition. Straight off, you must clarify what the Eye of the Plum Blossom is and seek that, and that alone!

My late Master, the Old Buddha, once said in verse,

> *Everything is so bright and clear,*
> *No need to seek some phantom in the Flowering Plum,*
> *Spontaneously creating rain and raising clouds in past and*
> *   present.*
> *Past and present are rare enough, and what ending will they*
> *   have?*

Thus, the creating of rain and the raising of clouds are functions of the Plum Blossom. Floating clouds and falling rain are the Plum Blossom's thousands of twists and turns and myriad masses of forms, as well as Its thousands of merits and myriad virtues. What is naturally ever-present is the Plum Blossom. Thus, we speak of the Plum Blossom as being forever.

The time-honored Meditation Master Hōen once said in verse:

> *The snow-laden north wind sets the valley trees to swaying.*
> *Everything is buried deep within, with little complaint,*
> *While on the mountain peak, the bright-spirited plum stands*
> *alone.*
> *Even before the twelfth month's heavy snows spew forth, I*
> *have the feeling of the yearly 'greater cold'.*[18]

Thus, without having penetrated what the movements of the Plum Blossom are, it is hard to know what the feeling of the greater cold is. Harmonizing the meritorious functioning of little bits of the Plum Blossom with the north wind is what has created the snow. Be very clear about this. It is the strength of the Plum Blossom that calls forth the wind, creates the snow, brings order to the year, and brings the valley woodlands, along with all other things, into existence.

The senior monk Taigen Fu expressed his awakening by saying in verse,

> *I remember from the days before I had awakened*
> *Whenever I heard the wail of the painted horn, it*
> *was like a cry of grief.*[19]
> *Now, when upon my pillow, I have no idle dreams*
> *And just trust to whatever the Plum Blossom may*
> *blow my way, large or small.*

---

18. Traditionally in China, there is a period around early November that is called 'the time of light snow' and, a month later, one called 'the time of heavy snow'. Similarly, a short while after the winter solstice there is a period called 'the time of the lesser cold' and, a month later, one called 'the time of the greater cold'.

19. The painted horn is the name of an ancient Chinese musical instrument.

Senior monk Fu was originally an academic lecturer. Having been shaken up by the Chief Cook of Mount Kassan, he had a great awakening. This was his Plum Blossom letting the Spring Wind blow as It would, large or small.

58

On the Whole Universe in All Ten Directions
(Jippō)

Translator's Introduction: In this discourse, depending on context, the Japanese word *'jippō'* is translated in various ways, such as the ten directions, the ten quarters, the ten domains, and the ten worlds, all of which refer to the whole universe not only in a literal, worldly sense but also in a spiritual one.

A Master's making a Fist signifies this whole universe of ours in all its ten directions.[1] This one instance of his manifesting his sincere heart <u>is</u> the whole universe—all ten quarters—in all its splendor. It completely pounds out the marrow from our bones.

Shakyamuni Buddha once proclaimed to His great assembly, "Within the Buddha lands in all ten quarters there is only the Teaching of the One Vehicle and no other." What He calls the ten quarters have produced the Buddha lands and they form the ten quarters. Therefore, unless we choose to make use of the Buddha lands in our training, we will not yet have the ten quarters. Because they are Buddha lands, we have taken the Buddha as our Master. This ordinary worldly country of ours is no different from Shakyamuni Buddha's Land. You need to explore through your training that when someone expresses what this ordinary worldly realm is, it is the six- or eight-foot-tall Buddha lands in all ten quarters, in the same sense that we clearly describe something as weighing either eight ounces or half a pound.[2]

---

1. A Master's making a Fist refers to a Chinese Zen Master's raising of his fist to direct a disciple away from a narrow way of thinking in order to have him encompass the whole of the universe, spatially and temporally.

2. That is, we use different terms for the same thing. In short, what we call the ordinary worldly realm is another name for the Buddha lands, depending on our perspective.

These ten quarters are contained within one single quarter and are contained within one single Buddha, which is why they have manifested as ten quarters. Because they are the ten worlds which is one world, and because they are this very world which is both one's own world and the world of the present moment, they are the Eye of the world, the Fist of the world, the supporting pillar of the world, and the stone lantern[*] of the world. The Buddhas of the ten quarters within these Buddha lands of the ten worlds are not something comparatively larger or smaller, nor are They something pure or sullied. Because of this, all Buddhas on Their own, along with all the Buddhas of the ten quarters, deeply admire and praise each other. Further, They do not slander each other or talk about each other's merits or weaknesses or each other's likes and dislikes as if They were turning the Wheel of the Dharma to express It. As Buddhas and the disciples of Buddhas, They help give rise to spiritual goals by making respectful inquiries.

In receiving the Dharma of the Buddhas and Ancestors, we explore It through our training, just as They do. We do not insult Them, or judge Them as being right or wrong, or say insulting things about Them as do non-Buddhists and the demon hordes. When we open and read the Buddhist Scriptures that have been passed on to China, and look at Shakyamuni Buddha's Teaching over the span of His life, we see that He never spoke of Buddhas in other domains as being inferior or superior to Him, nor did He say that They were not Buddhas. In short, we cannot find in any of the Teaching that He gave in His lifetime a word of His that criticized any Buddha.

Thus it was that Shakyamuni Buddha once addressed His great assembly, saying, "I, on My own, have come to know how It appears, as every Buddha in the ten quarters has also done."[3] You need to know that the appearance referred to in His statement "I, on My own, have come to know how It appears" is the appearance of That which is fully perfected. The appearance of perfection is, as the saying goes, "This cane of bamboo is on the tall side whereas that cane of bamboo is on the short side." The Way of the Buddhas in the ten quarters is synonymous with giving full

---

*   See Glossary.

3.   In this discourse, the various forms of the word 'appearance' carry the meaning of 'the form that something takes'.

expression to the saying, "I, on My own, have come to know how It appears, which was the same for Shakyamuni Buddha." It is "I, on My own, have awakened to this appearance, and Buddhas in Their own domains are also like this." It is the way 'I' appears, the way 'knowing' appears, the way 'this' appears, the way 'all' appears, the way 'this ordinary worldly country of ours' appears, the way 'Shakyamuni Buddha' appears.

The underlying principle of this is what the Buddhist Scriptures give voice to. The Buddhas, along with Their Buddha lands, are beyond duality, beyond being sentient or nonsentient, beyond being deluded or enlightened, beyond being good, bad, or neutral, beyond being pure or sullied, beyond being something created and beyond being something permanently abiding, beyond yearning for things and beyond there being nothing to yearn for, beyond permanence and impermanence, beyond existence and non-existence, and beyond self. They are apart from the four phrases— there is existence, there is no existence, there is both existence and non-existence, and there is neither existence nor non-existence—as well as apart from the one hundred ways of negating. They are simply nothing other than the ten quarters, nothing other than the Buddha lands. Thus, the ten quarters are nothing other than what they are, just as we humans are: we have heads but no tails.

Meditation Master Chōsa Keishin, when addressing his assembly, once said, "The whole universe in all ten directions is nothing other than the discerning Eye of a mendicant monk." What is being spoken of now is the discerning Eye of Gautama. The discerning Eye of mendicant monk Gautama is synonymous with 'the Treasure House of the Eye of the True Teaching, which is what I have'. Even though It is Transmitted to whomever, It is still mendicant monk Gautama's discerning Eye. The whole universe, all sharp-edged and raggle-taggle in all its ten quarters, is Gautama's very organ of sight. This whole universe in all ten quarters is the One Eye among the mendicant monk's eyes, and up and beyond this, He has ever so many eyes.[4]

> "'The whole universe in all ten directions' is a term that a
> mendicant monk is accustomed to."[5]

'Accustomed to' means 'familiar with'. Among words in common use in Japan, it would be described as 'everyday'. So, 'the whole universe in all ten directions' is an everyday phrase in a mendicant monk's spiritual family. Its words are accurate and the phrase itself is accurate. Clearly, you need to explore through your training the underlying principle that everyday words are the whole universe in all ten directions, and therefore 'the whole universe in all ten directions' are everyday words. Because these ten directions are inexhaustible, they are the ten quarters in their entirety. We use these words in their ordinary, familiar sense. It is like seeking for a horse, seeking for salt, seeking for water, seeking for a drinking vessel, or like offering a drinking vessel, offering water, offering salt, offering a horse.[6] Who would know that an awakened one, one whose perspective is beyond duality, has transformed his body and transformed his mental functioning within the stream of his words, for he has transformed his speech within the stream of his words? The accuracy of his words and the straightforwardness of his speech, which gives a mouth to the oceans and a tongue to the mountains, has an everyday familiarity. Thus, even were we to cover his mouth and blanket our ears, what he expressed about the ten quarters would still be true.

---

4. An allusion to the thousand-armed Avalokiteshvara Bodhisattva, personification of the all-seeing, all-helping compassion of Buddha Nature.

5. This is the first of five statements that Dōgen quotes. He then supplies a commentary after each.

6. The significance of what is sought and what is offered is the topic of Discourse 79: On 'The King Requests Something from Sindh' (Ō Saku Sendaba). It concerns a certain king whose servants could anticipate their master's desires without his having to specifically say what he wanted at any given moment.

> "The whole universe in all ten quarters is the whole body of a mendicant monk."

With one hand pointing towards the heavens, the Buddha showed what the heavens are and, with the other hand pointing towards the earth, He showed what the earth is, for this is the way things are. Even so, He said, "In the heavens above and the earth below, I alone am the Honored One." This is the whole universe in all ten directions, which is the whole body of a mendicant monk. The crown of his head, his eyes, his nose, his skin and flesh, his bones and marrow, each and every one, is totally the embodiment of a mendicant monk, one who has clarified and let go of the whole ten quarters of the universe. Without our having to set all the ten quarters into motion, the whole of them are no different for us. Without depending on the fictions constructed by the intellective mind, we come to realize the body of a mendicant monk as the whole universe in all ten quarters and view the whole universe in all ten quarters as comprising the body of a mendicant monk.

> "The whole universe in all ten quarters is what our radiantly luminous True Self is."

What we call 'the True Self' is our Nose before 'father' and 'mother' were born.[7] When we mistake what our True Self is, we call whatever comes to hand 'the whole universe in all ten directions'. Despite that, the emerging of the True Self is the spiritual question manifesting before our very eyes. It is our opening the Buddha Hall and encountering Buddha. At the same time, it is someone else exchanging your eyes with black nuts from a soapberry tree.[8] Be that as it may, you will precipitously

---

7.   "Our Nose before 'father' and 'mother' were born" is a Zen expression for one's innate Buddha Nature prior to the first arising of the discriminating mind which separates things into opposites such as 'father' and 'mother'.

8.   That is, one's voracious eyes are replaced by eyes that have a cleansing effect on self and others.

encounter the Great Master. Further, it is easy to call to That One, but it is difficult to do what is asked. Even so, when we hear the call, we turn our head. Of what use is it to go through the motions of arbitrarily turning our head? It is That One who makes our head turn. But when there is rice that is going uneaten and a robe that is going unworn, even though you are like someone groping about who has not yet made contact with That One, I shall, for pity's sake, deal you thirty blows.[9]

"The whole universe in all ten quarters resides within the
radiant luminosity of our True Self."

The eyelid of the Eye is taken for the radiant luminosity of the True Self. Its sudden opening is taken for something that resides within. What is seen as residing in the Eye is what people call 'the whole universe in all ten quarters'. However, though there are people who speak in this manner, only those who lie down in the same bed actually see where the bedding is shot through with holes.[10]

"In the whole universe in all ten quarters, there is not one
single person who is not the True Self."

Accordingly, among each and every trainer of novices and each and every Fist, there is not one who is not a True Self, just as the ten quarters are. Because they are their True Self, each and every one of these True Selves is the ten quarters. The ten quarters of each and every one of these True Selves delimits what the ten quarters are on a deep and intimate level. Because the lifeline of each and every True Self is in the hands of the True Self, each repays the original cost of his or her straw sandals.[11] Now, why is

---

9.   Uneaten rice refers to someone passing up the opportunity to ingest the Dharma; an unworn robe refers to someone who passes up the opportunity to adhere to the Precepts.

10. That is, only those who have awakened share the same insight as to the nature of things.

11. That is, a monastic earns his or her keep by ceaselessly doing the training wholeheartedly.

it that the Eye of Bodhidharma and the Nose of Gautama are newly born from within the Womb of some pillar* of the temple? It is because, as they say, they freely come into, and go out of, the ten quarters in all ten directions.

      Gensha Shibi once said, "The whole universe throughout all its ten directions is the One Bright Pearl." You need to clearly recognize the converse, which is that the One Bright Pearl is the whole universe throughout all its ten directions. Those with heads of gods as well as those with faces of demons take It to be their cavernous dwelling place, whereas the Dharma heirs of the Buddhas and Ancestors take It to be Their Eye. Ordinary folk take It to be the crown of their head or their own fists. Those with a beginner's heart and those who are present-day trainees take It to be their donning the kesa* and their eating rice.[12] My late Master made It into mudballs which he would use to pelt both those junior to him and those senior to him.[13] Further, even though this was just like placing a stone on a *Go* board, he would customarily be scraping out the eyes of those in our Ancestral tradition.[14] When he was scraping them out, not only would our Ancestors lend him a hand at it, but a radiance would stream out from within their Eye.

      The venerable monk Kempō was once asked by a monk, "A certain Scripture says, 'The World-honored Ones in the ten quarters are on one and the same road that leads to the gateway to nirvana,' but, I wonder, where does that road begin?"

---

12.   'Donning the kesa' refers to living by the Precepts, whereas 'eating rice' refers to ingesting the Dharma.

13.   The principle is that if the Master pelts trainees with sufficient Teaching, sooner or later some of it will 'stick', like mudballs.

14.   That is, he would help remove their worldly way of looking at things so that the Truth could shine through their Eye.

Kempō took his traveling staff and drew a circle, saying,
"It is in here."

His words, "It is in here," refer to the ten quarters. What he calls a 'World-honored One' is a veritable traveling staff.* 'Traveling staffs' are what is 'in here'. 'The one road' refers to the ten quarters. However, do not try to hide your staff in Gautama's nose. Do not try to stick your traveling staff into the nostrils of one who is a traveling staff. Even if you are acting in that way, do not conclude that the Old Fellow Kempō had already finished stewing on "The World-honored Ones in the ten quarters are on one and the same road that leads to the gateway to nirvana." He only speaks of it as 'being right here', but that doesn't mean that his 'being right here' is in some way deficient. If Old Fellow Kempō, right from the start, was not being deceived by his traveling staff, then well and good for him.

In sum, just explore through your training that living noses are the ten quarters.

Delivered to the assembly on the thirteenth day of the eleventh lunar month in the first year of the Kangen era (December 25, 1243) in Echizen Province at Kippō-ji Monastery.

Copied on the twenty-fourth day of the year's end in the third year of the Kangen era (January 14, 1246), whilst in the quarters of the Abbot's assistant at Daibutsu-ji Temple in Echizen Province.

Ejō

59

On Encountering Buddha

(Kembutsu)

Translator's Introduction: The Japanese word that Dōgen chose for the title appears with great frequency throughout this discourse and has numerous possibilities for translation, including to see Buddha, to meet Buddha, to encounter Buddha, a Buddha, the Buddha, Buddha Nature, one's own Buddha Nature, and someone else's Buddha Nature, among others. English, on the other hand, requires the choice of just one of these at any point in the text. While there are places where context aids in choosing the most likely nuance, there are other places where a translator picks somewhat more randomly from the list of possibilities.

The discourse itself offers some passages that are rather difficult to render into easily comprehendible English, the opening section being a case in point. Readers may find it helpful to keep in mind the following point which lies at the heart of what Dōgen is talking about: there is That which transcends all that we perceive to be appearing or arising, and that That is in no way excluded from what we perceive, as It encompasses both what appears (has form) and what does not appear (is beyond form). Hence, there is the way that things appear, which is what we perceive the world to be, and then there is That which transcends the forms that comprise our world. That which transcends these forms is, at the same time, not separate from them. Thus, appearance is part and parcel with what is Real. In more concrete terms, the That is synonymous with Buddha Nature.

Shakyamuni Buddha, in addressing His great assembly, once said, "When you see all material forms, which are provisional, as being part of That which goes beyond such appearances, you will then be seeing the Tathagata." [1] To see the forms of things <u>and</u> to see That which goes beyond such appearances is a realization experienced bodily, one which will free you from delusion. As a consequence, you

---

1.   'All material forms, which are provisional' refers to all thoughts and things, which arise, persist for a while, disintegrate, and disappear. 'That which goes beyond such appearances' refers to the Buddha Nature which embraces not only all forms in past, present, and future, but also what is not form (the Void). Also, in this discourse, all the quotes Dōgen attributes to Shakyamuni Buddha come from the Lotus Scripture.

will meet the Tathagata.[2] We treat as 'seeing Buddha' the manifestation which the Eye that sees Buddha has already brought forth. The ultimate way by which the Eye sees Buddha refers to the Eye by which we encounter Buddha. When we see Buddha Nature in other places and when we see our own Buddha Nature as being apart from Buddhas, then, even though everything seems to be all tangled up like overgrown vines, we first explore through our training what 'meeting Buddha' means. Then we work on dropping off 'meeting Buddha' until we realize the vital, living state of 'meeting Buddha'. Finally, we make use of our 'having met Buddha'. All of these functions comprise our encountering the Sun-faced Buddha and the Moon-faced Buddha.[3]

To see such Buddhas is to see an endless stream of countenances, bodies and minds, as well as hands and eyes. From the time of our giving rise to our intention to realize Buddhahood and our stepping forth, right up to our doing our daily practice now, all is the Living Eye and the Living Bones and Marrow rushing in to see Buddha. It is our doing our utmost in training to realize the Way until there is no gap between our own enlightenment and that of our Master. As a consequence, the whole realm of self and the whole domain of other—that is, this individual and that individual—are all doing their utmost to see Buddha. Those folks who lack an Eye for exploring the Matter[*] through training take up the Tathagata's phrases, 'all material forms' and 'That which goes beyond such appearances' and, fancying that the way things appear are not true appearances, imagine that they have encountered the Tathagata. Truly, some of those who are small-minded will take up studying His words like that, but the full realization of the Buddha's intent is not like this. You need to realize that to see the way things appear while concurrently going beyond the matter of how they appear is

---

2.   That is, it is a spiritual realization, not an intellectual one.

3.   The lifespan of the Sun-faced Buddha is 1,800 years, whereas the lifespan of the Moon-faced Buddha is twenty-four hours. This derives from a kōan story concerning Baso, who, when he was ill, was asked how he felt. He used the reference to the two Buddhas to express how he was experiencing time, which went beyond conventional, calendar measurements, in that his days seemed to drag on while his months seemed to fly by.

*   See Glossary.

to forthwith meet the Tathagata. There is the Tathagata within existence and there is the Tathagata that is beyond existence.

  The Great Meditation Master Hōgen of Seiryō-in Monastery once said, "If we see the way things appear as being devoid of form, then we will not see the Tathagata." Now, this saying by Great Master Hōgen expresses his encounter with Buddha. It contains what Hōgen personally said and what his encounter with Buddha imparted. To put the matter in the colloquial, it is like Hōgen and Shakyamuni Buddha coming head-on in competition and extending Their hands to each other in cooperation.[4] You need to listen with your ears to what Hōgen said, and, as to what his encountering Buddha imparted, you need to hear what he is voicing with your Eye. At the same time, those in the past who have explored this underlying principle through their training have said:

  All the ways in which things appear are appearances of the
  Tathagata. There is no single way in which the Tathagata appears,
  nor are the appearances of things and the appearance of the
  Tathagata ever to be confused with each other. And you should not,
  even provisionally, take these appearances not to be His appearance.
  Were you to treat them as not being His appearance, you would be
  as one deserting his father and running away from home.[5]

In other words, what these trainees are habitually saying is, "Because the appearances of things are the appearing of the Tathagata, the way things appear will be just the way things appear." Truly, this is a profound discourse on the Greater Vehicle;* it is what is awakened to in all ten quarters.

---

4. That is, the two of them are saying the same thing but in different ways.

5. An allusion to a parable in the Lotus Scripture, found in the fourth chapter entitled "Belief and Understanding", which describes how we spend so much of our lives running away from the Tathagata.

You should definitely settle the Matter by taking it on faith and then making it your training. And do not be like threads of gossamer blown hither and thither by every breeze.

"The way things appear is the way the Tathagata appears: He is not separate from form." You should thoroughly explore this statement until you encounter Buddha. Then, having settled the Matter and awakened to faith, you should accept the Teaching given in this statement and, reciting it, thoroughly penetrate its meaning. In this manner you should not let there be any time when your own eyes and ears are not observing and hearkening to it, or when you are not dropping off your own body and mind, bones and marrow, or when you are not letting go of your own self-created world with its mountains and rivers, for this is the daily behavior of Buddhas and Ancestors for exploring the Way through Their training. Do not think that because it is your own way of putting things, it could not possibly bring clarity to your own eyes. Turned around by one word of your own, you may see yourself dropping off your own concept of what Buddhas and Ancestors are, for such is the everyday Way of the Buddhas and Ancestors.

Hence, there is only one way to explore the Matter: 'the way that all things appear' has already gone beyond their not having appeared, and 'That which transcends what appears' is synonymous with the appearance of all things. Because That which transcends appearances is not separate from appearances, That which transcends appearances truly goes beyond what has appeared. You need to explore through your training that the appearance that is referred to as 'That which transcends appearances' and the appearance that is referred to as 'the way all things appear' are both the way that the Tathagata appears. Within what we are exploring there are the two Scriptural interpretations: that of going to visit Buddha and seeing Him, and that of going to visit Buddha and not seeing Him. These are what we explore with our vital Eye. If your Eye has not yet manifested in order to look at these Scriptural interpretations, yours will not be the Eye of thorough enlightenment. If It is not the Eye of thorough enlightenment, you have not encountered Buddha. In encountering Buddha, there is what is seen as form and what is seen as being beyond form: it is "I do not understand the Buddha Dharma."[6] In not encountering Buddha, there is what is not seen as form and what is not seen as being beyond form: it is what people who intellectually understand the Buddha Dharma have attained. This is what Hōgen's previously quoted statement is getting at, which demonstrates his realization of eighty or ninety percent of the Matter.[7] At the same time, in regard to the One Great Matter, we may say, "When you see all forms as the True Form, then you will straight off encounter the Tathagata." Such statements as this are entirely due to the influence of Shakyamuni Buddha: it is not the Skin and Flesh, Bones and Marrow of any other person.

> At that time when Shakyamuni Buddha was residing on Vulture Peak, He once addressed His great assembly through Bhaisajya Rājā, the Bodhisattva* Lord of Healing, speaking in verse:

> > *If we are on intimate terms with a Dharma Master,*
> > *We will surely arrive at the Bodhisattva Path.*
> > *If we learn by faithfully following this Master,*
> > *We will surely catch sight of Buddhas as numberless as*
> > *the Ganges' grains of sand.*

'Being on intimate terms with a Dharma Master' resembles the Second Chinese Ancestor Eka's attending on Bodhidharma for eight years, after which he got his Master's Marrow with his whole arm, and it is like Nangaku's training in the Way for fifteen years. Getting the Marrow of one's Teacher is what we mean by 'being on intimate terms'. 'The Bodhisattva Path' is synonymous with "I am also like this, and

---

6. The quotation is by Daikan Enō and refers to his not being content with having just an intellectual understanding of Buddha Dharma.

7. In Zen stories, realizing the Truth short of a hundred percent is not a negative judgment but actually high praise, as it expresses that someone has a more profound understanding than just what has been voiced.

you are also like this."[8] It is straightaway attaining the innumerable daily tangles that go along with Buddhist practice.

'Straightaway attaining' does not mean acquiring all that has been manifested from ancient times up to now, nor does it mean giving rise to some experience that has never arisen before, nor does it mean consciously grasping what is unbounded in the present; 'straightaway attaining' means dropping off the notion of acquiring intimacy. Thus, all attaining is straightaway attaining. 'What we learn by faithfully following our Master' means following in ancient footsteps as his attendant, something that we need to thoroughly explore. At the very moment when we do our daily Buddhist practice, we can realize what a Master can see. At that moment, it is our seeing Buddhas as innumerable as the sands of the Ganges River. "Buddhas as numberless as the Ganges' grains of sand" are just the moments when we are freely functioning, like fish darting about through water.[9] Do not keep chasing after seeing Buddhas as numberless as the Ganges' grains of sand by fawning on your Master. What you should do first off is strive to follow the teachings of your Master, for by following them you will attain the perspective of a Buddha.

Shakyamuni Buddha, in addressing all who were experiencing a genuine state of awakening, said in verse:

> Having profoundly entered into a state of
> meditative concentration,
> We see Buddhas in all directions.

The whole universe is profound because it is the Buddha Lands of the Ten Quarters. It is not broad, nor large, nor small, nor narrow. When we act, we act by following it. We call this meditative state 'complete absorption'. This is not seven feet or eight feet,

---

8. This quotation is part of a dialogue between Nangaku and his Master Enō, in which the latter speaks of being freed from stain, a condition that he equates with being one with the Buddhas and Ancestors.

9. That is, when we act like a Buddha, at that moment we are a Buddha, and we see all as Buddhas.

nor is it ten feet. It is encapsulated in the one phrase 'entered into', that is, it is complete absorption, without anything being left outside. This 'profoundly entered into' refers to meditative concentration, whereas 'having profoundly entered into meditative concentration' means 'to see Buddhas in all directions'. Because we have reached this state by profoundly entering That Place where no one can reach us, we see Buddhas in all directions. No matter what someone may try to distract us with, we would not chase after it and, as a result, Buddhas will manifest everywhere throughout the ten quarters. The state of 'entering profoundly' cannot manifest itself for a very long time. 'Seeing Buddhas in all directions' is simply Jōshū's seeing his Master Nansen as a reclining Tathagata.[10] And 'meditative concentration' is beyond something to be 'gotten into' or 'gotten out of'. In our leaping beyond any doubt or fear of the True Dragon, at that very moment when we see Buddha we will not radiate uncertainty. Because we encounter myriad Buddhas by our having encountered Buddha, we profoundly enter myriad states of meditative concentration by our having entered a state of meditative concentration. The underlying principle of such things as 'meditative concentration', 'seeing Buddha', and 'entering profoundly' was not something made up by people in the past who were leisurely in their efforts and then foisted it off to present-day folks. Nor is it some new, present-day item, for such an underlying principle is invariable. All instances of Transmitting the Way and accepting the Precepts have been like this. Exploring the Matter and obtaining Its fruits are also like this.

Shakyamuni Buddha once addressed Samantabhadra,* the Bodhisattva of Universal Goodness, saying:

> If there are any who accept and keep to these words of Mine on the flowering of the Dharma, who read or recite them, accurately remember them, put them into practice, or make copies of them, know that such persons have encountered Shakyamuni

---

10.   Dōgen recounts the story of Nansen's first meeting with Jōshū, from which this image is derived, in Discourse 34: On the Cypress Tree (Hakujushi).

Buddha just as truly as if they had heard what was said directly from
the Buddha's mouth.[11]

In general, all Buddhas say that to encounter Shakyamuni Buddha and to become
Shakyamuni Buddha is to realize enlightenment and to realize Buddhahood. This
realization by Buddhas has, from the first, been made possible by Their doing these
seven acts: accepting, keeping to, reading, reciting, remembering, putting into
practice, and making copies of what the Buddha said. Anyone who performs these
seven acts is 'one of those persons' whom we should by all means undertake to know:
they are 'such a one',* just as he or she truly is. Because this is how we encounter
Shakyamuni Buddha, hearing His words being recited is just like hearing the Buddha
speak directly to us. Shakyamuni Buddha has been Shakyamuni Buddha ever since
He encountered Shakyamuni Buddha. Thus, His eloquent tongue has enfolded the
three-thousandfold world far and wide. What mountain or ocean would not be a
Scripture of the Buddha? This is why 'such a person' who copies down His words
encounters Shakyamuni Buddha face-to-face. The Buddha's mouth has always been
open throughout myriad ancient times, so on what occasion has there not been His
voicing of Scriptures? Thus, only those who accept and keep to what He has expressed
may encounter Shakyamuni Buddha. The meritorious functioning of the sense organs
of such persons will be no different from this. And what is before and what after, what
is to the right and what to the left, what is given and what taken, as well as whatever
constitutes one's daily attitude of mind, will also be no different. How can we fail to
rejoice in having been born in a time when we have met this Scriptural Teaching of
His, which permits us to encounter Shakyamuni Buddha? It is our having been born
to meet Shakyamuni Buddha. Those who are diligent in body and mind, and have
accepted and kept to these words of His on the flowering of the Dharma, have read or
recited them, have accurately remembered them, have put them into practice, or have
made copies of them, all such persons will consequently encounter Shakyamuni
Buddha. Hearing these Scriptural words of His being recited is just like hearing the
Buddha speak directly to us, so who would not be eager to hear them? Those who feel

11. 'These words of Mine on the flowering of the Dharma' is a reference to the Lotus
     Scripture.

no compunction to be the best that they can be are human beings who are truly poverty stricken and lacking in good fortune and astuteness. Those who do their exploring and training are among 'those persons' whom we should by all means undertake to know, for, by doing so, we will consequently come to see Shakyamuni Buddha.

Shakyamuni Buddha, when addressing His assembly, once said:

> If you good men and women, upon hearing Me say that My life is immeasurably long, trust in what I say and awaken to it with a heart that is profoundly seeking, then you will see the Buddha as constantly existing on Vulture Peak, surrounded by His Bodhisattvas and shravakas, giving voice to the Dharma.[12] And you will see this everyday world as bedecked with lapis lazuli, ever calm, just, and proper.

This 'mind that is profoundly seeking' is our everyday world. Who, pray, would not trust in and thereby awaken to the Buddha's words that are so true and real? Your encountering these Scriptural words of His is an opportunity for you to trust in Them so as to awaken. Trusting and awakening with a heart that is profoundly seeking is what the flowering of the Dharma is. And so that we might trust in, and awaken to, His immeasurable life with a heart that is profoundly seeking That which is the Truth, He vowed to be reborn in this everyday land of ours. By means of His spiritual powers, the strength of His compassion, and His capacity for immeasurable life, the Tathagata has helped us to trust and awaken by inclining us towards our mind, by inclining us towards our body, by inclining us towards the whole universe, by inclining us towards the Buddhas and Ancestors, by inclining us towards all thoughts and things, by inclining us towards the True Form of all things, by inclining us towards skin and flesh, bones and marrow, and by inclining us towards birth and death, coming and going. These instances of trusting and awakening are 'seeing Buddha'. Thus, we know

---

12. Shravakas, here and later in the text, refer to those who, along with Bodhisattvas, stayed to listen to the Buddha's Teaching while others, being too proud, left in the middle of the Buddha's expressing the Dharma.

that we can encounter a Buddha with the eyes of the mind and that we can see Buddha with the Eye of trusting and awakening.

Surely, the fact that He speaks not only of our seeing Buddha but also of our seeing His continual existence on the Divine Vulture Peak means that the continual existence of the Peak occurs simultaneously with the Tathagata's life. So, seeing Buddha continually existing on the Divine Vulture Peak describes the continual existence in the past, present and future of both the Tathagata and the Divine Vulture Peak. Bodhisattvas and shravakas alike will have continual existence, and giving voice to the Dharma will also have continual existence. We will see the everyday world as bedecked with lapis lazuli, ever calm, just, and proper. Do not be troubled when seeing this everyday world, for what is high is on a level with whatever is high, and what is low is on a level with whatever is low. This land is a land of lapis lazuli. Do not disparage those eyes that see it as ever calm, just, and proper, for indeed the land of lapis lazuli is ever just so. If you treat this land as not being that of lapis lazuli, the Divine Vulture Peak will not be the Divine Vulture Peak, and Shakyamuni Buddha will not be Shakyamuni Buddha. To trust and realize that this land is lapis lazuli is the appearance of profound trust and awakening, for this is seeing Buddha.

Shakyamuni Buddha, in addressing His great assembly, once said in verse:

> *When those who wholeheartedly yearn to see the Buddha,*
> *Do not begrudge even their own lives,*
> *Then I, with all the Sangha,*
> *Will appear together on the Divine Vulture Peak.*

The wholeheartedness spoken of here is not the wholeheartedness, say, of ordinary folk or of those who follow lesser courses: it is the wholeheartedness derived from yearning to encounter Buddha. 'The wholeheartedness derived from yearning to encounter Buddha' refers to the Divine Vulture Peak, along with all the Sangha. When each individual, in private, arouses the desire to see Buddha, that person desires to see Buddha through devotion to the Heart of the Divine Vulture Peak. Thus, wholeheartedness is already the Divine Vulture Peak, so how could one's whole being not appear together with that Heart? How could it not be body and mind together as one? Our body and mind are already like this, just as are the years of our life and our life itself. Thus, we entrust our own regrets, which are merely our regrets, to the unsurpassed Way of the Divine Vulture Peak. Therefore, Shakyamuni Buddha said that His appearing on the Divine Vulture Peak, along with all His Sangha, is brought about by our wholehearted desire to see Buddha.

Shakyamuni Buddha, in addressing His great assembly, once said in verse:

> *If you give voice to this Teaching,*
> *This, then, is to see Me,*
> *As well as the Tathagata Whose Treasures Are Abundant,*
> *Along with all My many transformations.*[13]

What this Scripture is voicing is, "I continue to abide in this world, using My spiritual powers to make confused beings not see Me, though I am near." The Tathagata's marvelous spiritual powers, both visible and invisible, have bestowed upon Him the meritorious functioning expressed by "This then is to see Me," and so forth.

Shakyamuni Buddha, in addressing His great assembly, also said in verse:

> *Those who can keep to this Scripture*
> *Are persons who already behold Me*
> *Along with the Buddha Whose Treasures Are Abundant,*
> *As well as all My various bodily transformations.*

---

13. The Tathagata Whose Treasures Are Abundant is said to have appeared and praised Shakyamuni Buddha after the latter had given voice to the first ten chapters of the Lotus Scripture. The transformations spoken of refer to the many ways in which the Cosmic Buddha, Vairochana, manifests through Shakyamuni Buddha.

Because it is difficult to keep to this Scripture, the Tathagata urged us to do so as a matter of daily practice.

If there are people who, on their own, keep to this Scripture, they <u>will</u> encounter Buddha. You need to realize that the one who meets Buddha is the one who is keeping to the Scripture, and that the one who is keeping to the Scripture is the one who is seeing Buddha. Thus, someone who, upon hearing but a single verse or a single line, accepts and keeps to it is someone who will be able to see Shakyamuni Buddha, as well as meet the Buddha Whose Treasures Are Abundant and see all His various bodily transformations. And such a one will receive the Transmission of the Treasure House of the Buddha's Teaching, and acquire the True Eye of Buddha, and will see what the life of a Buddha is, attain the Eye to go beyond 'Buddha', get the fleshy topknot of a Buddha, and understand what a Buddha's Nose means.

The Buddha Whose Wisdom Has Flowered, Who is Lord of the Constellations, and Whose Voice Thunders Forth from the Clouds, in addressing the Lord of Wondrous Adornment, once said, "O Great Lord, you need to keep in mind that a good spiritual friend is a great persuader, one who guides us to change so that we may see the Buddha and give rise to the heart of supreme, fully perfected enlightenment."

At this time, the great assembly had not yet folded up their sitting mats. Even though we may speak of the Buddhas of past, present, or future, you should not liken these to the three temporal worlds of ordinary people. What <u>we</u> call 'the past' is what is in our minds, what <u>we</u> call 'the present' is our fist, and what <u>we</u> call 'the future' is what is in the back of our minds. So, the Buddha Whose Wisdom Has Flowered, Who is Lord of the Constellations and Whose Voice Thunders Forth from the Clouds, is seeing Buddha, which arises in the mind. The stock phrase 'to see Buddha right now' is just like this.[14] 'Guiding all beings to change' is seeing Buddha, and seeing Buddha is

---

14. That is, it is something that arises in the mind.

giving rise to the mind of supreme, fully perfected enlightenment. Giving rise to the mind of enlightenment is seeing Buddha from start to finish.

Shakyamuni Buddha also said in verse:

> *Those who practice deeds of merit*
> *And are gentle, honest, and forthright,*
> *All see Me in body*
> *And hear Me voice the Dharma.*

What He calls 'deeds of merit' is being dragged through the mud and being stuck in the water, following waves and chasing after billows.[15] He describes those who put this into practice as being gentle, honest, and forthright, as in "I am also like this, and you are also like this." Being so, they see Buddha within the mud and they encounter Buddha within the midst of waves, and they thereby participate in His existing here, voicing the Dharma.

At the same time, in present-day Great Sung China, the crowd that goes around calling themselves teachers of Zen is large indeed. They do not comprehend the length and breadth of the Buddha's Dharma, for what they have seen and heard is slight indeed. After learning by rote barely two or three sentences of Rinzai's or Ummon's, they fancy that they have obtained the whole truth of the Buddha Dharma. If the truth of the Buddha Dharma was totally exhausted in two or three sentences of Rinzai's or Ummon's, the Buddha Dharma would not have reached us today. It is hard enough to hear of Rinzai and Ummon being described as venerable from the point of view of the Buddha Dharma. How much less venerable are that bunch today who fall far short of Rinzai and Ummon! They are rabble not worth mentioning. Being too dull-witted, they can hardly clarify for themselves what the heart of the Buddha's Teaching is, so they go about arbitrarily slandering the Buddhist Scriptures, ignoring altogether the part about putting Them into practice and studying Them. Such people should be called non-Buddhist fishy folk. They are not the offspring of the Buddhas

---

15.   That is, undergoing whatever is necessary to help all sentient beings realize the Truth.

and Ancestors, much less have they reached the realm of having seen a Buddha! They are a bunch who have not even grasped the principles of Confucius and Lao-tzu. As you are offspring in the house of the Buddhas and Ancestors, do not associate with that pack who go around proclaiming themselves to be teachers of Zen. Simply train yourselves thoroughly until you experience the Eye that sees Buddha.

My late Master, the Old Buddha of Tendō, once quoted the following:

King Prasenajit once asked the Venerable Arhat* Pindola, "I have heard it said that you, O Venerable One, have personally met the Buddha. Is that so?"

As a sign of affirmation, the Venerable One used his hand to raise his eyebrow.

My late Master once wrote a eulogy to Pindola:

*Raising his own eyebrow in response to the question, he
    laughed,
Showing without guile that he had encountered Buddha in
    a familiar way.
For which he deserves gratitude from the four quarters up
    to this very day.
The Spring occurs within the twigs of the Plum, which,
    wrapped in snow, are ever so cold.*

'Encountering Buddha' does not mean that he saw his own Buddha Nature or the Buddha Nature of others; it means that he actually met the Buddha. Because 'one plum branch' is meeting 'one plum branch', it is the Flower's bursting open, bright and clear. The underlying principle that King Prasenajit is asking about now is whether Pindola had already met Buddha and whether he had become a Buddha himself. The Venerable One clearly raised an eyebrow in verification that he had seen Buddha, about which no one can be deceived. To this day, this underlying principle has not been abandoned. It is evident that Pindola deserves our gratitude due to his meeting Buddha as a direct experience, even though the experience left no visible trace. He is one of the three billion who had actually encountered Buddha.[16] The present reference is to that meeting with the Buddha, one that went beyond Pindola's merely seeing the Buddha's thirty-two marks. Who is so set apart from the realm of the thirty-two marks so as not to see them? There may well be great numbers of all sorts of ordinary humans, celestial beings, shravakas, and pratyekabuddhas* who do not know the principle of meeting Buddha. For instance, it is like saying that there are many who may be holding up a hossu, but there are not many who truly know what 'holding up the hossu' means.[17] 'To see Buddha' means 'to have the Buddha see us'. Even if one wished to conceal from oneself the signs of having met Buddha, they would already show, for this is the underlying principle of seeing Buddha. We need to thoroughly explore in detail the aspect of raising an eyebrow, making efforts as numerous as the sands of the Ganges with our body and mind. Even if we had dwelt together with Shakyamuni Buddha constantly, day and night, for hundreds of thousands of myriad eons, if we did not have the ability to raise an eyebrow, we would not see Buddha. Even though we are in a distant place some hundred thousand miles away from India, if we personally exhibit our ability to raise an eyebrow, it will be due to our having seen Shakyamuni Buddha from the time before the Lord of Emptiness,* for it is our seeing a branch of plum blossoms and seeing the Spring within the plum twigs. As a consequence, when we encounter Buddha face-to-face, we make three prostrations, or bow with hands in gasshō,* or let our face break into a smile, or make our Fist thunder forth, or sit cross-legged on our mat, doing meditation.

---

16. According to Nāgārjuna's commentary to the Mahāprajñāpāramitā, "The world is comprised of nine billion people, three billion of whom have encountered Buddha, three billion of whom have heard of the Buddha's coming into the world but have not actually met Him, and three billion who have neither encountered nor heard of Him."

17. The hossu is a ceremonial implement resembling an Indian fly-whisk. A monk who holds up a hossu is presumably one who is a genuine Master, but Dōgen is saying that many may hold it up, but that does not mean they know what they are doing.

The Venerable Pindola once went to a great gathering at the palace of King Ashoka for a meal. After the king had made an incense offering and had done his prostrations, he asked the Venerable One, saying, "I have heard it said that you, O Venerable One, have personally met the Buddha. Is that true?"

      The Venerable One brushed up his eyebrow with his hand and said, "Do you get it?"

      The king replied, "I don't understand." [18]

      The Venerable One said, "When the Dragon King of Anavatapta invited the Buddha to a meal, a poor humble monk like me was also among the number that participated."

The main point of King Ashoka's question, "I have heard it said that you, O Venerable One, have personally met the Buddha. Is that true?" was to find out whether the Venerable One was already a Venerable One. At that point and without hesitation, the Venerable One brushed up his eyebrow. This caused 'seeing Buddha' to appear in the world and caused 'becoming Buddha' to be personally seen. What he replied was, "When the Dragon King of Anavatapta invited the Buddha to a meal, a poor humble monk like me was also among the number that participated." Keep in mind that in a gathering of Buddhas, the Buddhas may well be as plentiful as rice, hemp, bamboo, and reeds, but no arhats or pratyekabuddhas may participate. Even were arhats and pratyekabuddhas to come, they would not be counted as being among the Buddhas. The Venerable One had already stated, "When the Dragon King of Anavatapta invited the Buddha to a meal, a poor humble monk like me was also among the number that participated." This is a statement about himself that arose naturally, for the principle of meeting Buddha is quite clear. 'Inviting the Buddha' refers not only to Shakyamuni Buddha but also to inviting all the Buddhas within the immeasurable and

---

18.   "Do you get it?" has a double meaning. The king took the question literally, whereas Pindola was asking a spiritual question: "Do you get It?" meaning "Do you not see my enlightened Buddha Nature?"

inexhaustible three temporal worlds, as well as all Buddhas in the ten quarters. To be included among all the invited Buddhas was his meeting Buddha as a direct experience, one that was unconcealed and beyond concealment. Pointing to 'seeing Buddha', 'seeing Master', 'seeing self', and 'seeing you' should be no different. What he called "the Dragon King of Anavatapta" is the Dragon King of Lake Anavatapta. In our country, Lake Anavatapta is called "The Lake Free of Suffering from Heat".[19]

Meditation Master Honei Jin'yū once praised Pindola in verse:

> *When our Buddha met Pindola face-to-face,*
> *The latter had eyebrows long, hair short, eyes fierce.*
> *But King Ashoka still had his doubts.*
> *Well, om mani śrī sūrya!* [20]

This eulogy is not a hundred percent right on, but I offer it because it is worth exploring as a possible point of view.

Jōshū was once asked by a monk, "I have heard it said that you, O Venerable Monk, personally had a face-to-face encounter with Nansen. Is that true?"

The Master replied, "In our Chinshū district, we grow really big daikon radishes."

What Jōshū is now showing through his response is his experience of intimately meeting Nansen. It is not that he has words for it or that he does not have words for

---

19. Lake Anavatapta is traditionally said to be in Tibet, and is considered to be the source of the four major rivers of India. The particular Dragon King referred to is one of four who resided in the lake and were converted to Buddhism. As a result he became free from the sufferings that dragon kings are otherwise heir to.

20. 'Om mani śrī sūrya' (Hail to him who is a veritable pearl that shines like the sun!) is a mantra praising and confirming the Buddhahood of Pindola.

it; it is not that they are words that a Master or disciple might utter or words that common folk might utter. It is not his raising an eyebrow, or his brushing up an eyebrow, or his face-to-face encountering of Nansen's eyebrow. Even though he was a person of excellent talents who walked his own way, if he had not encountered Nansen, he could not have been like that. Great Master Jōshū uttered the words, "In our Chinshū district, we grow really big daikon radishes," when he was Abbot of Shinsai-in Monastery in the Chōka Gardens of the Chinshū district.[21] He was later given the posthumous title of Great Master Shinsai. Because this was the way he was, he correctly Transmitted the Treasure House of the Eye of the True Teaching of the Buddhas and Ancestors after the Eye that sees Buddha had opened through his training. When there is a correct Transmission of the Treasure House of the Eye of the True Teaching, it manifests in one's everyday behavior as a softening, as an open-heartedness.

Delivered to the assembly at Mount Yamashibu on the nineteen day of the eleventh lunar month during the winter of the first year of the Kangen era (December 31, 1243).

Copied in the quarters of the Abbot's assistant in Daibutsu-ji Temple in Yoshida district, Echizen Province, on the sixteenth day of the tenth month during the winter of the second year of the Kangen era (November 17, 1244).

Ejō

---

21.   Jōshū's remark can be understood as follows: just as my Master Nansen was to me, his disciple, so I am to my disciples, who are like the daikon radishes that I cultivate in our monastery garden, in that they sit still within their growing place, becoming ever larger and more deeply-rooted, just like a daikon.

60

On Seeking One's Master Far and Wide
(Henzan)

Translator's Introduction: The term *'henzan'* conventionally refers to the practice of a novice monk's going throughout the country on a pilgrimage to seek a Master under whom to study and train, and possibly to spiritually awaken. As such, it might be rendered as 'seeking a Master far and wide'. Based on several kōan stories, Dōgen understands the term as referring to thoroughly exploring the Matter through one's training with one's Master, which does not require leaving one's training place. In this sense, one is seeking far and wide within oneself for the Master, which is one's True Self.

To practice the Great Way of the Buddhas and Ancestors is to become enlightened through and through, to go forth with no strings entangling our feet, with clouds appearing under our feet. Even though it has been described like this, when the Flower opens, the whole world is awakened. As Tōzan put it: "I constantly make the Way the important Matter."* This is why there is the saying that a sweet melon is sweet right to its stem and a bitter melon is bitter down to its roots: the sweetness of what is sweet is sweet right to its very stem. This is how Tōzan had explored the Matter through his training with his Master.

Great Master Gensha Shibi was once summoned by his Master Seppō, who said to him, "O Shibi, my austere monk, why haven't you gone out on a pilgrimage to seek a Master to train with?"

He replied, "Bodhidharma did not come east to China for that, nor did the Second Ancestor go west to India for that!" Seppō thoroughly approved of what Shibi had said.

---

* See *Glossary.*

In this dialogue, the conventional meaning that underlies the term *'henzan'* has been turned completely upside down. And furthermore, what Shibi said is not something found in holy writ. What yardstick could possibly be used to measure his awakening?

When Nangaku Ejō first visited the Old Buddha Daikan Enō, the Old Buddha said, "What is it that comes thus?"

Nangaku thoroughly explored this mudball with his Master during a span of eight years. Finally he made his move, which was his thorough exploration with his Master, saying to the Old Buddha, "I have realized what you meant when I first came here. Upon receiving me, you said, 'What is it that comes thus?'"

Thereupon, the Old Buddha Enō asked, "And, pray, just what have you realized?"

Nangaku then replied, "Were I to try to put the One Matter into words, they would miss the mark." This was the manifestation of his thorough exploration with his Master, his manifestation of his eight years of training.

The Old Buddha Enō asked, "And is this a substitute for training to become enlightened?"

Nangaku responded, "It is not that there is no training for enlightenment, but rather, there is nothing to be had that will stain It."

Thereupon, Enō said, "I am no different, and you are no different, and all the Buddhas and Ancestors of India were no different."

After this, Ejō explored the Matter with his Master, inside and out, during another span of eight years. Counting from beginning to end, it was during a span of fifteen years that he thoroughly explored the Matter with his Master.[1]

His 'coming thus' was his thorough exploration of the Matter with his Master. With his remark, "Were I to try to put the One Matter into words, they would miss the mark," he opened the door to the Temple and went in to meet the Buddhas and Ancestors: this too was how he sought far and wide for a Master. After entering the picture, he pursued his training with his Master, committing himself to turning away from multitudinous forms of delusion, which goes beyond casually entering one monastery upon leaving another. His going in and meeting the Buddhas Eye-to-Eye was his seeking a Master far and wide, and his earnest acceptance of the Teaching was his exploring the Matter with his Master. To see through, and beyond, the flesh of the Master's face is precisely what exploring the Matter far and wide with one's Master means.

      From the first, the purpose of Seppō's remark concerning visiting other Masters was not to recommend that Shibi leave the monastery, nor was it to recommend that he go traveling north or south. It was to help foster the kind of exploring far and wide that Shibi himself expressed by saying, "Bodhidharma did not come east to China for that, nor did the Second Ancestor go west to India for that!" Shibi's saying that Bodhidharma did not come east to China for that goes beyond any silly remarks about his coming not being a coming. It is the principle of the Great Earth not having a single clod to tread upon. What Shibi calls 'Bodhidharma' is but one part of the stream of life. Even if all the eastern lands had suddenly come to a full boil and had sought Bodhidharma out to serve under him, this would not be the same as his turning away from delusion nor would it be the same as his turning himself around within the outpouring of someone else's words. Because Bodhidharma did not

---

1.   By Japanese reckoning, he did not train for a full eight years but within the span of eight calendar years. Hence, the eighth year in which he trained before awakening was also the first year in which he trained after awakening.

come to the eastern lands for such things, he saw the Face in an eastern land.[2] Even though he saw the Face of Buddhas and the Face of Ancestors in an eastern land, this 'land' goes beyond his coming east to China, for that would have been like his grasping what the Buddhas and Ancestors are while losing sight of his own Nose.[3] In sum, 'land' is beyond being east or west: 'east and west' has nothing to do with lands.

As to our Second Ancestor, Taiso Eka, not going west to India, in that he thoroughly explored 'India' with his Master, he did not actually travel west to India. Had the Second Ancestor actually gone to India, it would simply be his 'having dropped off a forearm'.[4] Now, why did the Second Ancestor not go to India? He did not go to India because he had leapt into his Master's blue Eye. If he had not leapt into his Master's blue Eye, he certainly should have gone to India. Instead, he scraped out Bodhidharma's Eye as his thorough exploration of the Matter.[5] Going west to India or coming east to China is not thoroughly exploring the Matter with one's Master, nor is someone making a thorough search by proceeding to Mount Tendai or Mount Nangaku, or by going to Mount Godai or to the heavens above. If you do not see through, and rid yourself of, your concept of the four seas and the five lakes, yours will not be a thorough exploration with your Master.[6] Going back and forth between the four seas and the five lakes does not constitute a thorough exploration of the Matter. It just makes our path slippery and our feet sore, thereby causing us to fall and lose sight of our thorough exploration.

Speaking more generally, because we make our penetration into Master Chōsa Keishin's statement, "The whole universe in all ten directions is our True

---

2. A reference to his four Chinese disciples, all of whom awoke to the Truth.

3. 'Losing sight of one's Nose' is a Zen phrase for missing the vitally important part, namely, one's Original Self.

4. This refers to spiritually severing one's attachments in order to find the Truth.

5. To 'scrape out' Bodhidharma's Eye means to fully absorb his spiritual Teaching and to make It one's own.

6. 'The four seas and the five lakes' is a reference to the whole world with China as its center.

Body," our exploring of the Matter with our Master, this will be our study and practice of Bodhidharma's not coming east to China and the Second Ancestor's not going west to India. Thoroughly exploring the Matter with one's Master means that when a stone is large, it is large just as it is, and when a stone is small, it is small just as it is. Without setting stones in motion, we let the large ones do their training and the small ones do theirs. While training, to encounter a hundred thousand myriad things in a hundred thousand myriad places is still not thoroughly exploring the Matter. Turning ourselves around a hundred thousand myriad times within the outpouring of half a word is our thorough exploration of the Matter. For example, working the soil is simply working the soil, which is exploring the Matter thoroughly. To go from working the soil once to working the sky once and then to working the four quarters and eight directions once is not thoroughly exploring the Matter. When Gutei was exploring the Matter with Master Tenryū, he realized the realm of the One-finger, which was a thorough exploring of the Matter with his Master. Gutei's simply raising one finger was his thorough exploring of the Matter.[7]

       Shibi once addressed his assembly, saying, "I and Old Master Shakyamuni have done the same practice."
       There was a monk at the time who came forth and asked, "I wonder what person you encountered?"

---

7.   At the heart of Meditation Master Tenryū's Dharma was his teaching that All is One, which he would express by holding up his index finger. Tenryū's very young disciple, Gutei, took to imitating his Master's gesture but without understanding what Tenryū was expressing. On one occasion when Gutei raised his finger, Tenryū is said to have cut it off. Frightened by this, Gutei ran to leave the room. When Tenryū called to him, Gutei turned to face his Master, who then held up his finger. This triggered Gutei's awakening to the Truth. The cutting off of Gutei's finger, like Taiso Eka's cutting off his arm, is probably meant metaphorically as the dropping off of body and mind, since such physically violent acts are clearly serious violations of the Precepts.

The Master answered, "The Sha family's third son, while on a fishing boat."[8]

From start to finish, the genuineness of what our venerable Master Shakyamuni encountered is naturally the same as His encounter with 'Old Master Shakyamuni'. And because the genuineness from start to finish of what the venerable monk Shibi encountered is naturally the same as his encounter with the 'Venerable Fellow Shibi', our venerable Master Shakyamuni and the venerable monk Shibi have made the same encounter. Both our venerable Master Shakyamuni and the venerable monk Shibi explored to the utmost the sufficiency and insufficiency of their spiritual search, a practice which we take to be the underlying principle of thoroughly seeking one's Master.[9] Because our venerable Master Shakyamuni had the same kind of experience as the venerable monk Shibi had, He is an Old Buddha, and because the venerable monk Shibi had the same kind of experience as our venerable Master Shakyamuni had, he is one of His descendants. This principle should be thoroughly explored with one's Master, and in detail.

You need to clarify through your training the import of Shibi's saying that he met the Sha family's third son while on a fishing boat. That is to say, we explore through and through, with the utmost diligence, the instance when both our venerable Master Shakyamuni and the venerable monk Shibi had the same kind of simultaneous encounter with their Master. There was the venerable monk Shibi who encountered the Sha family's third son while on a fishing boat, and there was the Sha family's third son who encountered the shaven-headed monk upon Mount Shibi. Do your utmost to let yourself and others experience the sameness and experience the difference. The venerable monk Shibi and our venerable Master Shakyamuni had the same kind of encounter and did the same exploring far and wide. In order for you to have the same encounter, you need to explore far and wide the principle that 'the Sha's third son' and

---

8. An allusion to Shibi's meeting up with his own True Self while he was living on a fishing boat.

9. That is, their awakening to their True Self was fully sufficient and, at the same time, it was insufficient in that there is always the ever going on, ever becoming Buddha.

'I' have encountered a One beyond what words can describe. When the principle of seeking the Master far and wide has not yet arisen, one is unable to encounter one's Self and, lacking an encountering with one's Self, one is unable to encounter another and, lacking an encountering with another, one is unable to encounter 'such a person'* and, being unable to encounter the true 'I', one is unable to encounter a Master's Fist[10] and, being unable to encounter a Master's Eye, one is unable to let oneself hook one's Self and haul It up, and one is unable to let It come on board even before It is hooked.[11]

When we have completely exhausted our seeking far and wide, we drop off seeking far and wide. It is comparable to the saying, "When the sea has dried up, one does not see its bottom," or the saying, "When a person dies, the mind does not remain." 'When the sea has dried up' means 'when the whole sea has completely dried up'. At the same time, when the sea has indeed completely dried up, one does not see a seabed. 'Not remaining behind' and 'completely ceasing', together, comprise our human mind. The mind does not remain because it has customarily withered away into death. Hence, you need to recognize that the whole of a person is his mind and that the whole of the Mind is what a person is. In this manner, we thoroughly explore with our Master the front and back of each side of an issue.

There was an occasion when my former Master Tendō Nyojō, the Old Buddha, was asked to give a Dharma talk by his veteran fellow monks, who had come from all over. Having gathered together in his Lecture Hall, they were given the following Teaching:

---

10.   Some Zen Masters were in the habit of raising a fist to express That which goes beyond conceptualization or words.

11.   The references to fishing are connected with Shibi's 'catching his True Self' while he was living on a fishing barge. 'Fishing' itself has a metaphoric connection with doing one's meditation.

The Great Way has no fixed gate.

From out the crown of our heads, It leaps forth in all
directions.

Unbounded as space itself, It leaves no traces behind.

Still, It has found Its way into Seiryō's Nose.[12]

Even the bunch of you who would betray Gautama
encounter It thus,

To say nothing of those of you born from Rinzai's
woeful womb.[13]

Ho! In our great family we are tumbled about like
apricot blossoms set dancing by the spring
breeze.

Astonished, they fall, flying wildly in a riot of crimson.

For the present Dharma talk, veteran monks from all directions came to Seiryō Temple in Chien-k'ang Prefecture, where the Old Buddha who was my former Master was serving as chief priest. He and these fellow monks of long-standing were sometimes related like guest and host and sometimes they were simply fellow practitioners sitting side-by-side in meditation. They were such old friends. How could their number fail to be large? It was an occasion when they had gathered together to petition him for a Dharma talk. Veteran monks who were totally devoid of having anything concrete to say to him were not among his friends or among that number who had petitioned him. Although those old friends were themselves highly respected and prized, they waited upon him, requesting his Teaching.

      Speaking more generally, my former Master's practice of thoroughly seeking far and wide was not something fully mastered by those in any other place. In the last

---

12.   Seiryō is an allusion to Master Tendō himself, who at the time of this Dharma talk was
      chief priest at Seiryō Temple.

13.   The overall tone of Tendō's poem, as well as Dōgen's subsequent comments, implies that
      the preceding two lines are meant ironically.

two or three centuries in Great Sung China, there has not been an Old Buddha comparable to my former Master.

"The Great Way has no fixed gate" describes four or five thousand flower and willow lanes, and twenty or thirty thousand music pavilions.[14] At the same time, in letting one's whole self leap forth, we make no use of whatever may remain behind. It is our leaping forth from the crown of our head and entering into our Nostrils: it is these two together that we explore through our training with our Master. Those who have not yet leapt free through the crown of their head and have not yet turned themselves around within their very Nostrils are not persons who are exploring the Matter through their training with their Master, nor are they folks who are thoroughly seeking the Master far and wide. We should explore the essence of 'seeking the Master far and wide' just as Shibi did.

What the Fourth Ancestor explored through his training under the Third Ancestor during the span of nine years was, simply, seeking the Master far and wide. Meditation Master Nansen Fugan once resided in Chih-yang without leaving the mountain for some thirty years, which was his seeking the Master far and wide. Master Ungan Donjō and Master Dōgo Enchi, among others, diligently explored the Matter through their training at Meditation Master Yakusan's monastery for forty years, which was their seeking the Master far and wide. The Second Ancestor spent eight years exploring the Matter with his Master on Mount Sūzan and, through that training, thoroughly realized his Master's Skin and Flesh, Bones and Marrow.

---

14.   'Flower and willow lanes' is a common euphemism in China and Japan for a red-light district. Similarly, the term 'pavilion', particularly in association with some kind of entertainment, customarily refers to a brothel. Given the historic practice of monastic celibacy both in Chinese and Japanese Buddhism, it is unlikely that Dōgen is suggesting or encouraging monks to engage in behavior that would break their vow of celibacy. Even so, there is the teaching in Buddhism that after someone has fully awakened to the Truth, and the false self has completely dropped off, such a person can freely go anywhere, even into brothels or wine shops, without being tempted to partake of what was being offered, and without judging those who were engaged in such activities.

'To seek the Master far and wide' simply means 'just sitting there, dropping off body and mind'. It is as if at the present moment, one goes to where one goes and one comes from where one comes, without their being the slightest gap between them. This is seeking the Master far and wide with one's whole body: this is the whole body of the Great Way. 'To go on, beyond the top of Vairochana* Buddha's head' is the meditative state that is utterly still. Decisive attainment of such a state is Vairochana Buddha's going on. To thoroughly awaken to seeking the Master far and wide by leaping forth means that the gourd leaps forth from the gourd plant. For a long time, we have regarded the stem end of the gourd to be the training place for our 'uncorking Buddha'. Its lifeline is like a thread. We gourds thoroughly explore the gourd plant through our training with our Master. Our raising a single blade of grass is nothing other than our seeking the Master far and wide.[15]

Given to my assembly at my hermitage at the foot of Mount Yamashibu in Echizen Province
        on the twenty-seventh day of the eleventh lunar month in the first year of the
        Kangen era (January 9, 1244).

Copied in the chief disciple's quarters at the same hermitage on the twenty-seventh day of the
        twelfth lunar month in the same year (February 8, 1244).

Ejō

---

15. Dōgen's gourd metaphor probably derives from a saying of his own Master, "The vine of the gourd plant embraces the gourd," which is an allusion to the Master-disciple relationship. To paraphrase this closing passage, the vine is like the lifeline of the Buddhas and Ancestors, which threads its way to sustain the disciple. The training place for disciple and Master is like the juncture where the stem joins the vine. Coming to know one's True Master, that is, one's Buddha Nature, is like picking a ripened gourd, which 'uncorks' (lets out) the Buddha within the disciple. As Dōgen says elsewhere, "Picking up a single blade of grass, we make it into a sixteen-foot tall golden body." So here, our simple action of making a beginning by 'raising a single blade of grass' sets us on our way to seeking far and wide with our Master for the True Master who, when ultimately found, will be the fully erect golden body of Buddha.

61

On the Eye of a Buddha

(Ganzei)

Translator's Introduction: *Ganzei*, the title of this discourse, has several meanings. It literally refers to the physical organs of sight: the eyes. However, in most contexts its meaning is spiritual. For instance, in a story in which a disciple asks his Master to grant him the Eye, he is asking to be Transmitted, that is, to have passed on to him the Eye of the True Teaching. In other contexts, it refers to the Eye of Wisdom (Wise Discernment) or to the Eye with which one perceives that someone is 'such a person', that is, a person who has already awakened to his or her Buddha Nature. While the reader needs to be aware that the meaning of the word Eye in Dōgen's discourses does shift, which of these various meanings is intended is usually fairly clear from context.

When we take up our explorations of the Matter[*] through our training for billions of myriad eons and roll them into balls, they will make eighty-four thousand Eyes.[1]

When my late Master, the Old Buddha of Tendō, was residing as Abbot at Zuigan Monastery, he once said as part of his formal teaching to his assembly:

> *The autumn wind is cool, the autumn moon is bright,*
> *It lights up the Great Earth all with Its hills and streams.*
> *My eyes are atwinkle as we meet each other face-to-face,*
> *My blows and shouts mingle as I test my patch-*
> *robed monks.*

Now, 'testing patch-robed monks' means testing whether they too are Old Buddhas. The pivotal point is that he mixed his blows and shouts, using them to test

---

*   See Glossary.

1.   This is a 'recipe' for taking the fruits of one's training and using them to help others see with the Eye of a Buddha. It relates to a story about his Master, which Dōgen later presents.

his disciples. It is his Eye that manifests such vitality. The Great Earth with all Its hills and streams is the appearance of things as our Eye reveals them. It is the coolness of the autumn wind, which is inexhaustible. It is the brightness of the autumn moon, which is inexhaustible. Being the coolness of the autumn wind, It is beyond comparison with even the four great oceans. Being the brightness of the autumn moon, It is more resplendent than a thousand suns and moons. Its coolness and resplendence are the Great Earth with Its hills and streams which our vision perceives. Patch-robed monks are Buddhas and Ancestors. The one whose Eye does not opt for enlightenment, or for being unenlightened, or for being in some state before or after enlightenment, is one who is an Ancestor of the Buddha. 'Testing' is the Master's disclosing the Eye. It is the disciple's manifesting the One Eye. It is the living Eye itself. 'Meeting each other face-to-face' is the mutual encountering of Master and disciple. 'Mutually encountering' is the Eye being sharp; 'meeting face-to-face' is the Eye thundering forth. In short, do not think that if your whole body is large, your whole Eye must be small. Even those in past ages who have considered themselves to be ever so eminent have been in agreement that their body is large and their eyes are small. This is because they were not yet in possession of their Eye.

      Once when Tōzan Ryōkai was in the monastic assembly of Ungan Donjō, Ungan came upon him making straw sandals,[2] whereupon Tōzan spoke to Ungan, saying, "I pray that you will grant me the Eye, O Venerable Monk."[3]

      Ungan asked, "Who did you give yours away to?"

---

2.   The practice of making straw sandals is considered one of the secret meritorious practices, since such sandals were made for a fellow monk whose sandals had worn out. Without the maker letting it be known who he was, the sandals would be left where the chosen monk could find them.

3.   Tōzan is formally asking Ungan for the Transmission.

Tōzan replied, "This person never had One." [4]

Ungan then asked, "Supposing you had One, where would you turn in order to give It to someone else?"

Tōzan had no words.

Ungan then asked, "Is the Eye you are praying for your Eye or not?"

Tōzan replied, "It is not a matter of It being my Eye or not being my Eye."

Ungan responded, "Ahaaa!" [5]

So, fully displaying one's exploring the Matter through training with one's Master is asking for the Eye. Practicing the Way in the Cloud Hall, attending the Abbot's formal talks in the Dharma Hall, entering the Master's quarters to inquire of the Way, these are ways of asking for the Eye. [6] In general, following the assembly when leaving formal meditation and following the assembly when coming to formal meditation are ways of asking for the Eye as a matter of course. The underlying principle that the Eye is beyond self and beyond other is evident.

As the dialogue said, Tōzan had already requested help by asking the Master to grant him the Eye. Be clear about this: if the Eye is truly yours, you do not need to ask anyone for It, and if It is truly someone else's, you cannot beg It off that person.

Ungan pointed to this by asking, "Who did you give yours away to?"

There is the occasion of Its 'being yours' and there is the dispensing of It by 'giving It to whomever'. Tōzan's saying, "This person never had One," was his own way of

---

4. 'This person' is a humble way to refer to oneself and avoids the assertion of a personal 'I'.

5. Ungan's response was his way of affirming Tōzan's answer.

6. Making straw sandals as a secret meritorious practice would also be a way.

expressing his Eye.[7] You should take the time to explore through your training the Truth revealed by his manifesting the Way in this manner.

> Ungan asked, "Supposing you had One, in what direction would you turn in order to give It to someone else?"

The Eye in this expression signifies that the 'never had' of "This person never had One" is both to have One and to have turned in order to give It to someone else. To turn in order to give It to someone is to have It. You need to thoroughly explore that this is 'such an expression'.

> Tōzan had no words.

He was not dumbstruck. Rather, he was a victim of the sudden arising of dualistic thoughts due to past karma.*

> Pointing out the Matter for his disciple's sake, Ungan then asked, "Is the Eye you are praying for your Eye or not?"

This is a detail concerning the one-eyedness of the Eye. It is his vigorously shattering Tōzan's 'Eye'. The main point of what Ungan is saying is, "It is the Eye asking for the Eye." It is water pulling water along. It is mountains standing in rows with mountains. It is our going forth among those of unlike mind and our living amidst those of like mind.

> Tōzan replied, "It is not a matter of It being my Eye or not being my Eye."

This is his Eye singing forth of Its own accord.[8] Whenever body or mind, thought or knowledge, or form or rank are present, you should encounter those conditions as being the living Eye which is coming forth of Its own accord from beyond the duality of having or not having. All the Buddhas of the three temporal worlds are continually standing in the Dharma Hall listening to the Eye's turning of

---

7.   That is, there is no 'I' that has the Eye of the True Treasure as a personal possession, and everyone has It.

8.   This Eye is Tōzan's True Eye.

the Great Wheel of the Dharma and giving voice to It. In short, within the innermost realm of what we thoroughly explore through our training, we leap into the Eye as we give rise to the intention to realize Buddhahood, as we do the training and practice, and as we awaken to Great Wisdom. From the first, this Eye is beyond self and beyond other. Because It has no obstructions of any kind, the Great Matter is likewise free of obstructions.

In commenting on the preceding story, Rōya Ekaku, a Master of old, once said, "How wonderful indeed are the Buddhas of the Ten Quarters. From the first, They have been flowers within the Eye." What he called 'the Buddhas of the Ten Quarters' is your Eye. The flowers within the Eye are the Buddhas of the Ten Quarters. Your present activities of stepping forward and stepping back, of just sitting and just sleeping, are just such flowers. Be that as it may, you have inherited the power of the Eye Itself. It is your being stripped of your delusions and your being set loose to rid yourself of them.

My late Master, the Old Buddha, once said, "I'm going to scrape out the Eye of Bodhidharma and make It into mudballs to pelt you monks with." With a shout he said, "Yes! The sea has dried up, right to the bottom, and its waves are so high that they smite the very heavens!"

While in the Abbot's quarters at Seiryō-ji Temple, he made a point of this for the sake of the vast sea of assembled monks. This is why he spoke of 'pelting them', as if he were saying 'making them into a real person'. Because of his pelting, all the various monks would give rise to their True Countenance. He meant, for instance, that with the Eye of Bodhidharma he would make each of them into a 'real person'. And he has done so! This is what the underlying principle of 'pelting persons' is. Because each person is someone who has been struck alive with the Eye, the fist with which he struck someone in the Cloud Hall, the traveling staff* with which he struck someone in the Dharma Hall, and the lacquered hossu* with which he struck someone in the

Abbot's quarters are all the Eye of Bodhidharma. His gouging out Bodhidharma's Eye and making It into mudballs to pelt monks with is called today 'seeking an interview with the Abbot to ask for a spiritual boon' or 'getting up in the morning to do one's morning practice' or 'making the effort to just sit'. And what kind of person does he beat them into? "The sea has dried up, right to the bottom, and its waves are so high that they smite the very heavens!"

My late Master, the Old Buddha, once entered the Dharma Hall and spoke in praise of the Tathagata's realizing the Way, saying in verse:

> *For six years He stumbled on through the weeds of*
> *provisional truth with the determined spirit of a*
> *wild fox.*
> *He would leap forth with His whole body, only to become*
> *entangled in delusion's vines.*
> *Having totally lost His eyes, there was no place for Him*
> *to seek for It.*
> *Now He goes about deceiving others by saying that He*
> *was awakened by the morning star.*

That "He was awakened by the morning star" are the words of someone who had totally lost His eyes at that very moment. This was the entangled condition of His whole being, and so He easily leapt free from it. Seeking what is sought is seeking for that which does not exist in what manifests before our very eyes; It is seeking for that which does not exist in what has not yet manifested before our very eyes.

In the Dharma Hall, my late Master, the Old Buddha, once said in verse:

When Gautama finally lost His deceiving eyes,
There appeared in the snow a single blossom on one
bough of the Old Plum Tree.
What has now arrived is the growing of thorn-like spurs,
So that all the more I laugh at the spring winds which
send all things flying in disarray.

Gautama's eyes are not simply one or two or three eyes. To which eye or eyes does
this losing refer? It may be that there are eyes which are called 'losing one's eyes'.
Further, in such a situation as this, there is the Eye that is 'a single blossom on one
bough of the Old Plum Tree'. Before the spring arrives, this Eye discloses the heart of
spring.

Once when ascending to the Dharma seat, my late Master, the Old Buddha,
said:

Day after long day the pouring rain, then finally the sky
completely clear! The croaking of bullfrogs and the mumbling of
earthworms. The Old Buddhas have never passed away, displaying
for us Their diamond-hard Eye. Oh, dear! I've tangled the
entangled.

'The diamond-hard Eye' is the pouring rain day after long day; It is the sky's being
completely clear. It is the croaking of bullfrogs, It is the mumbling of earthworms and,
because They have never passed away, It is the Old Buddhas. Even if the Old Buddhas
were to pass away, it would not be the same as the passing away of those who are not
Old Buddhas.

My late Master, the Old Buddha, while giving a Dharma talk, once said:

> From the winter solstice on, the days grow longer as the
> sun moves farther southward. From within my Eye, a light pours
> forth, and into my Nostrils pours the breath of Life.

In the endless stream of present moments from the winter solstice to the summer solstice, though the days and months grew ever longer, he let go of measuring them. This is the light that was emitted from his Eye. It was his 'seeing mountains' in the light of day.[9] This is what everyday, dignified behavior was like among his assembly.

My late Master, the Old Buddha, when giving a Dharma talk at Jinzu-ji Temple in Lin'an prefecture, said:

> This morning is the first day of the second lunar month.
> The Eye of my hossu is bulging out; It is bright like a mirror and as
> shiny black as lacquer. With a dash, It leaps across heaven and earth
> and swallows them up, as both together are but a single form of It.
> You of this monks' assembly are still beating your heads against
> your walls and butting up against your fences. And, in short, to what
> end? I've given you my all, tossing It your way with a hearty laugh.
> I entrust everything to the Spring Wind, for there is nothing more
> that I need to do.

In this instance, his saying "beating your heads against your walls and butting up against your fences" means the whole of your walls are doing the beating and the whole of your fences are doing the butting. And there is this Eye. 'This morning', 'the second lunar month', 'the first day' are all instances of the Eye; that is, the Eye of the

---

9.   That is, his seeing that his assembly of monks was doing their training well.

hossu.[10] Because It leaps across every barrier with a dash, it is 'this morning', and because in thousands of myriad ways It swallows up the whole universe, heaven and earth, it is 'the second month', and when I've given you my all, tossing It your way, it is 'the first day'. Such is the life of one who is manifesting the Eye.

Given to the assembly on the seventeenth day of the twelfth lunar month in the first year of the Kangen era (January 28, 1244) while staying at Yamashibu Peak in Echizen province.

Copied by me on the twenty-eighth day of the same month (February 8, 1244) whilst in the quarters of the Abbot's assistant at the foot of the Peak.

Ejō

---

10. The hossu is used as part of the ceremonial connected with the disciples coming up in front of the whole community to ask the Master their spiritual question. This ceremony is customarily performed twice each month.

62

On Everyday Life

(Kajō)

Translator's Introduction: *Kajō* literally means 'what is habitual (*jō*) in one's home life (*ka*)'. Throughout the discourse Dōgen speaks of *sahan*, literally 'tea and cooked rice', as the staples of everyday living. While at one level this term simply points out that the Buddhas and Ancestors, in Their humanity, are no different from any other person, it also, more significantly, carries a deeper spiritual connotation, referring to the everyday ceaseless practice that has spiritually sustained and nourished Them and which has the capacity to do the same for us.

Generally speaking, in the dwelling places of Buddhas and Ancestors, taking tea and eating rice is what constitutes Their everyday life.[1] This custom of taking tea and eating rice has been passed on to us and fully manifests itself in the here and now. This is why the taking of tea and the eating of rice by Buddhas and Ancestors has come down to us as a way of living.

The monk Fuyō Dōkai, whilst on Mount Daiyō, once asked Tōsu, "The thoughts and sayings of the Buddha's Ancestors are like the tea and rice of everyday life. Putting these thoughts and sayings aside for the moment, is there any word or phrase you might have for the sake of others?"

Tōsu answered, "You, right now, say! The Emperor inside the capital rules it, so does he have to look back to previous emperors of legendary times, like Yü, T'ang, Yao, and Shun?"

Just when Daiyō was intent on opening his mouth, Tōsu picked up his ceremonial hossu* and covered Daiyō's mouth with

---

1. Taking tea and eating rice is a metaphor for partaking of the Dharma which spiritually nourishes us.

* See *Glossary.*

it, saying, "At the very moment when you gave rise to the intention to realize Buddhahood, you immediately deserved thirty blows."

Thereupon, Daiyō opened up to his enlightenment and, after having bowed in deepest respect to Tōsu, immediately took his leave.

Tōsu called out to him, "Come back a minute, acharya!" *

When Daiyō did not turn his head around, Tōsu said, "Have you, my disciple, arrived at the place where there is no doubt?"

Daiyō covered his ears with his hands and left.

So, clearly, we should preserve and take care of the teaching that the thoughts and sayings of the Buddha's Ancestors are the tea and rice of everyday life. The homely fare of everyday life is the thoughts of Buddhas and the sayings of Ancestors.² The Buddhas and Ancestors prepare the tea and rice, and the tea and rice help sustain and take care of the Buddhas and Ancestors. Since this is so, we, for our part, do not need to rely on anything apart from the potency of this tea and rice of Theirs. Simply, we do not squander the strength of the Buddhas and Ancestors that resides within the partaking of this tea and rice.

You would do well to explore with great diligence the remark about not looking back to previous emperors of legendary times such as Yü, T'ang, Yao, and Shun. You would also do well to explore how to let the question as to whether there is any word or phrase that you may have for the benefit of others spring forth from the crown of <u>your</u> head. You should experiment through your training with your Master to see if you can get it to spring forth.

When Great Master Sekitō Kisen was at his hermitage on Mount Nangaku, he once said:

---

2.   'Homely fare' (C. *t'su-cha tan-fan*), literally, 'coarse tea and thin gruel', is a conventional Chinese phrase used by a host as an apology for what is being offered to a guest.

> *I've thatched me a grass hut, without a coin to my name.*
> *Having finished eating rice, I feel content, and look to*
> *taking me a nap.*

His 'having finished eating rice', which he said time after time, over and over again, is the thought and saying of an Ancestor of the Buddha who has explored what rice is. Someone who has not yet eaten rice is someone who has not yet experienced satiety. At the same time, this principle of 'feeling content, having finished eating rice,' manifests before one eats rice, while one is eating rice, and after one has eaten rice. In a house where people finish eating up their rice, to fail to see that there is always the eating of rice is to explore through one's training only four or five measures out of ten.

My late Master, an Old Buddha, when expounding the Teaching to his assembly, once said:

> I can recall an incident in which a monk asked Hyakujō, "Just what sort of thing is the Wondrous Matter?"*
>
> Hyakujō replied, "He sits alone atop Daiyū Peak.[3] O my great assembly, this Fellow cannot be disturbed by anything, so let Him sit for a while in meditation, eliminating dualistic thought."
>
> If there was someone today, a novice, say, who suddenly asked, "Just what sort of thing is the Miraculous Matter?" I would simply turn to the person and say, "What Miraculous Matter is there?" In short, it is the 'What!' in the alms bowl of pure compassion which was passed on to me to use for eating my rice.[4]

---

3.   Daiyū Peak is an alternative name for Mount Hyakujō, where Hyakujō had his monastery.

4.   There is a play on words in this last sentence. 'The alms bowl of great compassion' can also be understood as an allusion to Tendō's alms bowl, which he had brought with him when he left Great Compassion Monastery in order to become Abbot of Tendō Monastery. The whole quotation was part of his inaugural Dharma talk to his new assembly.

In the everyday life of the Buddhas and Ancestors, without fail, there is the Miraculous Matter, which is Their so-called 'sitting alone atop Daiyū Peak'. Even though we now encounter that Fellow when we let Him sit in meditation and eliminate dualistic thinking, It is still what the Miraculous Matter is. And there is that which is even more miraculous: the alms bowl of great compassion being passed on to Tendō, from which he ate his rice. The Miraculous Matter is each and every thing everywhere 'eating rice'. Thus, sitting alone atop Daiyū Peak is precisely what eating rice is. The alms bowl is what we use for eating rice, and whatever we use for eating our rice is our alms bowl. That is why it is the alms bowl of great compassion and why Tendō ate his rice from it. There was his knowing what rice is after he had fully satisfied himself. And there was his being satisfied from having completely eaten the rice. And there was his full awareness of the rice satisfying him. And there was his having been fully satisfied and yet continuing to eat his rice.

Now then, just what could this alms bowl of his possibly be? From my perspective, it is not merely a wooden object, nor is it something black like lacquerware. Might it be the One of unyielding stone? Might it be the Iron Man? It is bottomless: it is beyond our own Nose. In its swallowing up empty space, empty space receives it, in gasshō.*

My late Master, an Old Buddha, once addressed an assembly whilst in the Abbot's quarters at the Zuigan Pure Land Meditation Temple in the Taishū District, saying, "When hunger comes, I eat rice, and when tiredness comes, I take a sleep. Forges and bellows fill the universe."[5] His phrase, 'when hunger comes' refers to the life of one who habitually 'eats rice'. The person who has never yet eaten rice is someone incapable of hungering for it. Hence, you need to realize that we for whom

---

5. 'Forges and bellows' is a traditional Zen Buddhist metaphor for the conditions and expedient means that intensify the heat of training, whereby a trainee is forged into a True Monk. As Tendō Nyojō points out, these conditions and expedient means are available everywhere. In other words, all things have the capability of teaching us the Dharma.

hunger may well be an event in our everyday life are persons who must have decided to eat rice to the full.

'When tiredness comes' refers to being tired within tiredness, which habitually fully springs from a tired head.[6] Nevertheless, it is the here and now, wherein the whole of our being is swept clean, turned around, and put in order within our daily life.

'I take a sleep' refers to letting the ego 'nap', having borrowed the Buddha Eye, the Dharma Eye, the Eye of Wise Discernment, the Eye of the Ancestors, the Eye of those who act as the temple's pillars* and stone lanterns.*

After my late Master, an Old Buddha, had gone by invitation from Zuigan-ji Temple in Taishū to Jinzu-ji Temple in Rin'an City, he once gave a talk in the Dharma Hall there, in which he said:

> *For half a year I ate rice as I sat atop a cloud-covered peak,*
> *Sitting there to break through the smoke and mist which*
> *arose a thousand myriad times over,*
> *When suddenly a resounding clap issued forth, as thunder*
> *rumbled o'er,*
> *And the heavens, with springtime glow, shone like apricot*
> *blooms all crimson red.*

All the methods of the Buddhas and Ancestors, as taught from the time of the Buddha, were Their 'eating rice whilst sitting atop a cloud-covered peak'. Thoroughly exploring how to carry on the Buddha's life of wise discernment was Their manifesting a life of eating rice. 'Sitting atop a cloud-covered peak for half a year' is called 'eating rice'. They do not know how much the smoke and mist, in which They are sitting in order to break through, has piled up. And, however sudden the clap of thunder may be, the springtime glow is simply the crimson of apricot blossoms.

---

6. That is, tiredness is a mental thing.

The term 'the heavens' refers to being open at every moment of now. And those moments are what 'eating rice' is.

The Cloud-covered Peak is the name for a peak at Zuigan-ji Temple.

My late Master, the Old Buddha, while in the Buddha Hall at Zuigan-ji Temple in Keigen City in the Minshū District, once expounded the Teaching to the assembly, saying:

> Right at this moment, put down the load you are carrying. 'The wondrous golden form' is putting on one's robe and eating one's rice: 'putting on one's robe and eating one's rice' is the wondrous golden form. Further, refrain from poking around, asking who is or isn't putting on their robe and eating rice. Do not talk about so-and-so being the Wondrous Golden Form. Should you so restrain yourself, it will be an expression of what Master Tendō meant when he said, "That is why I bow to you." As I am already eating my rice, so do your bow, with your hands in gasshō, and then eat your rice. We act like this because we earnestly shun going about while holding flowers aloft.[7]

The monk Chōkei Daian once addressed his assembly in the Dharma Hall, saying:

> I, Daian, stayed with Isan for thirty years. I supped on Isan rice. I urinated Isan urine. But I did not explore Isan's Zen. I simply raised one unsexed water buffalo. When it wandered off into the weeds, I'd haul it out. When it trespassed on someone's garden patch, I'd chastise it. As I had already bawled it out over a long time, people would treat it to such remarks as, "Oh, you poor creature."

---

7.   That is, going around acting holy.

Now it has changed and become a white ox right out in the open. It is constantly right before my face. All day long, it clearly shines forth, manifesting the Dharma. Even if one were to try to drive it off, it would not go away.

Clearly, we should accept, and keep to, this address to his assembly. His thirty years of endeavor within the assembly of an Ancestor of the Buddha was his eating his rice, unmixed with cares and worries. When you manifest a life of eating rice, there are, quite naturally, the signs of your rearing a single castrated water buffalo.

Great Master Jōshū Shinsai once asked a newly arrived monk, "Have you ever come here before?"

The monk replied, "Yes, I have."

The Master said, "Have some tea before you leave."

He also asked another monk, "Have you ever come here before?"

The monk replied, "No, I never have."

The Master said, "Have some tea before you leave."

The Prior of the monastery asked the Master, "Why did you say to the monk who had been here before, 'Have some tea before you leave,' and also say to the monk who had not been here before, 'Have some tea before you leave?'"

The Master gestured for the Prior to come to him. When the Prior complied, the Master said, "Have some tea before you leave."[8]

---

8. Jōshū's questions are double-edged. While it appears as if he were asking a commonplace question as to whether someone had come to Jōshū's monastery before, he is actually asking a spiritual question (one which Dōgen will explore), namely, "Have you ever arrived at the Here and Now?" Since both the two monks and the Prior all take Jōshū's

His 'here' is not something off the top of his head, nor does it refer to <u>his</u> Nose, nor does it refer to Jōshū.[9] Because he had leapt free of 'here', he had already arrived at the Here and Now and had not yet arrived at the Here.[10] <u>Right here</u> is where the What is, but those others merely talked about it in terms of 'having come before' or 'not having come before'. This is why my late Master said, "What person who takes residence either in a gilded tower or in a wine shop could come to call on Jōshū and drink his tea?"

And so it is that the everyday life of Buddhas and Ancestors is simply Their taking of Tea and Their eating of Rice.

Delivered to the assembly below Yamashibu Peak in Echizen Province on the seventeenth day of the twelfth lunar month in the first year of the Kangen era (January 28, 1243).

Copied by me in the quarters of the Abbot's assistant below the peak on the first day of the first month in the second year of the same era (February 10, 1244).

Ejō

---

question on a superficial level, Jōshū offers them tea (that is, the Teaching) before they go off to find That which is the Here and Now.

9. That is, the Here and Now is not an intellectual concept, nor is it a reference to Jōshū's own Original Nature, nor is it a personal reference to Jōshū himself.

10. That is, Jōshū had fully realized the Truth (his having arrived at the Here and Now) and at the same time, his training and practice continued with his 'always going on, always becoming Buddha' (his not yet having arrived at the Here).

63

On the Roar of the Dragon

(Ryūgin)

Translator's Introduction: The roar of the Dragon refers to a sound not unlike that of the wind blowing through a grove of barren trees. This sound may become audible during meditation when the meditator has dropped off body and mind, that is, has let go of the greed, anger, and delusion which form attachments to the five skandhas. The withered tree that Dōgen speaks of in this discourse is a common Buddhist metaphor for someone who has reached a deep level of meditation, a person whose passions have all but disappeared. This meditative state, however, is not to be confused with a quietistic or blissful condition, which is simply a passing phase that may arise in spiritual practice.

The title could also be rendered as the "Song of the Dragon", since it is also used to describe a particularly forceful expression of the Dharma, one that sets the Wheel of the Dharma turning.

> Great Master Tōsu Daidō of Shuchou Province was once asked by a monk, "Does the roar of the Dragon exist even within a withered tree?"
>
> The Master replied, "As I would put it, the Lion's roar exists within one's skull."

Talk of withered trees and dead ashes is something taught by non-Buddhists. Even so, you need to distinguish between withered trees that non-Buddhists speak of and withered trees that Buddhists speak of. Even though non-Buddhists talk about withered trees, they do not know what a 'withered tree' is, much less would they actually hear the Dragon's roar. Non-Buddhists imagine that a withered tree is something dead or dying. They have been taught that such a tree cannot experience the springtime.

We explore through our training the 'withered tree' that the Buddhas and Ancestors speak of as 'the ocean having dried up'. 'The ocean having dried up' is synonymous with 'the tree having withered up' and 'the tree having withered up' is synonymous with its having encountered the Spring. The tree's being unwavering is

887

a sign of its having withered.[1] Such trees as mountain trees, ocean trees, and sky trees are what withered trees are.[2] Their budding is the roar of the Dragon within a withered tree. Even those trees whose girth is measured in hundreds of thousands are offspring of some withered tree. Its form and its innate nature, its embodiment and the strength derived from its being withered comprise the long-lived withered trees which Buddhas and Ancestors speak of. At the same time, they go beyond being long-lived or short-lived. There are the trees of mountains and valleys, and there are the trees of fields and villages. The trees of mountains and valleys are conventionally called pines and cedars. The trees of fields and villages are conventionally called ordinary people and those in lofty positions. We explore through our training that those whose 'leaves grow from their roots' are called the Buddhas and Ancestors, and we explore the expression 'end and beginning here return unto the Source'.[3] What is just like this is the long Dharma body of withered trees and the short Dharma body of withered trees. Those who are not withered trees do not yet roar like a Dragon, and those who are not yet withered trees will not forget the sound of the Dragon. "How many times have I met the spring, my heart unswerving?" is the Dragon's song of one who is completely withered.[4] To be sure, this 'song' is not in the same category as the five tones in a conventional musical scale, but two or three of the Five Tones are in the sequence of the Dragon's song.

At the same time, by this monk's question, "Does the roar of the Dragon exist even within a withered tree?" it has been brought forth for the first time in immeasurable eons. It was his bringing forth his spiritual question. Tōsu's saying "As

---

1.   'Unwavering' in this context means not being shaken by the arising of delusive thoughts.

2.   This is a description of various types of meditators: mountain trees are those who are sitting as still as a mountain, ocean trees are those who are exploring the Depths, and sky trees are those who are exploring the Unbounded.

3.   The quotations in this sentence come from the Sandōkai, a poem by our Thirty-fifth Ancestor, Sekitō Kisen, which is customarily recited every day in Zen Buddhist monasteries.

4.   This quotation is from a poem by Daibai Hōjō, which Dōgen gives in full in Discourse 29: On Ceaseless Practice (Gyōji).

I would put it, the Lion's roar exists within one's skull" means "What place could there possibly be that is concealed from It?" And it means "We never rest from surrendering our self and from supporting others." And it means "Skulls are scattered everywhere in the fields." [5]

Great Master Kyōgen Chikan was once asked by a monk, "What is the Way?"

The Master answered, "The singing of the Dragon amidst the withered trees."

The monk replied, "I don't understand."

The Master said, "It is the Eye in skulls."

Later, there was a monk who asked Sekisō, "Just what sort of thing is this 'singing of a dragon amidst withered trees?'"

Sekisō replied, "Even now, there is Its being tinged with delight."

The monk then asked, "Just what is that thing about 'eyes in skulls?'"

Sekisō replied, "Even now, there is Its being tinged with consciousness."

There was also a monk who asked Sōzan, "Just what sort of thing is this 'singing of a dragon amidst withered trees?'"

Sōzan replied, "Its bloodline has not been severed."

The monk then asked, "Well, just what is that thing about 'eyes in skulls?'"

Sōzan replied, "They are not completely dried out."

The monk then said, "Oh, I don't know about that! Are there any who can hear it?"

---

5. That is, in the fields of training.

Sōzan replied, "There is not one person on the whole of the great earth who has not already heard It."

The monk retorted, "I'm not convinced. What verses does a dragon chant?"

Sōzan replied, "I do not know what those verses are, but those who do hear It bemoan the fact that others do not."[6]

The hearers and the chanters that these monks were just now talking about do not come anywhere near to those who actually sing the Dragon's song, for this melody is what the Dragon Itself sings. Being amidst withered trees or in a skull are not referring to something inside or outside, nor are they a reference to self or other; they are referring to the 'What' that is here and now and to the 'What' that has always been of old. Its being tinged with delight even now is the horns on Its head coming forth. Its being tinged with consciousness even now is Its completely shedding Its skin.

Sōzan's saying, "Its bloodline has not been severed," means that the Way is not concealed and that, within the sphere of words, there is the turning around of self. "They are not completely dried out" means that the drying up of the ocean has not completely reached the bottom. Because the drying out has not achieved completion, there is drying going on atop the dryness. The monk's asking, "Are there any who can hear it?" implies "Are there any who cannot?" As to Sōzan's saying, "There is not one person on the whole of the great earth who has not already heard It," I should have liked to ask him, "Putting aside, for the moment, your remark about there being

---

6. These three short dialogues are typical of many kōan stories that involve a Master and someone identified only as a monk. The monk—presumably a novice—asks a question based on an attempt to understand some saying by an Ancestor from a commonplace, literal perspective, whereas the Master gives a response as if the monk had asked his or her question from a spiritual perspective. This is done to help the monk break through a dependence on worldly ways of thinking. That is, in the above three cases the monks think that what they are quoting is somehow about mythical creatures called dragons, whereas the Masters are pointing the monks to a deeper meaning of the term 'Dragon', that is, they are pointing to one's innate Buddha Nature.

no one who has not already heard It, tell me, in the time before the whole earth sprang into existence, where was the roar of the Dragon then? Speak up! Quick, quick!"

"I'm not convinced. What verses does the Dragon chant?" is the question that needs answering for all our sakes. The roaring Dragon, quite naturally, is making vocal sounds and taking up the Great Matter* whilst in mud; this is Its taking in a breath through Its nostrils. "I do not know what those verses are" means that a Dragon exists within those verses. "Those who do hear It bemoan the fact that others do not" is sad indeed!

The roar of the Dragon that has now come forth through such Masters as Kyōgen, Sekisō, and Sōzan creates the clouds and makes the rain. It does not speak of the Way, nor does It speak of Eyes or skulls; it is just the thousands of songs, the myriad songs that the Dragon sings. Its still having delight is found in the croaking of bullfrogs, and Its still having consciousness is found in the mumbling of worms. Therefore, Its bloodline has not been severed; there is one gourd succeeding another.[7] Because Its skull is not completely dry, It is the chief pillar* of the temple from whose Womb is born the other pillars of the temple. It is the temple's main stone lantern* which is most conspicuous among all the stone lanterns in the temple.

Delivered to the assembly on the twenty-fifth day of the twelfth lunar month in the first year of the Kangen era (February 5, 1244), whilst beneath Yamashibu Peak in Echizen Province.

Copied at Eihei-ji Monastery on the fifth day of the third lunar month in the second year of the Kōan era (April 17, 1279).

---

*   See Glossary.

7.   The gourd refers to a Master as a vessel for the Water of the Spirit, which is passed on through the Transmission.

64

On Spring and Autumn:
Warming Up and Cooling Down

(Shunjū)

Translator's Introduction: This discourse is concerned with the teachings of Tōzan who, along with his Dharma heir, Sōzan, is considered a founding Ancestor of Dōgen's Sōtō tradition. Dōgen first presents a kōan story for which Tōzan was famous, one dealing with how to train with the opposites. He then makes mention of the *Five Positions* (J. *Goi*), in which Tōzan outlines the relationships between the transient and the Absolute—the Absolute within the transient, the transient within the Absolute, the transient itself, the Absolute itself, and the transient and Absolute in harmony. Dōgen quotes and critiques various Masters who have written poems expressing their understanding of both the story and the *Five Positions*. Since many of these poems contain Zen terms which would most likely have been understood in Dōgen's time but are unfamiliar to present-day Western readers, some effort has been made to clarify what these poems are pointing to, though Japanese scholarly commentators are not always certain of or in agreement as to the significance of some of the metaphors that the poem contains.

> Great Master Tōzan Ryōkai was once asked by a monk, "When cold or heat come our way, how are we to avoid them?"
> The Master replied, "Why don't you proceed to the place where there is no heat or cold?"
> The monk then asked, "What is that place where there is no heat or cold?"
> The Master answered, "When it is cold, my acharya,* give yourself up to the cold; when it is hot, my acharya, give yourself up to the heat."

Ever so many people in the past have given much thought to this dialogue, and many people in the present need to make every effort to train with it. The Buddhas and

---

*   See Glossary.

Ancestors have invariably come to explore it, and those who come to explore it are Buddhas and Ancestors. Many of the Indian and Chinese Buddhas and Ancestors in both the past and present have treated this story as an actual incidence of one's Original Nature manifesting. In this dialogue, Original Nature manifests as the spiritual question of Buddhas and Ancestors.

At the same time, the monk's question, "When cold or heat come our way, how are we to avoid them?" needs to be examined in detail. It is your taking a good hard look through your training at the very moment when cold comes and at the very moment when heat comes. This cold and heat come from a cold and heat that are entirely cold and entirely hot. Since they come from cold and heat, when they do arrive, they have come from a head that thinks in terms of cold and hot, and they manifest from eyes that see in terms of cold and hot. Above this 'head' is the very place where there is no cold or hot. Within these 'eyes' is the very place where there is no cold or hot. The Great Ancestor's statement, "When it is cold, my acharya, give yourself up to the cold; when it is hot, my acharya, give yourself up to the heat," refers to what was happening at that very moment. Even though 'when it is cold' refers to his saying 'give yourself up to the cold', 'when it is hot' need not necessarily be his way of saying 'give yourself up to the heat'. 'Cold' is fundamentally and totally cold; 'heat' is fundamentally and totally hot. Even though we may have been able to avoid experiencing them on myriad occasions, this is still just exchanging the head for the tail. Cold is what the living Eye of the Ancestors of our tradition is; hot is what the warm skin of my late Master was.

Meditation Master Tanka Shijun was the Dharma heir of the Venerable Monk Fuyō Dōkai. He once said:

> Among our monastic assembly, there are those who have deliberated among themselves and then made the assertion, "In this story, the monk's question has already sunk him into duality, whereas the Venerable Monk Tōzan's reply returns the matter to the position of the Absolute. Recognizing what is being sounded in Tōzan's words, the monk then enters into the position of the

Absolute, whereas Tōzan now responds by stringing along with the dualistic position." Deliberating in this way, those who assert such a view not only slander the late, saintly Tōzan but they also disgrace themselves. Have you not encountered the saying, "When you listen to the explanations of ordinary people, they may call up pretty pictures in the mind—all in reds and greens—but even though these may be beautiful when before your eyes, after continued repetition, they will ultimately sicken you?"

In general, my noble Buddhist travelers of the Way, if you wish to grasp this Great Matter,* you must first become conscious of this Highest Ancestor's Treasure House of the Eye of the True Teaching. The teachings uttered by the rest of those Ancestors of the Buddha are as meaningful as the sizzling sounds a cold bowl makes when hot water is poured into it. Even so, I dare to put it to you, what ultimately is the place that is without cold or heat? Do you understand?[1] A pair of kingfishers come to roost in the Jeweled Mansion, whereas the mandarin drake and his mate are allied with the Golden Palace.[2]

This Master is one of Tōzan's direct descendants, an outstanding personage in the seat of our Ancestors. As such, he rebukes the many who, dwelling within the cave of duality, bow down to our Founding Ancestor, Great Master Tōzan, for the wrong reason.[3] If the Buddha's Dharma had been Transmitted from such a position of duality,

---

1.   In accord with traditional Zen interpretations, these two questions could also be rendered as, "The 'What' is ultimately the place that is without cold or heat. Do you get It?"

2.   The pairs of birds—one male, one female—are a metaphor for the opposites, in the present case cold and hot. They come to rest in That Place which is beyond the opposites, and which is 'experienced' by kingfishers as a jeweled mansion and by ducks as a golden palace.

3.   That is, they do not grasp the true significance of Tōzan's teaching on the *Five Positions*, which ultimately transcends the duality of the transient and the Absolute.

how could It possibly have ever come down to us today? Be they feral kittens or farmyard clowns, they have not yet been thoroughly trained within Tōzan's inner chambers. Folks who have never crossed the threshold into the day-to-day training with the Buddha's Dharma have erroneously asserted that Tōzan came in contact with people by applying such things as a dualistic five positions. This is barbarous and irresponsible talk, which you should not pay attention to. You should just thoroughly explore through your training that this superior Ancestor of yours was, by all means, in possession of the Treasure House of the Eye of the True Teaching.

Meditation Master Wanshi Shōgaku of Mount Tendō in Chingyüan Prefecture was a Dharma heir of Abbot Tanka Shijun. He once said:

> When we discuss this matter which my Master Tanka has brought up, it is just like the two of us playing a game of *Go*. If you do not respond according to the move I made, I will have caught you off guard. If you experience that this is what has happened, you will be able to grasp Tōzan's intention right off. I cannot help but add the following comment in verse:
>
>> *When he looked inside himself, there was no cold or hot,*
>> *For, in an instant, the vast ocean had dried up to its very*
>>> *last drop.*
>> *I say that I can catch the Great Turtle by just picking It up,*[4]
>> *But I can't help laughing as you go fishing for It in the sand.*

For the moment, let's say that there is a game of *Go*. Well, how about these two players? If we call it 'a two-person game of *Go*', there could be an eight-stone handicap. If there is an eight-stone handicap, it would hardly be a game of *Go*, would it? But if I were to describe it, it would be something like the following: the game of *Go* is simply a player and his opponent encountering each other. Be that as it may, you

---

4.   The Great Turtle is a metaphor for Buddha Nature.

should keep in mind Wanshi's statement, "If you do not respond according to the move I made," focusing on it single-mindedly and, while cloaking yourself in it, make a thorough exploration of it. His saying "If you do not respond according to the move I made" is equivalent to his saying "You can never be me." Do not pass over his saying, "I will have caught you off guard." Within mud, there is the mud. The one who walks in it washes his feet, and also washes his chinstrap.[5] Within a pearl, there is the Pearl. When It is radiant, It illumines both oneself and others.

Meditation Master Kassan Engo was a Dharma heir of Meditation Master Goso Hōen. He once said in verse:

> *The bowl sets the pearl to rolling and the pearl rolls in*
> *the bowl:*
> *The transitory within the Absolute and the Absolute*
> *within the transitory.*[6]
> *The antelope holds onto a tree branch by its horns,*
> *thereby leaving no trace.*
> *When the hunting dogs circle the forest, uncertain, they*
> *seek it in vain.*[7]

The expression here, "the bowl sets the pearl to rolling," is unprecedented and incomparable. It has rarely been heard in past or present. Hitherto, people have merely spoken as if the pearl rolling around in the bowl were something unceasing. The

---

5.　That is, when you go through the mud of training to spiritually aid others, you do not stop at your ankles but go all the way up to your chin.

6.　These two assertions are the first two of the five positions.

7.　It is said that when the *reiyō* (C. *ling-yang*), a type of antelope, sleeps at night, it uses its horns to hoist itself up onto a tree branch. By keeping its legs above the ground, it leaves no trace of its whereabouts, so that hunting dogs cannot find it. This metaphor is used in Chinese Zen to describe someone who has dropped off body and mind, and thereby leaves no trace of an egocentric self for 'hunting dogs' to attack.

antelope is now using his horns to hang onto Emptiness, and the Forest is now circling the hunting dogs.

Meditation Master Setchō Jukēn of Shishō Monastery in Keigen City was a Dharma heir of Venerable Abbot Chimon Kōso. He once said in verse:

> *The dangling of the Master's hands, on the contrary, is*
> *like a veritable cliff ten thousand feet high.*
> *Why do the transitory and the Absolute necessarily need*
> *to be offered a fixed place?*
> *When the bright moon illumines the ancient palace of*
> *lapis lazuli,*
> *The keen black hound, in eager pursuit, vainly bounds up*
> *its stairs.*[8]

---

8. 'Dangling hands' refers to an ancient Chinese practice of raising children without using physical coercion. In Zen, it was used to refer to a Master's approach to training a disciple. Despite the seeming gentleness, it ultimately leads to the disciple ending up at the top of a high cliff, from which he needs to take responsibility for his actions and to step off in full faith. When taking such an action, he is no longer in the position of guest looking up to the Master (host position), but has assumed the host position (acting as a Master acts). This resembles the shift in the *Five Positions* from the perspective of the transitory to that of the Absolute. This is possible because the positioning of Master and disciple is not absolutely fixed.

    Until this shift takes place, the disciple is like a *kanro (C. han-lu)*, a type of black hunting dog associated with a small state in China named Han that flourished during the era of the Warring States (440-221 BCE). This highly intelligent dog was used to hunt down rabbits. In the present poem, the last two lines could be paraphrased as the following: When Buddha Nature shines forth like the full moon, It illumines all transitory things. A disciple, one who is as keen as a hunting dog, may attempt to pursue the Buddha Nature, but becomes confused and mistakes the illumined palace of lapis lazuli (the transitory) for what is Real (the Absolute, represented by the Moon) and vainly chases after that.

Setchō Jukēn was a third generation Dharma heir of Ummon. He could be described as a skin bag* who knew the full satisfaction of having awakened. In saying "The dangling of the Master's hands, on the contrary, is like a veritable cliff ten thousand feet high," he reveals an extraordinarily wondrous standard. Even so, dangling hands may not necessarily be as he describes. The present account of the monk asking Tōzan what he was pointing to is not necessarily about hands dangling or hands not dangling or about renouncing the world or not renouncing the world. Even less does it make use of expressions about the transitory and the Absolute. It is as though people could not lay a hand on this story without making use of the perspective of the transitory and the Absolute. It is like their not having been led by the nose to pay a visit to their Master to ask for instruction and, consequently, they do not arrive at the border of our Founding Ancestor's domain. They therefore fail to catch sight of the great ones of the Buddha Dharma in our monastic family. What is more, they should gather up their straw sandals and go pay visits to other Masters. And they should stop going around slandering the Buddha Dharma of our Founding Ancestor by saying that It is limited to the five positions of the Absolute and the transitory.

Meditation Master Chōrei Shutaku of Tennei Monastery in the Eastern Capital once said in verse:

> *Within the relative, there is the Absolute; within the*
> *Absolute, the transitory,*
> *As centuries by the thousands have drifted by within the*
> *human realm.*
> *How many times have I desired to go back, yet have not*
> *been able to turn back time.*
> *Before my gate, as of old, how luxuriant the weeds!*

Though he also gave full expression to the transitory and the Absolute, nevertheless he has picked up on something. Without denying that he has picked up on something, what is It that exists within the transitory?

Abbot Busshō Hōtai of Mount Daii in Tanchou Province was a Dharma heir of Engo. He once said in verse:

> *For my sake as a monk, you, Tōzan, showed me the*
> *place beyond cold and hot,*
> *And once again a dead tree brought forth a blossom.*
> *People who scratch a mark on their boat in order to*
> *locate their sword are laughable indeed!* [9]
> *To this very day they are still among the cold ashes.*

This expression of his has a bit of the ability to activate one's spiritual question and to pierce right through it.

---

9. An allusion to a story in the Chinese classic, *Spring and Autumn Chronicles*, from which the title of this discourse derives. A man once lost his sword while sailing down a river. He made a scratch on the side of his boat to mark the spot where the sword fell overboard. Despite his efforts to retrieve the sword by looking for it beneath the place where he had scratched, he failed to find it, as the boat had drifted downstream.

Meditation Master Tandō Bunjun of Rokutan once said in verse:

> *At times of heat, you gave yourself up to heat and, at*
> *times of cold, you gave yourself up to cold.*
> *You did not involve yourself with the whys and*
> *wherefores of cold and heat.*
> *Having done the practice until you saw what the*
> *whole wide world really is and remembering*
> *what worldly matters really are,*
> *Your head, my dear Master Tōzan, was crowned with*
> *a boar's-hide cap.*[10]

So, right now, let me ask, what for heaven's sake does he mean by not involving himself? Quickly say! Quickly spit it out!

Meditation Master Kazan Shujun of Huchou Province was a Dharma heir of Zen Master Taihei Bukkan Egon. He once said in verse:

> *The place beyond cold and hot is what Tōzan spoke of,*
> *But ever so many meditators wander off from there.*
> *When it is cold, I just huddle by the fire; when it is hot, I*
> *take advantage of whatever is cool.*
> *All my life, I have been able to escape, warding off both*
> *cold and heat.*

Although this Master is a Dharma grandson of Meditation Master Goso Hōen, his words are like those of a small child. Even so, his saying "All my life, I have been

---

10. 'Master', here, refers to someone who is beyond 'heat and cold', someone who is at one with True Nature. 'The boar's-hide cap' refers to that which is both hot and cold, since it keeps the head warm when the weather is cold. The transitory heat and cold simply ride above his True Nature.

able to escape, warding off both cold and heat" shows promise of his becoming an excellent Master later on. His saying 'all my life' means 'with my whole being' and 'warding off both cold and heat' means 'dropping off body and mind'.

Speaking more generally, even though there have been monastics from ever so many districts and ever so many generations who have beat their drum on both sides, making offerings of eulogies to the ancients, they have not yet caught even a glimpse of what our Founding Ancestor Tōzan was talking about. Were you to ask why, it is because they have not known what 'cold' and 'hot' mean in the everyday life of an Ancestor of the Buddha. So indeed, they vainly speak of huddling by the fire and of taking advantage of whatever is cool. The more the pity that you, Shujun, even though living amidst venerable senior monks, did not hearken to what 'cold' and 'heat' meant. How regrettable that what our Ancestral Master Tōzan said has been abandoned! When we truly know the forms of this 'cold' and 'hot', and have passed through periods of 'cold' and 'hot', and have continually made use of 'cold' and 'hot', it is then that we should make eulogies to the ancients and make commentaries on what our Founding Ancestor Tōzan's words were pointing to for our sakes. Those who have not gone this far cannot even compare with those who know their own shortcomings. Even the worldly are aware of the sun and moon and rely upon the myriad things that arise. And they distinguish among themselves between those who are saintly and those who are wise, as well as between those who are gentle folk and those who are foolish people. Do not make a mistake and mix up the 'cold and hot' that Buddhas speak of with the 'cold and hot' of foolish people. You need simply to be diligent in your practice forthwith.

Delivered to the assembly a second time in the second year of the Kangen era (1244), whilst deep in the mountains of Echizen Province.

I was expounding to the monks the teaching of revolving the Buddhist "Kirin Sutra" when one encounters a Buddha.[11] *As an Ancestral Master once said, "Although there may be many in the assembly who have sprouted a horn, one kirin will suffice."*[12]

---

11. The *Kirin Sutra* is an alternative name for the *Spring and Autumn Chronicles*, the only work directly attributed to Confucius. Dōgen may be expounding what he considers to be a Buddhist equivalent of that text. The *kirin (C. ch'i-lin)* is a fabulous, auspicious beast, considered to be the Far East equivalent of a unicorn. It has the body of a deer, the tail of an ox, the hooves of a horse, and one fleshy horn, with the hair on its back of varied colors and yellow hair on its stomach. It is a metaphor for a Dharma heir who is highly skilled in innumerable means to help others to realize the Truth.

12. This saying by Seigen Gyōshi means that it is fine to have many extraordinary disciples, but having just one Dharma heir will suffice.

65

On Why Our Ancestral Master Came from the West

(Soshi Seirai I)

Translator's Introduction: This short discourse focuses on the question that each trainee is presumably keeping in mind at all times: why have I come to train? This is the spiritual question that permeates everything that the trainee is doing. It is what the trainee needs to get his teeth into and to hold onto, like someone holding onto the branch of a tree with his mouth as he dangles over a thousand foot cliff. It is the Great Matter of life and death, the willingness to risk life and limb in order to realize the Truth.

Great Master Kyōgen Chikan was a Dharma heir of Great Master Isan Reiyū. He once said to his assembly, "Imagine someone climbing up a tree at the edge of a thousand-foot-high cliff.[1] He grabs hold of a branch with his mouth, since he cannot get a hold with his feet and he is unable to pull himself up with his hands. Just at that moment, a man at the bottom of the tree asks him, 'Why did Bodhidharma come from the West?' At such a time, were he to open his mouth to answer the man, he would lose his grip and forfeit his life. Were he not to answer, he would make a mistake due to the nature of what was asked.[2] Speak up! What, for goodness sake, should he do at such a time?"

At that moment, a novice monk named Kotō Shō came forth from the assembly and said, "I have no question about the time when the man has gone up the tree but, Venerable Monk, please tell me, what about the time before he has climbed the tree?"

The Master thereupon broke out in uproarious laughter.

---

1. 'Climbing a tree' is a metaphor for doing one's training and practice.

2. That is, by not answering a spiritual question, he would be acting contrary to the Bodhisattva vow to spiritually help all sentient beings.

Although this dialogue has sparked many discussions and commentaries, few of them have expressed its essence. I am afraid that people, by and large, have been bewildered by it. Even so, in thinking about it, if you make use of 'not deliberately thinking about it', as well as of 'not deliberately thinking about anything', your efforts on your meditation cushion will naturally be like those of our dear old friend Kyōgen.[3] When you sit as still as a mountain on your own cushion, as our dear friend Kyōgen has already done, you too will be exploring this dialogue in detail with him, even though he has not yet opened his mouth. Not only will you be making free use of our dear Kyōgen's Eye to look upon the dialogue, but you will also be using It to break through and see the meaning of Shakyamuni Buddha's Treasure House of the Eye of the True Teaching.

Imagine someone climbing up a tree at the edge of a thousand-foot-high cliff.

We need to thoroughly explore these words in a quiet manner. Who is it that he is calling a 'someone'? We should not say that whoever is not a temple pillar* must necessarily be called 'a piece of lumber'. Even though it was the exalted face of the Buddha along with the face of our Great Ancestor Makakashō that broke into smiles, we should not overlook the fact that we ourselves, as well as others, can also experience this mutual recognition. The place where the person was climbing up the tree was not the whole of the great earth, nor was it the top of a hundred-foot pole. It was a thousand-foot-high cliff. Even should the climber fall off the tree, it would still be within the context of a thousand-foot-high cliff. There are times when one falls and there are times when one climbs. In saying "Imagine someone climbing up a tree at the edge of a thousand-foot-high cliff," we need to recognize that we are saying that there is a time when one is climbing. During that time, the climber is a thousand feet

---

3.   The two methods Dōgen is recommending derive from a narrative concerning Abbot Yakusan Igen, which Dōgen quotes at the beginning of Discourse 26: On Wanshi's 'Kindly Advice for Doing Seated Meditation' (Zazen Shin).

*   See Glossary.

up and it is a thousand feet down. It is a thousand feet on the left and it is a thousand feet on the right. It is also a thousand feet from here and a thousand feet from there. Such a climber, as well as the tree being climbed, is also a thousand feet. The foregoing thousand feet will be just like this. Were you to ask me, "Just how much is a thousand feet," I would answer, "It is like the diameter of the Old Mirror, like the width of the Fireplace, or like the height of a monk's Seamless Stupa." [4]

He grabs hold of a branch with his mouth.

Just what is this 'mouth'? Even if we do not know the expanse of the whole Mouth itself, we may, just for the present, discover the whereabouts of the Mouth by moving along a branch of the tree, thoroughly exploring the branch by nipping off its leaves. It may be that by the very act of gripping the branch of the tree, his Mouth has taken form. Consequently, the whole of his Mouth is the tree: the whole of the tree is his Mouth. His whole body, through and through, is his Mouth: his whole Mouth, through and through, is his body. Because the tree already has a hold on itself, the Master said that the man's feet could not get a hold on the tree, which is like saying that the man's feet could not get a hold on his own feet. Because the branches are pulling themselves up with their branches, the Master said that the man was unable to pull himself up with his hands, which is like his saying that the man's hands were pulling his own hands up. Even so, his feet still go forward and back, and his hands still make a fist and open a fist.[5] Now, people may well think of the man as dangling in space, but how

---

4. That is, like the three examples, it is beyond measure. The 'Old Mirror' refers to the whole universe which, although limitless, constantly reflects the activity of our own mind. The 'Fireplace' is immeasurable because, when the fires of karmic consequence arise, the size of the fireplace is irrelevant in the face of the pain experienced. In construction and sewing, measurements are made along the seams of an object; therefore, a 'Seamless Stupa' is beyond our ability to measure.

5. That is, even though the trainee may not yet have awakened fully, he may still be able to give expression to the Truth.

could dangling in space be an improvement on grabbing hold of a branch with his
Mouth?

>Just at that moment, a man at the bottom of the tree asks
>him, "Why did Bodhidharma come from the West?"

To say that there was a person at the bottom of the tree at that moment is as if the
Master had said that there was a person who was inside the tree, as if there was
something called a 'human tree'. To say that underneath the climber at that very
moment there was a human being who was asking a question would be to express that
very thing. Accordingly, it is 'a tree asking a tree' and 'a man asking a man'. It is 'the
whole tree itself asking the whole question' and 'the whole intent behind
Bodhidharma coming from the West' asking 'why he came from the West'. The one
who is asking the question is the very Mouth grabbing hold of a branch and then
asking. If the Mouth were not grabbing hold of the branch, there could be no asking
of a question, nor any voice to fill the mouth, nor any mouth that was filled with
speech. When we truly ask why Bodhidharma came from the West, we ask by getting
our teeth into why he came from the West.

>Were he to open his mouth to answer the man, he would
>lose his grip and forfeit his life.

Now you need to become intimately familiar with the words, "Were he to open his
mouth to answer the man, he would lose his grip and forfeit his life." It sounds at first
as if the man could actually answer the other without opening his mouth. If this were
really the case, he would not lose his grip and forfeit his life. Even though he has the
choice between opening his mouth and not opening it, this choice will not interfere
with his Mouth's ability to grab hold of the tree branch. Opening and closing are not
necessarily the only functions of the Mouth, and the mouth is capable of both opening
and closing. Thus, grabbing hold of the branch is the everyday behavior of our whole
Mouth and it will not interfere with the mouth's opening and closing. Is 'opening

one's mouth to answer another' the same as 'disgorging the tree branch to answer another' or the same as 'disclosing the intent behind Bodhidharma's coming from the West to answer another'? If the climber does not disclose the intent behind 'Bodhidharma's coming from the West' in order to answer another, then he is not answering the question that was asked.

Not to have answered another is to grasp hold of life with one's whole being; it cannot be called 'losing one's grip and forfeiting one's life'.[6] And if one has already released his grip and forfeited his life, there will not be any answering of the question. Even so, Kyōgen's heart did not refuse to answer others; in all likelihood he had already loosened his grip and forfeited his life. Keep in mind that when we refuse to answer others, we are protecting ourselves and holding onto our life. When we answer in a flash, we turn ourselves around spiritually and activate our True Life. Clearly, what fills the mouth of each and every person is the Truth. We should answer others, and we should answer ourselves; we should ask others, and we should ask ourselves. This is our Mouth holding onto the Truth, for it is our Mouth holding onto the Truth that Kyōgen calls 'holding onto the branch'. When you give your answer to others, you open the Mouth within your mouth. If you do not answer them, even though this may not be in accord with what they are asking, it will be in accord with what you yourself are asking.

So, you need to realize that all the Buddhas and Ancestors have both asked and answered the question as to why Bodhidharma came from the West, and They have all experienced the moment of being up a tree holding onto a branch with Their Mouth, and They all continue to give the answer.

---

6.   That is, it cannot be called 'dropping off body and mind'.

The Venerable Abbot Setchō Jūken once said in verse:

> *It is easy to speak while high up a tree,*
> *It is hard to speak while beneath a tree,*
> *This old monk has climbed that tree,*
> *So come on, ask your question!*

Now, in response to his "Come on, ask your question!" it would be so sad if you were to employ all your strength and then ask your question too late, for your question will have come after his answer. Let me ask all the old sharp ones of past and present, "Is Kyōgen's uproarious laughter what he uttered whilst up the tree, or is it what he uttered whilst beneath the tree? Does it answer why Bodhidharma came from the West or not?" Let's see if you can give it a try!

Delivered to the assembly on the fourth day of the second lunar month in the second year of the Kangen era (March 14, 1244), whilst deep in the mountains of Echizen Province.

Copied on the twenty-second day of the sixth lunar month in the second year of the Kōan era (August 2, 1279), whilst at Eihei-ji Monastery on Mount Kichijō.

66

On the Udumbara Blossom

(Udonge)

Translator's Introduction: The udumbara tree is said to bloom once every three thousand years. It is used to illustrate how rare it is for a Buddha such as Shakyamuni to appear in the world, though many other Buddhas will arise as a result of Shakyamuni's awakening. Although there is a Buddhist tradition that understands His holding the udumbara blossom aloft as a literal fact, there is another tradition which understands this as His holding aloft the flowering of His Buddha Nature for all to see, and that His disciple Makakashō's breaking into a smile of recognition was his way of displaying his own Buddha Nature. All the others who were present on that occasion apparently assumed that only Shakyamuni Buddha could have Buddha Nature, whereas no one else could possibly have It.

Before an assembly of millions on Vulture Peak, the World-honored One held aloft an udumbara flower, His eyes atwinkle. At that time, Makakashō's face broke into a smile. The World-honored One then said, "I have the Treasure House of the Eye of the True Teaching, which is the Wondrous Heart of Nirvana, and I bestow It on Makakashō."

Just as all other Buddhas have done, the Seven Buddhas [*] have likewise held aloft the Flower. Through Their practice and awakening, They too have manifested the raising and holding aloft of Their Flower.

Thus, Their holding the Flower aloft encompasses the picking up of all Flowers by all Buddhas together, regardless of whether the Flowers are being raised or lowered, whether done in recognition of one's own Buddha Nature or of other's, whether pointing within or pointing without. This is the measure of the Flower, the measure of a Buddha, the measure of a mind, the measure of a body. No matter how many times the Flower has been held aloft, each instance has been a Transmitting of Truth to each and every genuine Dharma heir, for this is the very essence of Transmission. Once the Buddha held His Flower aloft, He never parted from It. And

---

[*] See Glossary.

once the Flower held aloft the World-honored One, at that moment the World-honored One became the Flower's Dharma heir. Because the time when one's Flower is held aloft is the whole of time, the whole of time is in harmony both with the World-honored One and with the holding aloft of one's Flower.

'The holding aloft of one's Flower' is the Flower holding the flower aloft; it is represented by such things as the plum blossom, the spring blossoms, the snow-covered blossoms, and the lotus blossom. The five petals displayed by the plum blossom are the more than three hundred and sixty other assemblies wherein He voiced the Dharma, the five thousand and forty-eight volumes of the Scriptures, the Three Vehicles,* the twelve divisions of the Canon, and the bodhisattva* stage of being 'thrice wise and ten times saintly'.* Accordingly, it is beyond the stage of just being thrice wise and ten times saintly. The Great Treasure House with Its extraordinary wonders exists, about which it is said, "When the Flower comes into bloom, the whole world arises." We call the effects of the five petals which open together as one flower 'the natural realization of the Truth', for it is the whole of oneself already being adorned with the whole of one's Self. Reiun Shingon's losing his worldly eyes upon seeing peach blossoms and Kyōgen Chikan's having his worldly hearing disappear at the sound of a pebble striking against a cane of bamboo are instances of their holding the Flower aloft. Great Master Eka's standing waist deep in snow and 'cutting off' his arm, and then later doing prostrations after having realized what Bodhidharma's Marrow is, was the natural opening of his Flower.[1] Enō's pounding rice in a stone mortar until it was purely white and then receiving Daiman Kōnin's kesa* in the middle of the night demonstrated his having already held the Flower aloft. Examples such as these are the roots of Life itself being held within the hands of the World-honored One.

Speaking more generally, holding the Flower aloft already existed before the World-honored One had realized the Truth, and it existed at the same time as the World-honored One's realizing the Truth, and it continues to exist even after the World-honored One's realization of the Truth. Accordingly, the Flower is the realizing

---

1. This reference to Eka's cutting off his arm may refer to giving up one's attachments rather than to a literal, physical act.

of the Truth. The holding of the Flower aloft goes far beyond these divisions of time. The Buddhas' and Ancestors' giving rise to the intention to realize the Truth, Their taking a first step, Their practicing until They awoke, and Their preserving the Truth well have all been instances of Flowers being held aloft, dancing like butterflies on the breezes of spring. Thus, because the World-honored Gautama put His Body into a Flower and concealed His Body within Space, we call His ability to grab hold of His Nose and to grab hold of Unbounded Space 'His holding aloft His Flower'. Holding aloft the Flower is holding It aloft with one's Eye, holding It aloft with the consciousness of one's mind, holding It aloft with one's Nose, and holding It aloft by one's holding aloft a flower.

Generally speaking, the great earth with its mountains and rivers, as well as the sun, moon, wind, and rain, along with humans and animals, grasses and trees, are all being held aloft. Namely, they are the holding aloft of the udumbara flower. Birth and death, coming and going, are also varieties of the Flower. Indeed, they are the brilliant radiance of the Flower. When we explore the Matter[*] in this way, we continue to hold <u>our</u> Flower aloft.

The Buddha once said, "It is like the udumbara flower, which All of Us love and delight in." His saying 'All' refers to Buddhas and Ancestors, both those who reveal Themselves and Those who do not. Theirs is a presence of brilliant radiance, one which grasses and trees, insects and bugs inherently possess. All of us who love this radiance and delight in it describe it as the Skin and Flesh, Bones and Marrow of all beings as they go about like fish freely disporting in the water. Hence, each and every one of us is ultimately an udumbara blossom, a condition that some call 'being rare indeed'!

'His eyes atwinkle' describes the occasion when the Buddha was sitting in meditation at the base of the Bodhi tree and He exchanged His worldly eyes for the brightness of the Morning Star. And there was the occasion when Makakashō's face broke into a smile. He had already broken into the smile, exchanging it for the face of one who was holding his Flower aloft. At that moment when the Tathagata's eyes twinkled, we quickly lost <u>our</u> worldly eyes. This twinkling of the Tathagata's eyes was

His holding the Flower aloft. The udumbara blossom signifies the natural opening up of one's heart.

At the very moment of the flower being held aloft, all Gautamas, all Makakashōs, all sentient beings, all of us, all together, are extending our hands and holding our Flower aloft, and this practice has not ceased even to the present day. Further, because we are in a meditative state in which our whole being keeps itself within our hands, we call this 'being' the four elements* and the five skandhas.*[2]

The Buddha's 'what I have' refers to what He bestows on others and what He confers becomes their 'what I have'.[3] Of necessity, what is given is restricted to what it is that He has.

Your 'what I have' is your crowning glory. When you hold your 'what I have' aloft and exchange it, in turn, for 'what I give you,' you are keeping to the Treasure House of the Eye of the True Teaching. Bodhidharma's coming from the West was his coming to hold the Flower aloft. His holding the Flower aloft is called his delighting in single-minded pursuit of the Way. Delighting in single-minded pursuit of the Way means just control yourself and sit there, dropping off body and mind. Becoming a Buddha or an Ancestor is called delighting in single-minded pursuit of the Way, and putting on one's clothes and eating one's meals is also called delighting in single-minded pursuit of the Way. In short, the most important matter for Buddhas and Ancestors is, without doubt, delighting in single-minded pursuit of the Way.

When those in the Buddha Hall mutually encounter each other spiritually and when those in the Monks' Hall also encounter each other spiritually, they all become more and more endowed with variety in their flowerings, and these flowerings become

---

2.   'Our whole being keeps itself within our hands' refers to our focusing our consciousness within our hands, which are being held in the traditional manner while doing seated meditation.

3.   Namely, the Treasure House of the Eye of the True Teaching, which is the Wondrous Heart of Nirvana.

ever more intense in their hues.[4] And what is more, within the Monks' Hall the wooden *han* is now taken and struck, reverberating to the clouds, while in the Buddha Hall the bamboo *shō* is now blown, reverberating to the bottom of the water.[5] At just such times, my late Master might inadvertently begin to recite a melodious poem about plum blossoms, such as the following:

> *When Gautama lost his worldly eyes,*
> *Only a single branch of plum blossoms appeared amidst*
> > *the snow.*
> *Now everywhere new branches have sprung up*
> *And, laughing, I delight in the spring wind's scattering*
> > *petals in wild disarray.*

The Tathagata's worldly eyes have inadvertently become a Plum Blossom, while the plum blossoms have now become thorny twigs, sprouting up everywhere. The Tathagata keeps His True Self hidden within His Eye, and His Eye keeps Its True Self hidden within the plum blossom, and the plum blossoms keep their True Self hidden within the thorny twigs. The plum blossoms, in response, are now blowing in the spring breeze. Even though this is how things are, it is in peach blossoms that my Master took his delight and joy.

My late Master, the Old Buddha Tendō, once said in verse,

---

4.   The Buddha Hall is the place in the monastery where ceremonies are performed, with senior monks doing the performing. Thus, 'those in the Buddha Hall' is associated with senior monks and 'those in the Monks' Hall' is associated with novices.

5.   A *han* is a wooden plate, or block, that is struck like a gong, whereas the *shō* is an organ-like wind instrument, producing dense, reedy chords. The clouds (J. *un*) and water (J. *sui*) refer to novice monks, who are commonly called *unsui*. Such reverberant, penetrating instrumental sounds are employed in monasteries to aid trainees in shaking themselves free from holding onto body and mind.

> *What Reiun saw were peach blossoms opening:*[6]
> *What I see are peach blossoms scattering.*

Keep in mind that the opening of peach blossoms is what Reiun saw. He expressed it in his poem as, "And straightaway—at that very moment—I arrived, never again to be in doubt." The falling of the petals of the peach blossoms is what Tendō himself saw. The opening of peach blossoms is aroused by the breezes of spring. These winds abhor the scattering of the blossoms' petals. Even though the spring winds abhor the peach blossoms scattering thus, this scattering may well equate with the dropping off of body and mind.

Delivered to the assembly on the twelfth day of the second lunar month in the second year of the Kangen era (March 22, 1244), whilst at Kippō-ji Temple in Echizen Province.

Copied on the sixth day of the second lunar month in the third year of Shōwa (February 20, 1314).

---

6.   The reference to Reiun Shigon is to his poem that capped his kenshō:

> *Thirty years I sought for Him, the Good Friend with*
> *His Sword of Wisdom:*
> *For so many rounds have the leaves fallen and the*
> *branches burst anew with blooms!*
> *But just one glance at those peach blossoms*
> *And straightaway—at that very moment—I arrived,*
> *never again to be in doubt.*

67

On Giving Rise to the Unsurpassed Mind

(Hotsu Mujō Shin)

Translator's Introduction: This discourse was given on the same day as was Discourse 85: On Giving Rise to the Enlightened Mind (*Hotsu Bodai Shin*). Considering the passage that describes how alms should be given to monastics, it is likely that this talk was given for Dōgen's lay disciples.

An important aspect of this discourse is Dōgen's opening remarks concerning metaphors, which offers a clue as to his use of such terms as a blade of grass, trees, tiles, stones, fences, walls, stupas, images of Buddhas, and Buddhas, all of which can readily be understood as references to what is experienced in terms of training disciples.

Our Highest Ancestor in India, Shakyamuni Buddha, once said, "The snow-capped Himalayas are a metaphor for the great nirvana." You need to know that He is speaking metaphorically about something that can be metaphoric. 'Something that can be metaphoric' implies that the mountains and nirvana are somehow intimately connected and that they are connected in a straightforward manner. When He uses the term 'snow-capped Himalayas', He is using the actual snow-capped Himalayas as a metaphor, just as when He uses the term 'great nirvana', He is using the actual great nirvana as a metaphor.

Our First Ancestor in China, Bodhidharma, once said, "Any mind and all minds are like trees and stones." 'Mind' here means 'mind just as it is'. It is the mind that encompasses the whole of the great earth. Therefore, it is the mind of self and the mind of other. Any mind and all minds—those of ordinary worldly humans, those of the Buddhas and Ancestors of the whole universe in all ten directions, those of celestial and demonic beings, among others—are precisely like trees and stones, and there is no mind apart from this. These 'trees and stones' are not made captive by the bonds of 'existence versus non-existence' or 'emptiness versus form'. By means of this mind of trees and stones, we give rise to the Mind that both seeks the Way and does the practice to awaken to It, because these are the trees of our Mind and the stones of our Mind. With the aid of these trees and stones of our Mind, we bring forth what we are thinking about here and now based upon not deliberately thinking about anything in particular. Not until we have encountered what our tradition voices concerning the trees and stones of our Mind can we go beyond the various teachings that non-Buddhists propagate. Before then, we are not on the Buddha's Way.

The National Teacher Echū once said, "The tiles* and stones of our walls and fences are precisely what the mind of Old Buddhas is." We should investigate in detail where, precisely, these tiles and stones of our walls and fences are, and we need to ask ourselves what it is that has appeared in this manner. 'The mind of Old Buddhas' is not something in the far-off fields of the Lord of Emptiness.* It is being satisfied with the morning gruel and being satisfied with the noontime meal. It is being satisfied with the grass and being satisfied with the water.[1] To treat your mind in this way and to sit like a Buddha and act like a Buddha is called 'giving rise to the mind that seeks Buddhahood'. Speaking more generally, the causes and conditions for giving rise to the enlightened Mind do not come from any other place than the mind that seeks to be enlightened, for it is our very mind that is giving rise to the intention to search for Buddhahood. What we call 'giving rise to the mind that seeks to be enlightened' is the offering of a single blade of grass and thereby creating a Buddha, and it is the offering of a rootless tree and thereby creating a Scripture. It is giving alms to a Buddha by offering a handful of sand, and it is giving alms to a Buddha by offering rice water. It is offering a ball of rice to some sentient being or offering five flowers to the Tathagata. To practice some bit of good at the suggestion of another, and to do bows to the Buddha upon having been annoyed by some demon, these too are our giving rise to the mind that seeks to be enlightened. Not only that, it is knowing that

---

* See Glossary.

1. Being satisfied with the grass and water describes a domesticated water buffalo, a metaphor for the contentment experienced by a well-trained and awakened trainee.

one's family home is not one's True Home, and so forsaking home life, leaving family behind in order to enter a mountain monastery and practice the Way, either by relying on faith or upon one's understanding. It is to fashion images of Buddhas and to fashion stupas.* It is to read the Scriptures and to keep the name of Buddha in mind. It is to give expression to the Dharma for the sake of all beings. It is to seek out a True Master and inquire of the Way. It is to sit in full lotus position, to bow to the Three Treasures, and to make "Homage to the Buddha" one's sole invocation.

The causes and conditions of the eighty thousand aggregates that make up the whole of the Dharma, as the preceding statements have expressed, are positively due to giving rise to the intention to realize Buddhahood. There are those who have given rise to the intention in their sleep while dreaming and have realized Buddhahood. And there are those who have given rise to the intention while in a drunken stupor and have realized Buddhahood. And there are those who have given rise to the intention and realized Buddhahood amidst flying flower petals or falling leaves. And there are those who have given rise to the intention and realized Buddhahood amidst peach blossoms or a bamboo grove. And there are those who have given rise to the intention and realized Buddhahood while high in the heavens. And there are those who have given rise to the intention and realized Buddhahood while deep within the ocean. In all these cases, they have given rise to the mind of enlightenment whilst within the enlightened Mind and have given rise to the mind of enlightenment whilst within body and mind. All Buddhas have given rise to an enlightened Mind whilst within body and mind, and They have given rise to an enlightened Mind whilst within the Skin and Flesh, Bones and Marrow of the Buddha's Ancestor, Bodhidharma.

Thus, our present-day fashioning of such things as stupas and images of Buddhas is undoubtedly due to our giving rise to our enlightened Mind; it is our giving rise to the intention to reach Buddhahood forthwith and without giving up midway. This spiritually beneficial activity is free of any attachments. It is a meritorious activity that is free of any striving. It enables us to see the True Nature of all things. This is seeing Dharma Nature. It is the meditative state that beckons to all the Buddhas. It is the invocation that finds all the Buddhas. It is the supreme, fully enlightened Mind. It is the fruition of arhathood.* It is the full manifestation of

Buddhahood. Apart from this, there is no other method that is free of all attachments and free of any striving.

At the same time, there are befuddled folks of the Lesser Course[*] who say:

> To fashion images of the Buddha and raise stupas is to undertake activities that involve attachments. We should put them aside and not engage in them. Bringing a halt to the functioning of the worldly, selfish mind and developing a tranquil spirit is what being free of attachments means. Being free from the cycle of arising and decay and being free from striving is what Reality is. Training oneself single-mindedly to see the Ultimate Reality of Buddha Nature is to be free of attachments.

Talking in this way, they have made this their customary, worldly way of study in India and China in both the past and the present. Accordingly, they do not fashion images or raise stupas, even though they have been fostering serious breakages of Precepts. Caught in the thickets of sensory defilements, they sully themselves, yet they fail to keep the name of Buddha in mind or to read the Scriptures. These are folks who have not only ruined their spiritual potential, which all humans of any sort have, but they have also dismissed out-of-hand the Buddha Nature of the Tathagata. Truly, how pitiful that at a time when they have encountered Buddha, Dharma, and Sangha, they have become sworn enemies of these Three Treasures. Though they have climbed on the mountain of the Three Treasures, they have returned empty-handed; though they have entered the ocean of the Three Treasures, they have returned empty-handed. Even were they to encounter a thousand Buddhas and ten thousand Ancestors coming into the world, there would be no hope of their realizing enlightenment, for they have lost the means for giving rise to that intention. Their situation is like this because they have not followed what is written in the Scriptures or followed a reliable spiritual guide. The situation of many people is like this because they are following non-Buddhist ways and false teachers. You should quickly discard views and opinions such as "Fashioning such things as stupas has nothing to do with attaining spiritual wisdom." Wash your mind clean, wash your body clean, wash your ears clean, wash your eyes clean, and you will neither look at nor pay attention to such views and opinions. Just follow the teachings of the Buddha, follow good spiritual guides, keep coming back to the True Teaching, and explore through your training with your Master what the Buddha Dharma is.

In the Great Way of the Buddha Dharma, the Scriptures of the whole universe exist within a single mote of dust, and all the Buddhas beyond measure exist within a single mote of dust. There is not a tree or a blade of grass that is separate from our body and mind. When the myriad thoughts and things do not arise, our whole mind also does not arise, and since this is the True Form of all thoughts and things, It is the true form of every single mote of dust. Accordingly, our whole mind is all thoughts and things, and all thoughts and things are our whole mind, our whole being. If there were a time when such things as fashioning stupas involved attachments, then the enlightenment that is the fruit of Buddhahood and the Buddha Nature, which is what is real, would also involve attachments. Because that which is real, namely, the Buddha Nature, is not involved in attachments, the fashioning of Buddhist images and the raising of stupas likewise do not involve attachments. Buddha Nature is the mind that is free of attachments and whose intention is to realize Buddhahood; it is the meritorious activity that is free of attachments and free of delusions. You should firmly trust and understand that such things as the fashioning of Buddhist images and the raising of stupas are simply a manifestation of the mind that seeks enlightenment. Such efforts to fulfill the wish to help rescue all sentient beings have been fostered over millions of eons, for they are the giving rise to the intention to realize Buddhahood over millions and millions of eons. We call this encountering Buddha and hearkening to His Teaching.

You need to keep in mind that gathering wood and stones, collecting up mud and earth, gathering gold and silver, as well as the seven precious jewels,[*] in order to fashion an image of the Buddha or to raise a stupa, and the gathering up of one's whole mind in order to fashion a stupa or fashion an image are our piling the Boundless upon the boundless to create a Buddha, our holding aloft the Mind of the mind to fashion a Buddha, our piling a stupa upon the Stupa to fashion a stupa, our making manifest the Buddhahood of a Buddha to fashion a Buddha. This is why the *Lotus Scripture* says, "When we pay attention to such matters, all the Buddhas in the ten quarters appear." Understand that when one person realizes Buddhahood by paying attention to such matters, all the Buddhas in the ten quarters appear by paying attention to such matters. And when one person realizes Buddhahood by one thought or thing, it is all thoughts and things realizing Buddhahood.

Shakyamuni Buddha once said, "When I saw the morning star emerge, I was enlightened simultaneously with the whole of the great earth and all its sentient beings." Accordingly, giving rise to the intention, doing the training and practice, awakening, and realizing nirvana will be giving rise to the intention, doing the training and practice, awakening, and realizing nirvana, and all at the same time. The body and mind of which the Buddha spoke encompasses grasses and trees, tiles and stones, as well as wind and rain, water and fire. Finding ways to make use of these in order to help realize what the Buddha said is precisely what giving rise to the intention to realize Buddhahood is. Fashion your stupas and your images of Buddha by taking hold of the Unbounded, and fashion your images of Buddha and your stupas by using both your hands to scoop up Water from the mountain stream, for such actions are your giving rise to supreme, fully perfected enlightenment. And so, throughout hundreds of thousands of myriad eons, this is how one person's giving rise to the intention to realize Buddhahood manifests, which is the same as doing the training and awakening to the Truth.

At the same time, when you hear that giving rise to the intention to realize Buddhahood is a one-time thing, after which one does not experience the rising of the intention again, and that even though one's training and practice are beyond measure, the fruits of awakening are a one-time event, you are not hearing the Buddha Dharma, you are not comprehending the Buddha Dharma, you are not encountering the Buddha Dharma. The intention that arises in the mind millions of times is, beyond doubt, an arising that is a singular arising of the intention. And the arising of the intention in millions of people is a singular arising of the intention. And a singular arising of the intention is millions of arisings of the intention. Training and enlightenment, as well as turning the Wheel of the Dharma, are also just like this. And it is like this because, if you were unaware of such things as grasses and trees, how could you possibly have a body and a mind? And if you had no body or mind, how could you possibly know of grasses and trees? And if you were unaware of grasses and trees, there would be no grasses and trees for you.[2] Practicing the Way by doing meditation is giving rise to the intention to realize Buddhahood. The arisings of the intention transcend sameness or difference. The instances of doing meditation transcend sameness or difference, and they transcend something occurring just two or three times, and they transcend being something to be rid of. You need to thoroughly explore each and every thing in this way. If the whole procedure, from beginning to end, of bringing together grasses and trees, as well as the seven treasures, in order to fashion stupas and Buddhist images were activities that involved attachments, then enlightenment would not be possible and the thirty-seven methods of training to realize enlightenment would also be activities that involve attachments.[3]

As to the matter of the body and mind of humans in the three temporal worlds—be they humble or lofty—if they were to undertake the training and practice whilst being all involved with attachments, it would not be possible for them to reach the Ultimate. Grasses and trees, tiles and stones, as well as the four elements* and the five skandhas,* are likewise 'just mind': they are likewise what the True Form of all things is. The whole universe in all ten quarters, as well as the True Nature of all things, which is Buddha Nature, are likewise manifestations of Truth. Within the True Nature of all things, which is Buddha Nature, how could there possibly be such things as grasses and trees? And how could such things as grasses and trees not be Buddha Nature, which is the True Nature of all things? All thoughts and things are not involved with attachments, nor are they free of attachments: they are the Real Form. The Real Form is the real form of all things just as they are, and being just as they are is synonymous with our body and mind at this very moment, here and now. By means of this body and mind of ours, we can give rise to the intention to realize Buddhahood. Therefore, do not despise treading on water or treading on rocks. While holding a single blade of grass aloft, we create a golden body sixteen feet high, and while

2.　'Grasses and trees' is a Zen term for all manner of things that sprout up and flourish for a while.

3.　These thirty-seven methods are the topic of Discourse 70: On the Thirty-seven Methods of Training for Realizing Enlightenment (Sanjūshichihon Bodai Bumpō).

holding aloft a single mote of dust, we construct a stupa for our dear Old Buddha. These activities are manifestations of our having given rise to the heart of Wisdom. It is our encountering Buddha, our heeding Buddha, our becoming Buddha, and our putting Buddha into practice.

Shakyamuni Buddha once said:

> You lay men and lay women who are my virtuous sons and daughters, make alms offerings to the Three Treasures—Buddha, Dharma, and Sangha—with the flesh of your spouses and children, and make alms offerings to the Three Treasures with your own flesh. How can all the monks who have already received the alms you've offered in good faith possibly fail to do their training?

So, be aware that making alms offerings to the Three Treasures of such things as food, clothing, bedding, medicine, lodging for monks, cultivated lands, and woodlands is your making alms offerings of your own flesh and skin, bones and marrow, as well as those of your spouse and children. Having already entered the Three Treasure's ocean of meritorious activity, you are therefore all of one and the same flavor. Because you are all of one and the same flavor, you <u>are</u> the Three Treasures. The meritorious activity of the Three Treasures has already manifested in the skin and flesh, bones and marrow of your own body, as well as that of your spouse and children, for it is your diligence in doing your utmost to practice the Way. Now, joining with the True Nature and form of the World-honored One, you should explore the Skin and Flesh, Bones and Marrow of the Buddha's Way. This present alms offering of your very being is your giving rise to the intention to realize Buddhahood, so how could those monks who received your offering possibly fail to do the practice, and do it correctly from start to finish? Accordingly, no sooner does a single particle of thought arise than your Whole Mind will in an instant follow suit and give rise to your intention. When your Whole Mind arises right off, Unbounded Space will soon emerge.

In short, even when saintly ones and arhats awaken to the Mind that gives rise to the intention to realize Buddhahood, they will be able, right off, to plant Buddha

Nature's seed.[4] Should they then do the training and practice devotedly by embracing the four elements and the five skandhas, they will realize the Way, or should they then do the training and practice devotedly by embracing grasses and trees, fences and walls, they will realize the Way because, in both their substance and their inherent nature, the four elements and the five skandhas are the same as grasses and trees, tiles and stones, and because they are also the same in mind and in life, as well as in body and in function.

Accordingly, within the assemblies of the Buddhas and Ancestors there have been many who did their utmost to practice the Way by taking up the mind that focused on grasses and trees. This is behavior arising from the Mind that seeks enlightenment. As a person of the Way, the Fifth Ancestor, Daiman Kōnin, once planted a pine tree. Rinzai made the effort to plant cedar and pine trees on Mount Ōbaku. And there was the old man of the Ryū clan who planted pines on Mount Tōzan. By practicing the constancy of the pine and cypress, they scraped out the Eye of the Buddhas and Ancestors.[5] This displayed their ability to take pleasure in their living Eye, which is the Eye enlightened.

Fashioning such things as stupas and images of Buddhas is the Eye taking Its pleasure. It is to taste the arising of the intention to realize Buddhahood: it is to make use of the arising of this intention. If there were no attaining of the Eye for such things as fashioning stupas, there would be no awakening to the Truth by the Buddhas and Ancestors. After attaining an Eye for fashioning Buddhas, one creates Buddhas and creates Ancestors. Were someone to say, "Such fashioned things as stupas are ultimately reduced to dust and dirt, and so they have no real merit, whereas cultivating 'nothing arising' is stable practice because it is not tainted by the dust and dirt of the world," these would not be the words of a Buddha. If stupas are reduced to dust and

---

4. 'Saintly ones and arhats' refers to those doing their training within the Lesser Course. The terms do not imply that such persons are necessarily monastics.

5. Because the pine and the cypress trees do not lose their foliage even in the severest of winters, they have been used in the East as a common metaphor for friends who remain constant in adversity. To 'scrape out' the Eye of the Buddhas and Ancestors means to fully absorb Their spiritual Teaching and to make It one's own.

dirt, then the state of 'non-arising' will also be reduced to dust and dirt. If the state of 'non-arising' is not reduced to dust and dirt, then stupas likewise will not be reduced to dust and dirt. <u>Right here</u> is where the What is! To give expression to having attachments is to give expression to being free of attachments.

The Tathagata said in the *Avatamsaka Scripture*:

> When Bodhisattvas[*] give rise to the intention to realize Buddhahood and make birth-and-death the foremost issue, they wholeheartedly seek enlightened Wisdom and, being steadfast, they will not waver. The meritorious functioning of that single-mindedness is deep and vast, knowing no bounds. If I were to analyze and explain it, I would be unable to exhaust the topic, even if I had eons to do it.

You need to be clear about this: using the issue of birth-and-death to give rise to your intention to realize Buddhahood is to wholeheartedly seek enlightened Wisdom. This wholeheartedness must be as a single blade of grass or a single tree, because it is your single moment of life and your single moment of death. Even so, the depth of this meritorious activity is beyond any bounds, and its vastness is also beyond any bounds. Even were the Tathagata to speak for eons of time describing this meritorious activity, He could not fully exhaust the topic even then. He could not fully exhaust it because one's Mind remains after one's death, just as the bottom of the sea remains after the sea has dried up. It is like seeking far and wide for the boundaries of this wholeheartedness, which is as boundless as the depth and vastness of a single blade of grass or a single tree, or of a stone or a tile. When the single blade of grass or the single stone is seven or eight feet tall, so such a one's wholeheartedness is likewise seven or eight feet tall, and his heart that seeks the Way is also seven or eight feet tall.

Thus, entering into the depths of the mountains to ponder the Buddha's Way may well be easy, whereas to fashion a stupa or fashion a Buddha is ever so hard. Though both approaches are ripened by diligence and strenuous effort, the one makes use of the mind and the other is being used by the Mind, which is different by far.

Time after time, giving rise to the enlightened Mind in this way makes the Buddhas and Ancestors manifest.

Delivered to the assembly at Kippō-ji Temple in Echizen Province on the fourteenth day of the second lunar month in the second year of the Kangen era (March 24, 1244).

Copied at Eihei-ji Temple on the tenth day of the third lunar month in the second year of the Kōan era (April 22, 1279).

Ejō

68

On the Universal Body of the Tathagata

(Nyorai Zenshin)

Translator's Introduction: This short discourse is based on passages from the *Lotus Scripture*. In it, Dōgen discusses the Buddha (the Awakened One) as the Tathagata (the One Who Comes Thus), that is, as someone who has completely dropped off self and now simply is, just as He is. The body of One who is a Tathagata is no longer a matter of something personal but embraces the whole universe and is, therefore, the Universal Body. This Universal Body incorporates all that the historical Buddha leaves behind, such as His relics. And His Universal Body includes not only these relics but also His teachings, particularly in the form of written, bound copies.

Once when Shakyamuni Buddha was residing on Vulture Peak at Rajagriha, He addressed Lord Bhaisajya the Bodhisattva*- Mahasattva* of Healing, saying, "Lord Bhaisajya, in every place where this Teaching of Mine is voiced, or read, or recited aloud, or written down, or stored where bound copies of the Scriptures are kept, you should erect a seven-jeweled* stupa,* one that is especially tall, broad, and well adorned. There is no need to install a relic within it.[1] And why? Because the Universal Body of the Tathagata already exists within this stupa. This stupa should be presented with alms, revered, highly honored, and eulogized by your offering all kinds of flowers and incense, jeweled garlands and silken canopies, banners and flags, music and songs of praise. If there are people who are able to catch sight of this stupa and thereupon bow in respect and offer alms, by all means you should

---

* See Glossary.

1. A relic (J. shāri; Skt. śarīra) customarily consisted of some physical part of a deceased Buddha or Ancestor, such as ashes, bones, or hair.

926

realize that they are approaching supreme, fully perfected enlightenment."

What He called 'bound copies of Scriptures' are like what has been voiced, what has been read, what has been recited, and what has been written down. Bound copies of Scripture are what True Nature is. The True Nature of the seven-jeweled stupa that needs to be erected is called the Stupa. As to the ultimate measure of Its height and breadth, that measure is, of necessity, the measure of True Nature. The Universal Body of the Tathagata that already exists within this Stupa refers to the bound Scriptures, which is synonymous with the Universal Body.

Accordingly, Teachings that have been voiced, read, recited, and written down are what the Universal Body of the Tathagata is. This is why we should make offerings to, revere, highly honor, and eulogize It by presenting It with all kinds of flowers and incense, jeweled garlands and silken canopies, banners and flags, music and songs of praise. Offerings may be such things as celestial flowers, celestial incense, and celestial canopies because these are all True Nature. Or they may be the choicest of flowers and incense, or kesas* and robes esteemed among ordinary people for these are all True Nature. Offerings of alms and offerings of reverence are what True Nature is.

You should erect a Stupa, reminding yourself that there is no need to install a relic within It, for you know that bound Scriptures are the relics of the Tathagata and are part of the Universal Body of the Tathagata. Beyond doubt, these Scriptures are golden words that came from the Buddha's mouth, and there can be no spiritually beneficial endeavor that surpasses seeing and hearing them. Be quick to accumulate merit and pile up virtuous acts. If there are people who bow in reverence to this Stupa and make an offering to It, keep in mind that they are all approaching supreme, fully perfected enlightenment. When we catch sight of this Stupa, we should, in all sincerity, respectfully bow and make an offering to It. Then we will all be close to supreme, fully perfected enlightenment. 'Being close' does not mean 'being close after being separate from', nor does it mean 'being close after coming together'; 'being close' refers to one's enlightenment being supreme and fully perfected. When we experience, here and now, the receiving and passing on, reading and reciting, understanding and expressing, writing and copying of Scriptures, it is our catching sight of this Stupa. We should rejoice, for we are all close to supreme, fully perfected enlightenment.

Well now, the bound copies of the Scriptures are the Universal Body of the Tathagata. Bowing in respect to copies of Scripture is bowing in respect to the Tathagata. To have encountered copies of Scripture is to have an audience with the Tathagata, for copies of Scripture are relics of the Tathagata and relics of the Tathagata are these Scriptures. Even if you have learned that copies of Scriptures are relics, if you do not know that relics refers to copies of Scriptures, then you have not yet arrived at what the Buddha was saying. The True Nature of all things here and now is what copies of Scripture are. The world of humans as well as celestial worlds, the oceans as well as empty space, this planet of ours as well as other worlds are all True Nature; they are all copies of Scriptures; they are all relics. Receiving and passing on, reading and reciting, understanding and expressing, writing and copying Scriptures creates relics and will open the way to enlightenment. This is what is meant by the phrase, 'following the Scriptures'. There are the relics of former Buddhas, and the relics of present-day Buddhas, and the relics of pratyekabuddhas,* and the relics of Wheel-turning Lords,* and the relics of those who are veritable lions among men, as well as the relics of wooden Buddhas, and the relics of painted Buddhas, and the relics of human beings. Buddhas and Ancestors during the present-day generations in Great Sung China are letting Their relics show while They are still alive, and many are producing relics with Their cremation: these are all copies of Scripture.

Once, when addressing a large assembly, Shakyamuni Buddha said, "The lifetime to which I succeeded by traveling the Bodhisattva Way has not even yet been exhausted, but will still be twice the past number of eons." Our present eighty-four gallons of relics are, frankly, what the life of a Buddha is.[2] A lifetime of practicing the Bodhisattva Way is, from the start, not limited merely to the three-thousand great-

---

2.   'Eighty-four gallons of relics' is an estimate of the average size of a human body.

thousandfold world; it can be something beyond calculation, as is the Universal Body of the Tathagata, and as are the bound copies of Scripture.

The Bodhisattva Who Accumulates Wisdom said:

> I have seen Shakyamuni the Tathagata pursue the Bodhisattva Way without ever ceasing, doing difficult and painful practices for incalculable eons, and thereby accumulating merit and piling up virtue. When I have looked at the three-thousand great-thousandfold world, there is no place even the size of a mustard seed where, as a Bodhisattva, He has not laid down his life for the sake of others. And because of that He was able to fully experience the path to enlightenment.

Be clear about this, this three-thousand great-thousandfold world is a single instance of a sincere and trusting heart, and it is a single instance of emptiness of self, and it is the Universal Body of the Tathagata, which does not depend on our laying down our life or on our not laying it down. Relics are beyond being something prior to a Buddha or after a Buddha, and they are not something that lines up beside a Buddha. Performing difficult and painful practices for immeasurable eons has been the daily activity of the Buddha's womb and the Buddha's hara;[3] these practices are the Buddha's Skin and Flesh, Bones and Marrow. As has been said of Him, "He has never ceased to be." Even after becoming an Awakened One, He practiced ever more vigorously, and even though He has transformed our great-thousandfold world, He still goes forward. The everyday life of His Universal Body is no different.

Given to the assembly at Kippō-ji Temple in the Yoshida district of Echizen Province on the fifteenth day of the second lunar month in the second year of the Kangen era (March 25, 1244).

---

3.   The Buddha's womb is the source from which all things are produced by one's Buddha Nature. The Buddha's hara is the place from which the Child of the Lord is born.

Copied while in the monks' quarters at Eihei Zen Temple on the twenty-third day of the sixth lunar month in the second year of the Kōan era (August 2, 1279).

69

On the Meditative State
That Is the Lord of Meditative States

(Zammai-ō Zammai)

Translator's Introduction: A meditative state is a state of the mind in meditation. In this discourse, Dōgen explores the ultimate form of these meditative states, one that arises when one understands seated meditation as more than what the mind or body experiences during formal seated meditation.

Throughout this discourse he uses the term *kekkafuza*, which is traditionally rendered as 'to sit in full lotus position', but such a translation is apt to be understood only on a literal, physical level. By contrast, when one's legs are folded into the lotus position, they indeed form a lotus, as the term implies. Hence one is, in effect, doing one's meditation while seated on a lotus. Iconographically, this is a traditional sitting place for Buddhas, and it is, more specifically, the meditation seat of Vairochana, the Cosmic Buddha, whom Scriptures describe as appearing atop Shakyamuni Buddha's head when He is doing seated meditation. Thus, to sit in meditation like Vairochana is to sit upon a lotus throne. This is true regardless of the physical posture of the body. To point to this non-physical aspect, the phrase *kekkafuza* is rendered in the present translation as 'to sit as if sitting within a lotus blossom'.

Further, as Dōgen has pointed out already on a number of occasions, 'doing seated meditation' has a broader meaning than just doing formal meditation sittings. It also refers to maintaining the mind of meditation in whatever one does. Dōgen expresses this broader meaning in the course of this discourse.

Going beyond the whole universe at full speed and then living a valued and greatly honored life within the dwelling place of the Buddhas and Ancestors is what sitting as if sitting within a lotus blossom is all about. Leaping over the heads of non-Buddhists and gangs of bedevilers and then, within the inner chambers of the Buddhas and Ancestors, becoming someone who has realized the intent of the Buddha Dharma is what sitting as if sitting within a lotus blossom is all about. In order to go beyond the outermost limits, which is where the Buddhas and Ancestors are found, there is just this one method. Therefore, the Buddhas and Ancestors have engaged in this method without having any other practice.

By all means keep in mind that the universe of seated meditation is something a long way off from other universes. Having clarified this principle, the Buddhas and Ancestors have undertaken to do Their utmost to give rise to the intention to awaken, to do the training and practice, and to realize spiritual Wisdom and the freedom of nirvana. At the very moment of sitting, you should thoroughly explore through your training whether the whole universe is that which is vertical or that which is horizontal.[1] At the very moment of sitting, just what is that 'sitting'? Is it our mind doing somersaults? Or is it like a fish freely disporting in water? Or is it thinking about something? Or is it striving after something? Or not striving after anything? No, it is sitting within sitting, sitting within body and mind, dropping everything off within sitting and within body and mind, and just sitting! In this way, you need to thoroughly explore through your training the thousands of aspects, nay, the hundreds of thousands of aspects of just sitting. Your body should just sit as if you were sitting within a lotus blossom.

My late Master, an Old Buddha, once said:

> Doing the practice of meditation is the dropping off of body and mind. To accomplish this, right off, is the purpose of seated meditation practice. "Just control yourself and sit there!"[2] You don't have to offer incense, do prostrations, chant the name of Buddha, repent of anything, or read Scriptures.

It is clear that over the past four or five hundred years, only my late Master has scraped out the Eye of the Buddhas and Ancestors and just sat within this Eye. There have

---

1.   'Vertical' refers to space, which at any given moment contains everything without anything being added or taken away, whereas 'horizontal' refers to time, which is the ever-changing flow of moments of now, wherein all is in constant flux. These two perspectives are explored in depth by Dōgen in Discourse 11: On 'Just for the Time Being, Just for a While, For the Whole of Time is the Whole of Existence' (Uji), which literally translates as 'Existence and Time'.

2.   This is a translation of the oft-used Japanese term shikan taza.

been few in China who stood head-and-shoulders with him. Few have clarified that 'just sitting there' was the method of the Buddha, whereas the Buddha Dharma is "Just sit there!" Even if some appear to understand physical sitting to be what the Buddha taught, they have not yet grasped that 'sitting there' means "Just sit there!"[3] Much less can they keep to and preserve the Buddha Dharma as the Buddha's Teaching!

Hence, there is the mind's just sitting there, which is not the same as the body's just sitting there. And there is the body's just sitting there, which is not the same as the mind's just sitting. There is 'just sitting there with body and mind having dropped off', which is not the same as 'just sitting in order to drop off body and mind'. To have already realized such a state is the perfect oneness of practice and understanding that the Buddhas and Ancestors have experienced. Maintain and safeguard your mind's functions of remembering, considering, and reflecting. Thoroughly explore through your training what mind, intent, and consciousness truly are.

Shakyamuni Buddha, in addressing His great assembly, once said:

> If you sit as if sitting within a lotus blossom, you will experience a meditative state within your body and mind which will have such dignity and virtue that people will respect and venerate it. This meditative state will be like a sun illumining the whole world. It will eradicate sleepiness, laziness, and brooding from the mind. The body will become light, without creating a feeling of fatigue. And whatever arises as enlightenment will also be light and accommodating. Your sitting peacefully will be like a dragon's coiling up. Just seeing a picture of someone seated within a lotus blossom is enough to frighten the Lord of Demons, and how much more so, should he actually see someone who is experiencing the Truth whilst sitting peacefully without any agitation?

---

3.   That is, neither trying to think nor trying not to think.

So, even the Lord of Demons is startled, troubled, and frightened when he encounters an illustration of someone seated within a lotus blossom.[4] How much more so were you to actually sit as if sitting within a lotus blossom, for the spiritual benefits from doing this cannot be measured. The joy and virtue of just sitting there on an everyday basis is beyond measure.

Shakyamuni Buddha, in addressing His great assembly, continued, saying, "This is why we sit as if sitting within a lotus blossom." The World-honored Tathagata then taught each of His disciples how they should sit in this way. Some non-Buddhists always stand on their tiptoes when seeking the Way, some always stand upright when seeking the Way, and some hike their feet up on their shoulders when seeking the Way. Confused and rigid minds like these sink into a sea of hindrances, their bodies knowing no tranquility. This is why the Buddha taught His disciples to sit as if sitting within a lotus blossom with their body upright. And why? Because when the body is upright, the mind is easy to set properly. When the body sits upright, the mind does not tire. Once the mind is regulated and its intent is proper, the mind is held to what is right before it. If the mind starts galloping off or becomes scattered, or if the body starts leaning or shifting about, sitting upright will remove these effects and bring you back. When you want to realize a meditative state and desire to enter into a meditative state, even if you are galloping off in all directions or are wildly scattered, sitting upright will bring all these completely back to normal. Doing the practice in this way lets you awaken to and enter the meditative state that is the lord of meditative states.

Be clear about this, sitting as if sitting within a lotus blossom is what the meditative state that is the lord of meditative states is; it is what entering into spiritual realization is. All meditative states are members of the family of the meditative state that is the lord. Sitting as if sitting within a lotus blossom means keeping your body upright, and keeping your mind upright, and keeping your body-and-mind upright, and keeping the Buddhas and Ancestors upright, and keeping your training and

4.   The Lord of Demons is often referred to as Māra and is the personification of the selfish self.

enlightenment upright, and keeping the crown of your head upright, and keeping the very pulse of your lifeblood upright.

Now, by forming a lotus with our human skin, flesh, bones, and marrow, we form a lotus within the meditative state that is the lord of meditative states. The World-honored One constantly maintained, and entrusted to us, the practice of sitting as if sitting within a lotus blossom, and Transmitted this 'sitting as if sitting within a lotus blossom' to His disciples, and had the practice of sitting as if sitting within a lotus blossom taught to ordinary people and to those in lofty positions. This is precisely what the Mind seal* that the Seven Buddhas* accurately Transmitted is.

Shakyamuni Buddha sat Himself under the Bodhi tree as if He were sitting within a lotus blossom as He let pass fifty small eons, then sixty eons, then immeasurable eons. Whether you sit as if sitting within a lotus blossom for three weeks or for a few hours, it is your turning of the wondrous Wheel of the Dharma and your lifelong edification of the Buddha. Further, when you do not flag or slacken, this will be your 'yellowed scrolls with their red scroll rods'.[5] This is the occasion of Buddha meeting Buddha. This is the very moment when sentient beings become Buddhas.

After his arrival from the West, our First Chinese Ancestor, the Venerable Bodhidharma, sat as if he were sitting within a lotus blossom while facing a wall at Shōrin-ji Temple on a peak in the Sū mountain range for nine autumns. From that time up to this very day, the Eye atop the crown of his head has spread throughout the whole of China. The lifeblood of our First Ancestor is, simply, being seated as if sitting within a lotus blossom. Before our First Ancestor arrived in China, the people there had not yet heard of sitting as if sitting within a lotus blossom. They only learned about it after our First Ancestor came from the West.

---

*   See Glossary.

5.   'Yellowed scrolls with their red scroll rods' is a Buddhist reference to the Scriptures. It describes the form in which Scriptures were originally preserved.

As this is so, just control yourself and sit day and night as if you were sitting within a lotus blossom, for the whole of your life and for myriad lives to come, without leaving your monastery and without doing any other practice, for this is what the meditative state that is the lord of meditative states is.

Delivered to the assembly at the Kippō-ji Temple in Echizen Province on the fifteenth day of the second lunar month in the second year of the Kangen era (March 25, 1244).

Written down in the quarters of the Abbot's assistant on the same mountain on the same night.

Ejō

Compared against the original and corrected on the first day of autumn in the first year of the Bun'ō era (August 9, 1260).

70

On the Thirty-Seven Methods of Training
for Realizing Enlightenment

(Sanjūshichihon Bodai Bumpō)

Translator's Introduction: These thirty-seven methods derive from early Buddhist scriptures. Although they have customarily been taken in a literal sense, Dōgen chooses to explore deeper spiritual implications of these Teachings.

Of particular notice in this discourse is Dōgen's discussion of the Noble Eightfold Path, in which he has added a lengthy and spirited commentary on Right Action. There are some who may be disturbed by the strong rhetoric that Dōgen uses in this section. There are times when a Zen Master uses strong language, as it may be the only way for a Master to help cut through their disciples' delusions so that they may reconsider what they are doing. Also, many of Dōgen's expressions would not have seemed as highly charged in his time and culture as they seem in today's Western culture. This section focuses on the relationship between those who are lay trainees and those who are monastics. Dōgen's target in this section is quite clear: that flattering and manipulating bunch who curry worldly favors, seeking to be labeled as a Zen Master by some sovereign or minister of state, simply because they go around spouting that there is really no difference between what is going on in the mind of someone involved in affairs of state and what is going on in the mind of a Shakyamuni Buddha. He then endeavors to point out what the difference is between those who have chosen to remain in home life (J. *zaike*) and those who have chosen to leave home life behind (J. *shukke*): even the best of lay trainees cannot realize supreme, fully perfected enlightenment (Buddhahood) unless they ultimately leave home life behind because the pull of secular demands is too great and time-consuming, and anything less than a full commitment will simply not be sufficient. He then takes up the cases of various lay people, specifically including Vimalakirti (J. *Yuima*) who had long served as a Zen Buddhist model for lay trainees, whom 'that bunch' claim had realized full Buddhahood without having to leave lay life behind. However, despite what may seem on first reading to be Dōgen's dismissal of lay trainees, with a closer reading it appears that what he is really attacking is the notion that, since there is no difference between the mind of a lay person and that of a monk, monastic life is irrelevant to the realization of Buddhahood and that, since lay people are enlightened just as they are, they therefore need not train. When this section of Dōgen's discourse is seen in relation to what he has been teaching so far, the relevance of his message for lay trainees might be summed up as, "Do not give up on your training, for training and enlightenment are synonymous, and do not do the practice in order to become a Buddha, but simply do it to fulfill your Bodhisattva vow to help all sentient beings, including yourself, realize their True Nature."

The Buddhas of old had a system of study, namely, the learning, practicing, and confirming of thirty-seven methods of training for realizing enlightenment. These methods deal with the variations and stages in training and are also the methods used for grappling with one's spiritual question. They are the means for producing all the Buddhas and Ancestors.

The Four Abodes of Reflection
also called the Four Focal Points of Reflection

First, reflecting on the impurity of body
Second, reflecting on how what our senses perceive
leads to suffering
Third, reflecting on the impermanence of our mental
functions
Fourth, reflecting on how all thoughts and things are
devoid of a permanent, unchanging self

'Reflecting on the impurity of body' means reflecting on our present fleshly body as being the Whole Universe in all ten quarters, because that is what our true Body is. The reflection that our body is impure is what springs up again and again when we are on the Absolute Way. Were it not to spring up, reflection upon it would not be possible. It would be as if we lacked a body. It would be as if doing the practice were impossible. It would be as if giving full expression to It were impossible. It would be as if fully reflecting on anything were impossible. But since you have already had manifestations of the possibility of reflection, you should recognize that it can spring up again and again. 'The possibility of reflection' refers to our everyday actions, such as sweeping the ground and sweeping the floor. Because we sweep the ground in any given month, and because we sweep the ground and sweep the floor punctually during the second lunar month, the whole of the great earth is just as it is.[1]

The body's reflecting refers to your reflecting on your own body. It is not using the body to reflect on anything else. And this very act of reflection means that That Which Is Superlative has appeared. When your reflecting on your body has appeared, your reflecting on your Mind may be searched for but you have not yet made contact with It, for It has not yet appeared. Thus, when you reflect on your body, it is the manifesting of the Diamond Samadhi and the Bravely Going On Samadhi, and these are both reflections on the body's not being pure.[2]

Speaking more generally, we call the principle of seeing the morning star in the middle of the night as seeing that the body is not pure. It has nothing to do with the issue of being clean versus being unclean. When there is a body, it is not pure; when bodily excretions manifest, they are not pure. To explore the Matter* in this way, when demons become Buddhas, they use their demon to defeat their demon in order to become a Buddha.[3] When Buddhas become Buddhas, They take up Their Buddha Nature to fathom Their Buddha Nature and become a Buddha. When ordinary humans become Buddhas, they take up their humanity to harmonize their humanity and become a Buddha. By all means, you should thoroughly explore the principle that there is a pathway to be taken up.

For instance, it is like the method of washing clothes. The water is dirtied by the clothes, whereas the clothes are washed clean. Whether we use this soiled water to do our laundry or change this water to continue washing, we are still using water and still washing our clothes. If the clothes do not appear to be clean after one or two

---

1.   That is, we do our daily actions, whether we are aware of what time it is or not. In the Japanese calendar, the second lunar month coincides with the beginning of spring.

2.   The Diamond Samadhi is the meditative state that is like the one described in the Diamond-cutting Scripture, whereas the Bravely Going On Samadhi is that meditative state described in the Scripture of Bravely Going On (J. Shuryōgon Kyō; S. Shurangama Scripture).

*   See Glossary.

3.   In Buddhism, the term 'demon' is often used to refer to defiling passions.

washings, do not stop from weariness and let the laundry pile up. If your water has been all absorbed, get more water; even if your robe appears clean, give it another rinse. When it comes to water, we use various sorts of liquids which are fine for washing robes. Thoroughly explore the principle that we know that water is unclean when there are fish in it. When it comes to robes, there are various types to be washed. Making such an effort out of washing your clothes is the arising of your kōan.* However, one will get a glimpse of what cleanliness is. The underlying point here is that soaking your clothes in water is not necessarily your original goal nor is dirtying the water with your clothes your original goal. It is in washing your clothes by using the dirtied water that the original goal of washing your clothes exists. Further, there are methods of washing clothes clean by using such things as fire, wind, soil, water, or air. And there are methods of cleansing earth, water, fire, wind, and air by using earth, water, fire, wind, or air.

The main point of the present 'seeing that the body is not pure' is also like this. Accordingly, what 'body' encompasses, what 'seeing' encompasses, and what 'not pure' encompasses comprise the kesa* that your mother gave birth to. If a kesa is not the kesa that your mother gave birth to, then the Buddhas and Ancestors do not use it—how could Shōnawashu have been the only one?[4] You should hold this principle in mind very carefully, exploring it through your training and dealing with it exhaustively.

'Reflecting on how what our senses perceive leads to suffering' means that suffering is nothing other than a sense perception. It is beyond a matter of what we perceive or what others perceive, and it is beyond a matter of being attached to one's own perceptions or not being attached to them. It is the sensations of a live body, and it is the sufferings of a live body. Say we replace a sweet, ripe melon with a bitter bottle-gourd. It is bitter, skin and flesh, bones and marrow. It is bitter to the mind of attachment and to the mind free of attachments. This type of reflecting is one step above spiritual abilities and above training to realize enlightenment. It is a spiritual ability that springs forth from the whole stem, that springs forth from the whole root. Thus, it has been said, "Sentient beings are thought to suffer, and here indeed is a

---

4.   The Third Indian Ancestor, Shōnawashu, is said to have been born wearing the kesa.

sentient being who suffers." 'Sentient beings' is beyond self and beyond other. We cannot deceive others, for ultimately there are sentient beings who are suffering. Sweet melons are sweet up to their calyx, whereas bitter gourds are bitter down to their very roots. Even so, what suffering is cannot easily be ferreted out. Ask yourself: precisely what is suffering?

Concerning 'reflecting on the impermanence of our mental functions', the Old Buddha Daikan Enō once said, "Impermanence is what Buddha Nature is." Thus, the various ways in which impermanence is understood are all Buddha Nature. Great Master Yōka Genkaku once said, "That actions are impermanent and that all things are empty of anything unchanging is what the Tathagata's great, fully perfected realization was." Your present day reflecting on the impermanence of your mental functions is itself the Tathagata's great, fully perfected realization, for the great, fully perfected realization is what a Tathagata is. Even if your mind does not intend to reflect, it pursues whatever is going by. Thus, wherever there is mind, there is reflection. To generalize, upon your reaching Supreme Wisdom, that supreme, fully enlightened state manifests simply as impermanence and the reflecting mind. The mind is not necessarily constant. Because it goes beyond the four lines of a Scriptural verse and transcends the hundreds of ways of negating, the tiles* and stones of our walls and fences along with their rocks of various sizes is our mind itself, and impermanence itself is reflection itself.

'Reflecting on how all thoughts and things are devoid of a permanent, unchanging self' means that whatever is long is the long Dharma body and whatever is short is the short Dharma body. Because they appear in a living manner, they are without an unchanging self. Buddha Nature does not exist for a dog, and a dog has Buddha Nature. All sentient beings lack having a Buddha Nature, and Buddha Nature is beyond all sentient beings. All Buddhas are beyond ordinary sentient beings, and all Buddhas are beyond 'Buddhas'. All Buddha Nature is beyond 'Buddha Nature', and all sentient beings are beyond being 'a sentient being'. Because this is the way things are, all thoughts and things are beyond being 'all thoughts and things', which we explore through our training as our reflecting on how all thoughts and things are devoid of a permanent, unchanging self. You need to remember to let your whole being leap free from entanglements with self.

Shakyamuni Buddha once said, "All Buddhas and bodhisattvas* reside peacefully within this Teaching, which They regard as a sacred womb." Both Buddhas and bodhisattvas treat these four abodes of reflection as a sacred womb. You need to know that there is the sacred womb of those who have reached the stage of All-knowing Enlightenment and there is the sacred womb of those who have reached the stage of Wondrous Enlightenment.[5] There are Buddhas and bodhisattvas who have already reached these stages, and there are Buddhas who have gone beyond Wondrous Enlightenment who likewise regard this as a sacred womb. And bodhisattvas who have leapt beyond the stages prior to All-knowing Enlightenment and Wondrous Enlightenment also regard the four abodes of reflection as a sacred womb. Truly, the Skin and Flesh, Bones and Marrow of the Buddhas and Ancestors are nothing other than the four abodes of reflection.

The Four Kinds of Cutting Off Evil
also called the Four Kinds of Right Effort

First, endeavoring to avoid whatever gives rise to evil deeds

Second, endeavoring to bring one's evil deeds to a halt when they arise

Third, endeavoring to do what produces merit

Fourth, endeavoring to do what increases merit

In 'endeavoring to avoid whatever gives rise to evil deeds', what we call 'evil deeds' do not invariably have set forms or exact definitions. They simply follow the customs of a country or are those established in a given land. Even so, preventing the arising of evil deeds that have not yet arisen is what the Buddha taught. It is what has been continually Transmitted accurately. It has been said that, according to the

---

5. 'All-knowing Enlightenment' is the fifty-first stage of bodhisattvahood, the one before becoming a Buddha. 'Wondrous Enlightenment' is the fifty-second stage of bodhisattvahood, the one of becoming Buddha.

understanding of non-Buddhists, the self that has not yet sprouted up is taken to be what is fundamental.[6] According to the Buddha's Teaching, it will not be like this.

Let's look into this matter a bit. In the time before evil deeds have arisen, where are they? Were you to say that they exist in the future, you would be on the false path of the nihilists forever.[7] Were you to say that the future becomes the present, that would not be the way that the Buddha's Teaching put the matter, for you would have confused what the three temporal worlds are. If you are unclear about the three temporal worlds, you will become confused as to what thoughts and things are. If you are confused about what thoughts and things are, you will become confused as to what the true appearance of thoughts and things are. If you are confused about their true appearance, you will be confused about what the saying 'each Buddha on His own, together with all Buddhas' is pointing to. Therefore, we do not say that the future later becomes the present.

Let's look a bit further. What should we call evil deeds that have not yet arisen? Who has known or seen them? If they were knowable and perceivable, there would be a time when they had not yet existed and a time when their not yet having arisen had not occurred. If this were so, we could not then call them 'thoughts and things that have not yet arisen'. We would have to call them 'thoughts and things that have already passed away'. You should set aside learning from non-Buddhists or such persons as shravakas* who follow the Lesser Course,* and just focus your practice on endeavoring to avoid whatever gives rise to evil deeds. We call the unrestrained accumulating of evil thoughts 'evil deeds that have not yet arisen', for that is what they are. What we call 'their non-arising' means 'yesterday expressing the Dharma of Certainty and today expressing the Dharma of Uncertainty'.

What 'endeavoring to bring one's evil deeds to a halt when they arise' refers to is what has already arisen being what has completely arisen, and what has completely arisen being what has half arisen, and what has half arisen being what is arising here and now. What is arising here and now is a hindrance that conceals what

---

6.   That is, the non-Buddhist view that there is a permanent, unchanging soul which exists prior to, and independent of, birth, the body being but a temporary abode for this soul.

7.   That is, one would be denying the Buddhist principle of causality.

is arising. It is an arising that springs forth from our mind. When we make this effort, we bring our evil deeds to a halt. It is like Devadatta, while alive, entering the realm of the hells and it is like Devadatta, while alive, receiving the promise of Buddhahood.[8] It is like the living body of Shakrendra being within the womb of a donkey, and it is like his living body realizing Buddhahood.[9] Making use of such an underlying principle, you need to explore through your training the principle of bringing about extinction of evil deeds. Extinguishing such deeds treats extinction as a leaping free and puts aside the delusion of extinguishing them.[10]

'Endeavoring to do what produces merit' is synonymous with the saying, "Being thoroughly content with one's countenance, just as we were before the duality of 'father' and 'mother' had arisen."[11] It is the time before thoughts and things have sprouted up. It is the understanding that precedes the Lords of Awe-inspiring Voices.

You need to understand that 'endeavoring to do what increases merit' is not the same as continuing to give rise to good that has already arisen. It is endeavoring to increase it. It is Shakyamuni Buddha Himself, once having seen the morning star, going on to help others see the morning star. It is one's Eye creating the morning star. It is, as Baso once put it, "After an aimless life, for thirty years I have gone on, never lacking for salt or vinegar." Because Shakyamuni was increasing merit, merit had already arisen. Thus, when the valley stream is deep, the handle of our dipper will be long. It is only because we already had It that Bodhidharma came.

---

8.   Due to his betrayal of Shakyamuni, Devadatta experienced hellish suffering during his lifetime, and, at the same time, Shakyamuni predicted Devadatta's ultimately realizing Buddhahood.

9.   In Discourse 87: On Taking Refuge in the Treasures of Buddha, Dharma, and Sangha *(Kie Buppōsō Hō)*, Dōgen will relate the story of the deity Shakrendra, who was reborn in the womb of a donkey.

10.   The delusional aspect arises from thinking that once one has brought one's wicked ways to a halt, one has brought them to an end for all times.

11.   'Being thoroughly content with one's countenance' refers to our complete acceptance of ourselves as being just what we are, without engaging in judgmentalism.

The Four Steps Towards the Marvelous Spiritual Abilities

First, longing to help others realize their marvelous
spiritual abilities
Second, having a mind to make the necessary effort
Third, being willing to keep one's focus on this goal
Fourth, doing all these through the mind of meditation

'Longing to help others realize their marvelous spiritual abilities' refers to the body and mind aiming to become a Buddha, to Baso's saying, "Having finished eating rice, I feel content, and look to taking me a nap," and to my Master Tendō's saying, "That is why I bow to you." In short, longing to help others realize their spiritual abilities goes beyond the causes and conditions of our body and mind. As Master Wanshi put it:

> *The water is now so clear you can see to its depths,*
> *As fish swim by at their leisure:*
> *The sky is now so clear it is boundless,*
> *As birds fly off, leaving no trace.*

'Having a mind to make the necessary effort' refers to the tiles and stones of our walls and fences, to the great earth with its mountains and rivers. It refers to the various arisings of the three worlds of desire, form, and beyond form, as well as to the brightly polished wood of chairs and bamboo.[12] Because this mind is able to make the necessary effort, there is the mind of Buddhas and Ancestors, there is the mind of the worldly and the saintly, there is the mind of grasses and trees, there is the kaleidoscopic mind. Your whole mind is synonymous with having a mind to make the necessary effort.

'Being willing to keep one's focus on this goal' is synonymous with being atop a hundred-foot pole and then stepping straight ahead. Where is the top of this

---

12.   That is, the mind that is required to help is just one's own ordinary mind, and does not require a mind that is somehow special or unique.

hundred-foot pole? As is said, we cannot find it without stepping straight ahead, and taking one step straight ahead is not something to be denied. This place is where the What exists, whether you explain it as advancing or as retreating. At the very moment when one is advancing towards spiritual abilities, the whole universe in all ten quarters follows upon these spiritual abilities and goes with them, and, following upon these spiritual abilities, we arrive.

'Our doing all these through the mind of meditation' means that, due to the vastness of inherent karmic* ignorance, even all the Buddhas and Ancestors possess nothing upon which They can rely. There is meditating on our physical being, and there is meditating on our mind, and there is meditating on consciousness, and there is meditating on straw sandals, and there is meditating on one's self as it was before there was the Kalpa* of Emptiness.

We also call these methods the four abilities of free will. As Shakyamuni Buddha once said, "When someone has not moved, yet arrives, we call that the miraculous spiritual functioning of free will." Thus, what is sharp is like the point of a needle and what has a square edge is like the side of a chisel.

The Five Roots of Training

> *First, the root of faith in the Dharma*
> *Second, the root of zealous spiritual endeavor*
> *Third, the root of mindfulness*
> *Fourth, the root of concentration*
> *Fifth, the root of wise discernment*

Keep in mind that the root of faith in the Dharma is beyond self, beyond other, beyond any forcing of oneself, beyond anything contrived, beyond anything others have hauled up in their minds, beyond any objective rules or standards, and therefore it was Transmitted, unseen, from West to East. What we call 'faith' is a faith that is forged with one's whole being. It is invariably following where faith goes from the perspective of Buddhahood, which is following our Self where It goes. Were it not based upon the perspective of Buddhahood, there would be no manifestation of faith. This is why it is said that we can enter the great ocean of Buddha Dharma by means of our faith. In sum, the place where faith manifests is the place where Buddhas and Ancestors appear.

'The root of zealous spiritual endeavor' is being alert to just doing meditation. It is resting even when unable to take rest. It is taking rest when taking rest. It is being someone who is terribly unimportant. It is being One who is not unimportant. It is being both important and unimportant. It is the First Moon and the second moon.[13] Shakyamuni Buddha once said, "I am always zealous in my spiritual endeavors. That is why I was able to realize supreme, fully perfected enlightenment." What He called His continual zealous endeavors was His doing it totally—from head to tail—through the whole of past, present, and future. His saying, "I am always zealous in my spiritual endeavors" is His way of saying, "I have already realized Buddhahood." Because it is His already having realized supreme, fully perfected enlightenment, it is His always being zealous in His spiritual endeavors. Were this not so, how could He have possibly been continually zealous in His endeavors? How could He have possibly already realized It? How can those who are academic teachers of Buddhism and those who write scholarly commentaries on Scriptures possibly encounter or hear about this principle, much less explore it through training with a Master?

'The root of mindfulness' is the circle of those withered trees of living flesh, for what we call the circle of those of living flesh are as withered trees.[14] Withered trees <u>are</u> the root of mindfulness. When we ourselves are groping about trying to hit the mark, this is mindfulness. There is the mindfulness when we have a body, as well as the mindfulness when our mind is free of attachments. There is the mindfulness of an involved mind, and there is the mindfulness when we go beyond body. The root of

---

13.   The First Moon is Buddha Nature, whereas the second moon is the reflection of Buddha Nature in all things.

14.   'The circle of those withered trees of living flesh' refers to the Sangha sitting together in meditation: they are alive, yet they are sitting as still and unaffected by what comes as a withered tree.

life of all humans on this great earth is the root of mindfulness, and the root of life of all the Buddhas in the ten quarters is the root of mindfulness. There are many people in one moment of mindfulness and there are many moments of mindfulness within one person. Even so, there are those who have mindfulness and those who lack mindfulness. It is not a matter of human beings always having mindfulness, nor is it a matter of mindfulness always being associated with human beings. Even though this is so, there is inexhaustible merit in being able to observe and thoroughly investigate this topic of mindfulness.

'The root of concentration' is being sparing with your eyebrow, and it is your lifting up your eyebrow.[15] Hence, you are not in the dark about cause and effect, and you are not free from causality, whereby one may enter into the womb of a donkey or enter the womb of a horse. You are like a jewel encased within a stone: one cannot say that it is all stone or all jewel. You are like a mountain crowning the ground: one cannot say that it is all ground or all mountain. Even so, you spring forth from the crown of your head and leap into It.

'The root of wise discernment' is the Buddhas of the three temporal worlds not knowing They have It, and it is feral cats and white water buffaloes being certain that they do have It.[16] You should not ask why it is thus, for it is beyond putting in words. There is inhalation and exhalation through the Nose, and there are fingertips within a Fist. The term 'donkey' maintains, and relies on, there being a donkey. The term 'well' is a mutual encountering with a well. In sum, a Root is the Dharma heir of a Root.

---

15. A reference to the Venerable Pindola's raising of one eyebrow which Dōgen recounts in Discourse 57: On the Plum Blossom *(Baika)*. The raising of one's eyebrow was a sign of confirming someone else's kenshō, a practice which, according to Dōgen, should be done sparingly.

16. 'Feral cats and white oxen' is descriptive of certain types of trainees who are heavily deluded.

The Five Strengths

First, the strength of faith in the Dharma
Second, the strength of zealous spiritual endeavor
Third, the strength of mindfulness
Fourth, the strength of concentration
Fifth, the strength of wise discernment

'The strength of faith' is being deceived by oneself and having no place to escape to. It is being called to by someone and having to turn one's head around. From birth to old age, it is simply being just This. It is stumbling seven times, then getting up and going on. It is eight times falling down and making use of it. Thus, faith is like a jewel, crystal clear as water. It is considering the Transmitting of the Dharma and the Transmitting of the robe to be acts of faith, as are the Transmitting of Buddhas and the Transmitting of Ancestors.

'The strength of zealous spiritual endeavor' is thoroughly expressing in words what cannot be put into practice and thoroughly putting into practice what cannot be put into words. Thus, being able to explain a little bit is nothing more than being able to explain a little bit. And being able to put into practice one line of Scripture is nothing more than being able to put into practice one line of Scripture. Getting strength from within one's strength is the strength of zealous spiritual endeavor.

'The strength of mindfulness' is the great slayer pulling someone by the nose. Thus, it was the Nose pulling the person.[17] The strength of mindfulness is also our relinquishing the jewel and redeeming the jewel, and it is also our relinquishing a tile and redeeming a tile. Further, it also means thirty blows for not having relinquished

---

17.   An allusion to Meditation Master Shakkyō Ezō yanking the nose of Master Seidō Chizō. Shakkyō was a great 'slayer' of the false self, who taught his fellow monk Seidō the meaning of the True Self (one's Nose). It was Shakkyō's True Self that did the pulling.

them. No matter how much we human beings may make use of the strength of our mindfulness, it will never erode.

'The strength of concentration' is like a child getting its mother and like a mother getting her child. And it is like a child getting 'child' and a mother getting 'mother'. Be that as it may, it is not exchanging our head for a face, nor is it buying gold with gold. It is simply our chanting from our concentration growing ever louder.

'The strength of wise discernment' is ever deeper and far-reaching as the years and generations pass. It is like ferrying a boat's crossing to the Other Shore. This is why in ancient times someone said, "It is like the crossing was getting a ferry." The heart of what this is saying is, "The crossing, beyond question, is the ferry." A crossing that does not get in the way of a crossing we call 'a ferry'. In spring, the ice dissolves of itself.

The Seven Branches Associated with Awakening

> *First, awakening to a preference for the Dharma*
> *Second, awakening to being zealous in one's endeavors*
> *Third, awakening to a delight in the Truth*
> *Fourth, awakening to eliminating one's rough edges*
> *Fifth, awakening to equanimity*
> *Sixth, awakening to concentration*
> *Seventh, awakening to mindfulness*

'Awakening to a preference for the Dharma' is synonymous with Kanchi Sōsan's saying, "Let but a hair's breadth of discriminatory thought arise and you have made Heaven and Earth strangers to each other." Thus, as he also said, "The Way to the Ultimate is not hard; simply give up being picky and choosy."

'Awakening to being zealous in one's endeavors' is synonymous with never having endorsed robbing others in the marketplace. Whether buying for one's own sake or selling for one's own sake, both have their fixed price, and there is recognition of one's worth. Even if we seem to be bending over backwards in recommending others, a blow to our body does not break us. In never ceasing to offer anyone a trigger word, you will encounter the Trader who offers you, on His part, the turning around of your heart.[18] So, before you have finished doing your donkey work, go about doing horse work.[19]

'Awakening to a delight in the Truth' is synonymous with the sympathy your grandma had when your blood was dripping from a cut. Leave the thousand hands and eyes of the Great Compassionate One to do their business. Plum blossoms are beginning to peep through the wintry snow—news of the coming spring. A great Master may still be cold, but even so, he will be freely swimming about, disporting like a fish, and overflowing with gales of laughter.

'Awakening to eliminating one's rough edges' means, when looking within yourself, not getting all absorbed in yourself, and, when looking outside yourself, not getting all absorbed in others. It means 'what I have gotten, you have not yet gotten.' It is ardently expressing It while going forth amidst all manner of beings.

'Awakening to equanimity' means that even though I have brought It, others may not accept It. It is just as the Chinese, when barefooted, learn to walk like Chinese, and as the Persians who go hunting for ivory tusks in the South Seas.

'Awakening to concentration' means before taking the initiative, preserving the Eye that exists before taking the initiative. It is our blowing our own nose. It is taking hold of our own tether and leading our own self. And, nevertheless, it is being able to let our domesticated water buffalo graze on its own.

'Awakening to mindfulness' means a pillar* of the temple going forth, walking the sky. Thus, even though we say that someone's mouth resembles a mallet and someone's Eye is like an eyebrow, still, this is a matter of burning sandalwood in a sandalwood forest or of a lion roaring in a lion's den.

---

18. A trigger word is some remark which serves another as a trigger, or catalyst, for an awakening to the Truth.

19. Donkey work is the day-to-day plodding through one's training. While still training, one should also do the horse work, which is one's going forth wherever needed to help all sentient beings realize the Truth.

The Eight Branches of the Right Path
also called the Noble Eightfold Path

First, the branch of Right View
Second, the branch of Right Thought
Third, the branch of Right Speech
Fourth, the branch of Right Action
Fifth, the branch of Right Livelihood
Sixth, the branch of Right Effort
Seventh, the branch of Right Mindfulness
Eighth, the branch of Right Concentration

'The branch of Right View' is our cherishing the Eye of our True Self, which resides within. At the same time, prior to our body's arising, we were already endowed with the Eye. Even though this view was magnificently realized in the past, it is our own spiritual question coming forth and it will be experienced intimately in the future. In short, if one does not cherish the Eye of one's True Self, such a person is not an Ancestor of the Buddha.

'The branch of Right Thought' is the coming forth of all the Buddhas in the ten quarters when we cultivate this mode of thinking. As a result, the coming forth of the ten quarters and the coming forth of the Buddhas is what the time when we cultivate this mode of thinking refers to. When we cultivate this mode of thinking, we are beyond self and transcend other. Even so, at the very moment that we are completely involved in thinking about the Matter, we have directed our course towards Varanasi.[20] The place where this mode of thinking exists <u>is</u> Varanasi. The Old Buddha Yakusan once said, "What I was thinking about was based on not deliberately thinking about any particular thing." A monk then asked, "How can what anyone is thinking about be based on not deliberately thinking about <u>something</u>?" The Master replied,

---

20. Varanasi, nowadays called Benares, was the place where the Buddha first gave voice to the Dharma after His awakening.

"It is a matter of 'what I am thinking about' not being the point." This is a matter of right thinking and right thought. Breaking your meditation pillow is what right thought is about.[21]

'The branch of Right Speech' is our Mute Self not being a mute. Those who are mutes among humans are not yet able to speak. Those in the realm of the Mute are not mutes. They do not admire themselves as saints, nor do they pile something spiritual upon themselves. It is their thoroughly exploring the Matter by hanging their mouths up on the wall. It is all the mouths being hung up on all the walls.

'The branch of Right Action' is our leaving home life behind and entering the Meditation Hall. It is our entering a mountain monastery to procure a realization. As Shakyamuni Buddha once said, "The thirty-seven methods of training are the actions of a monk." The actions of a monk go beyond the Greater[*] and Lesser Courses. There are various types of monks, such as Buddha monks, bodhisattva monks, and shravaka monks. Those who have not yet left home life behind do not succeed to the inheritance of the Right Action of the Buddha's Dharma. They have not received the authentic Transmission of the Great Course of the Buddha's Dharma. Even though those who have remained in home life may have done some study of the Way as lay men and women, they have not left behind any traces of having become expert in the Way. Whenever anyone has become expert in the Way, that person has invariably left home life behind. How can those folks who are not up to leaving home life behind possibly devote themselves to attaining the rank of Buddha?

At the same time, for the past two or three hundred years, there have been many in Great Sung China who call themselves monks of the Zen tradition, saying, "Those who have remained in home life to study the Way and those who have left home life behind to study the Way are just the same." That bunch have turned themselves into dogs just for the sake of making the excrement and urine of lay people

---

21.   'Breaking one's meditation pillow' is a metaphor for working hard at one's meditation practice.

their food and drink.[22] Sometimes they say to rulers of countries and their ministers, "Your mind when conducting the affairs of state is exactly the same as the mind of Ancestors and Buddhas, for there is no other mind." Rulers and ministers, still ignorant of what real Teaching and genuine Dharma are, take great delight in bestowing such titles as Master upon them. Monks who talk like this are veritable Devadattas. They come out with such wild and childish drivel just so they can feed off the chirping and spitting of such lay folk—better to call it a child's whimpering. They are not of the family of the Seven Buddhas,* but are a band of devils and beasts. They do not know what 'body and mind' refers to, nor do they explore the Matter through training with a Master, nor do they understand what it means to leave home life behind both in body and in mind. They are in the dark about the politics of rulers and ministers, and it is as if they had never encountered the Great Way of the Buddhas and Ancestors even in their dreams.

The lay practitioner Vimalakirti* resembled the Buddha when He was in the world, yet there were many ways in which what he taught was not yet complete, and there were a number of points which he had not yet fully mastered. The lay practitioner Hōon had a history of training under several Ancestors, but he was not permitted entrance into Yakusan's inner chambers, and he was never the equal of Baso, his ultimate teacher. His name is said to be linked with the term 'exploring through training', but his exploring through training was not real. With others, such as Ri Fuba and Yō Bunkō, each thought he was tranquilly residing within his spiritual awakening, but neither had yet partaken of sugar dumplings, much less of a painted rice cake, or even less, of the rice gruel of the Buddhas and Ancestors, for they still did not possess a monk's alms bowl. Sad to say, their whole life as a skin bag* was in vain.

What I am universally recommending to sentient beings in lofty positions, to ordinary beings, to erudite scholarly beings, and to all other types of sentient beings in all ten quarters is that they follow the Tathagata's ways from the distant past by quickly leaving home life behind and training in the Way, so that they may attain the

---

22.   In this context, 'excrement and urine' is a derogatory metaphor for 'words and opinions', that is, for what the judgmental mind excretes. In Japanese, this terminology does not carry the vulgar sense that it has in English.

rank of Buddha and the rank of Ancestor. Do not listen to the incompetent words of those so-called 'Zen Masters' and their ilk. Because they do not understand what body is or what mind is, they speak such words. As likely as not, they are utterly lacking in compassion for sentient beings and have no thought of adhering to the Buddha Dharma. Only desiring to devote themselves to feeding off the urine and excrement of those who remain in home life, they are like vicious dogs—dogs with human faces, dogs in human hides. Thus they speak as they do. Do not sit down with them, do not converse with them, do not stop to train under them. While their human bodies are still alive, they have fallen into the world of the animals. If someone who has left home life behind had urine and excrement in abundance, these dogs would say that such a monk was preeminent. But they talk as they do because the urine and excrement of monks does not come up to the standards of these animals. Over more than two thousand years, there has been no trace appearing in the texts of the more than five thousand scrolls of the Canon which says that the intentions of those who remain in home life and of those who have left home life behind are exactly the same, either in theory or in practice. No Buddha or Ancestor has ever proclaimed such a thing in over fifty generations of our lineage and during the more than forty ages.[23] Even if there were a person—one who had left home behind—who broke or neglected the Precepts, or did not keep to the Teaching, or was lacking in wise discernment, such a one would surpass the discernment and the keeping to the Precepts of one who had remained in home life, because becoming a monk is Wisdom itself, realization Itself, the Way Itself, and the Dharma Itself. Even though those in home life may have good spiritual roots and are behaving quite meritoriously, they may well overlook the good spiritual roots and meritorious behavior of a monastic's body and mind. During the Buddha's whole lifetime of teaching, not one person in lay life fully realized the Way. This was due to their home life not being a suitable place for them to learn the Way of the Buddha and because their worldly distractions were so many.

When we explore the body and mind of that bunch who assert that a mind which is engaged in myriad affairs of state and the mind of an Ancestral Teacher are

---

23. The fifty generations are from Makakashō through Tendō Nyojō, whereas the more than forty ages are from the first of the Seven Buddhas up through Daikan Enō and beyond.

the same, it is obvious that they never encountered the mind and body of the Buddhas and Ancestors, nor was the Skin and Flesh, Bones and Marrow of the Buddhas and Ancestors ever Transmitted to those folks. Sad to say, even though they were encountering the True Teaching of the Buddha, they nevertheless became beasts.

Because this is the way things are, Enō, the Old Buddha of Sōkei, immediately took leave of his mother in order to seek a Master: this was Right Action. Before he heard the *Diamond-cutting Scripture* and gave rise to the intention to realize Buddhahood, he lived at home, working as a woodcutter. After hearing the *Diamond-cutting Scripture*, he was infused with Its lingering fragrance. So, dropping off his heavy burden of wood, he left home life behind. Keep in mind that once body and mind become so infused with the Buddha Dharma, it is said that remaining in home life is no longer possible. It has been the same for all the Buddhas and Ancestors. That bunch who say that one does not need to leave home life behind are committing an offense even more serious than those of the five treacherous deeds* and they are even more savage than Devadatta. Know that what they are doing is even worse than what the six male monastics, the six female monastics, as well as the eighteen monastics did during the Buddha's time, so do not converse with them.[24] A whole lifetime is not that long. You do not have the time to converse with such devils and beasts. And what is more, you received these human bodies and minds of yours as a result of seeds from encountering and hearing the Buddha Dharma in past lives. They are like temple tools for public use. They are not to be turned into a band of devils, nor are they to be aligned with any band of devils. Do not forget your deep obligation to the Buddhas and Ancestors by listening to the baying of these ferocious dogs, but protect and preserve the virtue of the milk of the Dharma. And do not sit or sup with these wicked dogs.

When Our Founding Ancestor, the Old Buddha of Mount Sūzan,[25] left far behind the western Buddhist country of India to come east to the remote land of China, the True Teaching of the Buddhas and Ancestors was Transmitted through his person.

---

24. These three groups were comprised of monks who had difficulties with their training, and therefore left the assembly of the Buddha.

25. That is, Bodhidharma.

If he had not left worldly life behind in order to realize the Way, such a thing would not have been possible. Before he came from the West, human beings of all stations had never encountered or heard of the True Teaching. So, you should keep in mind that the true Transmission of the true Teaching was made possible due to the spiritually beneficial action of his having left home life behind.

Our Great Master, the revered Shakyamuni, graciously set aside the rank of his father the king and did not succeed him as his heir, but not because the king's rank was not valued. Rather, it was done that He might succeed as heir to the most precious rank of Buddha. The rank of Buddha is the rank of someone who has left home life behind. It is a rank which those in the three worlds of desire, form, and without form— both those in lofty positions and ordinary human beings—all bow to out of deepest respect. It is not a place whose seat is to be shared with a Lord Brahma or a Lord Shakra. How much less is it a rank whose seat is to be shared with earthly human rulers or scholastic lords of erudition, for it is the rank of supreme, fully perfected enlightenment. Those of this precious rank can give expression to the Dharma that carries beings to the Other Shore and can send forth their radiance which manifests auspicious signs. The actions of those who have left home life behind are the very stuff of Right Actions; they are the actions long-cherished by Buddhas, including the Seven Buddhas. It is a place that is not fully realized if it is not done by 'each Buddha on His own, together with all Buddhas'. Those who have not yet left home life behind should show their respect to those who have already left home life behind and serve them. They should bow their heads in homage to them and offer them alms, setting aside both body and life.

Shakyamuni Buddha once said, "To leave home life behind and accept the Precepts is to be the seed of a Buddha, for such a one has already become enlightened." So, keep in mind, what we call 'becoming enlightened' means leaving home life behind. Someone who has not yet left home life behind is, sad to say, one sunk in misery. In short, I cannot say how often during the Buddha's lifetime He praised the merits of leaving home life behind. Our honored Shakyamuni sincerely voiced this, and all Buddhas have certified it. Those who have left home life behind and who are breaking Precepts and failing to explore the Matter with their Master have realized the Way, whereas those who have remained in home life have not yet realized the Way. When royalty respectfully bow to male or female monastics, these monastics do not return the bow; when those in lofty positions bow to the ones who have left home behind, both the male and the female monastics never return the bow. This is because the merit of leaving home life behind is unsurpassed. It is like this because, if they were to receive bows from male and female monastics—that is, those who have left home life behind—the mansions and palaces of those in lofty positions would instantly fall into ruin and decay, along with all their resplendence and good fortune.

In sum, as the Buddha Dharma gradually progressed eastward, there were those who realized the Way by leaving home life behind; they have been as common as rice and flax plants, bamboo and reeds. But there was not even one of them who realized the Way whilst remaining in home life. Once the Buddha Dharma reached their eyes and ears, they immediately engaged themselves in leaving home life behind. I have come to realize clearly that remaining in home life is not a place for the Buddha Dharma to reside. At the same time, that bunch who say that the body and mind of those who are engaged in conducting affairs of state is exactly the same as the body and mind of the Buddhas and Ancestors have never encountered or heard the Teaching of the Buddha. They are criminals in the darkest of hells. They are foolish people who have not even seen or heard what they themselves are saying. They are traitors to their land. Their attempt to equate a mind that is engaged in worldly affairs with the mind of the Buddhas and Ancestors is done just for the delight of rulers; it is an attempt undertaken because of the preeminence of the Buddha Dharma. You need to remember that the Buddha Dharma is what is preeminent. Now, it may happen that the mind engaged with worldly affairs is temporarily in the same state as the mind of the Buddhas and Ancestor—and quite naturally—but whenever the body and mind of the Buddhas and Ancestors spontaneously resembles the body and mind of someone engaged with worldly affairs, Theirs will not be the body and mind of one engaged with worldly affairs. 'Zen Masters' and their like who say that the mind of someone engaged in worldly affairs is completely equivalent to the mind of Buddhas and Ancestors do not have a clue as to how the human mind works. And as to the working of the mind of Buddhas and Ancestors, well, they haven't seen that even in their dreams!

Speaking more broadly, Lord Brahma, Lord Shakrendra, human rulers, erudite lords of scholarship, demon lords, and the like—each and every one of them—need to give up their obsession with good fortune within the three worlds of desire, form, and beyond form, leave their home life behind, accept the Precepts, and then put into practice the Way of the Buddhas and the Ancestors, for this will be a cause for Buddhahood to be realized over vast eons. Do you not see? If old Vimalakirti had left home life behind, he would have encountered a monastic Vimalakirti who was even superior to the lay Vimalakirti. Today, it would be hard to encounter a Subhuti, or a Shariputra, or a Manjushri,* or a Maitreya,* let alone half a Vimalakirti, much less three, four, or five Vimalakirtis![26] Should it be the case that you are not encountering or coming to know three, four, or five Vimalakirtis, well, we are not encountering, or knowing, or supporting, or relying upon even one Vimalakirti. If we are not yet supporting or relying upon one Vimalakirti, then we are not encountering Vimalakirti as a Buddha. When we do not encounter Vimalakirti as a Buddha, Vimalakirti does not yet exist as a Manjushri, or as a Maitreya, or as a Subhuti, or as a Shariputra, to say nothing of a Vimalakirti being the great earth with its mountains and rivers, or his being grasses and trees, tiles and stones, or wind and rain, water and fire, or his being, past, present, and future! The reason that Vimalakirti's luminosity and meritorious virtues are not apparent is because he had not left home life behind. Had Vimalakirti left home life behind, he would have shown those meritorious virtues. The so-called 'Zen Masters' of the T'ang and Sung Dynasties and their like had never arrived at this point, so they vainly considered Vimalakirti as being right in whatever he did. These folks, sad to say, did not know the spoken Teaching and were in the dark about the Buddha Dharma.

Furthermore, many of that bunch went so far as to say that the words and ways of Vimalakirti and the Venerable Shakyamuni were equal. These too have never considered, much less known, the Buddha Dharma or the Way of the Ancestors, nor did they even know Vimalakirti himself. They say that what Vimalakirti's silence was pointing out to bodhisattvas by his not using words was comparable to the Tathagata's not using words for some person's sake. I would say that they are greatly ignorant of

---

26.   Subhuti and Shariputra were two of the Buddha's most preeminent disciples.

the Buddha Dharma and have little ability for studying the Way. The Tathagata's use of words was already different from that of others, and his not using words must also not be likened to that of others. Thus, the Tathagata's moment of utter silence and Vimalakirti's moment of silence should not even be considered analogous. When we explore the abilities of that bunch who imagine that the words Vimalakirti spoke to convey the Dharma were different from those of the Tathagata, but the silences of the two were undoubtedly the same, we see that they have not even come close to where the Buddha is. Sad to say, these people have not yet seen His form or heard His voice, much less have they experienced the glorious light that leaps forth from His form and voice. And even less do they know that they must learn what the Silence within silence means, to say nothing of their even hearing It! Generally speaking, people's understanding of movement and silence differ, so how can they say that the Venerable Shakyamuni is like any of these types or even different from them? That bunch who have not explored the Matter within the inner quarters of the Buddhas and Ancestors talk like this.

Again, many wrong-headed people fancy that spoken teachings and physical expressions are what is provisionally true, whereas silence and physical quietude are the real truth. This kind of talk is also not the Buddha Dharma. It is what those who pass on what they have heard about of the Scriptures and of the teachings of Brahma or Ishvara or their like speculate about. How could the Buddha's Teaching ever be mixed up with 'movement versus stillness'? Through your training you need to explore that there is movement and stillness within the Buddha's Way, <u>and</u> there is no movement and stillness therein! And that there is our encountering movement and silence, <u>and</u> there is movement and silence encountering us! You veteran trainees of this very moment, do not slacken!

When we look at Great Sung China today, those folks who are exploring the Great Way of the Buddhas and Ancestors through their training are all but extinct; there may not even be two or three left. There are just those who believe that Vimalakirti was right and as a result, he had total silence, whereas we today are lacking in total silence and therefore are far inferior to Vimalakirti. Moreover, such folks lack the vital, absolute Way. Likewise, there are those who hold to the opinion that Vimalakirti's total silence is in no way different from the Venerable Shakyamuni's utter silence. They completely lack the light of illuminating discernment. We must admit that none of the folks who say things like this have ever encountered, heard, or explored the Buddha Dharma through their training. Do not think that since they are people of Great Sung China, what they assert must be the Teaching of the Buddha. The reason for this can be easily clarified: Right Action means the actions of a monk, which is something that is beyond the ken of those who write scholarly commentaries on Scriptures and those who teach academic Buddhism. What we call 'the actions of a monk' is our doing our utmost whilst in the Meditation Hall, it is our bowing in deepest gratitude whilst in the Buddha Hall, and it is our washing our face in the wash-up shed. Furthermore, bowing with hands in gasshō,* burning incense, and heating water are all Right Action. Not only is it exchanging your tail for your head, it is exchanging your head with your Head, exchanging your mind with your Mind, exchanging 'the Buddha' with Buddha, exchanging 'the truth' with Truth, for these are all branchings of the Path of Right Action. If you mistakenly engage in just talking about Buddha Dharma, His eyebrows will droop down and His countenance will sadden.

'The branch of Right Livelihood' is early morning gruel and midday rice. It is staying in the monastery grounds and delighting in single-minded pursuit of the Way. It is the Master sitting on the wooden Dharma seat and directly pointing to the Truth. The fewer than twenty trainees in the assembly of old Jōshū is a manifestation of Right Livelihood. And Yakusan's assembly of less than ten was the lifeblood of Right Livelihood. And Fun'yō's assembly of seven or eight was also a place where Right Livelihood was anchored, because everyone there had kept clear of false livelihood.

Shakyamuni Buddha once remarked that shravakas—those who hear the Dharma and do not heed it, but seek a rigid code—have not yet attained Right Livelihood. Thus, the teachings, practice, and realizations of shravakas are still not Right Livelihood. At the same time, there are commonplace people of recent days who say, "We should not separate shravakas from bodhisattvas, but should adopt both their behavior and their precepts and monastic regulations." Using the standards of the shravakas of the Lesser Course, they pass judgment on the everyday behavior and practices of the bodhisattvas of the Greater Course. As Shakyamuni Buddha once said,

"A shravaka's keeping of a precept is a bodhisattva's acting contrary to a precept."
Thus, what shravakas consider to be their keeping of the precepts, when viewed from
the perspective of the Bodhisattva Precepts, are all preceptual breakages of the
shravaka precepts. The other everyday practices of maintaining one's concentration
and applying one's wise discernment are just the same. For instance, even though a
Precept like 'cease from killing whatever lives' naturally appears to be the same for a
shravaka and a bodhisattva, there is certainly a difference between them, one which
surpasses the separation of the heavens and the earth.[27] And how much less could the
principles genuinely Transmitted from Buddha to Buddha and Ancestor to Ancestor
possibly be the same as those of the shravakas! Not only is there Right Livelihood,
there is also Pure Life. So, by exploring the Matter through training with an Ancestor
of the Buddha, yours will become Right Livelihood. Do not adopt the opinions and
explanations of such people as scholarly commentators. Because theirs is not yet Right
Livelihood, they do not live an enlightened life.

'The branch of Right Effort' is the daily conduct of dredging out your whole
being. And through dredging out your whole being, you fashion a truly human
countenance. It is your entering the Buddha Hall, riding upside down on a water
buffalo, doing one lap around the hall, two laps, three, four, five laps, so that nine
nines comes out to eighty-two.[28] It is your repaying your indebtedness to others
thousands of myriad times over. It is your turning your head left and right, up and
down. It is your changing your countenance as it goes left and right, up and down. It
is your entering your Master's private quarters and your going to the Dharma Hall.[29]
It is your mutually encountering your true Master in Bōshū Pavilion, and your

---

27. The difference lies in the shravaka's practice of limiting understanding of the Precepts to
the literal, whereas the bodhisattva understanding goes far beyond just the literal, taking
the Precepts on the broadest and deepest levels possible.

28. That is, being willing to undertake what seems impossible or inconceivable.

29. Entering the Master's private quarters to hear a Dharma talk and to do private interviews
with the Master is a privilege for Transmitted monks, whereas all trainees, including
Transmitted monks, are expected to go to the Dharma Hall to hear the Master's Dharma
talks for the community.

mutually encountering your true Master on Useki Peak.[30] It is your mutually encountering your true Master within the Buddha Hall. It is just like saying, "When seeing one person reflected in two facing mirrors, there are three figures."

'The branch of Right Mindfulness' is our being aware that eighty or ninety percent of the time we are deluding ourselves. Learning to give rise to wise discernment within mindfulness is to abandon our father and run away from home. To study that wise discernment arises effortlessly within mindfulness is to tie oneself up in knots. To say that Right Mindfulness means being blank-minded is non-Buddhist. Also, you should not regard the spirits of earth, water, fire, and wind as forms of mindfulness, nor should you consider the turning upside down of the mental functions of consciousness, thought, and perception to be mindfulness. Remember, "You have gotten what my Skin and Flesh, Bones and Marrow are" is Right Mindfulness.

'The branch of Right Concentration' is the dropping off of 'Buddha' and 'Ancestor'. It is the dropping off of 'Right Concentration'. It is what others can rejoice in. It is your making a Nose by cutting open the crown of your head. It is the raising aloft the udumbara blossom within the Treasure House of the Eye of the True Teaching. Within the udumbara blossom are Makakashōs, their faces broken wide with smiles, on hundreds of thousands of petals. Having been made continual use of throughout His life for ever so long, Shakyamuni's wooden paddle finally broke. That is why He spent six years, dropping off whatever sprouted up, until that one night when His flower blossomed. When the conflagration at kalpa's ending is blazing up and the three-thousand great-thousandfold world is being totally consumed, we just follow upon what arises and go forth.

These thirty-seven methods of training to realize enlightenment are the very Eyes and Nose of the Buddhas and Ancestors, Their Skin and Flesh, Bones and Marrow, Their Hands, Feet, and Countenances. The Buddhas and Ancestors continually explored through Their training these thirty-seven methods of training to

---

30.   Bōshū Pavilion and Useki Peak are two scenic places on Mount Seppō used as meditation sites.

realize enlightenment, one by one. At the same time, they are the one thousand and sixty ways our spiritual question manifests: they are our methods of training to realize enlightenment. We should sit until we break through them, and then let them drop off.

Given to the assembly at Kippō-ji Temple in Echizen Province on the twenty-fourth day of the second lunar month in the second year of the Kangen era (April 3, 1244).

Copied by me in the office of the Abbot's assistant in the same temple on the ninth day of the third lunar month in the same year (April 17, 1244).

Ejō

Glossary

Āchārya: Sanskrit for 'teacher'; in Zen monasteries, a polite form of address for a monk with at least five years of training; applied to a disciple advanced enough to teach monks and laity, but not yet deemed a Master.

Arhat: In Zen, one whose heart is cleansed of all greed, hatred, and delusion but who has not yet fully realized wise discernment or compassion.

Asura: An inhabitant of one of the six Worlds of Existence; before conversion, a heaven stormer, one who is so absorbed in attaining power that he cannot hear the Dharma, much less comprehend It; after conversion, he becomes a guardian of Buddhism.

Avalokiteshvara (C. Kuan Yin, J. Kanzeon or Kannon): The Bodhisattva who hearkens to the cries of the world; the embodiment of compassion.

Before 'father' and 'mother' were born: That is, the time before dualistic thinking arises in the mind.

Bodhisattva: When not capitalized, it refers to one who is attempting to follow the Mahāyāna (Greater Course) as the Buddha Path; when capitalized, the personification of some aspect of Buddha Nature.

A broken wooden ladle: A Zen metaphor describing someone's mind which has become free of discriminatory thinking.

A dragon elephant: Originally, a term for a particularly large elephant; used in Zen texts to describe a particularly brilliant and discerning Master.

The five treacherous deeds: Murdering one's father, murdering one's mother, murdering an arhat, spilling the blood of someone who has realized Buddhahood, and causing disharmony in the Sangha, thereby creating a schism in the order.

The four elements: Earth, water, fire, and wind.

The four stages of arhathood: (1) Stream-enterer: someone who enters into the stream of Buddhist training by abandoning false views; (2) Once-returner: someone having one more rebirth before realizing full enlightenment; (3) Non-returner: someone never returning to the realm of sensual desire; and (4) Arhat: someone who has reached a state of enlightenment and is therefore free from all defiling passions.

Gasshō: A gesture made by placing the palms of the hands together, with fingers pointing upwards, signifying the unity of body and mind. It is an expression of reverence often used during ceremonies, as well as a form of greeting when two Buddhists meet and a gesture of supplication.

Greater Course (Greater Vehicle): A translation of the term 'Mahāyāna', used to designate the Buddhist traditions that place the awakening of all sentient beings above one's personal awakening.

Hossu: A scepter-like instrument in the form of a fly-whisk carried by a celebrant during ceremonies. It represents the flowing forth of the Water of the Spirit as an expression of the celebrant's compassion.

Hungry ghost (preta): One who resides in one of the three negative modes of existence, pictured as a being who is suffering from a hunger for the Dharma and has some metaphorical deformity, such as lacking a mouth, which makes it impossible to absorb It.

Icchantika: Someone who is erroneously thought to be so amoral as to be completely devoid of Buddha Nature. In Zen, there is reference to the Great Icchantika, which is an epithet for Buddha Nature itself.

Jambudvipa: In Buddhist spiritual cosmology, the Southern Continent where people are capable of doing Buddhist training.

Kalpa: An endlessly long period of time, roughly equivalent to an eon.

Karma: What results from any volitional action, according to the universal law of cause and effect.

Kenshō: The experience of seeing into one's true nature, that is, one's Buddha Nature.

Kesa: A cloak-like robe traditionally worn by Buddhist monastics since the time of Shakyamuni Buddha. A similar type of robe is given to committed lay Buddhists.

Kōan: A statement or story used by a Zen Master as a teaching device to directly address a trainee's spiritual question; also may be used to refer to that question itself.

Lantern (stone or temple): A term often used metaphorically for a monk who stays in a monastery or temple, serving as a light to help guide a trainee.

Lesser Course: Followers of the two 'lesser' courses, namely, the shravakas and the pratyekabuddhas. They are not 'wrong' practitioners of Buddhism, but by their following a 'lesser' course it will take a longer time for their spiritual seeds to germinate and grow into the realizing of Buddhahood, since they have not yet entered the Bodhisattva Path, which involves the doing of one's practice for the sake of all sentient beings. See also the Greater Course and the Three Vehicles.

Lion Throne (Lion's Seat): The seat where a Master sits when giving a talk on some aspect of the Dharma.

Lord of Emptiness: The first of the Seven Buddhas, the one who lived during the Age of Emptiness, that is, before duality had first arisen.

Mahāsattva: An outstanding bodhisattva.

Mahāyāna: The Greater Vehicle.

Maitreya: The Buddha Yet to Come. He is said to be waiting as a Bodhisattva in the Tushita Heaven. To realize one's own Buddha Nature brings Maitreya forth.

Manjushri: The Bodhisattva who personifies Great Wisdom.

Matter (the One Great Matter): The goal of spiritual training, namely, the realization of the highest Truth.

Monjin: The act of bowing from the waist with hands in gasshō.

A pillar of the temple: A monk whose training is so strong that it supports the spiritual function of the temple or monastery in which he trains.

Pratyekabuddha: One who becomes enlightened as a result of his own efforts but does not share his understanding with others.

Samantabhadra: The Bodhisattva who is the embodiment of patient, loving activity.

Seal (Buddha seal, Buddha Mind seal, Dharma seal, and seal of certification): 'The Buddha Mind Seal' refers not only to the document written on plum blossom silk which certifies both the Master's and the disciple's Buddha Mind but also to the fact that the Minds of Master and disciple coincide and are not two separate minds. The Transmission of this seal is often referred to in Zen texts as 'the Transmission of Mind to Mind' as well as 'the special Transmission that is apart from Scriptural texts and which does not depend on words'.

The Seven Buddhas: The historical Buddha and the six Buddhas that preceded Him.

The seven treasures (the seven jewels): The seven types of jewels from which Pure Lands are fashioned.

Shashu: The way that the hands are held when doing walking meditation. There are various forms of shashu, but most involve one hand being wrapped around the fist of the other.

Shravaka: One who, upon hearing the Dharma, affirms his allegiance to It but may not yet try to put It into practice, or may try to reduce It simply to a rigid code of 'right' or 'wrong' behaviors.

The six Worlds of Existence: Those of celestial beings, humans, asuras, hungry ghosts, beasts, and those in hellish states.

Skandhas: The five skandhas comprising a living being's physical form, sensory perceptions, mental concepts and ideas, volition, and consciousness.

Skin bag: An allusion to a human as a sentient being having a physical body. Dōgen often uses the term to characterize ineffectual trainees.

Staff: The traveling staff carried by a monk when traveling to another temple. Hence the phrase 'to hang up one's traveling staff' meaning 'to have found the temple in which to permanently seek the Truth under the abbot'; metaphorically, a monk who is willing to go anywhere in order to spread the Dharma and help all sentient beings.

Stupa: Literally, a reliquary for the ashes of a Buddhist, and metaphorically, the body of a Buddha.

'Such a one' ('such a person'): Someone who has realized the Truth and automatically shows the signs of having had such a realization.

The Three Courses (the Three Vehicles): Namely, the way of training done by the shravakas, pratyekabuddhas, and bodhisattvas.

The thrice wise and ten times saintly: Those who have attained the final stage of bodhisattvahood before fully awakening and becoming a Buddha.

The tiles and stones of our walls and fences: The bits and pieces of our experiences, which we use to fashion our perception of the universe.

Tripitaka: The three divisions of Buddhist Scriptures, namely, the Buddha's

Teachings (Sutras), the Precepts (Vinaya), and the commentaries on the Sutras (Abhi-dharmas); also, the whole of the Buddhist canon.

Vairochana (the Cosmic Buddha): The Buddha who is the personification of spiritual Light and Truth, the one who represents the Pure Buddha Mind.

Vimalakīrti: A wealthy lay Buddhist renowned for his profound understanding of Mahāyāna.

A wheel-turning lord: A ruler who turns the Wheel of the Dharma in his country by governing according to Buddhist principles.

Yojana: An Indian measure of distance, understood by some scholars as equivalent to twelve or sixteen miles.

Appendix of Names

Many of Dōgen's discourses in the Shōbōgenzō are based on accounts taken from various collections of kōan stories. For the most part, these deal with notable Zen monastics who are customarily identified in the opening sentence of the story. However, since these stories have come from various sources, the name given for any of these monastics may not always be consistent. All the various names attributed to these monks would have been known to those in Dōgen's assembly but may not all be familiar to modern-day readers. To help in identifying who is who, I have taken the liberty of using the most familiar Japanese name by which these historic monks are known. For instance, Daikan Enō is referred to in the translations as Enō, whereas in some of the original texts he is referred to as Sōkei.

Also, monastic Japanese names that end in –san or –zan (Ch. –shan) may refer to the mountain on which a monastery is built, or to the monastery itself, or to the monk who was the first head of the monastery. Only context can clarify which is intended.

The numbers in parentheses by each name indicate the chapters in which a kōan story or other major reference to the person appears.

Banzan Hōshaku, C. P'an-shan Pao-chi. Zen Master. (27, 43, 82)

Barishiba, S. Pārshva. (29)

Baso Dōitsu, C. Ma-tsu Tao-i. (11, 19, 26, 29, 53, 75)

Bodhidharma, J. Bodaidaruma, C. P'u-t'i-ta-mo. (8, 19, 23, 29, 34, 41, 44, 47, 51, 69)

Bokushū Chin, C. Mu-chou Ch'en. A Dharma heir of Ōbaku.

Busshō Hōtai, C. Fo-hsing Fa-tai. Zen Master under Engo. (64)

Busshō Tokkō, C. Fa-shao Te-kuang. Zen Master under Daie Soko.

Ch'ang Cho, J. Chō Setsu. Lay disciple of Sekisō Keisho. (44)

Chimon Kōso, C. Chih-men Kuang-tso. Zen Master. (27)

Chisō, C. Chih-tsung. (51)

Chōkei Daian, C. Chang-ch'ing Ta-an. Under Hyakujō. (29, 62)

Chōkei Eryō, C. Chang-ch'ing Hui-leng. Under Seppō. (29)

Chōrei Shutaku, C. Chang-ling Shou-cho. Zen Master. (64)

Chōsa Keishin, C. Chang-sha Ching-ts'en. Zen Master. (8, 21, 35, 54, 58, 89, 95)

Daibai Hōjō, C. Ta-mei Fa-Ch'ang. Zen Master. (29)

Daie Sōkō, C. Ta-hui Tsung-kao. Under Engo. (41, 72, 88)

Daigu, J. Kōan Daigu, C. Kao-an Ta-yü. Zen Master.

Daii Dōshin, C. Ta-i Tao-hsin. Zen Master. (21, 29)

Daiji Kanchū, C. Ta-tz'u Huan-chung. Zen Master. (29)

Daikan Enō, C. Ta-chien Hui-neng. Sixth Chinese Ancestor, often known by his posthumous name of Meditation Master Sōkei. (10, 12, 15, 16, 19, 21, 28, 31, 45, 51, 60, 72, 84)

Daiman Kōnin, C. Ta-man Hung-jen. Zen Master. (21, 50)

Daini, Tripitika Master, C. Ta-erh. (18, 78)

Daitaka, S. Dhītika. (82)

Daizui Shinshō, C. Ta-sui Shen-chao. Great Master. (20)

Dōan Dōhi, C. Tung-an Tao-p'i.

Dōgo Enchi, C. Tao-wu Yüan-chih. Zen Master. (27, 32)

Dōrin, J. Chōka Dōrin, C. Niao-k'o Tao-lin. Zen Master. (9)

Echū (National Teacher), J. Nan'yō Echū, C. Nan-yang Hui-chung. (6, 18, 36, 45, 54, 67, 78)

Egaku, C. Hui-chio. Monk. (8)

Eka, J. Taiso Eka, C. Ta-tsu Hui-k'o. (29, 41, 47, 51, 60, 89)

Engo Kokugon, C. Yüan-wu K'o-ch'in. Zen Master. (22, 33, 36, 77, 88)

Enkan Saian, C. Yen-kuan Ch'i-an. National Teacher. (29)

Fuke, J. Chinshū Fuke, C. P'u-hua of Chen-chou. Zen Master. Under Ummon. (21)

Fuyō Dōkai, C. Fu-jung Tao-chieh. (29, 62)

Fuyōzan Reikun, C. Fu-jung Ling-hsün. Zen Master. (44)

Gako, C. E-hu. Disciple of Seppō. (35)

Gantō, J. Gantō Zenkatsu, C. Yen-t'ou Ch'üan-huo.

Gensha Shibi, C. Hsüan-sha Shih-pei. Under Seppō. (4, 18, 19, 22, 23, 29, 31, 48, 49, 60, 78)

Genshi, C. Yüan-tzu. (15)

Gensoku, C. Hsüan-tse. (1)

Gichū, C. I-chung. Zen Master.

Goso Hōen, C. Wu-tsu Fayen. Zen Master. (29)

Gozu Hōyū, C. Niu-t'ou Fa-jung. Zen Master. (27)

Gutei, C. Chü-chih. Zen Master. (60)

Haku Rakuten, C. Po Chü-i. Poet of the T'ang Dynasty and a lay disciple of ZenMaster Bukkō Nyoman. (9)

Hannyatara, S. Prajñātāra. Bodhidharma's Master. (20, 50)

Haryō Kōkan, C. Pa-ling Hao-chien. Zen Master. (23)

Hō'on, C. P'ang-yün. Lay disciple of Baso. (24)

Hofuku, C. Pao-fu. Disciple of Seppō. (35)

Hōgen, C. Fa-yen. (1, 59)

Hōju Chinshu, C. Chen-chou Pao-shou. Venerable Abbot. (95)

Honei Jin'yū, C. Pao-ning Jen-yung. Zen Master. (59)

Hōtatsu, C. Fa-ta. (16, 20)

Hyakujō Ekai, C. Pai-chang Huai-hai. (21, 24, 29, 33, 62, 73, 74, 76, 88)

Iitsu, C. Wei-i. Retired Abbot.

Isan Reiyū, C. Kuei-shan Ling-yu. Also known as Daii. (8, 21, 24, 29, 62)

Jimyō Soen, C. Tz'u-ming Ch'u-yüan. Zen Master.

Jinshū, C. Shen-hsiu. Chief disciple of Daiman Konin.

Jizō Keichin, C. Ti-tsang Kuei-shen. (35, 48)

Jōshū Shinsai, C. Chao-chou Chen-chi. Great Master. (18, 20, 21, 29, 34, 38, 47, 59, 62, 78, 79)

Kaie Shutan, C. Hai-hui Tuan. Zen Master. (18, 78)

Kanadaiba, S. Kāḹadeva. (21)

Kanchi Sōsan, C. Chien-chih Seng-ts'an. Third Chinese Ancestor.

Kashō Buddha, S. Kāshyapa Buddha. (15, 86)

Kayashata, S. Gayāshata. (19, 28)

Kazan Shujun, C. Ho-shan Shou-hsüen. Zen Master. (64)

Kegon Kyūjō, C. Hua-yen Hsü-ching. (25)

Keichō Beiko, C. Ching-chao Mi-hu. (25)

Kempō, C. Kan-feng. (58)

Kinkazan Kōtō, C. Kung-tao. Zen Master. (19)

Kisei, C. Kuei-hsing. Zen Master. (11)

Kisu Shishin, C. Kuei-tsung Chih-chen. Zen Master. (44)

Koboku Hōjō, C. Ku-mo Fa-cheng. Zen Master. (73)

Kōtō, Vinaya Master, C. Kuang-t'ung.

Kozan Chi'en, C. Ku-shan Chih-yüan.

Kumorata, S. Kumāralabdha. (88, 89)

Kyōgen Chikan, C. Hsiang-yen Chih-hsien. (8, 24, 29, 63, 65, 79)

Kyōsei Dōfu, C. Ching-ch'ing Tao-fu.

Kyōzan Ejaku, C. Yang-shan Hui-chi. Zen Master. Disciple of Isan. (18, 21, 24, 51,78)

Makakashō, S. Mahākāshyapa. First Indian Ancestor. (23, 29, 31, 52, 66, 74, 77,81, 85)

Massan Ryōnen, C. Mo-shan. Master. (10)

Mayoku Hōtetsu, C. Ma-ku Pao-ch'e. Zen Master. (3, 32)

Moggallana, S. Maudgalyayana. Disciple of the Buddha.

Musai Ryōha, C. Wu-chi Liao-p'ai.

Myōshin, C. Miao-hsin. Monk. (10)

Nāgārjuna, J. Nagyaarajuna, C. Lung-shu, Lung-sheng, or Lung-meng. AncestralMaster. (21, 82, 84, 86, 91)

Nangaku Ejō, C. Nan-yüeh Huai-jang. Under Daikan Enō. (7, 19, 22, 26, 60)

Nansen Fugan, C. Nan-ch'üan P'u-yüan. Zen Master. Disciple of Baso. (21, 34, 59,79)

Ōan Donge, C. Ying-an Tan-hua. Zen Master. (49)

Ōbaku Unshi, C. Huang-po Yün-shih. Zen Master. (21, 27, 29, 50, 73)

Ōryū Enan, C. Huang-lung Hui-nan. Zen Master.

Ōryū Shishin, C. Huang-lung Ssu-hsin.

Reiun Shigon, C. Ling-yün Chih-ch'in. Zen Master. (8)

Rinzai Gigen, C. Lin-ch'i I-hsüan. (10, 21, 24, 25, 29, 32, 50, 51, 82)

Rōya Ekaku, C. Lang-yeh Hui-chüeh. (61)

Ryūge Kodon, C. Lung-ya Chü-tun. Master.

Ryūtan Sōshin, C. Lung-t'an Ch'ung-hsin. Zen Master. (17)

Sanshō Enen, C. San-sheng Hui-jan. Zen Master. (19, 51)

Seidō Chizō, C. Hsi-t'ang Chih-tsang. Zen Master. (75)

Seigen Gyōshi, C. Ch'ing-yüan Hsing-ssu. Zen Master. (11, 15, 23, 31, 51)

Seihō, C. Ch'ing-feng. Zen Master. (1)

Seizan, C. Seizan. (75)

Sekisō Keisho, C. Shih-shuang Ch'ing-chu. Master.

Sekitō Kisen, C. Shih-t'ou Hsi-ch'ien. (11, 23, 27, 28, 51, 62)

Sempuku Jōko, C. Chien-fu Cheng-ku. Zen Master. (74)

Seppō Gison, C. Hsüeh-feng I-ts'un. (4, 19, 22, 29, 31, 35, 38, 45, 49, 60)

Setchō Chikan, C. Hsüeh-tou Chih-chien. Great Master. (52)

Setchō Jūken, C. Hsüeh-tou Chung-hsien. (64, 65, 79)

Shakkyō Ezō, C. Shih-kung Hui-tsang. Zen Master. (75)

Shayata, S. Jayanta. Great Monk. (89)

Shikan, J. Kankei Shikan, C. Kuan-hsi Chih-hsien. Zen Master. (10, 29)

Shinzan Sōmitsu, C. Shen-shan Seng-mi. Zen Master. (41)

Shishibodai, S. Simhabodhi. Great Monk.

Shōju, C. Cheng-shou. (91)

Shōkaku Jōsō, C. Chao-chüeh Ch'ang-tsung. Zen Master. (8)

Shōnawashu, S. Śānavāsa. Third Indian Ancestor.

Shūgetsu, C. Tsung-yüeh. Venerable Master.

Sōgyanandai, S. Sanghananda. Great Monk. (19, 28, 82)

Sōun, C. Sung-yün.

Sōzan Honjaku, C. Ts'ao-shan Pen-chi. (27, 30, 63)

Sozan Kōnin, C. Shu-shan Kuang-jen. Zen Master. (45)

Sunakshatra, C. Zenshō. Disciple of the Buddha who returned to lay life. (82)

Tafuku, C. Ta-fu. One of Jōshū's Dharma heirs.

Taigen Fu, C. Ta-yüan Fu. (57)

Tandō Bunjun, C. Chan-t'ang Wen-chun. Zen Master. (64, 72)

Tanka Shijun, C. Tan-hsia Tzu-ch'un. Great Monk. (64)

Tendō Nyojō, C. T'ien-t'ung Ju-ching. Zen Master. (2, 7, 20, 29, 49, 54, 57, 59, 60, 62, 66, 71, 76, 77)

Tenryū, C. T'ien-lung. Zen Master.

Tō Impō, C. Teng Yin-feng. (79)

Tōba, C. Tung-p'o. Layman in Keisei Sanshoku. (8)

Tokujō, J. Sensu Tokujō, C. Ch'uan-tzu Te-ch'ing. Under Yakusan Igen.

Tokusan Senkan, C. Te-shan Hsüan-chien. Zen Master. Disciple of Sekitō Kisen.(17, 18)

Tokusan Tokkai, C. Te-shan Te-hai. Disciple of Seppō.

Tōsu Daidō, C. T'ou-tzu Ta-t'ung. (43, 54, 63)

Tōsu Gisei, C. T'ou-tzu I-ch'ing. Great Monk. (62)

Tōzan Dōbi, C. Tung-shan Tao-wei.

Tōzan Ryōkai, C. Tung-shan Liang-chieh. (20, 24, 27, 41, 54, 61, 64)

Ubakikuta, S. Upagupta. Great Monk. (82, 91)

Ummon Bun'en, C. Yün-men Wen-yen. (35, 39, 74)

Unchō Tokufū, C. Hsüeh-ting Te-fu. Zen Master.

Ungan Donjō, C. Yün-yen T'an-sheng. (24, 32, 54, 61)

Ungo Dōyō, C. Yün-chu Tao-ying. (20, 27, 52)

Utpalavarna, J. Upparage. (82, 84)

Vasubandhu, J. Bashubanzu.

Vimalakirti, J. Yuima. (31, 70)

Wanshi Shōgaku, C. Hung-chih Cheng-chüeh. A Dharma heir of Tanka Shijun.(26)

Yafu Dōsen, C. Yeh-fu Tao-ch'uan. Zen Master.

Yakusan Igen, C. Yao-shan Wei-yen. Great Master. (11, 20, 26, 28, 70)

Yōka Genkaku, C. Yung-chia Hsüan-chüeh. (88)

Zengen Chūkō, C. Chien-yüan Chung-hsing. Great Master. (45)

About the Translator

After obtaining his doctorate in theatre criticism and the phenomenon of theatre from the University of Washington in 1972, Rev. Hubert Nearman (aka Mark J. Nearman) spent the following decade broadening his knowledge of classical Japanese and Chinese in order to devote himself to making annotated translations of the so-called 'secret tradition' writings (Japanese *hiden*) by Zeami Motokiyo, one of the principal founders of the fourteenth-century Japanese Noh theatre tradition. In 1981, he was awarded a three-year National Endowment for the Humanities grant to make similar annotated translations of treatises by Zeami's son-in-law, Komparu Zenchiku. His translations of these documents on Japanese aesthetics were published in *Monumenta Nipponica*. Also during this period he held faculty positions at the American University (in Washington, DC) and at the University of New South Wales.

In 1988 he was ordained in the Order of Buddhist Contemplatives of the Sōtō Zen tradition by Rev. Master Jiyu-Kennett and in 1992 received Dharma Transmission from her. Since then, at her request, he has devoted himself to translating major Buddhist works, including Keizan Jōkin's "Record of the Transmission of the Light" (*Denkōroku*) and his "Instructions on How to Do Pure Meditation" (*Zazen Yojin Ki*), as well as "The Scripture of Brahma's Net" (*Bommō Kyō*), the dhārani from "The Scripture on Courageously Going On" (*Shurāôgāma Sutra*), Kanshi Sōsan's "That Which is Engraved upon the Heart That Trusts to the Eternal" (*Hsin Hsin Ming*), Yōka Genkaku's "Song That Attests to the Way" (*Cheng Tao Ko*), "Bodhidharma's Discourse on Pure Meditation" (*Kuan Hsin Lun*), "The Scripture of the Buddha's Last Teachings"(*Yuikyō Gyō*), "The Scripture on Fully Perfected Enlightenment" (*Engaku Kyō*), along with the present work.

Rev. Hubert was named a Master of the Order of Buddhist Contemplatives in 2010, and died in 2016.

CPSIA information can be obtained
at www.ICGtesting.com
Printed in the USA
LVHW080808141222
735073LV00004B/214